Nothing to Write Home About

Nothing to Write Home About

British Family Correspondence and the Settler Colonial Everyday in British Columbia

Laura Ishiguro

UBCPress · Vancouver · Toronto

28 27 26 25 24 23 22 21 20 19   5 4 3 2 1

Printed in Canada on FSC-certified ancient-forest-free paper (100% post-consumer recycled) that is processed chlorine- and acid-free.

Library and Archives Canada Cataloguing in Publication

Ishiguro, Laura, author
Nothing to write home about : British family correspondence and the settler colonial everyday in British Columbia / Laura Ishiguro.

Includes bibliographical references and index.
Issued in print and electronic formats.
ISBN 978-0-7748-3843-6 (hardcover). – ISBN 978-0-7748-3844-3 (softcover). – ISBN 978-0-7748-3845-0 (PDF). – ISBN 978-0-7748-3846-7 (EPUB). – ISBN 978-0-7748-3847-4 (Kindle)

1. British – British Columbia – Correspondence. 2. Colonists – British Columbia – Correspondence. 3. Immigrants – British Columbia – Correspondence. 4. Letter writing – British Columbia – History – 19th century. 5. Letter writing – British Columbia – History – 20th century. 6. Families – British Columbia – Sources. 7. British Columbia – Emigration and immigration – History – 19th century – Sources. 8. British Columbia – Emigration and immigration – History – 20th century – Sources. 9. British Columbia – Biography – Sources. I. Title.

FC3850.B7I84 2019   971.100441   C2018-906460-9
C2018-906461-7

Canada

UBC Press gratefully acknowledges the financial support for our publishing program of the Government of Canada (through the Canada Book Fund), the Canada Council for the Arts, and the British Columbia Arts Council.

This book has been published with the help of a grant from the Canadian Federation for the Humanities and Social Sciences, through the Awards to Scholarly Publications Program, using funds provided by the Social Sciences and Humanities Research Council of Canada, and with the help of the University of British Columbia through the K.D. Srivastava Fund.

Printed and bound in Canada by Friesens
Set in Galliard and New Baskerville by Artegraphica Design Co. Ltd.
Copy editor: Frank Chow
Proofreader: Lauren Cross
Indexer: Cheryl Lemmens
Cover designer: George Kirkpatrick
Cartographer: Eric Leinberger

UBC Press
The University of British Columbia
2029 West Mall
Vancouver, BC V6T 1Z2
www.ubcpress.ca

Contents

Illustrations

Acknowledgments

DEAR ALL,

I hope this book finds you well. I am finally settling down to write the best part, and how could I possibly do it but with a letter of acknowledgment? But now that I am here, I am finding it overwhelming too, this summoning of words that inevitably feel so small for expressing the feelings that run so large in them. It is always true to say that publication is not possible without the material, emotional, and intellectual help of many others, and certainly it is the case here. However, it is also true to say that I wrote this particular book in the very best and the very worst years of my life to date. Given that, I know just how much it owes to other people's labour stretching far beyond the usual – incredible, generous, unyielding support that I did not think possible, let alone in a profession that is not usually defined by a culture of radical care. So, although I have long claimed to be an island, I will admit here that it is not true. It is a pleasure to have the opportunity to recognize – with awe, gratitude, honour, humility, and respect – the archipelagos and peninsulas and bridge-builders who have kept this work, and me, afloat for so long.

Perhaps, though, I should begin with place. Like the letters it examines, this book was written in and between homes. I began it in England, a place that was partly but never quite my home. I finished it where I now live and work, on the territory of the xʷməθkʷəy'əm people, in what is currently called Vancouver. A significant portion of my research and writing also took place in the home of my heart, on the territory of the Lekwungen and W̱SÁNEĆ people, in Victoria and at my parents' small farm outside the city. Underpinning this book is my understanding that each of these claims to home is both personal and political, historical and contemporary. As a hāfu settler of Japanese and British descent, I could only have been made from entwined global trajectories of family, migration, and settler colonialism. Because of my own history, I feel most at home here, a settler occupying unceded Indigenous territory, and feel distant in every way from the far-flung homes of my ancestors. I am constantly learning what this means, individually and collectively; my work here is part of that process.

I also wrote this book while on the move outside of home. I typed parts of it cramped in airplanes, buses, and trains. I scrawled its ideas on napkins and receipts as I walked. I wrote for long stretches in a mall food court in West London, and in more cafés than I can count in London, Vancouver, and elsewhere. In a rare violation of holiday rules, I reviewed copy edits in a campsite in Yale First Nation Territory on the banks of that awe-striking artery, the Fraser River. Along the way, my work has been fuelled by baristas and farmers, supported by security guards and cleaners, given rhythm by musicians and podcasters, and produced in tangible form only because of people working in forests, paper mills, mines, and factories. This is not to suggest that they did this work for me personally, of course. Rather, it is to recognize that this book is a visible, privileged edge of work that ultimately relies on the too-often undervalued and dangerous labour of so many other people. This should not go without saying.

At the same time, this book also owes much to many people who more directly and intentionally impacted its production, form, and content. For one, the book would be nothing without its sources. I am grateful to the descendants and others who cared for these collections of correspondence and generously donated them to public archives so that we could learn from them. I hope that I have done justice to and with them. My thanks, too, to the archivists and staff at the BC Archives, the British Library, the City of Vancouver Archives, the City of Victoria Archives, Library and Archives Canada, the New Westminster Archives, and UBC Rare Books and Special Collections. Manager Bradley Froggatt copied and sent materials from the Fort Steele Heritage Town Archives. Krisztina Laszlo, Chelsea Shriver, and Weiyan Yan ensured the book would have photographs; I appreciate their kind, quick, and excellent work on this and so much else in UBC Rare Books and Special Collections.

Material support made such research feasible. My work on this book was supported in part by an Insight Development Grant from the Social Sciences and Humanities Research Council of Canada and by the University of British Columbia. With this funding, Megan Harvey provided perfect long-term research assistance that enabled me to expand significantly the book's scope. Her smart, knowledgeable, dependable, and flexible work made it richer, and her friendship made the process better. Lars Wibe Hagen also conducted useful research at UBC; his summer research assistant position was funded by the university's Work Learn Office and shared with my colleague Eagle Glassheim. Funding from University College London and the Overseas Research Studentships program also supported my research, and enabled me to live and learn in a country that challenged my understanding of the world. This, in turn, has made me a better historian. Knowing this, I not only recognize gratefully all of this support but also look toward a future when scholarly opportunities are not so confined, and unequally so, by the ability to cross borders.

The team at UBC Press made the book's publication possible with skill, professionalism, encouragement, and patience, all of which I needed at various moments along the way. Thank you so much to all, and especially to Darcy Cullen and Megan Brand. Copy editor Frank Chow made my writing better. I have long appreciated Eric Leinberger's careful and clear maps in UBC Press books, and I am glad for his work on mine here. I am very grateful to the reviewers, too, whose excellent, perceptive comments helped me to improve the book and, in the process, taught me more about doing this work.

Part of Chapter 4 was previously published as "'A Dreadful Little Glutton Always Telling You about Food': The Epistolary Everyday and the Making of Settler Colonial British Columbia" in *The Canadian Historical Review* 99, 2 (June 2018). A small section of Chapter 2 appeared in "Material Girls: Daughters, Dress and Distance in the Trans-Imperial Family" in *Colonial Girlhood in Literature, Culture and History, 1840-1950,* ed. Kristine Moruzi and Michelle J. Smith (Basingstoke: Palgrave Macmillan, 2014). Part of Chapter 5 draws from an earlier version published as "'How I Wish I Might Be Near': Distance and the Epistolary Family in Late-Nineteenth-Century Condolence Letters" in *Within and Without the Nation: Canadian History as Transnational History*, ed. Adele Perry, Karen Dubinsky, and Henry Yu (Toronto: University of Toronto Press, 2015). I am grateful to the *CHR* (University of Toronto Press Journals), Palgrave Macmillan, and University of Toronto Press for granting me the permission to use this material. Thanks, too, to the editors and reviewers who helped me to hone those pieces first. In addition, I am indebted to the many conference organizers who gave me opportunities to share earlier versions of this work and to the attendees of talks who made helpful comments. These include Angela Wanhalla, Erin Millions, Susie Fisher, and Ben Bryce who arranged for me to speak from this research in Dunedin, Winnipeg, and Prince George.

Many other people have offered incisive insight, deep knowledge, generous challenges, kind mentorship and friendship, open hospitality, and an unyielding presence in my corner throughout this project. From the beginning, Catherine Hall meant so much. Her support, knowledge, critical questions, and scholarship shaped both my work and me as an historian. This book has taken the form it has in part because of Catherine's model; I have always respected her commitment to asking the questions that are urgent in the place that she lives. In that spirit, my return to British Columbia in 2012 prompted me to rethink the earlier work I had done in London, and in particular, to grapple with the often profoundly different questions, meanings, and consequences of British imperial history writing in the United Kingdom and Canada – what translates well across the distances and what does not. The turn to focus on settler colonialism in British Columbia was an analytical direction urged by this process, and by a world-shifting question posed to me by Zoë Laidlaw. I am grateful to Zoë and to Elizabeth Buettner who both engaged closely with my earlier work on this project, gave me new ways to think about it, and thus shaped the form it has subsequently taken.

Years ago, I read Anne Lamott's *Bird by Bird*, and one part particularly stayed with me. When you are stuck, she suggests, write the book to someone who wrote the books that inspired you. My endnotes intend to honour the many people to whom I owe intellectual debts, of course. But when I struggled with the writing, I thought of, and with, the work of two historians in particular: Jean Barman and Adele Perry. Their scholarship has done so much to explain colonialism, family, and British Columbia, and to provoke my questions about these. In short, they have made one of my core fields possible, and they have made it immeasurably better. This, then, is my offering into conversations that exist because of them, with thanks to both.

Many other colleagues and friends around the world have supported me even as they have also discovered my ironic struggle to maintain communication over long distances. Esmé Cleall, Daniel Grey, Onni Gust, Emily Manktelow, Charlotte Riley, and Jonathan Saha: I would never have begun to understand Britain and its relationship to empire without your astute analysis and open-hearted welcome, and I continue to learn so much from you. Louise Carter, Maureen Haaker, Harvey Osborne, and Ed Packard: the magical year in your midst made me believe in good things, and it has sustained me more than you know. For solidarity and help of various sorts, thanks to Lara Campbell, Ken Corbett, Anne Dance, Crystal Fraser, Stefanie Ickert, Sherri Inouye, Erin Millions, Chantal Norrgard, Adele Perry, Coll Thrush, Jon Weir, and Aaron Windel. Jack Little and crew offered good conversation about British Columbia, history, and more. Kristine Alexander, Sean Carleton, and Onni Gust read parts of the manuscript at one of the busiest times of the academic year, and their smart and thoughtful comments helped me immensely. Many students have inspired my questions and stoked my enthusiasm for this work. I am particularly grateful to Alice Gorton, who shared my preoccupation with this history and taught me so much about it, and to Dane Allard and Nicole Yakashiro, who both read the manuscript so generously.

Colleagues at UBC have offered support in a range of ways, and I appreciate those who listened to and talked with me over the course of this project. The Canadianist cluster based in the UBC History department engaged closely with two chapters and, more generally, sustained a good community. Joy Dixon offered knowledgeable support that was much needed and perfectly calibrated to my anxiety. With his characteristic generosity and expert clarity, Michel Ducharme taught me more about doing this work than he will believe. To answer your question at last, Michel: "This is how my manuscript is going." Bob McDonald forged a path with his commitment to British Columbia's history and kept an eye out for me. Tamara Myers saved me over and over again, giving me perspective and, when I needed it, company and a place to stay. Conversation with Paige Raibmon never failed to simultaneously encourage me and shift how I thought about things. Late in the process, she also re-read a chapter and gave me suggestions that were both brilliant and helpful.

Over the years, many writing partners and groups have helped me to keep the manuscript moving forward with accountability check-ins, crisis management, and company in the everyday slog. Thanks especially to Onni Gust, Maddie Knickerbocker, Meghan Longstaffe, Kendra Maas, Laura Madokoro, Eryk Martin, Nicole Miller, Sarah Nickel, Amanda Petersen, and Anne Wallen. Maddie also provided crucial support with a problem late in the game, offering insightful questions and smart answers that helped me come up with possible solutions. Our conversation was essential for getting me to a point where I could let this go despite my fears. That was exactly what I needed and had not been able to do alone, Maddie; thank you.

Equally as important as my writing partners, Kendra Milne has been a heroic kind of anti-writing partner. Again and again, she has reminded me of an important world beyond the manuscript and not only told me to relax but also made real opportunities for me to do so. The sheer scale and significance of this feat should not be understated. Thanks, Kendra.

Sarah Nickel has been, along with my mother, my most important postal correspondent, and has never once complained (to me, at least) about my illegible handwriting or epistolary etiquette, some of which she might recognize from the nineteenth century described in this book. In addition to her friendship and collegial solidarity in general, I am particularly grateful that she walked the path to publication just ahead of me because it meant that she could answer every single one of my many questions about the process. She did so with the sort of patient kindness to which I can only aspire, all the while doing her own important work. Kukwstsétsemc, stemét.

The writing and publication process was made incalculably better by the existence of Team Laura. Laura Madokoro has been an absolute force of support and a role model in getting good work done. At one point, she went above and beyond the call of duty by helping with some emergency research in Ottawa. She, Tom, Eli, and Hanako also gave me the best place to stay while I did my own research and provided a perfect and much-needed escape during a prolonged illness. Thank you, Other Laura.

Eryk Martin is the definition of radical care. His unconditional support and wise perspective kept me going when I literally could not do it myself and stayed steady even when I could. He figured out what I needed, patiently refused my intransigent catastrophes, listened to me type more loudly than you can imagine, and watched me spill water on his computer. Throughout it all, he believed in me and the work and, more than that, he told me he did. In addition to talking through every part of the project with me, he read the whole manuscript at a critical moment and knew just what to say. Eryk, thank you for doing the everyday work with me.

I have not been the easiest relative during this project, but still, my family of origin got me here with their abiding patience and understanding, and their quiet belief, hope, and love. I know – certainly, this research has insisted I know – about the incredible variety of family out there. My family, we might be weird, but I would not choose a different one for all the world. To my parents especially, Ann and Ed Ishiguro: everything is possible because of you, my first teachers and my very foundations. ありがとう, thank you, I love you always.

And so, to my people, my family in all its forms: this is because of you and it is for you.

Yours in gratitude,
Laura Mitsuyo Ishiguro

Nothing to Write Home About

Introduction

In June 1860, Victoria merchant Robert Burnaby replied to a letter from his brother Tom, a member of the clergy in their home county of Leicestershire, England. Formerly a civil servant in London, Burnaby had arrived on the northern Pacific slope of North America on Christmas Day 1858, hoping to try his hand at business in the British colonies of Vancouver Island and, recently claimed on the neighbouring mainland, British Columbia. He settled and worked there until illness compelled his return to England in 1873, two years after the colony of British Columbia – united with Vancouver Island in 1866 – joined Confederation as a province of the Dominion of Canada. During his fifteen years in North America, Burnaby wrote dozens of letters to his family in the British imperial metropole. As early as 1860, however, his relatives had already begun to complain. His recent letters were uninteresting, they protested, being neither as "lively nor [as] full of incident" as his earliest colonial correspondence. Writing to his brother Tom in June that year, Burnaby acknowledged that they were right: his letters had started to reflect what he called the "monotonous round" of his everyday life. "Although doubtless one might hourly pick up phrases and anecdotes to amuse you hugely," he explained, "one gets deadened by the common-place and has no heart to record what comes day after day and ever the same."[1]

This book examines British family letters like Burnaby's, sent between British Columbia and the United Kingdom between 1858 and 1914, in order to tell a new history of settler colonialism.[2] Although Burnaby found his letters and life sinking into banality, this was far from an uneventful time in what became Canada's westernmost province. Rather, these were formative years for settler colonial British Columbia – a time that I call its early settler period, defined by the formation of a white British settler society from its mid-nineteenth-century tenuous aspiration and fragile nascency to its emerging confidence and dominance in the early twentieth.

In its broadest definition, settler colonialism is a distinct form of colonial power that aims for ultimate, uncontested, and indefinite settler control and belonging. A burgeoning interdisciplinary field identifies several priorities that characterize settler colonial projects. These include the arrival and long-term settlement of a significant group of non-Indigenous, historically often white, people who plan to stay permanently; their work toward the dispossession, marginalization, and intended or assumed eventual elimination of Indigenous peoples; their assertion of sovereignty over Indigenous land; and their establishment of a new political and social order that distinguishes and privileges themselves in contrast to Indigenous and other non-Indigenous people, the latter often people of colour.[3]

Although the parameters of settler colonialism can be more complicated in practice than in theory, British Columbia was radically reconfigured by a general shift to these priorities between 1858 and 1914. In these years, major political, social, economic, cultural, and demographic transformations combined to overlay – without entirely erasing – Indigenous and hybrid fur-trade worlds with the foundations of a settler colonial order that continues to structure the province today. A large body of scholarship investigates the historical roots of settler colonialism in Canada, including British Columbia in this period. Here, as elsewhere, the literature takes race and Indigenous-settler relations as the primary prisms through which to view settler colonialism. Reflecting the priorities of the international scholarship, this literature focuses on the connections between race, gender, sexuality, and space, and on racializing settler laws, policies, and practices, especially related to land or immigration. It examines the exercise of physical and non-physical colonial violence, the undercurrents of settler anxiety, and the actions and impact of Indigenous resistance to settler regimes.[4] In these ways, the field has shed critical light on the historical trajectories of racialization, dispossession, and resettlement in northern North America, which endure in shaping the Canadian present.

Robert Burnaby's June 1860 letter reflects much of what this scholarship has demonstrated about colonial discourses on race and settler constructions of "the Indian." Responding to his family's "hint" about his boring correspondence, Burnaby explained to his brother that he had decided to "devote this letter to some account of the Indian tribes" – a topic that he assumed his English relatives would find interesting. He then launched into a long description of Indigenous people from the northern Pacific coast (including Haida, Tsimshian, and Tlingit people) who travelled south annually in the mid-nineteenth century for a number of reasons, including to trade and work in the Victoria area. Burnaby's account included many tropes that characterized settler representations of Indigenous people during this period. For instance, he drew on widespread condemnations of Indigenous people's domestic spaces and on ideas of the "lazy Indian" to suggest that their "Lodges" and "huts" smelled "horrible and filthy," and that the people inside were "lying round," "basking in the sun," and "doing nothing." He emphasized violence, both in warfare and in what he framed as acts of individual savagery, and claimed that the men came south to sell "their" women, "whom they used formerly to kill as unprofitable." He commented on their use of "gaudy Blankets and showy silk handkerchiefs" as clothing. And he suggested that they had been damaged by colonialism, remarking that their "contact with white folks has taught them all the vices and positively none of the virtues of the superior race."[5] In all of these ways, Burnaby framed Indigenous people as fundamentally different from and inferior to white people, and did so by drawing on common elements of nineteenth-century settler racism inflected with ideas about gender, class, labour, and civilization. Overall, the letter is a representative example of the explicit racializing and racist discourses that underpinned the nascent settler project, which in turn corroborates many of the emphases and insights of the existing scholarship on colonialism.[6]

However, to read this letter's thick description in isolation from the rest of Robert Burnaby's family correspondence would be to miss its exceptional nature. Burnaby himself argued that it was anomalous. As he explained, he intentionally selected its topic as an interesting and extraordinary diversion from his usual "common-place" concerns. A close reading of his other letters confirms this. Of the forty-two surviving family letters that Burnaby wrote about Vancouver Island and British Columbia between 1858 and 1863, the June 1860 letter was the first of only two that offered any extensive description of Indigenous people at all.[7] Approximately one-third of his letters mentioned Indigenous people, and nearly all of these were very brief passing remarks. A characteristic example appears in his first letter from Victoria. Among otherwise detailed descriptions of his new surroundings, he merely noted that he had seen "Indians paddl[ing] about" as his steamer arrived.[8] Rather than focusing on race or Indigenous-settler people, the vast majority of his correspondence concentrated instead on other aspects of his colonial experiences and his relationships with family in England. While Burnaby's close description in June 1860 reflects scholarly discussions about settler colonialism and the discursive construction of racialized difference, in other words, it stands almost entirely alone in doing so.

In this respect, Burnaby's letter opens a window on a much broader pattern in the British family correspondence sent between British Columbia and the United Kingdom in this period, with consequences for how we might think about the history of British Columbia, Canada, and the British Empire. Personal letters were among the most widely produced and circulated sources on early settler British Columbia, and thousands have been preserved, archived, and made accessible in public institutions in Canada. Read individually and together, these letters shed light on the experiences and understandings of a diverse but privileged range of Britons as they and their families contributed to the making of British Columbia. Like Burnaby's correspondence, a significant majority was marked by a prevailing disregard of the topics that have dominated the scholarship on settler colonialism. (Indeed, seen in this wider context, Burnaby's letters were unusual for mentioning Indigenous people, even in passing, as often as they did.) Instead, letter writers focused on other elements of their everyday lives and on their trans-imperial families – that is, their long-distance relationships maintained across the British Empire.

So, what might historians make of these widespread sources, which reflect a pivotal period in the making of a settler colonial society but which remain largely silent on the topics that drive the scholarship? Certainly, epistolary inattention to Indigenous-settler relations should not be taken as an indication that these were unimportant. As with Burnaby's June 1860 letter, the exceptions reveal powerful, shared ideologies that drove colonial practices, while even brief references shed light on Indigenous people's lives and settlers' everyday interactions with them. At the same time, the more common silences serve as examples of settlers' discursive erasures of Indigenous people, which buttressed their claims to British Columbia as *terra nullius* (nobody's land) and their assertions of sovereignty on that basis. Extracting exceptions or reading silences against the grain can thus contribute to our understanding of Indigenous-settler relations, race, power, and knowledge in Canada and the British Empire. However, I maintain that pursuing such analyses in isolation from the primary content of family correspondence risks missing its full significance as a body of historical evidence.

This book investigates family letters sent between British Columbia and the British imperial metropole in this spirit. It is propelled by the contention that epistolary content and silence – what needed to be said, what could not be said, and what could go without saying – mattered together in the foundations of settler colonial British Columbia. To investigate this assertion, the book asks a number of questions. How did letters represent the settler everyday and the trans-imperial family? What was the relationship between these common concerns and their accompanying erasure of other topics? In the interplay between content and silence, what did correspondence render understandable or possible for British families engaged with British Columbia? And what do family letters thus reveal about how Britons built, sustained, and made sense of the settler colonial project during its foundational years? Each chapter addresses these questions by analyzing correspondence through a different approach and thematic lens. The result is a diverse reading of the content, contexts, and uses of family letters, ranging from the broad structures and generic parameters of postal communication to individual emotional descriptions of British Columbia as astonishing or boring; from epistolary expressions of love to heated conflicts over property; and from banal, detailed accounts of settlers' everyday meals to their sustained refusal to explain major facets of their lives.

Through this discussion, the book calls attention to the unexamined and interrelated significance of the everyday and the trans-imperial family in the local and global history of settler colonialism. Indigenous-settler relations, race, violence, resistance, and land and immigration policies were fundamentally important. On their own, though, these cannot explain how and why Britons actually moved in this period, or how they transformed themselves into settlers and colonizers – crucial elements in the making of settler colonial places.[9] In British Columbia, the emergent settler project of dispossession and resettlement was premised on white British people who individually and collectively planned to stay, materially benefit, and belong into an indefinite future. Without these people's commitments to leaving former homes, living long-term familial separations, and making new homes, an enduring settler society and economy could have been neither constructed nor sustained in these years. To understand this, it is necessary to examine the personal priorities through which Britons refracted broader colonial ideologies, and came to take for granted their power, prospects, comfort, and belonging in British Columbia. As this book demonstrates, family letters both facilitated and revealed this process.

More specifically, I argue that British family correspondence supported and reflected the personal normalization of a settler colonial order in British Columbia in two main and interconnected ways. First, letters served as the medium of ongoing family relationships for Britons separated across distances. Although not all relatives wrote, an absence of letters meant an absence of active connections, and confined families to memory and imagination. Those who did write used the post to express feelings, perform duties, negotiate conflicts, and share resources that together constituted and sustained trans-imperial families in everyday separations and moments of crisis. In so doing, they made distance an ordinary part of the family and enabled metropolitan relatives to maintain an emotional and material place in settler lives. Second, letters operated as a key vehicle through which Britons produced and circulated knowledge about British Columbia, a place otherwise at the limits of metropolitan attention and understanding. Typically silencing possible points of anxiety and vulnerability, letter writers instead constructed tenacious representations of settler lives as banal and unchallenged. In other words, Britons used the post to navigate the personal separations integral to their migration and settlement, and at the same time to produce and entrench shared understandings of British Columbia as an unremarkable settler place. As they rewrote British Columbia as a familiar and familial home, their letters formed a powerful part of the settler colonial project of dispossession, marginalization, resettlement, and erasure.

Trans-Imperial British Families and Early Settler British Columbia

This book's overall purpose, then, is to contribute to our understanding of settler colonialism by interrogating a significant body of sources that disregards or decentres Indigenous-settler relations – the main concern of the distinct but overlapping fields of settler colonial studies and Canadian colonial historiography. It takes trans-imperial British family relationships as its primary focus, entering into conversation with a rich body of scholarship that positions the family as central to imperial or colonial histories. Over the past two decades, this literature has investigated intimacy as a key site in which colonial constructions of race, gender, sexuality, and difference were defined, reproduced, and rendered powerful in the lives of so-called colonizing and colonized peoples.[10] In British Columbia, as elsewhere, related research has focused on the regulation and practice of sexual relationships (especially those crossing boundaries of race or heterosexual marital monogamy), the development and imposition of settler law related to family, and biographies of individual families. This work has traced how sex, marriage, child rearing, and other intimate relationships were subject to state regulation and social sanction in the nineteenth and early twentieth centuries, as governments and communities intervened in family lives in an attempt to craft a respectable and self-reproducing white settler society.[11] The resulting research has revealed much about the gendered and intimate nature of settler colonialism, as it was specific to British Columbia and as it was connected to broader histories of Canada and empire. At the same time, it has largely focused on relationships in proximity – within households, nuclear families, and British Columbia itself. Aside from a very small number of case studies, the scholarship has not yet attended to the widespread significance of family relationships lived across distances and borders.[12] Building on and expanding the scope from these case studies, this book offers a new lens into the place and significance of trans-imperial families in the making of British Columbia. Distant relatives remained materially and emotionally salient in the lives of British people who built and benefited from early settler British Columbia. As the feminist adage maintains, and the scholarship on family and empire underscores, the personal was political in the settler colonial project – and sometimes this personal was trans-imperial too.

So, what exactly do I mean by trans-imperial British families? I understand the family as a varied and flexible category, broadly constituted of interlinked relationships rooted in blood and marriage, or alternative connections like adoption. A wide range of people called themselves family, including spouses, children and parents, grandchildren and grandparents, siblings, cousins, aunts, uncles, nieces, nephews, step-relatives, and in-laws. In general, these were relations defined by a combination of what historians Leonore Davidoff, Megan Doolittle, Janet Fink, and Katherine Holden explain as "blood, contract, and intimacy," within an institution that historian Adele Perry points out was assumed to be both "hierarchical and communal."[13] Specific relationships differed according to the contexts and individuals involved, marked variously by expressions of affection, demonstrations of familiarity, expectations of material or emotional support, efforts to control or influence others, stiff formality, or overt hostility. By encompassing extended as well as nuclear relatives, and non-sexual as well as conjugal connections, my framing of family includes a wider range of relations than the scholarship on British or colonial families usually considers. It also recognizes that families of origin remained significant for many people into adulthood and after marriage – a point that can be obscured by a focus on nuclear families or households, and by women's practice of changing surnames after marriage. To acknowledge the latter point, I follow Adele Perry's choice in her work on the Douglas-Connolly family by using women's surnames of both birth and marriage when known. This is a convention that some members of the Douglas-Connolly family used, but it is not authentic to the naming practices in the families that I investigate. However, it does allow me similarly to recognize and underscore married women's multiple and enduring family connections.[14]

In addition to their claim to family, the subjects of this book shared several defining points, including a general identification as British. I focus primarily on English, Scottish, and Welsh letter writers. I also briefly discuss one settler with familial connections to Ireland and explore a case study linked to the Isle of Man, which is part of the British Isles but not the United Kingdom; in the latter case, I examine letters that span a period of transition from direct British rule on the island to its self-governance as a British Crown Dependency. As a whole, the people in this book may or may not have understood themselves as British. Sometimes they defined themselves with this term, sometimes prioritized local or regional belonging, sometimes associated with nations either within or independent of Britain, and most often did not articulate how they positioned themselves within these layered categories of identity. While acknowledging this complexity, I use the term "British" here to refer broadly to those who claimed the British Isles as their home or homeland, and who were generally racialized as white (while recognizing that not all people in Britain were white). Critical for this book, they or their relatives were also seen as British in British Columbia where they contributed to and were particularly empowered by the emerging settler political, legal, and social structures on that basis. This is a capacious definition of Britishness, which risks flattening distinctions within it. However, for these people and the British Columbia with which they were engaged, Britain did particularly matter – a major and desired source of white settler migration, a political centre, a cultural point of reference, and a personal and familial home. In a period when the majority of British settlers were migrants, their place in British Columbia cannot be fully understood in isolation from their continued connections with the metropole. In this sense, even as it was not a natural, uniform, or simple category, I maintain that Britishness serves as a meaningful marker of identification for these families, invested with particular power in British Columbia and the imperial world with which they were involved.[15]

In Britain, these families came from a range of backgrounds, mostly from the middle classes. Over this period, the middle classes grew in size and influence and came to encompass two main groups: the upper middle class (including physicians, lawyers, clergy, leading civil servants, bankers, and industrialists) and the lower middle class (including lower-ranking civil servants, retailers, managers, and clerks). In general, they shared access to improved living standards, increased leisure time, and more disposable income, and tended to be defined by lower birth rates.[16] A smaller number of families in this book came from the working classes. In rural areas, the expansion of large-scale agriculture and other changes contributed to the decline of the family farm; in the Scottish Highlands, this period was also marked by the clearances, or forced displacement of tenant farmers. In the final three decades of the nineteenth century, British agriculture also suffered a major depression. With these regional rural struggles and the increasing availability of urban industrial factory work, large numbers of working-class people moved to cities. Though there was a significant rise in real wages for many working-class Britons by late century, they often continued to work for an income that barely covered subsistence needs and, despite expanding attention to public health, still experienced poor living and working conditions and high rates of disease.[17] Finally, this book also includes several members of the gentry. By the turn of the twentieth century, many of these families found their estates and wealth in relative decline, while nouveau-riche industrialists began to press into their exclusive world. Despite these shifting conditions, though, the gentry retained much of their extensive political, social, and economic power in this period.[18]

Over the past three decades, the scholarly study of nineteenth-century British families has shed light on the intimate relationships that rested at the heart of a changing country. This work has developed rich analyses focused on metropolitan nuclear families and households. It has less often offered substantial considerations of empire as influencing either the broad cultural ideas or the individual experiences of these families.[19] However, family life was far from necessarily proximate in this period. Industrialization, urbanization, new transportation technologies, and imperial expansion meant that Britons of all classes were more mobile than ever, both within and beyond the country's borders. Between 1815 and 1914, approximately 22 million emigrants left the British Isles. A significant proportion went to the United States or settler colonies and dominions such as Canada, Australia, and New Zealand. Many others moved back and forth between the metropole and imperial sites like India without formal or permanent emigration.[20]

There were many personal reasons for such mobility, but generally potential migrants were attracted to places that promised opportunities that seemed unavailable to them in the metropole. For middle-class Britons, for instance, migration could hold the promise of economic gain and security, as well as land ownership, political power, and social status beyond their aspirational reach in a metropole still rooted in class exclusivity. For working-class Britons, a move could offer the possibility of economic and social mobility, and an escape from rural clearances, dangerous and underpaid factory work, poverty, and overcrowded cities. For the gentry, migration could provide opportunities to sustain families' declining fortunes, lifestyles, and status, as well as personal advancement that might be less accessible at home, especially for younger sons.[21] Whatever the specific motivation, virtually all families had at least one relative who left Britain in this period.[22]

As a result, by the second half of the nineteenth century, British families could no longer be (if they ever had been) imagined as defined by proximity, confined by the borders of the nation, or uninfluenced by the wider empire. Instead, a large number of Britons forged trans-imperial relationships that remained active long after migration, weaving distances into the fabric of their family life. In turn, these people – both powerful and so-called ordinary Britons – played an active role in building and sustaining a global empire. The people in this book were among them. While many of these families had more extensive experiences with migration around the world, British Columbia was one node in their larger imperial and extra-imperial networks. Although their connections to other places were significant too, I concentrate here on the ties that connected British Columbia and the United Kingdom as one focused lens into the wider history of trans-imperial families.

In British Columbia, these Britons encountered and contributed to a place in flux. The northern Pacific slope of North America had been Indigenous territory since time immemorial. Non-Indigenous people first arrived by water in the late eighteenth century, in diverse crews including white, Black, Asian, and Indigenous people from around the world, largely headed by white European and American men intending to explore, trade, and profit in the region.[23] Until the mid-nineteenth century, Indigenous-newcomer relations were primarily defined by the fur economy. In 1843, the fur-trading Hudson's Bay Company moved its regional centre of operations from the Columbia River (now in the northwestern United States) to a new fort, Victoria, on the southern tip of Vancouver Island. Six years later, the British government asserted formal colonial claims to the island. Hoping to maintain a strategic foothold in the north Pacific without much investment of money or effort, the Colonial Office then granted the company proprietary rights to the colony in exchange for its promised encouragement of white settlement. However, the numbers of non-Indigenous people remained low in the 1840s and early 1850s, and company interests dominated the island colony for nearly a decade. Chief factor and colonial governor James Douglas pursued fourteen treaties with Indigenous people in the early 1850s, but only in key areas of white settlement and company activity around Victoria, Nanaimo, and Fort Rupert (now Port Hardy). Otherwise, Vancouver Island and the neighbouring mainland remained in practice largely uncontested Indigenous territory, and mostly beyond the knowledge, control, or active intervention of the Colonial Office and its agents.[24]

A major turning point in the area's history came in 1858 – the opening point of this book – with rumours of the discovery of gold on the Fraser River on the mainland. The news soon reached discontented prospectors in California and a diverse range of others around the world. Fort Victoria was quickly overwhelmed. The arrival of 450 prospectors on one ship in April 1858 increased its non-Indigenous population by more than half in a single day, while the ensuing months brought tens of thousands more. Responding to this major demographic change and the Hudson's Bay Company's corresponding assertion of British interests in the mainland territory, the Colonial Office declared it a colony, British Columbia, on

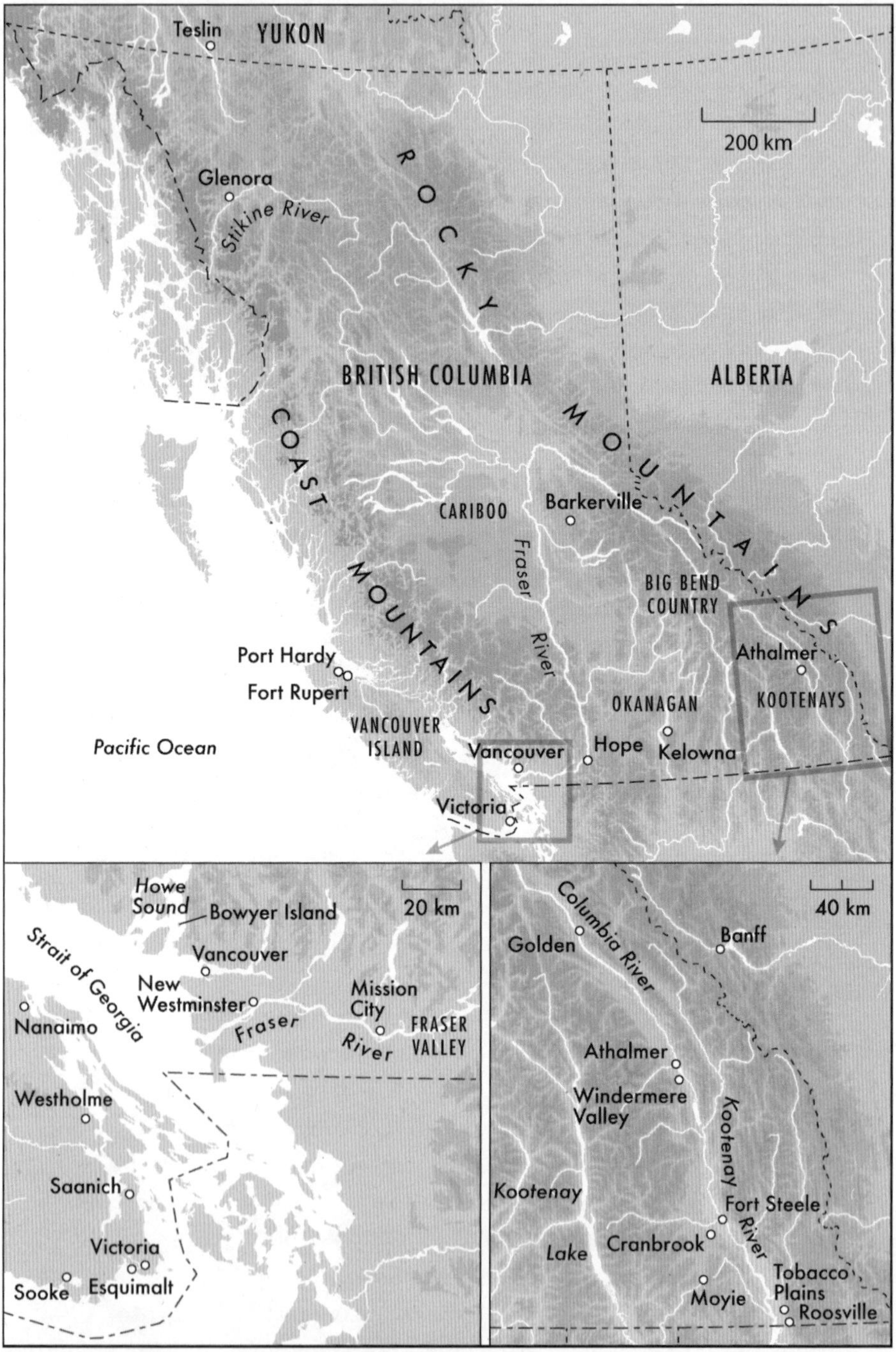

FIGURE 1 Early settler British Columbia | Map by Eric Leinberger.

2 August 1858. The island and mainland colonies were not especially well understood by the metropolitan government, nor were they priorities in a period dominated by British concerns with more lucrative or volatile areas of the empire. As the colonies became more economically precarious, the Colonial Office first united them in 1866, then urged British Columbia to join the new Dominion of Canada, which it did in 1871. The western province was connected to the rest of the dominion by the transcontinental Canadian Pacific Railway after the mid-1880s, and to the Pacific and Atlantic worlds beyond Canada's borders by rail connections to steamship lines. Among various significant effects of the advent of rail, the decision to end the Canadian Pacific Railway on Burrard Inlet provided the stimulus for a new city, Vancouver, which overtook the provincial capital of Victoria in size and economic power by the turn of the century.[25]

It was not merely the arrival of many new people that reconfigured British Columbia in these years. Rather, between the Fraser River gold rush in 1858 and the outbreak of global war in 1914, this place was fundamentally remade by a series of transformations that together laid the foundations of a colonial order rooted in Indigenous dispossession and marginalization, and non-Indigenous resettlement and white supremacy. During these years, British imperial and Canadian dominion claims to sovereignty were overlaid onto diverse Indigenous territory, though on the ground, Indigenous and fur-trade orders continued in influence and practice too. Settler governments grew significantly in power as they imposed new political and legal systems that distinguished among Indigenous people, non-Indigenous people of colour, and white people, and institutionalized the most privileges for the latter. New British and Canadian laws denied Indigenous title to the land, prioritized private ownership, and enabled individual settlers to acquire property through pre-emption or purchase. At the same time, colonial, provincial, and dominion governments worked to restrict Indigenous people to smaller and smaller reserves on land that did not impinge on settlers' economic interests. After the early 1850s, settler governments pursued no further treaties in British Columbia except for Treaty Eight (1899), which included the northeastern corner of the province. In the dominion era, the Indian Act (1876) defined Indians and their relationships to the state under Canadian law, while new assimilatory policies in this period included the introduction of a residential school system and bans on significant ceremonies like the potlatch.

These changes were bolstered by widely shared settler discourses on culture, race, and civilization, as well as physical, non-physical, and threatened state and individual violence.[26]

In concert with these transformations, an embryonic settler economy and society emerged in British Columbia between 1858 and 1914. In this early settler period, successive gold rushes and other resource booms sparked waves of immigration and sudden incursions of non-Indigenous people into new areas. The rapid extension of settler capitalism and resource extractive industries refashioned the environment and economy, and entrenched forms of labour and wealth that defined people's identities and everyday lives. Immigration promotion campaigns, perceived economic opportunities, and evolving transportation infrastructure (especially the Canadian Pacific Railway) facilitated the significant growth of a non-Indigenous population in British Columbia. Indeed, there was a demographic transformation in these years, as the number of non-Indigenous people exploded from a few hundred in 1858 to nearly half a million in 1914. By the end of the nineteenth century, non-Indigenous – and especially white British – people dominated the population due to immigration and, to a lesser extent, childbirth, as well as colonial practices and new pathogens that contributed to high death rates in Indigenous communities. Broadly speaking, by 1914 these points contributed to the foundation of a confident settler colonial project in British Columbia that was propelled by white Britons and connected to the wider process of settler nation building in Canada, with deep ramifications for Indigenous and non-Indigenous people.[27]

Even as they had significant impacts, however, widespread aspirations to an exclusionary and ongoing white society also remained far from achieved in early settler British Columbia. Although government officials and colonial commentators hoped for a stable population of white British settler families engaged in long-term agricultural work, for example, much of the land was inappropriate for farming, and resource extractive industries predominated instead. This led to uneven regional colonization, with isolated clusters of transient non-Indigenous settlement driven by industrial booms and busts. This in turn attracted (and disappointed) a diverse range of migrants who were mostly men, often single, and not necessarily white or British. Many sought short-term opportunities rather than long-term settlement. As early as 1859, an Emigration Office staffer in London suggested that the goal of attracting "a population firmly attached to the British Crown" made up of "married men of steady habits" might be entirely impossible on Vancouver Island.[28] Governments, churches, and charitable organizations tried to counter the low numbers of white women with assisted emigration schemes, but despite these efforts a marked settler gender imbalance continued.[29]

More broadly, the white settler population remained a minority through almost all of this time frame. Records vary, but most historians draw from evidence suggesting that in 1871 there were about 8,500 white people, 1,500 Chinese people, 500 Black people, and more than 25,000 Indigenous people in the new province. By 1881, the number of white settlers had grown to approximately 17,000 out of 53,000.[30] Still, despite devastating epidemics, colonial policies, and mass immigration, Indigenous people outnumbered white settlers until the end of the century, and the new economy fundamentally depended on their labour and knowledge.[31] In addition, as suggested by the 1871 data, newcomers of colour arrived in significant numbers in this period. They included but were not limited to Chinese, African American, Japanese, and South Asian people, all of whom played a critical role in British Columbia even as they encountered racism, labour exploitation, and exclusionary policies aimed at the making of a white settler society.[32] Taken together, all of these factors posed significant challenges to British aspirations to an affluent, enduring, and exclusive white settler colonial society rooted in heterosexual nuclear families, small-scale agriculture, and the dispossession and disappearance of Indigenous people.

Given these points, the British Columbian relatives in this book played an important role in the settler colonial project during its foundational years between 1858 and 1914. In the absence of an established, stable, and self-reproducing white population, they were individually and collectively regarded as essential to the future of British Columbia, whether as long-term settlers or as short-term workers and administrators. Political, legal, and social structures made it easier for white Britons like themselves to cross borders into British Columbia or Canada, and (for men especially) to acquire land, participate in the political system, and engage in a range of jobs with comparatively strong remuneration once there. On the ground, they served as symbolic and embodied markers of British or Canadian sovereignty. They were reproductive sources of future generations of settlers, and white British women were particularly and anxiously imagined as such. And they performed the labour of dispossession and resettlement in a range of other ways too, from enforcing settler laws to building fences on land they had pre-empted. Broadly, while these individuals differed in their explicit support for colonialism, the state, and white supremacy, British Columbia's developing settler structures enabled and encouraged their lives there.

Within these general parameters, the British Columbian correspondents in this book varied in their circumstances, intentions, and experiences. Nearly all were immigrants rather than British Columbia–born. Many moved directly from the British Isles, while others arrived by more circuitous routes, especially through the United States or other imperial sites like Australia, India, and New Zealand – personal histories that could shape their expectations and lives in British Columbia in a range of ways. Most were young men who arrived alone, either because they were single and had left their families of origin, or because they had left their families of marriage, often intending to reunite later in British Columbia or the United Kingdom. Still others arrived with family members, including spouses, children, adult siblings, or aging parents. Some but not all intended to stay as long-term settlers. Many planned to exploit short-term opportunities such as gold mining, or to complete specific government or military assignments. Their plans could differ from results, of course; some intended sojourners settled for life, and some supposedly permanent settlers left. In addition, many remained mobile within British Columbia as employment opportunities and personal circumstances changed. Their families and backgrounds tended to be broadly middle class, but this could look very different in British Columbia, where there were new possibilities for social and economic mobility (both upward and downward) and for remaking oneself, albeit within limits. In this sense, settlers' class identities could be particularly precarious and multiple, as their cultural ideas and personal pasts diverged from their lived, material circumstances in a new place. In British Columbia, these Britons became ranchers and mothers, missionaries and loggers, powerful policymakers and failed prospectors – and at the same time, they continued to be relatives to distant family. In sum, they were diverse individuals connected by their comparative privilege as white Britons in an incipient settler society, their trans-imperial family relationships, and their simultaneous engagement with multiple places, especially the United Kingdom and British Columbia. While these settlers have long been the traditional subjects of historical studies, I contend that we have not yet grappled with the everyday, affective, and trans-imperial familial foundations of their power in western Canada – work that I undertake here.

In its trans-imperial framing, this book also speaks to scholarly conversations about Britain, British Columbia, migration, and empire in three additional ways. For one, it suggests that family correspondence was a powerful and widespread, if thus far under-examined, way in which the empire penetrated metropolitan Britons' daily lives, fashioned their knowledge and consciousness of distant colonial places, and configured their personal relationships. In this, I engage with a field termed the "new" imperial history. This is now a large and diverse body of scholarship that generally centres race, gender, and sexuality, and considers culture, emotion, intimacy, and the everyday as critical sites of imperial power and resistance. It examines networks or webs among imperial metropoles and colonies, tracing how these not only connected places but also came to constitute the empire itself. Many scholars in this field have argued that there is not a distinct division between domestic and imperial histories; rather, the empire made Britain as it permeated all aspects of metropolitan life. This has been a contentious position, with other British historians maintaining that the empire did not have as significant an impact on metropolitan society or consciousness as the new imperial history has suggested.[33]

Like other work associated with the field, this book underscores the significance of family, affect, and the everyday. I understand the post as a global and imperial network, and trace how correspondence produced a configuration of family that cannot be reduced to colony, province, or nation. And, positioning Britain and British Columbia in the same frame, I maintain that correspondence reflected and helped to make the two sites in relation to one another (in addition to places beyond this dyad). From the British perspective, letters were common routes through which metropolitan residents came to understand and connect with lesser-known colonial sites like British Columbia, which did not often feature in novels, newspapers, major political debates, or other sources of information about the empire. For these relatives, empire was not merely something that happened "out there" beyond their attention and familiarity. Rather, through migration and the post, empire came home into the personal lives and everyday knowledge of metropolitan Britons.

At the same time, by arguing that early settler British Columbia cannot be fully understood without attention to its wider British imperial context, this book also joins a small body of work that connects the often distinct historiographies of Canada, Britain, and empire.[34] As a colony and province, British Columbia was a comparatively minor player in the British Empire – economically precarious and politically marginal and located far from centres of imperial and dominion power. Reflecting this, it has also played a comparatively minor role in the wider scholarship on the British Empire. At the same time that it was on the empire's largely forgotten fringes, however, British Columbia was also in the middle of an important pattern of imperial expansion in the nineteenth and early twentieth centuries. From its founding as a colony, it joined other nascent white settler societies on the Pacific Rim identified with Anglo-Saxonism and connected by shared aspirations to exclusionary, enduring whiteness. In this, its early settler period was part of an intensifying transnational project to make "white men's countries."[35] As such, British Columbia's history not only reveals how colonialism worked on what Adele Perry calls the "ragged margins" of the British Empire but also elucidates the trajectories and limits of a particular form of imperialism that expanded and flourished in these years.[36]

This has significant implications for how we approach the study of settler colonialism too. By its very definition, settler colonialism requires settlers who "come to stay," in anthropologist Patrick Wolfe's phrasing.[37] Existing studies of settler colonialism have generally focused on the logics, policies, and practices that enabled settlers to stay in a given colonial site, and their consequences for Indigenous and non-Indigenous people. But for settlers themselves, staying also necessarily meant leaving elsewhere. For white Britons in early settler British Columbia, this "elsewhere" was often the imperial metropole, which retained salience not only as a site of political power but also as a personal and familial home. In this sense, this book's trans-imperial framing reveals that migration and settlement – at the very heart of the colonial project in early settler British Columbia – was a fundamentally multi-sited, personal process.

Overall, then, this is a study of British families as they engaged with the imperial metropole and early settler colonial British Columbia. Through their mobility and epistolary networks of communication, these families helped to connect and remake both places, while turning themselves into settlers in a nascent settler society. In this focus, this book is situated at the intersections of several fields, and intervenes in numerous scholarly conversations. It traces diverse forms of long-distance family, underscoring their critical significance to colonial processes. In the spirit of the new imperial history, it highlights the importance of intimate networks between the metropole and colonial places. It suggests that metropolitan Britons understood, normalized, and engaged with the wider imperial world in part through epistolary family relationships. At the same time, it demonstrates that the migration on which local settler projects depended must be understood as both trans-imperial and personal. And by investigating British Columbia's particular place in the expansion of white settler colonialism in this period, it traces the affective, everyday, and trans-imperial workings of this formation of power as it developed in one site. In all of these ways, this book argues for the entwined significance of family and empire, Britain and British Columbia, settler colonialism and the post.

Letters

By focusing on families that were sustained through the imperial mail, this book takes letters as its main source as well as a key subject of analysis. It draws on research investigating thousands of family letters that are now located in Canadian and British repositories (including the British Columbia Archives, the British Library, the City of Vancouver Archives, the City of Victoria Archives, Library and Archives Canada, the New Westminster Archives, and the University of British Columbia's Rare Books and Special Collections) or that have been published in transcribed form. Specifically, it focuses on the correspondence of just over fifty families – approximately two thousand letters in total, now primarily archived in British Columbia. Some of these family collections are vast, spanning decades and comprising hundreds of letters between multiple relatives. Others are small or fragmented, in some cases containing only one or two letters, which might have been the only ones ever written or the only ones preserved and archived. Most consist of correspondence written in one direction rather than two-way conversations; it is sometimes but not always possible to reconstruct the other side of the communication, at least in terms of general content. To place these letters in context, I draw on myriad other sources, including diaries, memoirs, newspapers, court records, etiquette manuals, and government papers. In addition, my analysis is informed by some comparative engagement with British family letters written beyond the British Columbian context in the nineteenth and early twentieth centuries. This research includes published collections of correspondence between the United Kingdom, North America, Australia, and New Zealand, as well as archived letters sent to and from South Asia, now held in the British Library's India Office Private Papers.[38] Taken together, these sources and research strategies enable a focused analysis of family letters written between Britain and British Columbia that recognizes both their specificity and their connections to wider contexts, patterns, and issues.

These collections of correspondence represent an important cluster of settlers, but they do not reflect a full cross-section of British families engaged with early settler British Columbia. Most obviously, families who did not write any letters are left out. An inability to read and write may have impeded some families' epistolary communication; these would have been disproportionately members of the working classes. However, literacy rates were rising rapidly by the second half of the nineteenth century, and archived letters do indicate that Britons with diverse capabilities were able to communicate by post.[39] Other relatives may have chosen not to write out of hostility, disinterest, or diverging lives. Such a group likely came from as broad a range of backgrounds as those who did write. Although this book focuses on families who maintained trans-imperial connections by post, and can say less about those who did not do so, the final two chapters flesh out some of the forms and consequences of epistolary silence.

The nature of the correspondence analyzed here is also a product of the racialized, gendered, classed, and partial colonial archive.[40] Its depth and density – that so many personal records of white British settlers have been archived at all – reflects the writers' comparative social and cultural power. With some notable exceptions, men produced most of the letters from British Columbia. Rather than indicating a gendered letter-writing practice per se, this results from the disproportionate number of settler men and the markedly gendered nature of the archive. Class and status also matter. The metropolitan branches of these families tended to cluster in the middle classes, while the British Columbian relatives were often important figures in local or provincial politics, business, or society. Again with some significant exceptions, many sources in this book have been publicly archived because of the settlers' diverse but comparative influence in British Columbia. Finally, the vast majority of archived collections have been donated by descendants to Canadian rather than British repositories. This regional asymmetry reflects a particular postcolonial production of imperial archives, in which the colonial histories of former settler dominions have been largely unmoored from a sense of ongoing relevance in the metropole. The records of settlers and their families are now seen as more at home in Canada, important or interesting as stories of province and nation building rather than of empire or Britain – the latter being the primary focus of acquisitions for repositories in the United Kingdom. In this sense, settler records, as well as settlers themselves, have come to claim primary belonging in British Columbia.

These archival parameters matter because they reflect configurations of colonial power in past and present, and shape the possibilities and emphases of research. By using existing archival collections, this book prioritizes families who maintained connections by post, and focuses on the personal records of a comparatively privileged segment of the settler and metropolitan populations. At the same time, I also look to push beyond a common scholarly emphasis on prominent families, intentionally seeking out a range of Britons whose letters have been archived. By considering the records of less influential or so-called ordinary settlers, as well as the correspondence of powerful members of the political and social elite, I underscore the fact that the settler colonial project was not only a matter of policymaking and governance; it was also built on the everyday, affective lives of a larger, more varied, but still privileged group of white British settlers and their families.

To analyze these sources, the book builds from the insights and approaches of a large scholarship on letter writing. Like this body of work, I understand letters as texts and material objects that reflected, shaped, and reveal their wider historical contexts. As correspondents consciously and unconsciously decided what to write and how, they crafted senses of self, performed identities and relationships, and articulated individual and shared ideas about the world.[41] Historians have used family letters in many ways. While a significant number have considered letters together with various other kinds of sources, some have focused specifically on correspondence as a particular genre or form of relationship.[42] In Western Canada, historians Jean Barman and Ryan Eyford have examined epistolary case studies that point to the rich potential of family letters for casting new light on the region's history of migration and colonialism.[43] Picking up these threads here, I expand the scope to investigate a broader range of people, relationships, and letter-writing practices that contributed to the foundations of British Columbia, as well as to the United Kingdom and the wider British imperial world. The result is the first substantial study of letters as a widespread and influential body of sources in this context.

Undertaking this work, I examine family correspondence as a distinct and significant form in its own right. Broadly, I consider the content, style, function, materiality, and symbolism of correspondence for these families and the colonial project with which they were engaged. Within this general scope, I focus especially on letters' textual context, interrogating what correspondents wrote, how, and why. In this, I draw inspiration from anthropologist Ann Laura Stoler's discussion of reading "along the grain" and literary scholar Sharon Marcus's methodology of "just reading." Both respond to analytical trends in their fields (critical colonial and Victorian literary studies, respectively) that read into sources' silences and against authors' intentions. Interrogating and reconstructing silences, as well as seeking traces of suppressed voices, scholars have used these strategies while working with the partial and powerful colonial archive. Stoler suggests, however, that reading only against the grain risks assuming that we already know the dispositions and concerns of the authors, and the particular configurations of power they enacted. Similarly, Marcus highlights the importance of attending to sources' content and intentions as well as, or before, reading into their silences. In a similar spirit, I embark on a commitment here to take seriously "what texts make manifest on their surface," in Marcus's framing.[44] In my research, I have not approached letters with the intention of extracting specific topics that I have assumed will be present and significant, but rather have sought to understand first what characterizes this correspondence. Recognizing that the majority of letters ignore topics that populate the scholarship on colonialism, I have worked to identify common epistolary concerns and forms, and then to investigate patterns and variations in their representations, before finally interrogating the silences embedded in them.

The result is a wide-ranging exploration of the contours, intentions, limitations, and significance of epistolary content. By concentrating on what the majority of letters did say, this book centres on what historian Alan Conway once called the "dross" that dominates family correspondence.[45] I probe the very qualities in letters – generic conventions, expressions of affect, and prevailing banality – that might seem most unremarkable or familiar to contemporary readers. For instance, anyone who has lived far from places they call "home" might recognize themselves in settlers' letters that long for familiar comforts, even as technologies of communication, common attitudes, and wider contexts have changed dramatically in the intervening century and a half. This is certainly true for me, living between British Columbia and Britain over the course of this project, stretching and sometimes breaking my own personal relationships across this same distance. At the same time, I write with a sense of a different intimate familiarity too, as a settler raised on Vancouver Island on W̱SÁNEĆ (Saanich) territory, and now living in Vancouver on xʷməθkʷəy'əm (Musqueam) territory. Both surrounded by and embedded in the legacies of the history in this book, I am conscious of the enduring power of the settler everyday that remains built into Canada's very foundations. From this position, it seems unsurprising that so many Britons looked away from the human consequences of the colonial structures from which they benefited, and looked toward other aspects of their lives. This is, after all, an impulse of disregard that sustains many structures of inequality and violence, both then and now.

This familiarity matters. For one, it makes impossible any oversimplification of colonizers as mere "avatars of ideas and ideologies," in geographers David Lambert and Alan Lester's phrase.[46] Instead, these letters call attention to the complicated humanity of the people who drove, sustained, and profited from settler projects. In making this point, my intention is not to evoke sympathy or disgust for Britons as colonial agents and settlers, but rather to understand better their roles in British Columbia and in a wider imperial world. More specifically, I take this approach in order to explicate the powerful politics of affect and the everyday that are complicit in settler colonialism at its roots. Embedded in these sources is the familiarity through which settlers came to be at home with the colonial order in British Columbia. In historians Catherine Hall and Sonya Rose's framing, being "at home with the empire" was to wield a form of power, as Britons took for granted their place and role in an imperial world. While Hall and Rose develop this idea in a collection that focuses on how the British Empire was "infused" and made comfortable in metropolitan lives, this also mattered in other colonial places.[47] Settler contexts were built on the normalization of the colonial order, as white Britons both claimed these places as home and came to feel at home with them. The affective and banal concerns of family letters reveal this process at work, as white settlers and their families learned to take for granted British Columbia as a comfortable home.

Weaving together these points, this book positions correspondence as a subject, a source, and a methodological device through which to investigate the relationship between trans-imperial British families and the foundations of settler colonialism in British Columbia. Moving from general to particular, it first develops broadly scoped analyses of epistolary themes, with the early chapters considering examples from a wide range of families. It then progressively deepens its focus, with the later chapters fleshing out magnified case studies of family stories, playing with a more personal analytical voice, and conducting closer readings of individual letters that nuance the wider argument. Each chapter ends with what I call a coda, which – like its musical counterpart – serves as a longer closing section with an additional, climactic element and personal reflection to complete the argument, as well as doing the work of a conventional conclusion. Taken together, the range of approaches draws on both the breadth and depth of my research, balances a diversity of examples and detailed cases, and engages with the representative and the exceptional in archived correspondence. By employing this shifting analytical and vocal style, I also seek to demonstrate multiple registers on which historians might approach letters as telling sources and subjects, not only examining different epistolary themes but also modelling different ways to investigate the content, voice, form, purpose, and context of correspondence.

Part 1 focuses on broad structures and uses of the post. Chapter 1 outlines the postal systems that connected Britain and British Columbia, and introduces the general contours of the letters that moved through them. It shows that these postal structures and letters worked together to fashion settler British Columbia as part of the infrastructure of empire and a tool of white British migration. Turning to focus on the familial uses of letters in more detail, Chapter 2 then explores how relatives used letters to develop, maintain, and define long-distance relationships. Through the post, Britons navigated the personal impacts of distance, enabled the ongoing salience of metropolitan relatives in settler lives, and rendered letter writing and the trans-imperial family mutually constitutive.

Part 2 examines patterns and variations in the specific content of letters, considering their role in crafting trans-imperial family understandings of British Columbia as everyday or normal. Chapter 3 focuses on emotional description as a site for colonial knowledge production and circulation, tracing how settlers' letters moved from initial declarations of astonishment to prevailing representations of tedium. This was an affective move that reflected their growing ability to represent and sustain British Columbian lives as unremarkable, and their power to disregard settler violence, anxiety, or vulnerability. Chapter 4 then zooms in on one common, concrete epistolary topic. In discussions about food, correspondents produced meanings for the settler everyday that normalized their experiences, made them relatable across imperial distances by defining them in comparison with metropolitan norms, and ultimately claimed settler comfort and belonging while erasing Indigenous people's presence, practices, and competing claims.

Turning from the earlier chapters' emphasis on familial connection, Part 3 fleshes out the contours of epistolary rupture, conflict, or secrecy, and their significance for trans-imperial relationships and colonial knowledge. Chapter 5 focuses on letters about death, investigating how relatives performed collective grief and redistributed (or argued about) property in its wake. Several case studies reveal how relatives delineated the emotions, responsibilities, and relationships that constituted trans-imperial families in crisis. They show that families were defined by fracture as well as the everyday, hostility as well as affection, and individual material interests in imperial places as well as emotional claims to connection between them. Finally, Chapter 6 delves into a single case of epistolary silence, investigating a secret that was maintained among relatives but shared as gossip outside the family. It reveals that gossip and silence were strategies for maintaining relationships in circumstances when colonial and metropolitan lives, and families of origin and marriage, seemed otherwise irreconcilable. Correspondents managed information in order to shape knowledge and relationships, and in the process revealed divergent ideas about race, gender, and intimacy in a critical colonial moment.

Taken together, the chapters trace general postal structures and uses, emotional tones, and common topics, as well as particular cases of trouble, change, and silence in long-distance family lives. Through a range of approaches, they uncover comparatively consistent discursive strategies and family forms that underpinned a period of change in British Columbia, the United Kingdom, and the British imperial world. They demonstrate how Britons maintained trans-imperial relationships in everyday separations and times of crisis, and made sense of the personal distances necessary to migration and settlement. They also reveal how British settlers produced and circulated family forms of knowledge about British Columbia, while almost entirely disregarding topics that preoccupy the scholarship on colonialism. Individually and together, the chapters argue that family letters both explained and facilitated the foundations of settler colonialism as Britons rewrote British Columbia into a banal, livable, and sustainable home. Recognizing that this colonial logic has enduring power and resonance in the present – a point to which the Conclusion returns in more detail – this book ultimately seeks to explicate its historical roots in what Robert Burnaby's June 1860 family letter called the "common-place" of settler life, and, in so doing, unsettle its ongoing, normalized familiarity today.

Part 1
Relative Distances

1

"Bind the Empire Together"

The Postal System, Family Letters, and British Columbia

In February 1896, British Conservative Member of Parliament John Henniker Heaton made an impassioned plea for postal reform, the topic that dominated his nearly three-decade political career. In this case, he called on Secretary of State for the Colonies Joseph Chamberlain to establish a universal imperial penny post system. This would set a uniform, affordable, and preferential postal rate across the British Empire and, he argued, ameliorate a number of challenges to Britain's global imperial rule in the process. With the florid rhetoric of late-nineteenth-century new imperialism, Heaton proclaimed:

> What we want is some cheap and ready means of bridging over the chasm of distance between our people and the millions of their colonial kindred, of restoring the broken arch in their communications and the severed link in their sympathies, of weaving the innumerable delicate threads of private and family affection into a mighty strand that shall bind the Empire together, and resist any strain from our foes or the Fates. We want it now, while we are threatened.[1]

For Heaton, the postal system mattered because it had the power to strengthen and solidify the political, economic, and social connections that made the British Empire work, while poor or inaccessible mail services had what he called a "dissolvent effect on the Empire."[2] To underscore the pressing consequences of disunity, he repeatedly emphasized the growing challenges to British trade and rule in this period, as imperial competition and anti-colonial movements intensified around the world. At this particular moment, Heaton insisted, reforming the postal system was not only an important political issue but also an urgent one. At stake was the very future of the British Empire.

Although Heaton crafted these arguments in order to cultivate support for postal reform in a specific period of imperial jingoism, recent scholarship has investigated and confirmed one of his key underlying points: the postal system did play a significant role in British political, economic, and imperial history in the nineteenth century. More specifically, historians have demonstrated, the postal system and its reforms were integral to the making of a modern liberal state in Britain, while letter writing and communication networks facilitated colonial governance and the extension of British commerce around the world.[3] However, the scholarly work on postal systems has paid comparatively less attention to another central element of Heaton's argument – that what he called the "innumerable delicate threads of private and family affection" also mattered in the postal systems that "[bound] the Empire together."[4] To consider this point in its broader context, this chapter outlines the forms and entwined impact of postal systems, personal letters, and colonial structures in British Columbia, a place rarely mentioned in the wider scholarship on the post. How did associated (British, British Columbian, imperial, and international) postal systems develop and shape their various contexts in this period? What were the general contours of family letters sent between the United Kingdom and British Columbia, and what relationship did they have to the postal systems in which they moved? And what role did postal systems and family letters play together in shaping the broad structures of settler British Columbia and its integration into the British imperial world?

Drawing on these questions, this chapter introduces the core sources and general historical structures that underpin this book's exploration of family correspondence and early settler British Columbia. It first explains the important role of postal systems in British and British Columbian history in the nineteenth and early twentieth centuries. It then identifies common patterns in family correspondence, which I suggest were both products of a wider culture of letter writing and effects of changing postal structures. Finally, it examines the relationship between the postal system, family letters, and one critical branch or precondition of the settler colonial project: the migration of white British people. As I show, families strategically and explicitly used the postal system in order to shape migration to British Columbia. Their actions combined with changing postal structures to enable the foundations of settler British Columbia and bind these to the wider British imperial world.

"This All Important Question": The Postal Systems

The transmission of mail between Britain and British Columbia depended on the internal structures of multiple postal systems. These included the British Post Office and Royal Mail, the colonial and dominion mails of Vancouver Island, British Columbia, and Canada, and in some cases the American postal service. These systems were connected in a complex network shaped by international and imperial agreements, and arrangements between state institutions and private interests. Between the mid-nineteenth and early twentieth centuries, this communication network was reconfigured by remarkable changes, including major policy and legal reforms, technological developments, and infrastructural growth. Postal history was also linked to an incredible range of broader social and political transformations in the long nineteenth century, from changing education policies and literacy rates to the expansion of state bureaucracy. For the subjects of this book, these transformations mattered for two reasons: they facilitated a thriving culture of personal letter writing, and they produced a global system of communication that not only connected the metropole and colonial sites around the world but also reconfigured them in relation to one another. Indeed, postal structures were vital to the making of British Columbia as part of the British imperial world – a foundational point for its settler project and for the place of family letters within that project.

In the nineteenth and early twentieth centuries, industrialization, urbanization, and related changes transformed Britain.[5] Embedded in this wider history were a series of reforms that remade Royal Mail and the British Post Office. Before 1840, mail services were governed by a confusing and inconsistent series of regulations, rates, and procedures that varied across the country. In this system, the recipient of a letter usually paid its postage. Rates were based on distance and the number of sheets, with the latter point discouraging lengthy social letters. Even for short letters, the rates were high enough to be a major hardship, or even prohibitive, for significant swathes of the population. Given these costs, Britons found creative ways to communicate while evading the formal system, for example, by sending mail with unofficial carriers or transmitting coded messages in newspapers, which were not subject to the high postage of letters. By the 1830s, there were widespread concerns about the state of the postal service. In addition to issues of cost and usage, reformers argued that improvements were critical to the social, moral, and economic well-being of an industrializing country. For instance, they pointed out that more and more Britons lived in physical separation from relatives and acquaintances, in many cases leaving struggling family farms and moving to factory towns for work. As these politicians and social commentators suggested, an accessible and reliable postal system would enable such people to remain in touch with family, share their earnings, improve their literacy, and still move to where their labour was needed.[6]

In the middle decades of the nineteenth century, such arguments contributed to important changes that impacted many Britons' relationship to the post. The year 1840 marked the major turning point. Brought in that year, the new Uniform Penny Post set a standard, prepaid, and comparatively low postage rate based on weight – one penny for all mail under half an ounce sent within the United Kingdom. These lower rates helped direct more mail toward the state system and away from underground forms of communication, while subsequent reforms further extended and improved postal services. In the second half of the century, developing rail networks also facilitated the faster and more consistent delivery of mail across the country. The telegraph was integrated into the national Post Office system in 1870 and grew in popularity for political and business correspondence in the final years of the century. Beyond such forms of communication, though, use of the telegraph remained relatively limited, and letters in the official postal system served as the primary form of long-distance social communication in the United Kingdom in the late nineteenth and the early twentieth centuries.[7]

These changes were closely entwined with a number of broader transformations in British political, economic, and social life. As historian Patrick Joyce demonstrates, the reformed postal system facilitated the growth of the modern British state and its bureaucracy in numerous ways, for example by systematizing communication between government branches and extending their reach into new parts of the country. In the process, the Post Office became the largest employer and state institution in Britain in the second half of the nineteenth century.[8] At the same time, political dissent could also draw on a more accessible postal system to spread information, coordinate protests, and gain further support. The penny post played a pivotal role in the spread of the anti–Corn Laws movement in the 1840s and the laws' comparatively quick repeal, for example.[9] In this period, the Post Office also became integrated into many people's personal financial lives through its banking, insurance, and money order schemes. Companies profited from rapid and reliable communication that enabled them to coordinate trade, markets, and services. Postal reform also changed streetscapes and the built environment. Since postage was prepaid after 1840, mail no longer required delivery to a person. Impersonal forms of delivery contributed to the growing presence of house numbers, street signs, and mailboxes in Britain, and the increasing significance of numerical addresses as central identifiers of people and places.[10] These examples underscore a core point: postal reforms both reflected and participated in major changes across the country in this period.

Interwoven with these transformations was a revolution in the use of the British postal system. In the early nineteenth century, reformers had argued that the system needed to change so that so-called ordinary Britons could better access the mail. The ensuing reforms not only responded to an interest in social correspondence but also facilitated its remarkable growth. Lower postage rates meant that more people could afford to send mail, while the maximum weight for the penny post permitted longer letters. The reforms thus contributed to a culture of personal letter writing that encompassed a much wider range of Britons than ever before, including growing numbers of working-class families over time. The volume of mail sent within the United Kingdom jumped 122.4 percent in the first year of the penny post alone. The number of letters doubled, from 400 million to 800 million, between 1853 and 1870, and the number of all types of postal packets grew from 82 million in 1839 to 3.723 billion in 1900.[11] Rising literacy rates supported (and perhaps were partly shaped by) this expanding appetite for correspondence. Literacy in Britain, approximately 93 percent in 1890, was nearly universal by the turn of the century. While there was not a simple equivalence between letter writing and these numbers – official statistics may not have reflected functional literacy, while letter writing could also have been a collective project rather than something dependent on individual ability – there is a strong correlation between the growing ability of Britons to write and read letters, the increasing accessibility of the post, and the exceptional expansion in mail.[12] This was, as literary scholar Catherine Golden terms it, a "postal revolution" that fed a thriving culture of letter writing.[13]

The growing interest in correspondence was not circumscribed by national borders, especially given Britain's high emigration rates and imperial expansion in this period, as well as other countries' subsequent pursuit of similar postal reforms.[14] A series of international congresses and treaties connected the British postal system with an increasingly integrated global communication network. Most prominent among these was the 1874 creation of the General Postal Union, which aimed to convert a messy array of national regulations and bilateral treaties into a single unified international postal territory. The General Postal Union drew inspiration from the British reforms of 1840, and set uniform and prepaid rates. Its members agreed to carry mail in transit between other member countries without requiring additional postage. The United Kingdom was a founding signatory, and Canada joined in 1878, the same year that the organization was renamed the Universal Postal Union in recognition of a markedly expanded membership. By 1914, 135 states and colonies had joined the agency, which oversaw the transmission of approximately 25 billion letters a year and linked Canada and the United Kingdom in a global network of mail.[15]

The postal connections between British Columbia and the United Kingdom were also shaped by specific imperial priorities and practices. In 1846, the British government established a policy that gave it jurisdiction over mail arrangements across the empire, while individual colonies controlled their internal postal systems.[16] Within this wider imperial terrain, British Columbia's mail had a particular history, changing over the course of the nineteenth century from a very rudimentary system to a more reliable combination of post, parcel, and telegraph. The earliest transmission of mail from the United Kingdom to the region currently known as British Columbia operated in the early nineteenth-century fur-trade world, carried along Hudson's Bay Company lines by ship and brigade. Around 1850, the California gold rush prompted a regular service from the United Kingdom to San Francisco by the Panama route. This was then expanded northward to the Columbia River and Puget Sound (now in the northwestern United States), from which point Hudson's Bay Company boats carried letters to Fort Victoria and beyond. With the advent of the Fraser River gold rush in 1858, the secretary of state for the colonies proposed a regular post from the United Kingdom to British Columbia via British and American routes.[17] However, despite many government discussions, unstable gold rush conditions hindered the establishment of an effective internal state system, and the postal connections between the colonies and the metropole – what Vancouver Island governor Arthur Kennedy called in 1864 an "all important question" – remained unreliable, inconsistent, and heavily dependent on American services.[18] In this context, individuals and companies vied for internal delivery contracts, and express companies like Wells Fargo and Company extended north from California to carry the post within British Columbia.[19] Overall, during the colonial period, there was only a piecemeal postal system, governed by little (in the case of British Columbia) or no (Vancouver Island) legislation, maintained by private interests, and reliant on positive relations between the United Kingdom and the United States.

In the colonial period, British settlers frequently remarked on this postal system and its impact on their correspondence. In the mid-nineteenth century, these discussions most often focused on criticisms of the irregular, unpredictable, and slow service that connected the colonies with the metropole. Writing from Victoria in 1859, shortly after her arrival with her husband's Royal Engineers detachment, Mary Hawks Moody echoed many others when she complained to her sister in northern England that "the Mails are very uncertain & the arrangements *very* bad."[20] Settlers often blamed delays on the complicated transnational nature of the colonial post, specifically finding fault with what they called the "Yankee mails" or the Panama route, both outside of British control.[21] Occasionally, delays also resulted from their relatives' incorrect use of the postal system. In 1859, civil servant and aspiring colonial merchant Robert Burnaby informed his relatives in Leicestershire, England, that six of their letters had taken nine months to arrive in Victoria as they were "insufficiently stamped" and therefore sent by the slow Cape Horn route.[22] Even when the post worked smoothly, however, it still took a long time in the colonial period. In an average estimate, settler John Christie noted in 1861 that letters took about six weeks to two months to travel between his relatives in Scotland and him on Vancouver Island.[23]

When British Columbia entered Confederation with Canada in 1871, the dominion government took over the postal system and standardized and de-privatized the skeletal colonial structures.[24] However, British Columbia's mail still remained closely integrated with the United States postal system, and continued to be carried through American territory until the mid-1880s, when the completion of the Canadian Pacific Railway further regularized British Columbia's postal connections with eastern Canada and the United Kingdom, and reduced (but did not eliminate) the demand for American routes.[25] The 1887 *Official Postal Guide* for Canada summarized the options: mail was "forwarded daily to and from British Columbia via the Canadian Pacific Railway," or was "dispatched weekly, by steamer, between San Francisco California, and Victoria." Transatlantic mail routes similarly involved either Canadian or American ports, as letters for the United Kingdom left weekly by steamer from Quebec or Halifax, and biweekly from New York.[26]

These changes generally made the postal system more reliable and regular in the early provincial years. In 1883, English physician and prospective settler Charles Newcombe celebrated the fact that mail arrived in Victoria "3 or 4 times a week from Canada & the European countries" – a point that made Vancouver Island an attractive possible home for his family.[27] In the 1890s and 1900s, the Langley-Kidner family letters took approximately two weeks to travel between southern England and southwestern British Columbia.[28] Likewise, in 1899 Leonard Witherby noted that his parents' letters travelled from England to his Victoria home in an average of seventeen days.[29] However, for settlers who lived further away from cities or rail lines, delivery within British Columbia could still be frustratingly poor or inconsistent. Kootenay rancher Tommy Norbury complained to his mother in 1898 that "the mail service is about as bad as ever if not worse ... & the worst of it is, there is no remedy as the Govt. take no notice of petitions or anything else."[30]

While provincial mail delivery continued to be uneven on a local level, the British imperial postal system changed as a whole at the end of the nineteenth century with the 1898 institution of the Imperial Penny Post – a victory for postal reformers like John Henniker Heaton. As the Uniform Penny Post had done nationally in the United Kingdom in 1840, this important turning point set a low, standard, and prepaid postage rate that was calculated by weight. Its regulations applied across the empire except New Zealand and Australia, which joined in 1900 and 1911, respectively. In 1899, Canadian postmaster general William Mulock reported that there had been "greatly increased correspondence between Canada and the United Kingdom" as a result of the penny post – perhaps even a 150 percent growth. The British Post Office questioned Mulock's statistics but still found a significant increase. Whatever the specific numbers, they agreed, the penny post had assisted the proliferation of an already extensive level of correspondence that connected Canada with Britain and the wider imperial world at the turn of the century.[31]

While important, this postal system was not the only method of communication between the United Kingdom and early settler British Columbia. For one, Britons sometimes sent letters with travelling relatives or acquaintances, as well as through the official state system, although examples of the more informal delivery method are rare in the archive.[32] By the end of the nineteenth century, the telegraph was also a viable option between British Columbia and the metropole. In 1902, the existing telegraph system was extended across the Pacific, further integrating Canada, Australia, New Zealand, and the United Kingdom in an effective and rapid imperial communication network. This was more expensive but much quicker than letters: telegrams could travel between Britain and British Columbia in approximately two or three hours at the turn of the century. However, since telegrams conveyed only short messages at higher costs, families typically used this system only at times of urgent need or significant news, such as requests for a loan or notifications of a birth.[33] Throughout this period, letters sent through the official postal system remained the primary form of familial communication between the United Kingdom and British Columbia.

This history of long-distance communication mattered to the development of early settler British Columbia and its place in the British Empire. When John Henniker Heaton advanced his argument for imperial postal reform at the end of the nineteenth century, he was acknowledging a much larger point: put simply, writing and its circulation were key practices of colonialism. In a wide range of forms – from travel writing to newspaper articles, missionary reports to histories, company documents to bureaucratic files – paper and ink helped people to know, work, rule, revolt, and live in the empire.[34] Writing that was sent across vast distances mattered in particular ways. On a basic level, Britain's claim to a global empire fundamentally depended on a communication network that connected administrators in the metropole and the colonies, and enabled them to send reports, queries, instructions, budgets, legislation, declarations of war, and other papers critical to long-distance imperial governance. In this sense, a system for moving letters and documents around the world should be seen as an important form of imperial infrastructure – another of what historian Daniel Headrick has called the "tools" that facilitated and shaped colonial rule around the world.[35] Thus, written texts not only constitute a rich archive that tells us about empire and colonialism today but, in their circulation, were also part and parcel of it.

This was certainly true for early settler British Columbia, which was both physically and psychologically distant from the centres of imperial and dominion power. In Ottawa and London, civil servants, politicians, military officers, and others depended on writing to know and govern from afar. In 1849 and 1858, official imperial proclamations in London declared pen-and-paper sovereignty over Vancouver Island and British Columbia. Metropolitan imperial administrators then crafted policies for the colonies using information that travelled to them through the post, and communicated their decisions through official despatches in return. Through this process, political correspondence produced and circulated knowledge about the colonies and shaped the implementation of British governnce there. At the same time, the mail's slow and sometimes ineffective nature could mean that politics on the ground could be very different from that which was imagined and directed from afar, not least because local colonial administrators and provincial politicians often made decisions and acted without waiting for instruction from London or Ottawa. In this sense, the mail could suggest forms of British and Canadian confidence or control that were belied by much more complex situations in practice. Overall, this process of long-distance communication and governance, as well as its limits, shaped the developing settler state through what Christopher Bracken has termed "postal-colonialism."[36]

The mail also played a critical role in the growth of imperial and regional economies. For instance, early settler British Columbia was shaped by strong north-south postal connections with the western United States and, until late in the nineteenth century, comparatively weak connections with eastern North America. This contributed to British Columbia's marked reliance on San Francisco's markets, trade, and products throughout the colonial and early provincial years.[37] In addition, social uses of the post played an important role in the scattered and peripatetic careers of many Britons across the empire, including British Columbia. As Henniker Heaton suggested, a range of administrators, merchants, soldiers, missionaries, and settlers claimed that their imperial lives were more thinkable or sustainable because of the post, through which they kept in touch with distant friends and relatives. At its heart, writing and the post helped to construct colonial knowledge, facilitate the communication and implementation of imperial policies, negotiate markets and enact trade, plot resistance, support migration, and otherwise connect and shape the far-flung places claimed by Britain.

The remainder of this book expands on the social uses and significance of the postal system. As I have suggested, however, this was only one part of a broader role played by the mail in shaping early settler British Columbia as part of the British Empire. Overall, the postal systems between the United Kingdom and British Columbia changed significantly in the nineteenth and early twentieth centuries. These transformations were also entwined with much wider developments at local, national, and international scales. In the context of British Columbia, the postal system facilitated long-distance imperial and dominion governance, shaped the reach of the settler state and capitalist economy, and integrated British Columbia – albeit in sometimes uneven ways – with larger imperial and international communication networks. These changes were spurred in part by a growing interest in social correspondence in Britain and the empire and, in turn, the increasingly affordable and effective postal system contributed to a burgeoning shared culture of personal letter writing in and between these places.

"A Few Lines": Family Correspondence

While these personal letters varied by individual writers, relationships, intentions, and contexts, their general forms were remarkably similar across the more than half-century covered in this book. Archived family correspondence sent to or from early settler British Columbia is marked by common patterns in materials, structure, language, and content. These patterns reflected a shared set of generic conventions that were characteristic of a wider British culture of social correspondence in this period. Along with practices, they were encouraged by the postal reforms in the nineteenth and early twentieth centuries that made epistolary communication more feasible and familiar for a range of Britons, including families engaged with British Columbia.

In general, the family letters in this book were constructed from similar materials, including mass-produced steel pens, pencils, notepaper, envelopes, and adhesive stamps – all of which were developed or improved because of nineteenth-century industrialization.[38] The vast majority were written in pen on standardized stationery, with each sheet folded in half, creating four panels that were filled like a book. Some notepaper featured personal or business letterhead, and mourning stationery – used after a death – had printed black edges around the envelope and first panel.[39] More unconventional materials reflected correspondents' limited access to stationery, or helped relatives share local information more easily. For instance, Nanaimo schoolmaster Cornelius Bryant received an 1859 letter from his mother written on the back of the year's "Dudley Circuit," a

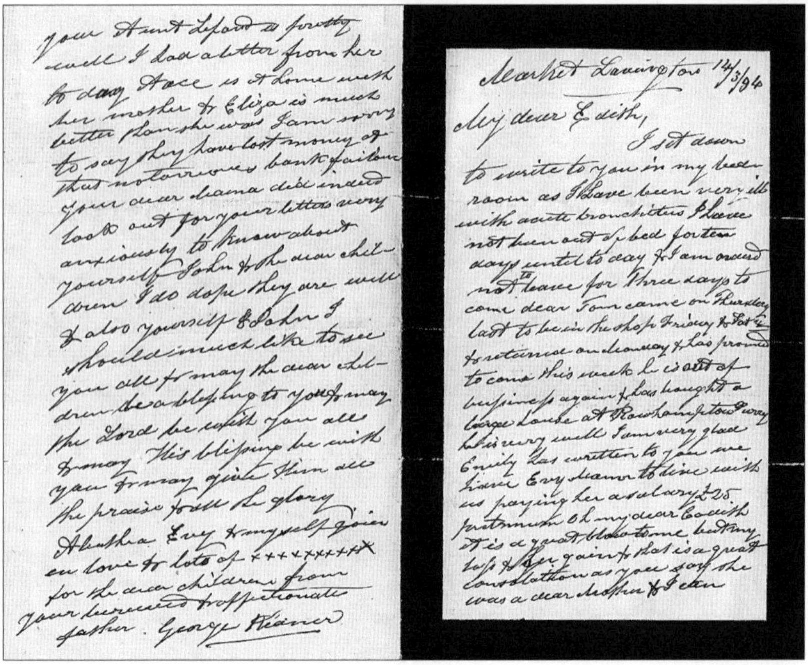

FIGURE 2 Letter on mourning stationery | Langley-Kidner family. George Kidner to daughter Edith Kidner Langley, Market Lavington, 14 March 1894, UBCSC, RBSC-ARC-1322, Langley family, box 1, file 1.

printed schedule for Wesleyan services around her home in the English West Midlands.[40] Such variations were rare, though, and letters' material forms were generally very similar.

Archived envelopes indicate a consistent, standard form as well. They typically matched the notepaper inside. Stamps were placed in the top right-hand corner, and postmarks – origin, destination, and sometimes post offices in between – appear on either the front or back.[41] Envelopes also featured the destination address centred on the front. Destinations sometimes included house numbers and street names, but were more often listed only as house names, post offices, or towns. In general, numerical addresses were more common on letters sent to the United Kingdom, but British Columbian addresses also grew more specific over the period as settlements expanded and mail delivery became more systematized. In their letters, settlers sometimes instructed relatives how

FIGURE 3 Envelope for letter on mourning stationery | Langley-Kidner family. George Kidner to daughter Edith Kidner Langley, Market Lavington, 14 March 1894, UBCSC, RBSC-ARC-1322, Langley family, box 1, file 1.

to address envelopes to British Columbia since it involved navigating an unfamiliar postal system and context. For instance, in 1901 Kootenay resident Harold Nation instructed his mother to stop addressing letters to him in "Canada." Although this contradicted official regulations, he explained that it was a matter of local identity. "Glancing at your envelope, I see that you put B.C. Canada," he wrote. "B.C. is quite enough as we think we are just as well known as Canada, which to us, is the name of the eastern Provinces."[42] While Nation pointed to the possibility of individual deviation in the details, archived envelopes generally reveal the availability of standardized stationery, the gradual systematization of addresses, and the growth of settlement in British Columbia over this period.

The letters themselves were almost always handwritten, though by the end of the period a small number were typed.[43] Correspondents used abbreviations such as "yr" (your), "cd" (could), "inst." (instante mense), and "ult." (ultimo mense), the latter two to reference the current and previous months respectively. The extensive use of such abbreviations without explanation indicates that they were widely understood, part of a common linguistic knowledge. Beyond abbreviations, spelling varied,

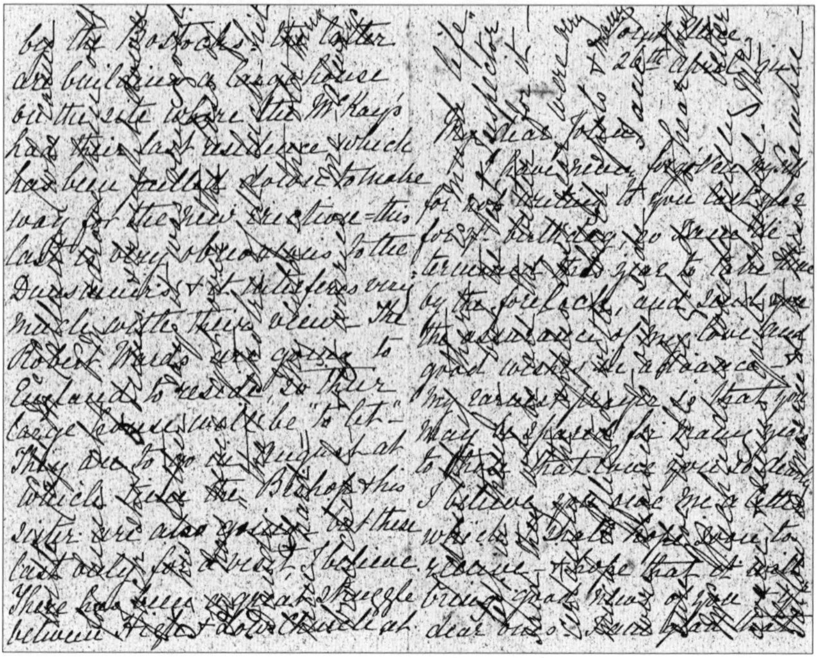

FIGURE 4 Cross-hatched letter | Trutch-O'Reilly family. Caroline Trutch O'Reilly to brother John Trutch, Victoria, 26 April 1894, UBCSC, RBSC-ARC-1561, Trutch family, box 2, file 6.

sometimes reflecting specific accents or educational experience. This was particularly true in the mid-nineteenth century, when correspondence more often featured diverse spelling and their writers had widely varied levels of formal schooling.[44] Individual hands could also indicate correspondents' confidence and familiarity with writing, often associated with their class, age, and education. In other cases, though, varied handwriting had less to do with experience or social position. While metropolitan relatives were generally able to write letters under consistent conditions, such as at a household desk, British Columbian correspondents sometimes explained that their writing was shaped by less favourable circumstances, such as a wet tent or a moving train.[45] Finally, a number of archived letters are cross-hatched – a technique in which a page was filled with two overlapping, perpendicular sets of writing. Correspondents chose to cross their writing like this in order to save paper.[46]

A decline in cross-hatching over this period was one effect of the nineteenth-century postal reforms, since under penny post regulations, postage was no longer calculated by the number of sheets in a letter. Changing postal regulations shaped correspondence in numerous other ways, too. For example, the 1898 institution of the Imperial Penny Post enabled some families to feel that they could afford to send more letters overall. Just before the penny post began, Mary Jane Matthews of Rock Ferry, England, scolded her son James in Vancouver for spending too much on postage. "You naughty boy," she wrote, "why do you put so many stamps on your letters." Immediately after the new regulations came into effect, her husband, Herbert Matthews, wrote James to celebrate: "Now the penny post has come in fine, to Canada, it will be strange if we cannot find time to write more letters."[47]

While some suggested that the penny post's cheaper standard rates encouraged more correspondence after 1898, the frequency of letters varied by family throughout the early settler period. Some relatives wrote rarely, and even when there was significant news to share, they might not do so right away.[48] Others wrote regularly, even weekly. Many chose to write the night before the mail was scheduled to leave, and for those in British Columbia, the unexpected arrival of a mail ship – often unpredictable, especially in the mid-nineteenth century – might mean writing a hasty letter in order not to miss it. To avoid such last-minute scrambles, other correspondents preferred to write letters over the course of several days or weeks, adding a few sentences at a time.[49] A number of settlers kept diaries over a longer period, which they later drew on for epistolary content, shared as excerpts, or addressed to relatives as a complete document.[50] When regular correspondents knew that they might not write for a while, they warned relatives. For settlers, this was often because they planned a journey into rural areas, away from regular access to the post, for gold prospecting or work in resource camps.[51] If they received no warning or a silence continued for longer than expected, metropolitan relatives sometimes contacted acquaintances in British Columbia to inquire after those who had failed to write.[52] The worst-case scenario befell the Rowell family in the early twentieth century, when Kootenay logger Wilf Rowell disappeared. His mother's letters were returned to her when he did not call for them at the post office, and finally, after years of silence, his brother had him declared officially deceased, using the family's final correspondence as evidence in the process.[53]

Responsibility for writing varied by family. The signatories of the letters in this book were men, women, and sometimes children who came from a range of class backgrounds and lived in diverse locations in British Columbia and Britain. Although it is possible, there is no indication that any of these letters were written by someone other than the people who signed them. When there were multiple relatives in a given place, they could each send separate letters, or one person could take on the role of primary correspondent while others passed on messages or enclosed short notes.[54] The named recipients likewise varied. In some families, letters were addressed to the same person from week to week, while other correspondents cycled through relatives – writing to their father one week, their mother the next, a sister the following, and so on, before repeating the cycle.[55]

Regardless of the named recipients, however, there was a general understanding that family letters would be read aloud, or even copied and sent onward to relatives in other places. Correspondents sometimes made this expectation explicit. In 1860, Anglican minister David Pringle wrote to his wife, Louie, who had remained in England while he established himself in Hope, British Columbia. He closed the letter by suggesting that she might "tear off" its personal content and send the rest to other relatives. "I cannot write this all again," he wrote, "& yet I s[houl]d like it to be known by many of our mutual belongings."[56] In 1890, Kootenay rancher Tommy Norbury similarly reminded relatives to share his letters, and in 1898, English physician and would-be Klondike prospector Roger Hicks asked his daughter to correct any mistakes when she copied his "scrawls" to send to others.[57] Sometimes families even passed correspondence over long transnational distances. In 1898, Norbury's mother sent a letter and a book to his brother Coni in Bermuda, who was then supposed to forward it to him in British Columbia.[58] The same year, Herbert Matthews sent his son James in Vancouver an extract of a letter from his other son Martin in Chile, and asked James to forward anything that Martin sent to him.[59] This strategy enabled letter writers to maximize their coverage and connection in an extended family network.

Given the widespread expectation that letters would be shared, correspondents specifically marked letters as private when they contained sensitive content. In the 1860s, naval officer Edmund Verney frequently wrote his father his personal opinions about Vancouver Island governance, British military affairs, and other political matters. In these cases, he indicated that letters were "private" at the top of the page, and elaborated on this in the main text.[60] Writing to his sister about his marriage plans in 1868, Victoria settler Samuel Beeman did the same, marking the letter "Private and Confidential," then writing: "In many long letters I have written *as ever* fully & freely to *yourself & dear Thomas* but let this be to *yourself*."[61] Without such indications, family letters might be shared not only in personal networks but also more widely. For example, a number of Cariboo prospectors addressed letters to relatives, who then published them in Welsh newspapers. Although it is impossible to determine from their content alone, these letters may have been written with the expectation that they would be published.[62] Others discovered that relatives had sent letters for publication without instruction or permission. To his horror, David Pringle learned that his wife had submitted his letters from Hope to the new literary journal, the *Cornhill Magazine,* in 1860. He responded:

> You hav [*sic*] put me in "a state" by dreaming of sending my letters for *publication.* 1st They were private & not intended to be made public. 2nd They were unfit for it. I remember asking you to publish a few things through my Father the pith & substance of one letter – but Louie, you must hav [*sic*] been dreaming when you wished to *show up* your husband in this style.[63]

Whatever their intended or actual audiences, the main content of letters contained many common features. As more Britons participated regularly in social correspondence over the nineteenth century, they built on an older, more exclusive tradition of letter writing and developed a more widely shared understanding of the genre.[64] It is possible that some drew on etiquette manuals to guide them in producing conventional correspondence. It is also likely that many Britons learned how to write letters in part from immersion in the practice. By the early twentieth century, some children were taught to write letters in school too.[65] However they learned to do so, these correspondents clearly shared expectations of the genre, rendering their letters generally similar to one another while also enabling relatives to deviate from norms in order to craft messages for specific contexts. Decisions to reject or revise conventional phrases could affect a letter's tone or spark emotional responses in readers, for example, by highlighting humour or affection, or suggesting distance or formality.[66] Deviation from conventions could also be deemed worthy of disapproval when it appeared sloppy rather than having a particular function. In 1899, Lucy Mathias of Putney, England, criticized her Victoria cousin, physician and collector Charles Newcombe, for a letter that included "*no* date & *no* address" at the top – a feature that was almost universal in family correspondence in this period.[67]

Besides the date and location, the most formulaic parts of these letters were their salutations and valedictions. Letters generally opened with a version of "My dear" or "My dearest," followed by the relationship and/or name of the intended recipient. Colonial civil servant and merchant Robert Burnaby addressed his letters in this style, beginning them, for example, with "My dearest Mother," "My dear Rose," "My dearest Harriet," and "My dear Tom."[68] This form remained remarkably consistent across the period and a broad range of writers. Valedictions and signatures were more varied, but typically included a form or combination of "Believe me," "Ever your most affectionate," or "I remain your loving," followed by the writer's name and/or relationship to the recipient. Some letters also featured a longer closing section in which correspondents explained that they missed their families or homes, inquired after acquaintances, requested more letters, and sent wishes, prayers, or love to relatives. Examples of these varied forms are again apparent in Burnaby's correspondence. For instance, he hurriedly closed an October 1861 letter to his mother as the mail steamer was threatening to depart: "Always remaining, dearest Mother, with fondest love to all, Your ever affect. Son, Rbt. Burnaby." Two and a half months later, he ended a Christmas letter to his mother with a more extensive closing passage:

> God bless you and all my darling Mother, and pray let me hear from you all. your mind, believing as I do that without *your* approbation and blessing which have always been my stay and comfort in life, I never could be really happy, and God bless you all dear brothers and sisters and surround you with all the comfort and happiness you can desire and find in the society of your children and each other. Your fondly loving Robert Burnaby.[69]

For Burnaby, this was an unusually embellished valediction, perhaps reflecting the particular emotional intensity of the holiday letter. In any case, most valedictions fell somewhere between the two versions, taking individually varied but broadly similar forms.

After the salutation, the first paragraph frequently concerned the correspondence itself. Here, relatives summarized their purpose for writing, or in the absence of a particular reason, they might explain that they were merely taking the opportunity to write "a few lines."[70] A discussion of recent correspondence often followed: what letters had been sent and received, what the writer thought of the latest letters, and general updates about the postal system. One example can be found in New Westminster farmer John Brough's 18 March 1862 letter to his sister. In his first paragraph, Brough noted that a 1 January letter from Scotland had arrived on 13 March. Before that, he had not received anything since May 1861, when his brother James's letter dated 16 March had arrived. Unlike some writers, Brough did not take an explicitly accusatory tack when discussing the family's infrequent correspondence. Instead, he referred to the unreliable postal service, wondering if some letters had been "in some way or other mismanaged in their transmission to this quarter of Her Majesty's dominions." Finally, remarking that his relatives had not indicated which letters they had received from him, he listed what he had sent in the same period so that they could account for each one.[71] In general, such discussions enabled relatives to track a correspondence, remark on one another's commitments to letter writing, and assess the effectiveness of the postal system.

As for the main bodies of letters, it is more difficult to make anything but the broadest generalizations, as writers addressed a wide range of topics in diverse styles for a number of purposes. On the whole, letters were concerned with maintaining relationships, explaining experiences, and discussing the familial, social, economic, and political worlds in which correspondents moved. They usually sought subjects that were interesting to both writers and readers, although they were probably not always successful.[72] Within these parameters, the following chapters identify and trace several specific threads in epistolary content. As I show, relatives performed family relationships through the post, as they expressed feelings, advised and argued with one another, and negotiated finances, wills, and businesses (Chapters 2 and 5). Correspondents also explained the mundane and the unusual in their lives, described their surroundings, and asked and answered questions about British Columbia (Chapters 3 and 4).

Along with their diverse content, letters varied in tone depending on a writer's circumstances, relationships, and intentions. On the one hand, some settlers clearly sought to reassure relatives that they were placed respectably, safely, happily, and prosperously in British Columbia. Shortly after arriving on Vancouver Island in 1899, the young English settler Leonard Witherby assured his mother that he had found good work with the Barkley family at Westholme. He elaborated on this in insistently positive and comforting terms: "It will teach me a splendid lot & will be awfully nice. I like the life more than I can possibly express & I hope you understand that I am most comfortably placed with a lady & gentleman."[73] On the other hand, rather than focus on justifying or defending their choices to migrate, many settlers dwelt on difficult aspects of their lives in British Columbia. For example, in 1898 English doctor Roger Hicks wrote a series of letters to his daughters focusing on the "vile" weather on his way to the Klondike, the frustrating and challenging travel conditions, and his "miserable" experiences in camp each night. While his letters spoke volumes about the Stikine region's environment and its impact on his daily life and work, they likely did little to reassure his children about his safety, happiness, or prospects in the province.[74]

Finally, family correspondence did not consist only of textual tone and content, as relatives frequently also enclosed small items or sent larger parcels in the post. Common gifts included personal portraits (Chapter 2) as well as photographs or drawings of houses and landscapes.[75] Relatives often enclosed items from their local environment too. When sent from Britain, these included flowers, pressed plants, or seeds from home gardens and familiar places. When sent from British Columbia, they were more often selected because of their novelty and ability to represent unfamiliar places, such as the "chips which the beavers cut out of the trees" that Harold Nation sent his sister from the Kootenays in 1901.[76] Metropolitan relatives also mailed items that were useful but difficult for settlers to obtain. Kootenay rancher Tommy Norbury requested that his father send a pair of glasses "from some big London man" for a fellow settler, and even approximated a prescription by post: "Sight as follows. Can see anything very plainly a long way off and can see to read in the day time, but cannot at night unless it is big print and then he has to hold it at arms length."[77] Parcels of clothing (Chapter 2) and food (Chapter 4) supplemented limited British Columbian wares. In addition, metropolitan relatives sometimes sent items to support settlers' commercial endeavours. For instance, in the late 1850s, Cornelius Bryant requested a list of goods from his parents – from telescopes and dolls to pearl buttons and accordions – that he planned to trade with Indigenous people in Nanaimo.[78]

Money orders also constituted a significant part of the material exchange between British relatives across the empire, including British Columbia.[79] The specifics varied. A few letter writers used the post to arrange or return loans from relatives that paid for passage to British Columbia.[80] Some settlers sent part of their British Columbian incomes to support metropolitan relatives. For example, Harold Nation sent his mother money from the Kootenays whenever he could, knowing that she was struggling in England without the support of his estranged father. To his horror, however, he was not able to earn and send enough to spare her from having to do washing work.[81] Indeed, British Columbia was far from a steady source of income for many settlers, and money was as likely to flow from Britain to sustain their lives as it was to move in the opposite direction. In the late 1880s, Tommy Norbury initially relied on the financial support of his Worcestershire parents, and the family regularly used the post to send money and negotiate budgets.[82] In these cases, as in many others, the trans-imperial exchange of family capital supported metropolitan lives and made possible certain kinds of settlement in British Columbia.

Overall, the letters at the heart of this book were part of a flourishing culture of personal letter writing. Over the nineteenth and early twentieth centuries, increasingly accessible postal systems – along with growing literacy, cheaper writing materials, and other developments – enabled a broad range of Britons to write and send longer social letters to one another, as well as parcels and money orders. In so doing, they built and strengthened a shared understanding of epistolary conventions and the post. The result was a dense trans-imperial network of family letters that, while diverse in many ways, were also constituted of generic forms, similar materials, shared phrases, and common threads.

"Don't Advise Anyone to Come Out": Family Letters and Migration

Family letters were politically significant to early settler British Columbia beginning with their intimate relationship to British migration. Migration is a necessary element of settler colonialism, which is partly defined by the mass movement and long-term settlement of non-Indigenous people in a new place. During the late nineteenth and early twentieth centuries, British Columbia's establishment as a settler colonial society was only made possible through ongoing migration, as the vast majority of British settlers were new arrivals rather than locally born. Although prospective settlers selected their future homes for a range of reasons, a significant number drew on family letters to determine whether, how, where, and when to move. Correspondents provided critical details about British Columbia, advised on migration, and arranged for letters of introduction or loans to assist with the travel and settlement of others in their personal networks. At the same time, while many supported chain migration, others used family letters to counter positive reports that appeared in the metropolitan press or immigration promotion literature, and instead discouraged further migration there. Whether representing it as a land of opportunity or a place of dashed hopes, settlers framed their letters as important and trustworthy sources, and instructed relatives to circulate their information in order to influence others. Overall, families used the postal system and personal correspondence to shape British migration and, in so doing, their letters contributed materially the foundation of settler colonial British Columbia.

For imperial and dominion politicians as well as many other Britons, early settler British Columbia was part of an emergent "Anglo-Saxon" community on the Pacific Rim, destined to become part of a "white Canada" in northern North America. In this vision, British migration was a political and social imperative, with British Columbia's future contingent on a significant, ongoing, and stable population of white settlers, including women and reproductive families, who would be loyal to the United Kingdom (or at least accept British and Canadian sovereignty) and identify culturally with Britishness.[83] As outlined in the Introduction, however, this imagined future remained far from certain on the ground. British Columbia's newcomer population grew, but it also remained comparatively small, largely male, racially diverse from myriad places, and significantly outnumbered by Indigenous people.[84] This clash between settler expectation and demographic reality rendered the migration and long-term resettlement of white British people an anxious priority that shaped government policies and immigration promotion campaigns throughout the period.[85]

To date, comparatively little scholarly attention has been given to why and how individuals chose to move to British Columbia within this larger political context. Certainly, white Britons could consider migrating because imperial and settler colonial structures facilitated it, empowered them in legal and political systems, and encouraged their cultural confidence that they belonged there. But individuals did not make the decision to move merely because they could. They also had personal reasons that prompted them to leave their current locations and try British Columbia, believing it to be a place of opportunity and adventure, material benefit or profit, and comfortable success. Some – such as colonial secretary Arthur Birch and Royal Engineers colonel Richard Moody and his family – moved there because they (or their relatives) were assigned particular, short-term jobs.[86] Many others moved based on personal speculation and aspiration, hoping to take advantage of the gold rushes, the possibility and affordability of land for white settlers, or other perceived opportunities that seemed less attractive or available to them elsewhere. Some made this choice with comparatively little information. In the summer of 1858, for example, John Christie decided to move after reading one Scottish newspaper article on the Fraser River gold rush.[87] In 1912, newlyweds Jack and Daisy Oxley Phillips were attracted to British Columbia by a promotional company brochure that suggested they could acquire land, a house, a profitable orchard, and a good life in the Windermere Valley – opportunities they did not anticipate for themselves in England.[88] Although it is less clear on what exact information he based his decision, Welsh-born James Skitt Matthews moved to Vancouver in 1898 after spending part of his youth in New Zealand and working for several months in Tacoma, Washington. He anticipated several advantages in British Columbia, particularly finding work, returning to what he saw as British soil, and being able to elope with his fiancée, Maud Boscawen, whose Auckland, New Zealand, family disapproved of the match (Chapter 2).[89] More rarely, Britons moved without any plan, as in the case of George Fawcett Drabble. In 1862, the English farmer left his Midlands home and travelled to Liverpool to say goodbye to emigrating friends – and then boarded the ship and left too, apparently impulsively.[90] As these stories suggest, there were as many reasons for moving to British Columbia as there were individual settlers, but broadly, Britons looked to take advantage of economic and social opportunities that they believed would be available to them there.

What made them believe that British Columbia held such opportunities for white British settlers? Again, there are many answers. While Christie and the Phillipses built their expectations from metropolitan newspapers and advertising, a number of British politicians suggested that personal correspondence could be a critical factor in migration and settlement, which were necessary components of the empire itself. Certainly, this was a powerful rhetorical device in the fight for postal reform. British MP John Henniker Heaton, for example, stressed that the "power and wealth of the Empire" was contingent on settlers who were willing to be "separated for life from members of their families."[91] He and other postal reformers argued that it was an accessible mail system that made such migration and separation thinkable, even attractive, for many Britons, in ways that government policies alone could not. To this end, Canadian postmaster general William Mulock suggested in 1897: "An encouraging letter from a friend in Canada to an intended emigrant from Great Britain would have more influence in determining the destination of such an Emigrant ... than would arguments of strangers though speaking with the authority of Governments."[92] By taking this position, these politicians cast personal letters as powerful elements in the British Empire, not only providing the demand and revenue to support the reforms they desired but also playing a symbolic and practical role in spurring migration and, through it, making the empire work.

The British Columbian case indicates that this was not mere rhetoric; family letters could indeed be materially important in migration. Some of the evidence for this is indirect. For instance, there are countless examples of settlers who, on moving to British Columbia, reunited with relatives. In the late 1850s, railway clerk Cornelius Bryant left the English West Midlands for Nanaimo, where he joined his aunt and extended family.[93] In the 1880s, Michael Wilkinson moved to live with his uncle Sam Brighouse, an early Vancouver settler. Brighouse had urged his English nephew to migrate in order to help with his business and inherit the estate (Chapter 5).[94] Jessie Chambers travelled from London with her husband and daughter in 1891 to join her uncle Alfred on Bowyer Island in Howe Sound.[95] And in 1913, the Murdochs moved to Kelowna from Tunbridge Wells, England, because Marjorie Carruthers Murdoch's brother, Ted, had already found success there. This was not the first example of chain migration in the family. Ted Carruthers had moved from Inverness, Scotland, around 1889 because his mother's cousin had promised him work in British Columbia.[96] Although the direct evidence has not always been archived, letters undoubtedly played a role in arranging many of these moves, given the unavailability of other methods of trans-imperial communication. At the very least, these examples suggest that familial networks played an important role in encouraging and facilitating Britons' migration to British Columbia, and to specific locations within it.[97]

Some archived letters do reveal intentional discussion about the possibility of chain migration. British Columbian letter writers sometimes sent valuable information for potential migrants, and requested that recipients circulate these details in wide personal networks in the United Kingdom. Such letters explained the prospects for settlement in certain regions or work in specific industries, and even claimed to predict the next economic booms in British Columbia. They also included general information about the economy, climate, land system and prices, transportation infrastructure, employment prospects, and costs of living. When Victoria resident Radcliffe Quine wrote to his siblings on the Isle of Man in 1861, for instance, he provided a lengthy explanation of Vancouver Island and British Columbia, and the possibilities of material success there. Among other points, he listed the typical pay for different jobs in dollars and pounds so that his relatives could compare colonial work with metropolitan wages.[98]

Even more directly, some correspondents assessed the benefits or drawbacks of British Columbia for specific family members or acquaintances who were considering migration. English physician Charles Newcombe's letters to his wife, Marian, provide one example. He travelled to western North America in 1883 in order to investigate the Pacific coast as a possible future home for their family. His letters were intended to help them consider the advantages and disadvantages of each place he visited (see also Chapter 3). In October that year, he provided a thorough report on Victoria and its surrounding areas. He was optimistic about the environment and its possibilities for comfortable leisure, but feared that the city could not ensure their prosperous future. Although Victoria had "no rows of any sort," he noted, it also had "little enterprise." Concluding that there was "but little prospect of occupation here," he determined to "look round Oregon & California." Later in the month, Newcombe wrote his wife again. Having travelled throughout the region and gathered advice from local settlers, he determined that southern Vancouver Island "seem[ed] to offer the most advantages" after all. Although the family would not make this decision immediately, they moved to Victoria in 1889, where they settled for the long term.[99]

Besides assessing British Columbia's prospects, letter writers also provided specific assistance with migration. In particular, settlers advised metropolitan relatives and acquaintances on the best routes, methods, and dates for travel, the approximate costs, and key items to bring, and sometimes even made arrangements for them. Some sent financial assistance or organized metropolitan loans to support others' passage to British Columbia, a process that could be assisted by the new postal money order system. As one example, in 1859 Anglican minister David Pringle requested a loan from his father to support his wife Louie's travel to join him in Hope. He then provided Louie with detailed instructions for her journey, including an estimated budget for each section of the trip via the Panama route. He explained that he had developed the plan in consultation with "Mrs. Gordon & Mr. Crease," and that he "concur[red] entirely" with their advice. In so doing, Pringle cast his information as authoritative expert knowledge, emphasizing that it was drawn from known sources and personal experience.[100]

In addition to providing an itinerary and information for Louie's passage, David Pringle noted that other settlers had suggested she would need "good introductions" to ensure her comfort, safety, and success while travelling without him. He promised: "I will now stir myself to obtain introductions for you."[101] Personal letters of introduction were also important for new settlers after their arrival.[102] When Tommy Norbury moved to the Kootenays in 1887, he brought an introduction from a family acquaintance in England who had helped him plan an initial stay with her brother, Michael Phillipps, at Tobacco Plains. This proved to be key for Norbury's local success. Phillipps was a prominent and knowledgeable settler in the region, and he recommended Norbury for jobs and guided him to good land nearby for pre-emption (Chapter 6).[103] In 1904, twenty-year-old Wilf Rowell moved to Canada, similarly supported by introductions to friends' relatives.[104] In these and other cases, letters provided useful information and facilitated valuable connections for prospective settlers, both on their journeys and after arrival in British Columbia.

While some correspondents encouraged chain migration in these ways, many settlers actually did little to promote British Columbia in their metropolitan networks, and indeed actively criticized it as a potential destination for others.[105] This was particularly true in the mid-nineteenth century, when settlers had often moved with little knowledge besides positive newspaper reports on the gold rush or promotional travel guides.[106] After arrival, many wrote disappointed letters about the troubled economy, high unemployment, poor living conditions, and frustrating goldfields. In 1859, for instance, Robert Burnaby reported to his mother that although

British Columbia was a "land of promise," Victoria was "at a standstill," he had "not been able to make one penny," and there was a "riot going on amongst the miners" on the Fraser River.[107] Mary Hawks Moody had anticipated neither wealth nor long-term opportunities in the colony when she accompanied her husband, Richard, in his temporary position as colonel of the Royal Engineers detachment near New Westminster. However, she wrote about others' despair. In 1859, she noted to her sister Emily: "Settlers, Miners & all Classes are leaving the Colony, I know nobody who does not regret having come out, many return by the next boat."[108] In 1866, New Westminster farmer John Brough warned his brother that the goldfields were no place for men seeking to "make their fortune."[109] In 1867, Nanaimo settler Alexander Papley informed his siblings in Stromness, in Orkney, Scotland, that their brother Peter (also in Nanaimo) had been "out of work for this long time," while he too struggled: "The place [is] very dull hear now[.] the coal mines [are] all stoped for some time but for how long i can't tell[.] i get a Days work now and again But not constant." Given this, he concluded: "i don't think i will be home for a little while as yet for the place [is] very dull at present a man can only Barely make a living."[110] Similarly, in the 1870s, Cariboo prospector John Evans repeatedly told his children that he could not return to Wales to see them because, without a major find, he could not make enough money to pay for his passage.[111]

Recognizing that the tone and content of their letters could be influential, settlers directed relatives to circulate these negative reports in personal networks in order to inform others that migration was not worth it.[112] Thus, colonial secretary Arthur Birch wrote to his brother John that the "gentlemen" in his metropolitan circles should avoid British Columbia, as there were few opportunities for them to gain status, wealth, or respectability there – and indeed, they were more likely to lose these things. He explained:

> Don't advise anyone to come out here on speculations as we are overrun with decayed gentlemen – the boots at the Hotel is the son of a Dr in Harley Street and has met me in "Society"[,] Clifford the son of a Clergyman in Somersetshire is chipping wood for the Public Offices, half the stokers on the River Steamer are decayed gentlemen & the numerous loungers about the place are all Captains or Majors.[113]

More concerned with working- or middle-class migration, Harold Nation wrote to his English mother about high settler unemployment in the Kootenays in 1900. The railway had "brought in the cheap men by the hundred," he explained, and "next year it will be ten times as bad!" "For goodness sake, don't advise any friends to send their sons out," he urged. In this assertion, he claimed both objectivity and comparative privilege. "These are dry facts and do not constitute a grumble on my part, for I have the most comfortable quarters," he wrote, before adding a less reassuring remark: "tho I am not getting any pay."[114]

When making such criticisms, settlers often emphasized that their letters were reliable and authoritative corrections to impersonal or indirect sources of information about British Columbia. During the 1860s, for example, many letter writers railed against glowing reports of the goldfields that, for a brief period, appeared in the metropolitan press. Writing to his Stromness siblings in 1867, Alexander Papley reported that their brother Joseph had gone to the goldfields at Big Bend, in eastern British Columbia, but that "the gold mines [is] not the thing that it [is] reported to be for one man that makes any thing good [there is] ten that comes Back with nothing and you may think the Orknes [is] a poor place but I believe it [is] a better place."[115] Like many Cariboo residents, Welsh prospector William Jones specifically criticized the *Times* of London for its positive representations of the gold rush there, intimating that (unlike his letters) the newspaper's information was neither local nor trustworthy. "If the Times correspondent was here, many would make sharp work of him; he resided in this place but is now, I expect, in London, writing Articles on British Columbia," he wrote, declaring: "He would be made an example of ... for writing such articles to delude people from their homes."[116]

Negative reports clustered in the mid-nineteenth-century colonial period, but even in the early provincial years, some settlers positioned their letters against the positive but limited representations of British Columbia in other sources, seeking to provide clarification based on their own experiences. At the end of the century, English physician Roger Hicks struggled to reach the Klondike goldfields through British Columbia, and wrote a series of frustrated letters to his daughters. "The lies that appear in the few Victoria & other Canadian papers one sees here are too bad," he remarked in one case; "one reads reports praising up the route & saying that men & pack trains are going daily out to Teslin, whereas nothing, or at any rate very little is being done."[117] In 1912, Jack and Daisy Oxley Phillips moved to the Windermere Valley, attracted by land company advertising. Discovering that the brochures had been misleading, Jack Phillips reported to his English mother-in-law that the company was "not quite ready for us" and the land was "a little more than I expected to give." He explained that other settlers told him that it was "a terrible place where the fruit trees won't grow and where nothing that was advertised in the pamphlets is ready."[118] In such cases, the accessible postal system and the growth of family correspondence enabled the significant expansion of information about British Columbia that was available to people in the United Kingdom. Adding to the few metropolitan sources on British Columbia, and challenging their positive representations of settler opportunity, these writers situated themselves as local experts on the ground, and framed their letters as critical and trustworthy counter-sources.

In a range of ways, then, British correspondents sought to produce mobile forms of knowledge about British Columbia and circulate these in extensive trans-imperial personal networks. Some politicians argued that this kind of epistolary information influenced migration decisions – a contention that played a role in the process of postal reform – while archived examples of British Columbian letters suggest that this could indeed have been the case. Correspondents discussed British Columbia to report on their own prospects, successes, or failures, but also with the intention of shaping further migration. Responding to specific queries and guiding others' plans, they framed their letters as reliable conduits of information. They explained economic and employment conditions, political and social structures, the environment, and various opportunities or challenges that newcomers could expect. They also offered specific advice on where to go, how to travel, how much it would cost, and what to do on arrival. In addition, money orders and letters of introduction facilitated migration, while acquaintances and relatives also arranged travel, employment, and accommodation for new settlers through the post. In other cases, correspondents discouraged migration, emphasizing that their personal experiences contradicted other representations of British Columbia in the metropole. Whatever their specific position, settlers claimed to be local authorities who were able to confirm or reject less personal and more limited sources, and to expand significantly the knowledge of British Columbia in their metropolitan personal networks. In the process, these correspondents both framed family letters and used the post as key tools for producing information and shaping the migration of other Britons – a linchpin of the early settler colonial project.

Coda: On the Archive

As British family letters moved through the infrastructure of empire and shaped the settler colonial project in British Columbia, they shared general contours that are strikingly similar when considered through the wide lens taken in this chapter. Although each archival collection reveals a different voice and personal story, my research has also made it clear just how much these letters share forms, language, and even content with one another. But at the same time, this scale of analysis – an understanding of common patterns and representativeness – has been possible only because of the breadth and depth of the publicly available epistolary archive. It still seems remarkable, even miraculous, that I have been able to read thousands of letters from this period.

In part, this is my sense of wonder that so many people wrote at all, committing hundreds of hours to pen and paper, and learning to navigate an often frustrating postal system. It is also about the particular nature of the sources, unlikely survivors of a century or more. These letters are thin sheets of paper folded into precarious envelopes. Adhesive stamps and town names were enough to direct them with precision to recipients half a world away. Through a coordinated (if sometimes inefficient) global system, these letters moved across national borders, stuffed into mailbags that survived ocean voyages and tossed from still-moving trains that rolled from community to community.[119] Not every letter reached its destination; some were lost to shipwrecks, misplaced or misaddressed, or never picked up from the post office. With few exceptions, though, the letters in this book were ones that were delivered as intended.[120]

These are also the letters that have been preserved, generation after generation. For much of this time, I imagine them stored in trunks and shoeboxes, surviving decades of closet moths, attic rats, and basement floods before reaching the archive. Perhaps envisioning the same, many people have responded to my research with the same surprised exclamation: "But where do you find all of this correspondence?" I have no doubt that thousands of letters remain in the hands of descendants, not to mention the thousands more that have been lost or destroyed. For this project, though, I have relied on dozens of publicly accessible collections, usually donated by families and now mostly held by libraries and archives in British Columbia. In many cases, settlers' local prominence or success made it more likely that their personal records would be given to or accepted by these institutions. But the archive also owes much to the families' affective labour, and their willingness not only to preserve but also to share these personal records. Even as I trace their generic and structural significance, then, I am humbled by the persistence of these sources, and by their vulnerability. Here, I have read thousands of letters, identified their patterns, and considered their relationship to the infrastructure of empire. But this analysis must also be seen as a reflection of a much more intimate archive – one that is powerful, personal, and fragile, as intimacy is.

In sum, working with this archive from the broadest perspective of the book, this chapter has underscored three critical and connected points about family correspondence and settler colonialism. First, there would have been no letters without mail ships or rail lines, or the larger postal systems that organized epistolary exchanges. Changing postal systems played an important role in shaping the United Kingdom and British Columbia in this period – facilitating their connections with one another, the Canadian dominion, and an imperial and international network. Second, the letters transmitted through these systems were diverse, but they also had many common features. These epistolary patterns reflect the emergence of a wider genre and culture of personal correspondence, which both encouraged and was supported by changing postal structures in Britain and its empire. Finally, postal systems and family letters worked together to influence a key ingredient of the settler colonial project: migration and settlement in British Columbia. Correspondents intentionally, strategically, and explicitly used the post to shape the migration decisions of relatives and acquaintances. In these ways, the postal systems, family correspondence, and migration together made possible the settler colonial project and bound British Columbia to the British imperial world. Building on this foundation, I turn next to the content of these letters in more detail, focusing first on their familial uses and intimate significance.

2

"Affection Can Overstep Distance"

The Letter as Trans-Imperial Family

On 10 March 1859, Robert Burnaby wrote his mother, Sarah Meares Burnaby, in Leicestershire. The previous week, he had moved from Vancouver Island to the mainland colony of British Columbia in order to take up work as the private secretary of the Royal Engineers colonel Richard Moody. The letter was full of local detail as Burnaby recounted his move, reported on new acquaintances, and described the environment around his new home. Then, after writing at length about the forest and the weather, he changed tack: "It is an inexpressible feeling of delight to me as I write in this lonely spot and so far away from you, dearest Mother, to feel that affection can overstep distance and outlive time, for now my heart is warming to you as really and lovingly as if I were sitting by your side by the little fire at home."[1] In this evocative passage, Burnaby claimed a continued sense of intimacy with his mother while "so far away." More specifically, he argued, he could feel and communicate emotional closeness through the act of writing to her. In making this suggestion, Burnaby – like many Britons in British Columbia – used correspondence both to discuss and to address a question at the heart of the trans-imperial family: what constituted relationships between settlers and their metropolitan relatives, and what work did it take to maintain them across distance?

This question cuts to the core of this chapter. Existing scholarly discussions of empire, settler colonialism, and the family tend to focus on sexual relationships or nuclear units contained in one place, or on the move together.[2] Similarly, much of the literature on nineteenth-century British families concentrates on cohabiting relations within the metropole.[3] Although there has been some attention to families maintained across imperial distances, the literature most often positions physical proximity as a norm – not a universal experience, but an assumed or usual familial feature.[4] However, in a period of remarkable imperial expansion and migration, familial distance was not an aberration. Rather, a significant number of Britons – including virtually all British settlers in British Columbia – experienced some form of separation from relatives in this period. For them, distance could mean a wide range of things, including a normalized part of the extended family's life, a welcome opportunity to cut ties or gain independence, a barrier to carrying out mutual obligations, or a difficult challenge to emotional closeness. Much more remains to be understood about these various meanings and forms of long-distance family relationships, as well as their significance for the various places in which the separated relatives lived.

Taking up this point with a focus on British Columbia, this chapter investigates trans-imperial epistolary relationships as a particular configuration of family. For most British settlers, the decision to move to British Columbia was driven by the long- or short-term opportunities that they believed would be available to them there. They did not necessarily intend to cut family ties, but few anticipated imminent reunion with metropolitan relatives – or even any reunion at all. Some experienced familial separation with relief, others with grief, and possibly many felt a combination of these. Relatives could draw on memory or imagination to think about one another, but if they wanted to maintain active, reciprocal relationships, they had few available strategies for doing so at a distance. In this context, the post served as an important (and often the only) tool for British settlers looking to maintain ongoing familial connections. Archived correspondence varied as much as relationships themselves: a one-time effort to solicit financial support, an eruption of conflict, an occasional explanation of major personal news, a short-lived project to explain a new home after migration, the regular or intermittent negotiation of family business, or a steady exchange saturated with information about everyday activities and claims to continued affective bonds. In each of these circumstances, Britons relied on the post to enact and sustain their families, however they understood them, as well as explaining explicitly what they saw as the connections between family and the mail.

Tracing these discussions, I consider here how a range of Britons used the post to develop and enact long-distance relationships, and, simultaneously, to comment on what they understood the trans-imperial family to entail. Drawing from Davidoff and colleagues' definition of the family as a combination of "blood, contract, and intimacy," I ask how relatives translated each of these elements into epistolary form between British Columbia and the United Kingdom.[5] What did these letter writers say about the connections between family and the post? How did they frame correspondence as a performance of affective connections and obligations central to their relationships with one another? How did they use the post to understand the family as it changed over time, and as its membership was transformed? Taken together, what do these epistolary discussions reveal about British families and settler British Columbia? As this chapter explains, Britons who chose to write to relatives, and whose letters have been archived, repeatedly and explicitly framed the post as integral to the forms, emotions, and duties of their long-distance families. Throughout this period, relatives argued that letter writing became a new familial obligation or expectation in the context of physical separation, enabling them to feel closer to one another and serving as material evidence of their continued commitment to the family. In addition, Britons used the post to establish relationships with new members and to maintain knowledge of relatives' changing lives over time. Finally, they also delivered epistolary advice that clearly articulated expectations of their relationships over distances, and sought to protect their families' collective interests. By developing and performing these epistolary forms of affect, duty, advice, and relationship, British correspondents both struggled against distance and sought to incorporate it into their understandings of family – ultimately defining letter writing and the active trans-imperial family as mutually constitutive.

Through this discussion, the chapter shares a broad project with other studies of family letter writing, which similarly seek to understand the epistolary reconfigurations of intimacy, obligation, and relationship across distances.[6] Investigating these shared concerns in a different historical context, it traces the specific forms and significance of epistolary families for Britons engaged with early settler British Columbia, thereby laying the groundwork for the remainder of this book. At the same time, it not only tells a particular history of letter writing linked to British Columbia but also elaborates on two larger, fundamental points about the parameters of British families in the late nineteenth and early twentieth centuries. First, while the scholarship tends to emphasize relationships contained within one site, letters point to another significant and common familial form: the long-distance, trans-imperial, epistolary family. Archived correspondence indicates that for many people, families of origin remained important well into adulthood, and after marriage or migration. From affectionate comfort to probing advice to material support, metropolitan relatives retained salience for many settlers in British Columbia. In addition, even as correspondents may have expressed yearning for the idealized intimacy of proximity, the extent of archived correspondence and its shared concerns for family also serve as a reminder that distance was not an exceptional experience for Britons during this period. Physical separation could mean many things for individuals and families beyond what they committed to paper, but the epistolary archive makes clear that the post did play an important and widely acknowledged role in incorporating distance into many family relationships.

"We Do Not At-all Feel We Are So Far from Home": Letters as Closeness, Affect, and Duty

Whatever they actively felt about familial separation, many Britons who wrote to relatives idealized letter writing in the same way as Robert Burnaby – as a key form of familial affect and duty that could diminish the sense of distance and maintain relationships. While some of these correspondents aspired to replicate conversation or proximity through letters, others embraced the distinctiveness of the post as a medium of relationship. In either case, they argued that letters were evidence of relatives' commitment to family, and their long-distance performance of the emotions and obligations that constituted it. They suggested that poor letters could be signs of poor relationships, while the absence of correspondence both indicated and produced a serious break in the family. Overall, these correspondents explained, letters were material measures and textual performances of trans-imperial family relationships that sought to overcome or incorporate distance.

Although the families in this book differed by class, region, and individual relationships, most were broadly influenced by nineteenth-century British middle-class discourses on gender, generation, work, and home. In this period, a range of metropolitan media imagined the family as a potent symbol of stability, a refuge from external pressures, and the heart of a moral order in a rapidly changing society. To make the family work, relatives were supposed to act in complementary ways, offering forms of material and emotional support deemed appropriate to their gender, age, and relationship. As wives and mothers, for instance, women were expected to serve as moral and spiritual guides for the family while running the household, raising children, and fostering the domestic environment of the home. As husbands and fathers, men were expected to be authoritative figures at home, as well as breadwinners who protected and supported the family by navigating the business of the outside world. Such discourses were powerful, but they could also be flexible or ignored. In other words, the family and its constituent members and relationships were subject to a set of common ideals, which shaped but never determined personal experiences in nineteenth-century Britain.[7]

These ideas also guided British representations of letter writing in this period. Within this broad cultural milieu, correspondents and commentators typically idealized both the intimacy of physical proximity and the ability of letters to recreate this intimacy. To this end, nineteenth-century letter-writing manuals regularly argued that correspondence enabled people to replicate conversation, which they framed as the preferred model of communication or relationship.[8] Many individual correspondents in British Columbia and Britain expressed similar hopes that their letters simulated physical closeness and performed emotional closeness. Travelling in London in 1876, for example, Victoria bishop Edward Cridge described a letter to his wife, Mary, as a conversation in spiritual proximity when they could not be physically near. "My heart prompts me to sit down in spirit by your side, and share your cares and sadness & talk together," he wrote.[9] Corresponding with her son at school in England in 1878, Victoria settler Sarah Lindley Crease similarly referred to a letter as a way to "spend a little time" together.[10] Good letters intentionally replicated proximity, as former colonial governor James Douglas instructed his daughter Martha in 1872. "When you write to Mamma," he directed her, "write and speak to her, as you know how, and when you write to Papa, write and speak to him, as if he was before you; and then you will write well."[11] Underpinning these statements was the idea that proximity facilitated desirable intimate knowledge, connection, and interaction – and that distance was a potential barrier to these positive elements of relationships. Correspondents wrote, they suggested, in the hope that they might overcome the challenges of distance by reproducing the intimacy of closeness.

Settler correspondents also claimed that receiving letters from the metropole helped them feel closer to family there and, in the process, made their lives in British Columbia seem easier. In 1859, shortly after her arrival in Victoria, Mary Hawks Moody wrote her mother in northern England: "We do not at-all feel we are so far from home, now we have our letters regularly."[12] In a series of letters to her sister from Athalmer in the early twentieth century, aspiring orchardist Daisy Oxley Phillips repeatedly and similarly emphasized that letters helped her "feel very close." Separation did not "lessen affection," she argued, but rather "bind[s] us closer together." Specifically, she suggested, it was the mail that produced "a very strong bond," because letters confirmed her relatives' commitments and tightened their connections to her. In the process, Phillips explained, her family's letters also fortified her for the difficulties of settlement in British Columbia. "Sometimes I have to be terribly plucky and it is then the home letters are so good," she wrote.[13] Whether or not these statements were straightforward reflections of what writers felt or experienced, they were very common types of claims about the value of family correspondence. Mobilizing them in these ways, correspondents agreed that letters had a symbolic role in shrinking distance and facilitating settler lives.

Sometimes much longer passages, or even whole letters, were devoted to discussing this idea. In April 1859, the English lawyer Henry Crease wrote a letter from Victoria that elaborated on the notion that the post had special material and affective power to overcome distance, conjure closeness, and substantiate relationships. He had recently moved to Vancouver Island while his wife, Sarah Lindley Crease, remained in England with her family of origin. She intended to join him after he had established himself in the colony and was ready to support a family there. During their separation, they used the post to maintain a relationship and share information about their possible colonial future (see also Chapter 3). His April 1859 letter acknowledged a parcel from London that he had just received, containing a range of items that she and the family had anticipated he might need. He did more than merely express thanks. He explained his contact with the parcel as touching in both senses – an experience that was embodied and emotional. Even the news of a "huge box" had left him "bursting with curiosity & heart beating with the thoughts that my *dearie's* handiwork might be there," he explained. The letter then re-performed the box's unpacking in text, offering vivid detail for an audience who had not been there to witness it. When he "ripped up the cover," he touched each item "with moistened eye." Thinking of each person "swell[ed] the heart," most of all when he considered "the little darling of all was there presiding over the packing & rejoicing that so many useful things would cheer up a loving Hubby – and the one pure link in the Chain of Love which ties our hearts in one – *across the World*!" Here, Crease translated the parcel's seemingly unremarkable objects into powerful "mementos" of his distant loved ones, thereby positioning the post as important not only because it exchanged "useful" items or information but also because of its comforting affective power to represent connections "across the World."[14]

Even as they insisted that they felt closer or connected because of the post, Britons also implicitly and explicitly recognized that correspondence was not the same as proximity. On a basic level, letters called attention to distance because they were typically produced when the intended recipient was not nearby. In addition, and despite idealized claims to the contrary, correspondence was different from face-to-face communication. Sometimes, writers embraced the particular nature of letters, arguing that they could express feelings or ideas that would be harder to say in person. Sarah Lindley Crease made this point in a letter to her father, London botanist John Lindley, in 1864. By then, she had joined her husband in the Vancouver Island colony. Her father was ill, though, and Sarah feared that he would die an atheist – a sensitive concern that she claimed she could articulate from her home in Victoria better than the relatives who were closer to him:

> I know not whether those dear ones near you, have ventured to speak of these things to you – but certain I am their hearts are bursting with longings to do so – but very possibly they may lack the *opportunity* – which this long distance gives to me – for well I know – how much harder it is to *speak* of what we so deeply feel – than to *write* the same.[15]

While Crease framed distance as a possible advantage here, this did not necessarily indicate that she actually preferred to live far from family in this moment. Rather, by evoking the benefits of distance, Crease strategically evaluated, discussed, and used the particular nature of the post as she saw most fit for the relationship and circumstances.

More often, correspondents framed letters as insufficient forms of communication and connection. They struggled to evoke connection in a divided present, conscious of the long time lag between sending a letter and receiving a reply. Some tried to imagine what a letter's recipient was doing at the same moment they were writing, only to realize that it was a different time of day across the world and, often, that they knew little about their relatives' lives in practice.[16] Sometimes they urged one another to visit since letters could never "tell you *all* [the] news," as Lucy Mathias wrote in one letter from Putney, England, to her cousin in Victoria, Charles Newcombe.[17] When rancher Tommy Norbury was debating his long-term plans in the Kootenays, he weighed his options in a letter to his parents in Worcestershire, England, before determining that "it is impossible to discuss these matters on paper and I have therefore decided to ... come home as soon as everything is satisfactorily arranged and discuss the matter over with you."[18] Writing from Rock Ferry, England, in 1898, Herbert Matthews did not anticipate or call for reunion with his Vancouver son, James. Still, he described letters as unsatisfactory compared with conversation, exclaiming: "How many things I should like to say to you that somehow or another we cannot convey in writing!"[19] Daisy Oxley Phillips also expressed her frustration with letters even as she acknowledged her family's dependence on them. "I feel if I were at home I could talk and discuss things just now and perhaps we could help each other to be cheerful," she wrote her sister Freda in 1912, adding: "If you want to let off steam you could always scribble to me."[20] Such passages idealized proximity and framed distance as a barrier to intimacy and immediacy. In so doing, these relatives framed letters as indispensable yet inadequate for approximating physical closeness and claiming emotional closeness – stated or assumed to be the ambition.

Not all Britons explicitly described their correspondence as a demonstration of affective connection that struggled against distance and disintegration in the family, however. Some likely implicitly intended their letters to perform this work, but did not remark specifically on it. Others wrote comparatively few letters, which made limited emotional claims or engaged little with the intimate details of one another's lives.[21] These people tended to call on family as a safety net in times of need, or as an occasional obligation to share vague personal updates, rather than as a regular enactment of affective communication. Although it is difficult to know for certain, these epistolary relationships likely reflected more emotionally distant relationships in general, and certainly the relatives involved do not seem to have protested infrequent or undemonstrative correspondence. In other words, different approaches to letter writing indicated and reproduced the varied individual relationships that constituted family. Correspondents used the post to perform their particular understandings of affect, duty, and relation with specific relatives, whether this was best articulated as yearning for intimate proximity or fulfilled by occasional contact or requests for assistance.

However, while some Britons seem to have been satisfied with minimal contact, irregular correspondence sparked significant concern and controversy when one relative expected or desired more frequent letters than the other. In such cases, disappointed or worried correspondents argued that letters were not only an opportunity to connect but also the only thread that enabled and affirmed their ongoing relationships with family, and the only material evidence of relatives' continued commitments to one another. Letters that only came "like Angel visits – far between," as New Westminster farmer John Brough described them, could suggest that one was neglected or forgotten by relatives.[22] To this end, Tommy Norbury grumbled to his mother in 1895 that his brother, Coni, "appears of late to have forgotten his relation in these parts," and Vancouver Island settler John Christie, in his diary in 1861, bemoaned the fact that "since I received my B[rother] W[illia]ms Letter last year I have had no word from Scotland so I am pretty much forgot by them all."[23] In this framing, a lack of regular letters indicated and potentially hastened the deterioration of reciprocal relationships.

Indeed, correspondents explained, writing constituted a particular form of obligation for separated relatives. The failure to meet a relative's letter-writing expectations could reflect one's negligence of family duty and relationships more generally. In 1866, for example, Whitechapel, London, resident Catherine Mittler Helmcken scolded her son John, the Victoria physician and politician, for his sporadic correspondence. "I received your kind letter after waiting anxiously for it," she wrote, adding: "I was very much disapointed at you not answering you[r] brother Williams[']: William[']s letter."[24] Others made the point more explicitly. When an acquaintance received only one letter after she moved to British Columbia, Mary Hawks Moody literally underscored her response. This was "a *great shame,*" she wrote to her sister, and it was "really *very wrong* of them not to write."[25] Writing from Leamington, England, Caroline Robinson called her Victoria son Ernest "lazy" for not writing to her, then similarly underlined her expectations of him: "do not be so *long again* before you write. I expect all your laziness is gone."[26] In addition to criticizing quantity, correspondents also argued that poor-quality correspondence – or what colonial secretary Arthur Birch called "very shabby letters" – implied that relatives did not value their family relationships.[27]

Some Britons elaborated further on the idea that letters served as the medium of reciprocal relationships, framing the post as the measure of a trans-imperial family itself. To this end, in 1899, Putney, England, resident Lucy Mathias responded to a short and rare letter from her Victoria cousin, Charles Newcombe. Here, she argued that it was their shared responsibility to write to one another. In not doing so often or well, he failed to live up to her standards and put their relationship at risk:

> I was very pleased to hear from you as [I] thought you never meant to write again & you had owed me a letter for so long. I answered your last one (Jan 26 1898) within 3 days! ... I have preserved that specimen of your handwriting & tho' I have not got it by me remember its contents[.] You wrote about your plans for the future and asked my advice about them. Naturally I felt honoured and replied to the best of my ability and that was the last news of you ... This letter is a noble return for your half-sheet to me, but I'll make no more allusions to that if you sit down at once and send me a good long letter ... I shant write to you again till I hear from you – so there.[28]

There are many possible reasons why Newcombe wrote to Mathias less often. Perhaps he did not feel as close to her, or he did not write as many letters as she did in general. In any case, whether intended earnestly or inflected with humour, her reproach in this letter not only sought to compel a good response from him but also clearly outlined her expectations of their correspondence, and equated his letters with his demonstrated commitment to their relationship. Not writing left him in emotional debt to her; he owed her, she emphasized. Similar complaints and rebukes were common.[29] Equating a lack of letters with a lack of relationship, correspondents framed the act of writing as a family duty, material evidence of affection, and a demonstrated commitment to distant relatives.

Either explicitly or implicitly in response to these expectations, relatives sometimes acknowledged and sought to justify their own poorly constructed or infrequent letters. They usually emphasized that inadequate letters were due to limited local markets, poor writing conditions, or busy settler lives rather than an absence of care for their relatives. Thus, Mary Hawks Moody in Victoria apologized for a blotted letter to her sister Emily in 1859. Explaining that she had "contrived to spill the Ink stand" at her desk, she asked her sister to "excuse blots" because she did not have time to re-write it and could not "waste [her] paper."[30] From a moving train in 1899, the young emigrant Leonard Witherby told his English mother to "excuse the writing" because "it is rather hard to write well when you are travelling at the rate of 50 miles per hour."[31] In 1913, Daisy Oxley Phillips acknowledged that her family letters had become "rather irregular," but assured her sister that this did not indicate a deteriorating relationship. "My thoughts are constantly with you and you are woven into so much that I am doing," she emphasized.[32]

Given her usually regular letters, Phillips may have been more successful in this reassurance than Radcliffe Quine, who first wrote to his siblings from Victoria in 1861, more than sixteen years after leaving them on the Isle of Man. His letter opened with a frank admission of his silence:

> I take this oportunity of adressing you for the first time Hoping that these few lines will find you and your Family in good Health as my Health is very good, thank god, when i looke Back to the Date of my leaving, my Native Home, i feel the most poignant sensations of shame and regret, i will not aggravate the impropriety of my omissions by amusing you with Childish excuses of illness and buisiness, but confess that an unaccountable negligence and Foolish Habit of Procrastination, have made me so inattentive. I throw myself on your kindness, to Excuse my fault.[33]

Here, Quine recognized that his siblings might interpret the absence of correspondence as a sign of a lack of commitment to family, and that he was at the mercy of their decision whether or not to forgive it. Chapter 5 explains the ramifications of not writing: Quine's siblings had declared him legally dead in his silence, which undermined his place in the family and barred him from accessing his inheritance. As highlighted starkly here, separated relatives did not always write to one another – a point that is usually hard to see and measure in the archive. Since letters were the primary medium for maintaining active relationships across distances, the decision not to write could be taken as dereliction of duty and cause family fracture.

The archive also contains rare examples of one-way correspondence in which a relative wrote letters in the context of a near or total lack of reciprocity. These again make a similar point, as writers anxiously pleaded for correspondence as a marker of continued relationship, and expressed concerns about the absence of return letters as a sign of familial conflict. The letters of Welsh miner, Cariboo prospector, and member of the provincial legislature John Evans serve as one example. Evans had left his wife and four children in Wales when he moved to British Columbia in 1862.

His wife died four years later, and his children grew into adulthood in England and Wales while he remained and remarried in the Cariboo region. Evans became an important member of the Welsh settler community in British Columbia, helping to establish a community hall in Barkerville and participating in religious meetings there.[34] But at the same time, he struggled to maintain connections with Wales from afar. During his time in British Columbia, he received some letters from his children, but the family's correspondence became increasingly one-sided as the years passed. Evans did not accuse his children of neglecting their filial duty as a way to urge their responses, as other correspondents did. Instead, he worried in his letters, asking them again and again to explain the silence and assuring them that they remained an important part of his thoughts at a distance. In a letter from Davis Creek in October 1873, for example, he wrote:

> I hope you do not think I am indifferent about your affairs[.] on the contrary I am utterly unhappy as I have not had a letter or paper from either of you since last May ... [A]fter anxious weeks of suspense I wrote to John enquiring the reason of the universal silence but not a word, and each time the mail is due I go up to Town to be disapointed.[35]

Two years later, he wrote to his daughter Mary Ellen: "I have not heard a word from either of you for a long time," adding: "I hope there is no cause for it, my mind is constantly with you whether I am busy or at leasure."[36] He then opened a December 1875 letter to his children: "Is it possible that anything has transpired to come [between] you and me or having you imbued the idea that I am indifferent to your welfare, or what can be the matter that I am not permitted to hear anything from any of you? What means this silence?"[37] Embedded in these repeated queries was Evans's understanding that silence shattered the possibility of long-distance relationships. It did not necessarily mean that people disowned their family members or no longer felt connected in their own imaginations. Without letters, though, he knew that his relationships could not continue and develop through ongoing interaction.

Taken together, these examples of correspondence between British Columbia and Britain reflected the writers' understandings of family, and their efforts to maintain relationships across and in relation to distances. Idealizing emotional closeness and connection, many framed letters as an opportunity that could approximate face-to-face contact or at least partially overcome the perceived barriers of separation. Since it was their primary form of ongoing and active relationship, they argued that letter writing was a particular obligation for separated relatives. They described poor letters as reflecting and producing poor relationships, while the absence of correspondence could break a family altogether. Overall, specific epistolary relationships varied, as did family relationships in general, but a range of correspondents broadly agreed that letters served as material evidence of continued connection and textual manifestations of relationship, affect, and duty. When British Columbian lives necessitated personal separation, in other words, settlers and their metropolitan relatives framed letters as the medium of family and a central vehicle through which they could strategically navigate the impact of distance on their relationships.

"Give Me a Place in Your Warm Heart and Write": The Post and the Changing Family

Britons also sought to develop and adapt their relationships in the context of familial change over time. Settlement in British Columbia often meant long-term separation. As these relatives understood well, individual lives and bodies changed, new members entered through marriage or birth, and once-familiar homes and families became unfamiliar or even unrecognizable as time passed in separation. Such changes – unwitnessed because of distance – could challenge relatives' understandings of one another and their continued sense of belonging in the family. Britons thus used letters, photographs, and parcels as central, strategic tools that enabled them to update their knowledge of relatives and to establish relationships with new family members. In so doing, they used the post to understand, discuss, and incorporate change into trans-imperial families.

At the most general level, letters typically included major and minor family news that otherwise would not be learned at a distance. There are countless examples. In the letter that opened this chapter, for example, Robert Burnaby updated relatives in Leicestershire, England, on his 1859 move from Victoria to New Westminster.[38] In 1905, Vancouver settlers Edward and Alix Dalgleish Lloyd sent a telegram, newspaper clippings, and letters informing his parents in Pembrokeshire, Wales, about the birth of their son Iowerth (named for Edward's father).[39] Correspondents in the metropole – more often central nodes in extended family networks –

frequently included news gathered from a number of relatives in Britain, or even beyond. In 1866, the Victoria physician and politician John Helmcken received one such letter from his mother. Among other updates reflecting the experiences of a struggling working-class family in London, she reported that John's sister Elizabeth could not "let her shop" and her children were "ill with a lowe fever." In addition, his sister Ann had "lost the first joint of one of her fingers," his brother Henry was "rather slack of work," and his cousin Elizabeth had recently found a position as a housemaid near Clapham Common.[40] When such thorough reports were not forthcoming, settlers might request "home" news. In the early twentieth century, Kootenay logger Wilf Rowell inquired after his family's new house in Teignmouth, England, their pet dogs, and his brother Hugh in South Africa, who had fallen out of touch with him.[41] Such exchanges enabled relatives to maintain some familiarity with each other's lives, even as the information could be very partial and general, and did not provide the detail that they might have expected or idealized from proximity.

By the late nineteenth century, photographs were an additional accessible and popular medium for Britons who sought to explain their changing lives and bodies to relatives.[42] Sent in the post and discussed in letters, personal portraits of relatives were regularly described as material and visual symbols of familial connection that could be displayed in distant homes or integrated into jewellery and worn close to the body. As letter writers explained, photographs helped relatives to update their knowledge, incorporate change, and accurately picture one another in ways that the text of correspondence never could. Thus, after receiving portraits of her mother and sister in Windsor, England, Daisy Oxley Phillips declared from the Windermere Valley in 1912: "Now ... I can picture you exactly as you are."[43] Most correspondents responded to pictures with grateful, delighted assessments, but photographic exchanges also rendered distant changing bodies open to familial criticism and concern. In 1874, for example, military bandmaster John Bayley thanked his sister Carrie for a portrait that she sent to him from Victoria, but concluded: "If the likeness is a good one, you are not so pretty as you used to be."[44] While sending a portrait opened up one's body to familial scrutiny, both positive and negative, letter writers consistently represented photography as a valued form of connection and communication, because it not only symbolized continued relationships but also helped them to understand bodies and lives as these changed over time.

Given the value that they placed on photographs, some correspondents pleaded for portraits and complained bitterly if they did not receive them. This was a heated topic for Cariboo prospector John Evans, who, as explained earlier, already worried about the implications of infrequent letters from his children. When his son Caradoc mentioned in a rare letter that Mary Ellen's husband would send portraits of the family, Evans clung to the idea. For him, these promised portraits represented his children's interest in communication and relationship with him, and would enable him to picture new members of the family (his son-in-law and grandchild) whom he could not meet in person. The photographs never arrived, however, and his letters then featured repeated and frustrated attempts to compel them, at one point writing: "Where are the portraits that were so long promised of my Son in Law & grandchild?"[45] Two years later, he wrote to his daughter: "Your husband and my dilatory Soninlaw promised me his portrait and I have been expecting mail after mail for a letter containing one." He then declared that "if ... my *penstiff* Soninlaw will not send me his [photograph] – I will never ask again."[46] He did ask again, though, writing in another letter Finally, he described himself as resigned to not receiving the portraits, but still did not abandon the topic: "I have ceased asking my Soninlaw for the favor I have so often troubled him about, and give it up now as a bad job."[47]

Even as he sought their photographs, Evans promised to send them his own portrait. He emphasized how much his children would find him changed. "You will scarcely know the gray headed old man," he wrote in one letter, and reiterated the point in another: "You will find it very different to those you have of me, my hair almost as white as wool."[48] Evans may have hoped that the photograph would provide his children with an opportunity to update their memories of him, which might in turn reinvigorate their relationship – otherwise plagued by poor communication – and help them foster changing connections across distance. In any case, he framed the exchange of portraits as an important and tangible form of communication for relatives who increasingly knew little about one another. Although the potential but incomplete exchange carried particular weight for Evans in the context of his family's asymmetrical correspondence, he was not alone in his interest in photography in the post. Many letter writers shared his insistence that portraits were valuable forms of continued connection in changing families that otherwise risked divergence and fragmentation over time.

While photographs and letters helped to explain the changing bodies and lives of distant relatives, correspondents also used the post to address the entrance of new people into the family circle. After receiving word of an engagement or marriage, for example, the extended family often responded with letters that included the (intended) spouse. When this did not happen, newly engaged or married Britons instructed relatives to write to their new spouses or to address future letters to both parties.[49] Frequently, the resulting letters were intended as congratulations that welcomed newcomers to the family. Many named and claimed the new relationship in salutations or valedictions. In 1871, for example, Emily Trutch Pinder White wrote to congratulate her new sister-in-law, Zoe Musgrave Trutch, after the latter married John Trutch in Victoria. White addressed this letter to "My dear sister Zoe" and signed it "Your affect[ionat]e sister."[50] When she heard that Cecilia Douglas had married her son John in Victoria, Catherine Mittler Helmcken similarly opened her letter of congratulations with "Dear Daughter" and signed it "From your True and Affectionate mother." These were conventional epistolary phrases that took on special meaning as correspondents signalled their acceptance of a new relative at a distance. This familial reception could be expressed in other ways too. In addition to calling Cecilia her "daughter," Helmcken also enclosed a lock of hair as a potent material and bodily symbol of their new connection.[51]

In other cases, letter writers sent briefer congratulations that welcomed newcomers to the family in more abstract terms. These writers sometimes explicitly recognized that their relationships would be limited across distances, and indeed, they might never meet their new relatives by marriage. In 1879, for example, Tottenham, England, resident Henry Hawkins sent his "kind love" to his brother and new sister-in-law in British Columbia, but concluded: "I Dont expect as ever I shall see her."[52] Writing to her son Ernest from Leamington, England, in 1876, Caroline Robinson recognized that she was unlikely to meet his new wife in Victoria, although she might still have gained new personal networks closer to home as a result of the marriage. Sending her "kind love" to her daughter-in-law, Robinson also inquired after her "native place" and "friends in England" so that "we may find them out in our travels."[53]

Other Britons wrote more extensive letters of welcome that elaborated on the recipients' new place in the extended family and detailed how distance might shape their relationships. When Peter Peebles announced his imminent marriage in New Westminster in 1886, his mother, Jane Murie Peebles Leighton, wrote to his fiancée Angusta Grant from Aberdeen, Scotland. "I take the liberty to address you this owing to Peters last letter," she began. "He told me that you are his promised Wife and that I was to get another Daughter." She then implied her blessing and hope for the match, explaining: "I think when young people makes up there [*sic*] minds to go together the old folks should give there consent." I sincerly hope you will both be happy and that neither of you will ever have cause to regret the steps you intend to take." In this letter, Leighton sought to set the terms of the new relationship. Promising that she would treat her daughter-in-law well, she also recognized that they were unlikely to meet, and at a distance, their relationship would remain limited:

> if it should be gods will that we ever meet you may be sure I will love you as I should ... it is two often the case that a young Wife does not get justice from her Mother in Law[.] at least I have seen so. but that will not be the case with me. you are far away but I will try to think well of you ... I will be glade [*sic*] to hear from you when convenient but I will not promis [*sic*] to write very often but I will do my best.[54]

For the Grant-Peebles family and others, letters provided the only means of establishing a new relationship at a distance. In times of marriage, then, the post played an important role in aiding family formation and adaptation, as relatives used correspondence to claim ties and reshape the changing parameters of family membership.

At the same time, these new epistolary relationships could be taken up (or not) in a range of ways. When English military bandmaster John Bayley became engaged in 1874, he wrote to his sister Carrie in Victoria from his base at the time in Dublin. He described his fiancée, Cissie, in detail so that Carrie could picture her future sister-in-law: "She is of medium height, dark hair, and eyes, I think her pretty well educated ... speaks French, plays and sings well ... She has not got curls, but in loving her there are so many good points to admire that I lose all fancy for any adornments." He urged Carrie to write to Cissie in order to solidify their new bond as sisters. Epistolary style mattered in forging family, he emphasized, so "let the letter be nicely worded, not stiff but friendly and girl like, don't be the least bit afraid to tell her all about yourself and how you pass your time."[55] Two and a half months later, John determined that his sister's effort had been valuable but not adequate given its importance, since the post was the only point of connection between the two women. "Cissie sent your letter for me to see, she is very glad you have written to her, only I think as the distance is so great you might have made it longer," he commented.[56] The following year, Cissie wrote to Carrie requesting more letters as a marker of their relationship and her acceptance in the Bayley family. "Do not stand upon any ceremony now dear, but give me a place in your warm heart and write to me sometimes," she pleaded. "Let me feel that though far away from each other you are willing to welcome me as a new sister."[57] In each of these letters, the Bayleys argued that correspondence was an essential way to reconstruct the transimperial family as its parameters changed, while simultaneously recognizing that letters were at best a fragile method of establishing ongoing, reciprocal, and meaningful relationships at a distance.

Correspondents also used the post to maintain or develop changing relationships between adults and children over time. Some settler children were sent to school in the United Kingdom, and in these cases, correspondence played an important role in sustaining existing connections between them and their parents who remained in British Columbia.[58] The post also helped to establish or represent extended familial connections between children and adults who had never known one another in person.[59] The Hawks-Moody extended family serves as one such example. The Moody family was stationed at the Royal Engineers camp in New Westminster in the late 1850s and early 1860s. For them, parcels offered material items that represented affective connections to a distant English home. "You do not know how much we value a parcel fr[om] 'home' out here," Mary Hawks Moody wrote to her mother in northern England in September 1861, explaining that "all the things seem to be doubled in value at once."[60] In these parcels, her mother and sister frequently sent clothing that fit her children's growing bodies, approximated metropolitan standards, and supplemented limited colonial markets. These exchanges also symbolized and facilitated connections between Moody's English family of origin and her young children in British Columbia. For example, in 1859 she requested a frock for her daughter Josephine (Zeffie) and enclosed "a pattern of her present body."[61] In its evocative materiality, this pattern enabled Zeffie's distant relatives to maintain some level of familiarity with her, or at least imagine her changing body, as she grew up in British Columbia, offering a limited substitute for the immediate, detailed knowledge that would have accompanied physical proximity.

In her letters, Moody represented the parcels as especially powerful symbols of family for her young children, who received clothing gifts from a "home" that they otherwise did not know. Her youngest children, Susan, Mary, and Meggie, had been born in British Columbia and had never met their metropolitan relatives, while their elder siblings had spent only a small portion of their lives in England. However, Moody repeatedly reported to her mother and sister that Susan described items of her clothing as made by her "Aunt Emmy" in "England" (even when they had not been).[62] In this, she emphasized her young daughter's rehearsal of these phrases as signs of Susan's imagined connection to both "family" and "England." In these repeated declarations, at least as her mother presented them, Susan seemed to grasp that she should have some relationship with people and places elsewhere. In this sense, clothing gifts helped young Susan Moody to understand the extended family, albeit vaguely, at a distance. In other words, the post helped to materialize relationships and evoke the extended family for young children who might otherwise feel unconnected to their relatives in the metropole.

As separated relatives declared again and again, distance made it difficult to understand and come to terms with changing bodies, lives, and membership in trans-imperial families. For those who wanted to maintain connections with family over time, the post mattered because it provided a way of performing relationships and communicating about change. Specifically, Britons used letters to welcome new relatives and establish relationships with them, to update knowledge about one another, and to assert their continued place and belonging in the family. In addition to textual content, photographs, clothing, and other items represented familial relationships and offered relatives tactile and visual knowledge of changing bodies and lives. Although the resulting relationships varied, these Britons generally used and described the post as the primary available (if also a fraught and limited) means of navigating and incorporating change into their understandings of family.

"Trying to Read You a Lecture": Epistolary Advice and Family Formation

Nineteenth-century Britons widely understood giving advice to be a component and role of the family. Translating this expectation into epistolary form, distant relatives used correspondence to advise one another on a wide range of personal issues, from fashion to finances to letter-writing etiquette itself. Parents and elder siblings particularly positioned themselves as moral guides, and suggested that it was their special obligation to advise their children or younger siblings. A subset of this larger pattern, marriage and courtship advice was a common feature of correspondence. By intervening in their relatives' marriage decisions, Britons both enacted their perceived responsibilities to each other and tried to protect the family's collective interests. In the process, their letters both explained and lived their understandings of what made good husbands, wives, parents, siblings, and children. Metropolitan relatives also tailored marriage advice to their concerns about distance and British Columbian society. Arguing that settlers were at particular risk of being led astray, far from the watchful eyes of relatives and living in a place that they understood to lack important features of British society, metropolitan correspondents reminded their British Columbian relatives to be cautious and attentive to the family's interests. Overall, their courtship and marriage advice reveals epistolary strategies for retaining influence in settler lives, communicating relationship expectations, and ultimately trying to ensure a respectable and mutually responsible trans-imperial family.

In general, this epistolary advice was shaped by societal attitudes toward marriage in Britain between the mid-nineteenth and early twentieth centuries. Of course, individual experiences and ideas differed, and were variously influenced by class, religion, and location. In the broadest sense, though, most Britons in this period assumed that marriage was a heterosexual union, and a patriarchal institution rooted in the authority of church and state.[63] Although coverture had long rendered women legally dependent on their husbands in the United Kingdom, this was increasingly criticized in the nineteenth century and the Married Women's Property Acts (1870, 1881, and 1882) enabled married women to own and control property under certain conditions. However, these legal changes did not erase widespread and ongoing beliefs in gendered difference and men's authority in marriage. Many Britons continued to understand women as naturally suited to the domestic sphere and men to the public. In addition, while middle-class ideals increasingly linked courtship with romantic love and individual choice, personal preference and happiness were not necessarily involved in the arrangement of a marriage or its results. Indeed, marriage was understood not only as a relationship between individuals but as a critical collective strategy of family formation. It impacted families' social status and respectability, advanced or impeded their economic interests, affected the distribution of property, produced and shaped future generations, and changed who was considered a relation at all. Because of this, relatives often sought to encourage, forbid, or arrange matches for one another in what they believed to be the best interests of the family as a whole.[64]

At least some of the correspondents in this book understood marriages as fundamental to the formation and future of their families, but they found that physical distance complicated (or made impossible) their oversight, arrangement, or approval of specific matches. Metropolitan relatives knew that it was likely that British Columbian settlers would not marry within their extended family or a known, trusted, and respected group of acquaintances – strategies particularly common to middle-class British families in this period.[65] They also understood that it was possible for settlers to avoid familial expectations that they share information, respond to advice, or even gain relatives' blessings before marrying while far away. Sometimes these vague fears became reality. In early 1899, for example, twenty-year-old James Skitt Matthews – under the age of majority in Vancouver – was able to get special dispensation to marry without his parents' permission since they were in England.[66] Relatives over the age of majority would not even need the special dispensation, nor would they necessarily need to inform their relatives of a marriage in British Columbia at all; distance could enable them to harbour such secrets if they chose (see Chapter 6). In this context, metropolitan parents and siblings wrote letters expressing fears that they had less influence over their relatives' behaviour and their family's respectability, and worrying about the gap between what was deemed acceptable in Britain and what seemed plausible in British Columbia. In the hopes of mitigating what they saw as the worst possibilities there, relatives also used the post to intervene or participate in distant marriages – or to attempt to do so, at least – in a range of ways.

Some Britons sought to facilitate their relatives' marriage arrangements from afar. The Victoria marriage between John Sebastian Helmcken and Cecilia Douglas offers one example. Raised by working-class German parents in East London, John Helmcken had trained as a doctor and was working as a medical officer for the Hudson's Bay Company in Victoria. The daughter of colonial governor James Douglas and Amelia Connolly

Douglas, Cecilia Douglas had mixed ancestral roots in Scotland, Cree territory, and Guyana's community of free people of colour. In this respect, both Helmcken and Douglas stretch the limits of my definition of Britishness, revealing its inability to capture the complexity of multiple and layered identities among families with connections to the United Kingdom and making lives across the diverse spaces of empire. In turn, their marriage crossed lines of race and class – exactly the kind of match about which some families in this book expressed anxieties or disapproval, or even kept secret from each other (see Chapter 6). However, this does not seem to have been the case for either the Douglases or the Helmckens. James Douglas did require that Helmcken prove himself to be a man of good character before marrying Cecilia. As part of his response, Helmcken's mother, Catherine, sent a note from London to "certify" that her son had been single when he moved to North America, and to grant her consent to his marriage in the colony. Once this exchange had been completed, the marriage went ahead.[67]

In other cases, metropolitan writers used the post to urge their relatives in British Columbia to return "home" in order to marry respectable family acquaintances there. George Robinson wrote to his Victoria-based son Ernest from Dudley, in the English West Midlands, in 1875. He noted that he could "recommend a young lady to [his son's] notice." The woman in question was "the daughter of an old friend," and after describing her, Robinson proposed that he send "her portrait" in the hopes that his son would be persuaded to return to England.[68] Some settlers responded directly to these suggestions, informing their metropolitan relatives that they had no plans to act as expected or advised, and rejecting what they framed as undue meddling. For example, Kootenay settler Harold Nation responded to his mother's "gentle hint ... to wait for England, Home and Beauty" by telling her that if he did that, "there will be a dead bachelor about fifty years from now."[69] In other cases, settlers more openly reassured their distant relatives about their marriage plans or prospects in British Columbia. In 1887, Tommy Norbury informed his Worcestershire family that he was considering marriage in the Kootenays. In a rare exception to a general epistolary silence about race, he specified explicitly that he did not plan to wed an Indigenous woman, presumably understanding that this was one of their unspoken fears about a British Columbian marriage.[70] In these ways, settlers and their metropolitan relatives negotiated family involvement in or knowledge of marriage arrangements through the post.

John Bayley's letters to his sister Carrie reveal in more detail one individual's epistolary strategies for shaping distant courtship behaviour and marriage arrangements, and communicating expectations for a respectable and mutually responsible trans-imperial family. In 1873, when his archived letters begin, twenty-six-year-old John was working as the bandmaster of the 46th (South Devonshire) Regiment of Foot, and eighteen-year-old Carrie was living with their grandmother in Victoria. Written following their father's death, John's letters situated him as the elder brother and the new head of the family, with special responsibility to instruct his younger sister and secure her future in British Columbia, even from afar. In a June 1874 letter, he staked a clear claim to his right to advise when he criticized his father's decisions about Carrie's education. Claiming that "I as your brother can speak in an unconstrained manner" about this matter, he argued that he now needed to ensure that she did what was best. He then delivered a series of general instructions for how she should act, ranging from "waste no time in idle frivolity" to "make all love you and at the same time be chary of your affection." In general, this letter expressed little faith in Carrie's ability to make good, independent decisions. John concluded by trying to justify its tone: "You will think I am trying to read you a lecture, but it is not so. I only want you to take particular good care of yourself."[71]

While these passages served as general life guidance, most of John's epistolary advice was tailored specifically to courtship, as he tried to ensure that Carrie would find a husband who was acceptable to him, and implied that she might not do so without his help. Broadly, he instructed her not to "select anyone simply on account of his good looks or oily tongue" and to "try to school [her] heart against flattery and stupid infatuation." Her actions mattered not only to herself, he reminded her; she also had a responsibility to the family as a whole. To this end, he wrote: "I always consider you a real credit to the family, and hope if you marry your husband may be a worthy man."[72] John's advice also revealed his particular anxieties about the nature of Vancouver Island society in the early settler years. He suggested that his sister might be easily led astray in a place with so many more white settler men than women, imagining these men as desperate and aggressive suitors without easily apparent class and family backgrounds for her to assess. In this context, he feared, his sister might be fooled into an unrespectable match. He used letters to instruct her on how to avoid this possibility, in one case expressing special concern about her potential interest in men whom he called "those stupid asses of navy officers." Describing them as risky or poor suitors, he directed her not to "take any notice of them beyond being civil," and explained that "they will try to make themselves very agreeable to you, because there are few young ladies on the Island, and they have so much time on their hands, there is nothing else to do, for amusement but spooning girls[.] I know the tinkers[.] take my advice and dont go taking walks or receiving letters from them." He warned that she was "apt to get a little bit infatuated with them" because they were officers and "they always represent themselves as gentleman [*sic*] coming from good families in England when in the strict sense of the word they have no right whatever to the appellation of gentleman and as far as birth is concerned they are perhaps the sons of some well to do cheese or fishmonger." Rejecting the idea that such a man could make an acceptable match for his sister, he instructed Carrie to be attentive to local respectability and character, while recognizing that this might look different from Britain. Specifically, she should seek

> the acquaintanceship of a respectable mercantile man who is settled out there, and you can see for yourself what position he occupies in society and don't be particular as long as he is a true honest industrious man, such a one would be far preferable to one of those brainless idiots, with nothing but a midshipman's bunk and about five shillings a day.[73]

The archive does not include Carrie Bayley's responses to her brother, although about five years later, she married the retired Royal Engineers officer and Queen's Printer Richard Wolfenden in Nanaimo.[74] Whatever role her brother's advice might (or might not) have played in this match, his letters clearly reflected his understandings of Vancouver Island's early settler society, and how respectability, class, and courtship could be configured there. At the same time, these letters represented his efforts to fill his role as the patriarchal head of a trans-imperial family, and to protect his sister's reputation and future – and by extension, his own. Overall, John Bayley justified his advice as a long-distance fulfillment of his particular familial obligations and rights, and emphasized that it was his sister's duty to be a "credit" to the family by making an appropriate marriage choice in turn. In so doing, he wrote his letters in the hopes of shaping the form and future of his family from afar.

While John Bayley's letters focused on his sister's behaviour in courtship, other metropolitan Britons sent their advice after they received news of an engagement or marriage in British Columbia. Fathers typically sent marriage advice to sons, whereas mothers were more likely to advise daughters or future daughters-in-law. Men often focused on how to provide a stable home for dependent wives, while some women framed their advice as shared secrets for negotiating power in relationships. When Jane Murie Peebles Leighton heard that her son planned to marry in New Westminster, for example, she advised her future daughter-in-law not to "give him all his own way to begin with."[75] More generally, epistolary marriage advice was usually embedded with parental claims to authority and the duty to advise, as writers explained that it was their obligation to share knowledge and experiences in order to support their children's future. In this way, epistolary advice after an engagement revealed letter writers' specific and gendered understandings of both marriage and parenthood.

Again, this broad point can be fleshed out with a case study. Between late 1898 and early 1899, Herbert and Mary Jane Matthews wrote a series of letters from Rock Ferry, England, in response to the surprising news that their son, James, was engaged to be married in Vancouver. James had arrived in North America from New Zealand in April 1898. His fiancée, Maud Boscawen, followed him from Auckland in November, probably without the blessing of her father, who disapproved of the match. Although this was never made explicit in the archived letters, she was soon pregnant with twins, which likely led to their decision to marry in January without the consent of James's parents.[76] Between receiving news of the engagement in November and the marriage in January, Herbert and Mary Jane wrote a number of advisory letters to their son. Their initial response was cautiously congratulatory, but they soon openly disapproved and advised the couple to delay the marriage until they were financially stable. Herbert wrote bluntly to his son in early December:

> I certainly do regret that both of you were so unwise as to have taken the course you have done. Had you asked us, or given us the slightest idea of your intentions, I should most strongly have advised you to wait ... I must tell you plainly, had you consulted your mother and I about your marrying, we should have used all our influence to persuade you to do no such thing, until you were settled.[77]

Here, he underscored his fears about his son's inability to support a wife yet. In addition, he recognized that with limited knowledge at a distance, he had been unable to advise his son about the engagement, as he felt was his duty and as he might have done in proximity.

This letter was not unique. Herbert and Mary Jane Matthews repeatedly explained that distance made it difficult to communicate their opinions and to help James and Maud navigate a challenging situation without misjudging it, hurting feelings, or damaging relationships. In December 1898, Herbert wrote a "gloomy" letter in which he explained: "We are so far away, our hands are tied that we cannot help you both, and that makes troubles so much harder to bear." Mary Jane worried that her future daughter-in-law had taken offence at her frank disapproval of the marriage, given that they did not know one another and she was unable to clarify in person. "You understand me I know," she wrote to James. "I trust you to explain whatever dear Maud may not understand. If you were only nearer to us."[78] Given the circumstances, though, Mary Jane and Herbert had only the post through which to respond to the intended marriage and shape the relationships that constituted the family, and so they translated their advice into epistolary form.

In general, the Matthewses' advice outlined the qualities James would need in order to be a good husband. Broadly, both parents drew on the notion that a husband should be a responsible provider for the family, framing marriage as a form of dependency for women as well as a kind of partnership. To this end, Herbert argued that, most of all, his son needed to recognize that he was now required to care for the woman who had "trusted herself to" him, to consider Maud in all major decisions, and to share openly with her. These instructions were specifically tailored to their understanding of James. Herbert and Mary Jane repeatedly admonished their son for a past in which he had been "hasty" with important choices and poor with money. Restraint mattered to middle-class domestic masculinity. In this spirit, Herbert emphasized that a good husband was obliged to practice frugal financial sense, instructing his son to "strive against your careless way with money, for her sake," to "be a strong man and govern yourself – not let your every inclination govern you," and simply to, "be a man James."[79]

This advice also reflected the Matthewses' understandings of parent-son relationships. Herbert repeatedly argued that his and Mary Jane's experiences granted them the knowledge to advise, while their role as parents meant that they had an obligation to do so. He explained that "after 26 years of married life I can surely speak with some authority" on the topic, and argued that James should listen to him about money because he had proved himself to be "*capable*" with the family finances. It was the parents' role to help their sons by delivering such advice, he argued: "What mother and I have always been trying, for you & Martin to do is, to save you finding out by your own hard experiences, what we have learnt before you." In turn, he wrote, James needed to understand that his parents' advice was both sound and caring: "You cannot drive the world before you and that you will discover by bitter experience, unless you listen to advice from those who have your best interests at heart and are qualified by experience to give you advice."[80]

Indeed, Herbert and Mary Jane reminded James that he had particular responsibilities to them as a son, and argued that he had violated these by rushing into a marriage without consulting them, instead ignoring their advice and withholding information. They were especially critical that he had asked to borrow money from them, though they did grant the request. In addition to indicating poor financial sense, they argued, his appeal for a loan suggested his lack of concern for his parents' financial security and future. They had a responsibility to advise and support their children, but, in turn, James had a duty to respect their needs, and they were hurt that he had not done so. "I cannot understand it a bit," Herbert wrote, "for I dare not think you would thoughtlessly throw away what your mother and I have so much need of." Again and again, Herbert and Mary Jane returned to this issue, claiming continued love and concern for their son, their simultaneous duty, desire, and inability to help him further, and his responsibility to respect their needs and act with manly and filial restraint.[81]

The parents also repeatedly criticized James's decision not to inform them of the probable reason for the loan – to pay for Maud's passage from New Zealand to Vancouver – and more generally, to withhold information about the possible marriage until after it was decided for certain. In so doing, they argued, he had violated the expectations and trust that underpinned their relationship. Herbert bemoaned the fact that James had not "made a confidante" of his mother, as he had always done before when he "had anything important to decide." Similarly, Mary Jane pleaded with her son: "Why is it James that you have lost all confidence in me.

Why did you not tell me in your old honest straight-forward way." Here, she reminded him of his obligation to be truthful and open with them in exchange for "the confidence we have in your word." She outlined her expectations of their relationship, which rested on reciprocity. "I hope you will give us your old love and confidence in return for what we cannot help feeling for you," she wrote.[82] Taken together, the Matthews parents' letters reflected their concerns about their continued duties, fading influence, and troubled relationships with their son, as well as their own finances. In what they saw as a crisis for the family, Herbert and Mary Jane Matthews used the post to articulate their expectations of themselves and their son, and in so doing, to guide their relationships in the future, even at a distance.

Like John Bayley and the Matthews parents, many Britons used letters as a vehicle for advising and admonishing relatives. Courtship and marriage were important foci for this, since they impacted a family's respectability, finances, and relationships as well as an individual's happiness and success. Epistolary advice on these topics reflected letter writers' understandings of settler society and their realization that relatives could simply ignore their guidance from afar. In addition, it revealed attitudes toward gender and family – in particular, the obligations of a good husband, wife, parent, child, or sibling. Overall, this epistolary advice demonstrates the efforts of British letter writers to articulate and extend familial responsibilities across distances, and to influence relatives' behaviour in British Columbia. The letter writers sought to retain a place in settler lives at a distance, and to shape the formation and future of respectable trans-imperial families at a potentially vulnerable juncture.

Coda: On Distance

In this chapter's opening anecdote, Robert Burnaby framed distance as something that could be "overstep[ped]" with affectionate letter writing, enabling him to maintain and articulate closeness with his English family while he was in British Columbia. He was far from the only correspondent to make such a claim. The epistolary archive is fixated on the idea of overcoming separation with long-distance forms of affection or obligation. There are many reasons for this. It was frequently a sense of duty or love that compelled these Britons to write to one another in the first place. Although recipients undoubtedly then kept letters for a range of motives, sentiment probably loomed large in many cases, a common reason why recipients and their descendants preserved the records for so long. Other letters might have been lost or destroyed because they were not part of relationships inflected with this kind of intimacy, obligation, or commitment to maintaining an ongoing relationship. This is, of course, speculation; it is impossible to say what preoccupied the letters that have not survived, and so I cannot to assess the extent to which publicly archived correspondence is representative in its approach to the long-distance family. Nonetheless, working with the existing archive, it is clear that there is a very common element shared across these letters: an expectation of, or yearning for, closeness in the context of familial separation. By tracing how Britons both discussed this issue and used correspondence to address it, this chapter has largely reinforced their common framing of distance as a problem for the family, to be solved in part by the post.

But distance was never as simple as archived letters suggested. For one, correspondence could not replicate proximity, even as it often aspired and even claimed to do so. In the yawning time lag between the sending and receiving of a letter, entire personal worlds could change: one could receive letters from the long-dead, send best wishes for a job already lost, lose track of a relative altogether. In colonial Victoria, Henry Crease may have quivered with excitement as he opened a parcel from his wife in London, as he later described to her, but the caress of an envelope was a long way from the touch, or voice, or sight of a loved one. In this light, the post could be a treasured thread of connection, but it was also one that emphasized its own thinness, its own fragility and insufficiency in overcoming distance.

In addition, settlers could also find distance useful, whether or not they admitted it in writing. It is less often apparent in the archive, but distance could facilitate a welcome break in the family, either temporarily or permanently. Distance could also allow relatives to keep certain secrets from one another, to lie or to massage the truth, or to act outside the bounds of one another's approval or surveillance, while still maintaining connections in other ways. It could foster disconnection and conflict as relatives fell out of touch or misunderstood one another, but it could also ease hostility by giving relatives space to pursue their own lives. In other words, there was no simple relationship between distance and families, even though letter writers repeatedly cast physical separation as a challenge for relatives that they desired and sought to overcome through the post. Chapters 5 and 6 take up some of these points by exploring examples of conflict and silence as key elements that were built into epistolary families and helped to define their limits. In the meantime, I maintain here that although affection and obligation are critical and obvious parts of the epistolary archive, they should be understood as a reflection of what people wrote and kept rather than a straightforward equation between closeness and family. Epistolary claims to connection were significant and common, but between the lines, the idea of distance was complicated because families were complicated.

In sum, tracing epistolary discussions of trans-imperial relationships, this chapter has shown that Britons regularly articulated their understandings of familial emotion, obligation, and membership through the post. They suggested that sending and receiving letters shrank senses of distance, enabled them to feel closer to relatives, and made challenging lives in British Columbia seem easier. They argued that letter writing was critical to ongoing relationships and a new family duty at a distance. Conversely, poor or infrequent correspondence symbolized and caused family conflict, neglect, or disintegration in the absence of other possible media for continued relationship. In addition, correspondents used the post to understand the changing lives and bodies of distant relatives, and to establish relationships with new members of the family. And they used letters to deliver advice, especially about courtship and marriage, which outlined their expectations for particular relationships, asserted the family's continued importance, and sought to protect its future in both the United Kingdom and British Columbia. This did not mean that all families were built on affection, connection, and well-received advice; these epistolary relationships were only one form of family. Nonetheless, they were a significant one. Overall, these correspondents framed the post as an essential vehicle for active relationships and used letters to incorporate distance into the meanings and forms of family itself. That so many settlers undertook the work of correspondence suggests the ongoing salience of metropolitan relatives in their lives, whether this took the form of material support, obligation, advice, or affection. In turn, these families mattered for the making of early settler British Columbia. Taking up this point, the next part of the book turns to the role of these epistolary relationships in shaping trans-imperial families' affective and everyday understandings of British Columbia.

Part 2
Colonial Commonplace

3

"Absolutely Nothing Going On"

Epistolary Emotion and Unremarkable Colonial Knowledge

In July 1889, Tommy Norbury wrote to his brother Coni from Fort Steele in southeastern British Columbia. Apologizing for what he called a "rotten letter," the young rancher declared: "There is absolutely nothing going on here & no news."[1] Read on its own, Norbury's claim of "absolutely nothing" initially seems like mere epistolary filler to be skimmed on the way to an analysis of something more remarkable. But this statement assumes greater significance with the realization that he was far from alone in such declarations. British family letters are saturated with similar claims, which included stock phrases and general apologies about "no news" to write, and specific descriptions of personal boredom, monotony, and banality in British Columbia. I find these to be strikingly at odds with dominant scholarly explanations of British emotional experiences in, and affective knowledge of, the British Empire. This scholarship tends to centre on fear and anxiety – an analytical focus that obscures the critical work of a much wider range of emotions through which Britons encountered, interpreted, sustained, and participated in imperial projects. Certainly, I contend here, it cannot explain how or why settler family correspondence articulated not traumatic fear or persistent anxiety but rather the quotidian power to be bored in British Columbia.

To do so, this chapter focuses on epistolary emotion, and specifically emotional description as a site of colonial knowledge production and circulation. Here I am not concerned with how letter writers actually felt, examining instead how they expressed or suggested particular feelings as a way to explain their lives in British Columbia to distant relatives. How did correspondents represent their lives and surroundings as personal emotional experiences? What was the relationship between epistolary boredom and other feelings, such as anxiety or fascination? When, how, and why did correspondence come to focus on the dull? And what do changing epistolary emotions and repeated descriptions of the unremarkable reveal about the genre of family letters, settlers' engagement with British Columbia, and the trans-imperial production of colonial knowledge? Considering these questions, I trace the changing affective contours of colonial description and familial knowledge, as letters moved from interest to indifference and Britons settled and made a new home in British Columbia.

More specifically, I begin with epistolary fascination. Detailed representations of astonishment and curiosity were usually confined to a small number of long letters written shortly after an individual's arrival in British Columbia, and focused especially on depicting unfamiliar environments, Indigenous people, and Chinese people. These letters served as early explanations of colonial difference and strategies used by Britons to make knowable an unknown place. This initial excited interest faded very quickly from correspondence, however, and settlers increasingly filled their letters with declarations that they had nothing to say and nothing to do. Some of these claims represented a common convention in nineteenth- and early-twentieth-century British and Irish family correspondence around the world, and were not specific to British Columbia. Others were detailed personal complaints about British Columbia as a specific settler place normalized to the point of tedium. By narrating it as "nothing," these epistolary emotions were integral to the settler project, as they both reflected and bolstered British understandings of British Columbia as a place of enduring personal belonging and collective security – an affirmation of a colonial status quo. As this chapter concludes, this process inherently left much unremarked. The epistolary power to claim boredom was also the power to look away from the possibility of racialized violence, settler anxiety, or colonial vulnerability. Overall, tracing these emotional representations and silences, this chapter argues that the shift from epistolary fascination to boredom reflected the growing ability of Britons to represent and sustain their lives in British Columbia as unremarkable and normal.

This discussion offers a new history of emotion, empire, and settler colonialism. A diverse body of work has sought to understand the historical meanings and significance of emotion as it was individually experienced and expressed, collectively understood and regulated, and influential in shaping wider social and political contexts.[2] While the new imperial history has long understood colonialism as "tense and tender" in a range of ways, the recent scholarship on empire has especially emphasized the ubiquity of fear, insecurity, and vulnerability for colonizers around the world. This work frames British anxiety, panic, or even trauma as constitutive (if sometimes also destructive) of its imperial project.[3] Scholars have also investigated the specific relationship between anxiety and settler colonialism. In his influential theorization, historian Lorenzo Veracini has suggested that settler colonialism is characterized by "ongoing [settler] concerns with existential threats and a paranoid fear of ultimate decolonisation," "a fear of indigenous revenge," and "apprehensions" about issues including "racial contamination" and "inappropriate demographic balances," among other "neurosis-generating settler anxieties."[4] In the most focused study of settler anxiety in British Columbia, historian Kenton Storey has recently traced how the Vancouver Island press expressed fears about potential Indigenous violence in the mid-nineteenth century.[5] Taken together, such work has shed light on British understandings of their own vulnerability, the contingencies of imperial rule, the motors of colonial policies, and the significance of Indigenous people's survivance (or active presence) and resistance as challenges to settler power.[6]

While recognizing the value of this work, I have found that British family letters require a different explanation. The language, content, and tone of correspondence suggest that fear and anxiety may not have been the dominant (and certainly were not the only) affective lenses through which settlers understood colonial projects. Letters expressed a wide range of other feelings in relation to British Columbia – including confidence, astonishment, excitement, disgust, boredom, happiness, and loneliness – far more often than they implied fearfulness. To be clear, settlers may have felt anxious. Indeed, many likely did, at least about their own futures, if not also about British Columbia as a whole. It is also possible that they repressed concerns in their texts and consciousness for various reasons. Given these points, it might be worthwhile to read against the grain in order to identify symptoms of settler anxiety, unease, or fear. Ultimately, I see this as a suggestive but fraught methodology. For one, it risks assuming that we already know that settlers were afraid underneath it all, despite what they said, and that we can recognize the parameters and significance of colonial anxiety even in its absence from the text – a true feeling that was denied or silenced but still traceable between the lines. In addition, an emphasis on reading against the grain for repressed anxiety risks missing the significance of the feelings that *were* expressed in letters. In this spirit, this chapter approaches the study of imperial emotion by reading for the feelings correspondents claimed, asserted, and actively sought to spark in their readers.

"This Is Where We Are Going to Live!": Fascinated Initial Description

In the mid-nineteenth century, Anglican minister Alexander David Pringle moved to British Columbia without his wife and children, planning to establish himself and set up a church in the town of Hope before they joined him. His early correspondence from the colony informed his English relatives about the unfamiliar place, reassured them that he was well, asked for help when needed, and prepared his wife for what she would encounter when they reunited there. To assist with these goals, his first letters offered lengthy descriptions of his surroundings and experiences of settlement. In one case, he drew a very rare concrete connection between these detailed letters and his feelings of worry without his family in what he called "in a new & far off land." Writing to his father in April 1860, he explained: "My extreme anxiety has made me acutely observant."[7] This comment is exceptional; other correspondents did not claim or even imply "extreme anxiety" as Pringle did. However, their initial letters from British Columbia were also "acutely observant," and consistently so throughout the early settler period. These detailed first letters were examples of a different epistolary emotion, astonishment.

Initial epistolary descriptions focused especially on the environment and Indigenous and Chinese people. Long letters framed these topics as telling symbols of local difference. These were not merely descriptive representations of British Columbia, however; they were also narrations of emotional encounters with the place, as settlers depicted themselves as fascinated or curious in relation to these topics. Through these passages, letter writers emphasized that relatives should not interpret British Columbia as a dangerous threat or source of anxiety; these colonial descriptions were intended not as causes for concern, they underscored, but rather as interested and interesting ways to explain an unfamiliar place. These may have been rejections of their uncertainty, denials of anxiety, and attempts to manage their families' fears. But it is remarkable and telling how letter writers recounted their first encounters with British Columbia in the same enthusiastic terms. With their detailed and comforting fascination, these initial letters stand apart from the later banality of family correspondence, and complicate the scholarly focus on settler anxiety by emphasizing the possibility of a comfortable and safe, if interesting, home.

In their first letters, British settlers most often offered appreciative assessments of the environment in whatever region of British Columbia they had arrived.[8] For example, English physician Charles Newcombe penned a positive representation of the environment after his arrival in Victoria in 1883. He had travelled to British Columbia to assess its potential for his family's settlement, while his wife, Marian Arnold Newcombe, remained in England. In this, he (like David Pringle) was one of many men who took on the role of familial scout and settler vanguard while wives and children stayed behind in Britain. These men typically took on the responsibility of assessing British Columbia's potential for the family's settlement, finding a job, establishing a business, or building a home before women and children joined them. These gendered arrangements rested on the ideas that migration to unfamiliar British Columbia was a significant risk as well as a potential opportunity, and that men were well placed to undertake this work as an extension of their public and financial role in the family. Since women often lived with their parents while their husbands travelled, these arrangements also reflected the significance of extended relatives in supporting a family's collective interests – or at least those of the women and children, who were not necessarily guaranteed either material provision from or reunion with the men who had left.[9]

For many of these men, the post was a useful and valuable tool for evaluating British Columbia as a place of settlement, passing on this information to metropolitan relatives, and explaining their steps to establish themselves as settlers and to create future family homes. Newcombe's long and detailed letters are a clear example of this gendered subgenre. In addition to maintaining his relationship with his wife from afar, his first letters from British Columbia were intended to help her consider life in the province – a future that the family would choose to pursue several years later. In these letters, Newcombe framed the environment as an important part of his appraisal of Victoria as a possible home. In his first letter from the city, he described it as having "the most magnificent scenery I have ever clapped eyes on." He claimed not only wonder here but also hope. Imagining how his family might live in Victoria, Newcombe represented it as a beautiful and pleasant place, finding special comfort in its safe availability for settler leisure. "This is a lovely place, wood, water, mountain & meadow all in one place, & sunshine to brighten all," he wrote, concluding: "I am sure you will like the place if we settle here. There are splendid walks & drives in every direction & innumerable inlets & islands for boating."[10]

Whereas Newcombe emphasized Victoria's soft and safe environment for his family's future leisure, naval officer Edmund Verney anticipated only a short-term posting in Esquimalt and was less concerned about its long-term possibilities for his settlement. Nonetheless, he too wrote positively about the southern Vancouver Island environment. In 1862, he wrote his first letter to his father, explaining: "You will want to know what I think of the place, and how I like my appointment: well, at present everything promises to be very delightful." He then described his surroundings: "I think the scenery here is beautiful: this exquisite little harbour is surrounded by little hills and bushes and pine trees growing down to the water's edge." Although he noted that "those who have been here some time think the pine trees very ugly," he did not yet claim this judgment himself. Instead, he framed trees as notable markers of a distinctive local landscape, concluding that "they certainly give the land a ragged and quite unique character."[11]

In such descriptions, settlers represented themselves as interested in their new surroundings, and framed the environment as comforting, appealing, or intriguing. Sometimes, to help them explain the place to distant relatives, they drew on comparisons to mutually understandable British and European environments, describing British Columbia as potentially familiar yet even more astonishing or beautiful than known places. For example, Verney's second letter to his father continued along the same appreciative lines as his first, beginning: "I am much charmed with the great beauty of this country." He then expanded his description:

> The living trees generally, grow to a much greater size than we are accustomed to in England, for I think we usually consider the pine to be a light stemmed, brittle tree, but here they grow to a gigantic size, both of height and of circumference ... The forest is in most places pretty thick, but here and there it opens into park-like enclosures, and large masses of rock crop out, bare of all but moss, a little soft turf in the hollows, and the most exquisite wild flowers, among which one recognizes in great abundance the calcilaria, the violet, the sweet-briar, and the strawberry: indeed the forest is as full of wild strawberries as possible.

Here, Verney drew comparisons between colonial and English plants, and through this strategy, described the environment as both remarkable and recognizable to himself and his readers. Enclosed sketches or objects could also help orient relatives and familiarize them with a new place, its plants, and its animals. In this case, Verney promised that he would later send "the girths of some of the largest" trees and "some cones" as interesting tokens of the environment.[12]

Other correspondents also compared environmental features between British Columbia and Europe as a narrative tactic to heighten their claims to local wonder. In 1899, nineteen-year-old Leonard Witherby arrived on Vancouver Island. His first letter from Victoria was twenty pages – a remarkable length that warranted special mention in the archived letter-book copy. Explaining his impressions of the city and its surroundings, he reported to his father:

> I think the best view I have ever seen is from Beacon Hill[;] the geography of this place is very difficult to understand & I cannot get hold of it very well however. You stand on B.H. & look straight across a piece of water for 40 miles & you see the State of Washington U.S.A. staring you in the face in the shape of the most splendid range of "all the year round" snow clad mountains I've ever seen, they look most magnificent. I saw them yesterday, as the sun was setting, & have never seen anything so grand, the shadows thrown by the sun, & the colours made by the snow looked most awfully fine, but I cannot describe them ... I am sure that it must beat Zwitzerland & other places into fits.[13]

In such passages, Witherby's letter depicted him as enthusiastic, moved almost to wordlessness by the local environment, while the Swiss comparison especially conveyed magnificence and wonder.

Witherby was not alone in choosing Switzerland as an impressive point of comparison to emphasize astonishment in British Columbia. When English settler and aspiring orchardist Daisy Oxley Phillips arrived in 1912 with her husband, Jack, she penned fascinated and awed descriptions of the environment. In her first letter to her mother from her new home in southeastern British Columbia, she enthused:

> We left Calgary at 8 o'clock, and then I had one of the days of my life. The scenery through the Rockies is the most beautiful and glorious you can

> possibly imagine, and when you are passing through it all day at the rate of 40 miles an hour you simply cannot imagine the size and vastness of it all. There is a wonderful spiral tunnel that is a marvel of engineering skill, and the Kicking Horse Pass is too glorious for words. Switzerland is a tiny little place on a postage stamp after it all, and to think this is where we are going to live! ... The scenery was lovely the whole way as the valley runs between the Rockies and the Selkirks. You have snow-peaks on each side, and the country is like Chobham Common or Bagshot with the river running through as well, and the colours like Switzerland ... It is a most lovely spot, like Lake Windermere in England, with snow-peaked mountains on each side of us.[14]

Like Witherby, Phillips described herself as stunned by local mountains, which she too framed as overwhelming the Swiss comparison, and like Verney, she sought to identify familiar English parallels to render this unfamiliar place comprehensible to her distant relatives.

Whether they represented British Columbian environments as comfortingly familiar or astonishingly different, letter writers generally emphasized that they felt their new home was safe and knowable, not a source of anxiety. After three days in Victoria, Charles Newcombe penned another letter to his wife, Marian. This time describing the cityscape and local society, he framed Victoria as a place of quaint difference from England and the United States, and emphasized that it could be delightful because of this difference:

> They are wonderfully behind the Yankees here in respect to Hotels & business facilities, but enjoy life in an easier & more healthy way. With magnificent climate, scenery & good natural productions in abundance, the Victorians lead a pleasant unspeculative sort of existence, & seem to look forward with dread to the waking up they will soon have to undergo. Lots of Canadians are coming in from the East & many Englishmen too.

In addition, he explained: "The forests come down to the waters edge here, & rocks jut out just as they do at Windermere ... Lots of geraniums are out still, also roses, fuchsias honeysuckle, gladiolus &c &c. Humming birds abound in summer."[15] Here, Newcombe dwelled on tamed and curious difference that would neither discourage his wife from joining him nor jeopardize their future as settlers. Indeed, the place was already familiar, he suggested; the "rocks jut[ted] out" as they did at their home near the English Lake Windermere, and English settlers were arriving in significant numbers. In sum, he represented Victoria as a secure and "healthy" place that could become a known family home.

In addition to discussing the environment, some British settlers or prospective settlers included descriptions of Indigenous and (to a lesser extent) Chinese people in their first letters from British Columbia. Often, this was the only point in a correspondence when people of colour were mentioned at all. These letter writers rarely described personal encounters with individuals, but rather drew from a wider pool of racialized and racist representation that constructed Indigenous and Chinese people as "others," framed them as uncivilized or unattractive, and belittled them as inferior (see also Chapter 6). In the process, they positioned themselves as observers – but deeply interested, curious, and sometimes disgusted ones. For example, in December 1887, Tommy Norbury wrote to his mother from the Kootenays:

> The Indians are no believers in work. You may perhaps come across a man who will work for 2 days but never longer. They make their wives do whatever there is to do, hauling wood, putting up tents, while they sit down either gambling or looking on. They are all spoilt by gambling, nobody stops them on the American Side. They will gamble off ½ dozen horses & all their blankets at a sitting, & then live, till they have raised some money somehow on begging from the white man.[16]

Here, Norbury reproduced common racialized and gendered abstractions, including representations of the "lazy Indian," Indigenous men as idle gamblers, and Indigenous women as overworked drudges.[17] He was not alone in drawing on such tropes to condemn what he portrayed as uncivilized gender roles and racialized inferiority or savagery. In his first letter from Esquimalt, for instance, Verney developed a similarly cutting and sweeping judgment, describing Indigenous people there as "hideously ugly and atrociously dirty: their customs are beastly, manners they have none."[18]

British settlers' representations of Chinese people tended to construct "otherness" in distinct ways, often less viciously disparaging but still focused on racialized and cultural difference. These passages especially emphasized Chinese men's queue hairstyle, labour and living conditions, and limited or accented use of the English language. In a letter written from the train on his way to the Pacific coast, for example, Leonard Witherby mentioned a Chinese man travelling with him. "There is a Chinaman in the car with us, with a great pig-tail on," he noted first. "Some fellows in my car gave the remains of their food to the Chinaman today, & they gave him a rather lot of things, & he said 'too muchee.'"[19] Writing again from Victoria, Witherby reported to his father: "There are 3 names that I saw stuck up, they are all washing men, 'Yee Wo' 'Sang wo Lee' 'San Sing' [;] out of every 10 people you meet, 4 will be Chinamen. They have some quarters of their own in a certain part of the city." Here, he did not dwell on descriptions of racialized bodies, but largely rendered Chinese people as an impersonal or even inhuman curiosity that made the cityscape of Victoria notable in their ubiquity, adding: "Everyone here has a Chinaman & telephone in his house."[20] In each of these cases, Britons framed Indigenous and Chinese people as points of local difference. In producing such epistolary representations, letter writers called on a wider set of ideas about race, culture, and difference, which both assumed and asserted white settler superiority. In order to pass judgment, writers framed these passages through epistolary emotion, as they both expressed and sought to spark curiosity, fascination, and disgust.

Critically, these affective depictions also asserted confidence, as letter writers explicitly and implicitly assured distant readers that there was no need for anxiety. Describing Victoria, for example, Charles Newcombe wrote to his wife: "The streets are thronged with Chinese & Indians in various costumes but all seem quiet & orderly."[21] Given that he was assessing the possibilities of settlement in the region, the tone of reassurance was significant. Here, Newcombe spoke directly against the possibility of violence and denied any need for familial fear. Other letters depicted Indigenous people as passive figures, or as threats to themselves rather than to settlers. In an 1864 letter to his brother, for example, colonial secretary Arthur Birch used the power of his official position to underscore that "with our 40,000 natives ... we manage to keep them fairly quiet," unlike other sites of empire like New Zealand.[22] Such descriptions did not articulate significant anxiety about the potential threat of Indigenous people, either to individual letter writers or to a larger colonial project. Correspondents may have intended these passages to offset relatives' concerns. But whatever their underlying feelings about the place, British settlers asserted and reinforced a confident sense of security rather than echoing such worries.

Taken together, Britons' first letters from British Columbia shared many common characteristics. Notably long and detailed, they included enthusiastic or stunned descriptions of local environments, and curious, disgusted, or unconcerned representations of Indigenous and Chinese people. These settlers (or prospective settlers) wrote with the conviction that their readers would be as fascinated as they were, and with an underlying goal of making an unknown place familiar. In their appreciative explanations of landscapes and confident dismissals of people of colour, these first descriptions aimed at reassurance too. The place was spectacular and remarkable at first encounter, letter writers explained, but it was also safe and knowable and potentially theirs. In this way, early epistolary descriptions produced a shifting vision of hope, conviction, and curiosity through which correspondents circulated family knowledge about British Columbia as interesting and strange, yet a possible settler home.

"No News": The Unremarkable as Generic Convention

Across a wide range of family collections, this initial emphasis on settler fascination quickly faded into the unremarkable. Letters soon came to repeat two kinds of declarations instead: general statements that claimed correspondents had nothing to write, and specific place-based descriptions of boredom and monotony. In the first type, settler letter writers regularly used brief stock phrases about "no news" to open and close letters, or sometimes to shift tone and topic in the middle. On the surface, these statements implied a lack of subjects of interest for writers or recipients. Instead of reading them as straightforward affective assessments of British Columbian lives, however, I suggest here that general statements about "no news" were more enactments of a wider epistolary convention. Research into other family collections from Britain, Ireland, India, and North America shows that a diverse range of nineteenth- and early-twentieth-century correspondents used the same or similar phrases in identical ways as British Columbian letter-writers. These passages may have reassured relatives, but they were not necessarily reflections of letters' content or judgments of their writers' lives. Rather, their common usage points most to the generic consistency of family correspondence in this period.

This chapter opened with Tommy Norbury's July 1889 declaration that there was "absolutely nothing going on and no news." This phrasing was not unusual. He and his brother Billy – who lived with Tommy for a time –

regularly used such passages in their family letters from the Kootenays. On 29 June 1889, for example, Billy wrote:

> My dear Mother. It seems a very long time since I wrote a letter that I nearly forgot how to write but I suppose that Tommy tells you all the news, though there is not much ... I am afraid this is not much of a letter but there is such a scarcity of news around here.[23]

Tommy included similar phrases in his salutations and valedictions, closing one letter to his mother with: "There is really no news. Love to all, Your loving son Tommy."[24] He similarly ended a letter to his brother Coni: "This is a fair specimen of a dull letter but stuck of anything amusing. Your loving bro Tommy."[25]

Comparable declarations pervaded other letters too. Writing to her English mother and sister from the Royal Engineers detachment near New Westminster, Mary Hawks Moody repeatedly apologized that her letters were "so short & stupid," in one case explaining that "we are going on in such a quiet same like sort of way that there is really nothing new to tell you."[26] In another letter, she remarked: "I don't think I have much to tell you, we are going on, now, very steadily."[27] In early 1864, naval officer Edmund Verney wrote to his father over the course of four days. His 4 February contribution opened, in part: "I know that my letters are stale and unprofitable, but I cannot invent news, and really nothing of any interest goes on here."[28] Regular correspondents like Norbury, Moody, or Verney might have felt that they had run out of fresh topics, but similar passages characterized the letters of many less frequent writers too. In an 1866 letter from New Westminster, farmer John Brough reported to his brother James that he had little to add to the "scanty news" that he had sent more than two months earlier.[29] In 1890, Vancouver settler John Morton wrote in the only archived letter to his wife in Britain: "I have not much news to tell you."[30] And on his way to the Klondike in 1898, Roger Hicks noted to his daughters halfway through one diarized letter: "Nothing much has been done since my last few lines."[31]

These claims may have depended in part on the definition of "news." Most narrowly, correspondents used the term to refer to vital events like marriages, births, and deaths, and they did not often have such updates to report. However, they also used the term in a more capacious sense that included local and international politics, and personal activities, plans, and finances. Sometimes they may not have felt they had news in this sense either. However, the rest of the letter was frequently full of such material, even when its salutation or valediction declared the opposite. Tommy Norbury's very first letter from the province, written from Golden in September 1887, is one striking example. Its valediction included the statement: "I am afraid there is not much in this letter but news is scarce." He also added a postscript that reiterated: "This is the piece I did not send last week. There is not much in it but it may as well go." Despite this suggestion, however, the letter was richly detailed, with typical initial expressions of fascination, as Norbury explained his new surroundings and his plans for settlement for an audience unfamiliar with the Kootenays.[32] In such cases, it is clear that declarations about the "scarcity" of "news" were not reflections of the content and tone of the rest of the letter, nor were they necessarily expressions of how correspondents actually interpreted their lives.

With this point in mind, I read these passages in a less literal way, focusing more on how and where they appeared in correspondence. Although they were not included in every letter, such phrases were very common. Typically at the beginning or end of letters – and more rarely, in the middle as a transition sentence between topics – these passages were used in the same ways across a range of letters and families, while still being flexible enough to accommodate individual voices and circumstances. Their usage reflected a wider pattern of self-deprecation in letters too, as correspondents regularly disparaged their own letters as short, long, late, or otherwise poor.[33] Because of their common forms and usage, I propose that these general claims to "no news" or deprecations that writers had "not much to say" are best understood as conventions of the genre of British family letter writing in the late nineteenth and early twentieth centuries (and perhaps beyond) rather than as specific to British Columbia.

A review of other family letters supports this suggestion. For example, letters written to recipients in British Columbia echoed the same phrases as the letters written by them. Catherine Mittler Helmcken closed an 1853 letter from London to her daughter-in-law Cecilia Douglas Helmcken in Victoria by noting: "I have no news to write."[34] In 1875, Worcestershire, England, resident George Robinson opened a letter to his son Ernest, a printer in Victoria: "Having a few leisure moments I avail myself of them to write you a few lines – not that I have anything of great importance to write about."[35] At the end of the century, Herbert Lewis Matthews wrote an anxious letter from Rock Ferry, England, to his son in Vancouver. Telling James that he had recently hurt his mother's feelings by sending her a curt postcard, Matthews then turned from family conflict to family news in the remainder of the letter. To signal this shift in tone and topic, he used the transition sentence: "Everything here, going on much as usual."[36]

A published collection of undelivered letters to Hudson's Bay Company employees on the North American Pacific coast further suggests the use of this epistolary convention by diverse British and Irish correspondents earlier in the nineteenth century. For example, in 1850, Alexander Rose, who was struggling for employment in Nairn, Scotland, wrote his brother James in the Sooke River settlement on southern Vancouver Island in part to inquire about the possibility of joining him. As his letter shifted from his financial concerns to updates on their metropolitan acquaintances and relatives, he signalled the change by writing: "I am sory [*sic*] that I have not more news to give you at present."[37] Robert and James Wilson were brothers, both employed by the Hudson's Bay Company in the 1830s. In 1833, Robert wrote to James from York Factory, on Hudson Bay: "I have no particular news to inform you of at present."[38] In 1844, London resident Elizabeth Carrack wrote to her son William: "I have not any News to send you this time."[39] Similarly, in 1847, sailor Charles Wallis's sister Susannah opened a letter to him from Bromley, England, with "there is not much news at Present to tell."[40] Cornish newspaper employee William Nicholls opened a long letter to his brother Robert, who worked as a seaman for the Hudson's Bay Company: "I have procured a large sheet of paper to write to you all the news (which by the bye I do not know how to fill up)."[41]

Likewise, British family letters from South Asia reflected similar patterns in the second half of the nineteenth century. Nearly six years after Norbury's complaint that "absolutely nothing" was happening in southeastern British Columbia, military officer William Lawrence Beynon penned the very same complaint from Gilgit, now in northern Pakistan. "Absolutely nothing going on here now," he wrote to his mother. "Everything as flat as ditch water."[42] The following year, he bemoaned again from northern India: "There is absolutely no news of any kind, so my epistle won't be long or interesting."[43] Writing from Bombay in 1858, a Peninsular and Oriental Steam Navigation Company employee, Franklin Kendall, apologized to his mother for "a very uninteresting letter but there is really nothing to say."[44] In the 1860s, British Army doctor Allie Beveridge noted in one letter from Pune, "Nothing new going on," then from Mian Mir near Lahore, "No news here," then from Rawalpindi, "It is some time now since I wrote to you but one can't make bricks without straw."[45] A former English domestic servant and a regular correspondent from her husband's military station in Sialkot, Pollie Keen frequently drew on similar phrases. For instance, she began an 1890 letter to her mother: "There is nothing much to say again this week."[46]

In all such examples, claims to "no news" were only brief parts of longer letters. As in the British Columbian cases, they were not necessarily reflections of the letters' content, and could even be written directly alongside remarkable topics. In the 1840s, Jonathan Buck was working for the Hudson's Bay Company on the Pacific coast. In the middle of the famine that struck his home country of Ireland, his half-sister Faithy began a letter to him thus:

> dearest Jonty[,] I suppose all the news that I could tell you has been written by other friends. I have but little of any importance to say. I suppose you read of all the starvation our country endured[.] everyone has suffered[.] your humble servant is seldom exempt from suffering[.] my tenant is beginning the last year to pay very badly[.][47]

Here, Faithy's letter produced a striking contrast, as she moved seamlessly from a deprecating claim that she had "little of any importance to say" to a discussion of significant suffering, both personal and collective, that was afflicting a home that her brother had left. In the process, her unremarkable salutation repeated a much wider pattern in British and Irish family correspondence in the nineteenth and early twentieth centuries – one in which a declaration that there was "no news" served as a way to open, close, and shift letters on conventional terms, regardless of the rest of their content.

There are a number of ways to read these phrases. This may have been simply a reflexive and normalized part of the genre, simply something one wrote. In some cases, they may have reflected individual correspondents' feelings or interpretations of their lives, or their struggle to find topics of mutual interest and understanding as their lives diverged from those of distant relatives. Some correspondents used such phrases to underscore their dutiful commitment to the epistolary family: they were doing the work of writing despite the absence of "news," they emphasized. To this end, Edmund Verney opened one letter to his father from Esquimalt: "It seems right that I should have some sort of a letter ready to send to you by every mail, even when I have not much to say."[48] Some writers also explicitly framed their supposedly uninteresting letters as a form of comfort for recipients. Writing from Victoria, Robert Burnaby apologized that one letter was "rather barren of incident," but suggested that its banality would allow his sister to "learn ... of my well being, and of the hopeful state of affairs just now."[49] In such cases, conventional claims to "no news" could help to cast letters as committed and comforting, if generic, performances of familial connection and duty.

Letters rarely hint at how readers interpreted such passages. Perhaps relatives skimmed over these generic claims and focused on the main body of letters. Or, as Burnaby urged, they may have offered some reassurance since they were at least surface claims that a family member was doing well; no news is good news, they seemed to imply. This point was likely only superficially comforting, though, as relatives were well aware of the possibility of silences or lies in letters (see Chapter 6).[50] In any case, correspondents occasionally suggested that they appreciated the comfort of epistolary banality – and certainly desired it if the alternative was no letter at all. Writing from Ealing, England, for instance, Lucy Mathias rejected her Victoria cousin Charles Newcombe's claim to an uninteresting letter. "You began your letter by saying you had 'nothing of interest to write about,'" she wrote, "but you know it's just the ordinary, everyday things that interest one – what you read & weather you ever play your violin & all the family events &c &c."[51]

Along similar lines, Mary Hawks Moody implored her English relatives to write to her in the colony. In particular, she instructed her mother to tell her sister Emily that "she must not fancy it is no use writing because *she fancies* she has nothing to say." Moody explained:

> I am sure I might do the same [i.e., fancy there was nothing to say] for the "moral" of this letter is the same as the last (so if you do not get either, you will have lost nothing) [.] The moral is "Richard is still at Queenborough [*sic,* New Westminster] we are all well, Baby & Charlie are teething ..." nothing very extraordinary in that is there? and still I know Em prefers "the twice told Tale."

Recognizing that her English family appreciated her correspondence even if it was "nothing," Moody emphasized that their letters – however unremarkable they claimed to be – were even more "invaluable" to her because they represented and confirmed her connections to family, home, and England from afar.[52] In this, Moody emphasized that for recipients as well as writers, the affective value of letters was not in their content or supposed interest level, but in their very existence, production, and reception.

Read together, these claims to "no news" are striking in the frequency and consistency with which they were used by British and Irish correspondents from a range of backgrounds and locations in the nineteenth and early twentieth centuries. Although they comprised only one part of letters, the common use of these conventions further suggests that, by the second half of the nineteenth century, British settlers in British Columbia were fluent in a larger epistolary culture, which shared generic expectations and standards of family correspondence. These conventions could help separated relatives perform connection, reassurance, and familial duties through letters.

"Deadened by the Common-place": The Unremarkable as Boredom

While general claims to "no news" reflected a broad culture of letter writing, settler correspondence could also be full of complaints that described British Columbia as specifically boring, monotonous, and "absolutely nothing." These passages represent a significant change in epistolary descriptions of settler lives. At first, Britons' interest had seemed boundless. A month after his arrival on Vancouver Island, Edmund Verney had enthused: "I find plenty to do here, and am never idle: there is so much interesting country to see that one does not easily tire of it."[53] But his letters would in fact tire quickly, as would so much family correspondence. As novelty became familiar, letter writers increasingly described themselves as struggling to interrupt an endless march of quotidian monotony. This was not a precise, uniform, or total shift, and it did not necessarily mean that feelings of astonishment or fascination disappeared from settlers' lives. However, it was a clear trend. Over time, letters worked to construct and circulate family knowledge of an unremarkable British Columbia. In so doing, they reflected an emerging individual and collective sense of feeling safe and at home, represented by the comfortable power to be bored or uninterested.

While a complicated and multi-faceted emotion, boredom is primarily rooted in personal perceptions of an absence of interest, event, or variation. These perceptions are often situated in the gaps between expectation and experience – where interest is anticipated but not felt. According to the existing scholarship, this boredom emerged as a modern construct from the mid-eighteenth century, and in Britain was closely linked to shifting ideas about the individual and new expectations of leisure and adventure in a period of industrialization, modernization, and rapid change.[54] Extending these insights to the empire, historian Jeffrey Auerbach has explored the trajectories of what he calls "imperial boredom," suggesting that elite British men increasingly experienced and expressed boredom with their lives and work in India and Australia in the late nineteenth century. Investigating the specific work of imperial boredom in a study of Sir James Mackintosh, historian Onni Gust has argued that his insistent representations of dullness framed early nineteenth-century Bombay as a "void" and the metropole as the height of "civilization" from which he lived in exile.[55] Similarly embracing the analytical possibilities of imperial boredom, I consider here a wider range of Britons and their representations of boring colonial lives, understanding these epistolary emotions as powerful productions of knowledge rather than as experienced feelings per se. This approach reveals a specific form of imperial boredom that was significant in settler colonial contexts. For Mackintosh, dullness signalled his refusal to belong in Bombay; for settler letter writers, I maintain, it reflected their ability to imagine places like British Columbia as normal, potential or future homes.

As their daily lives became routine and the unfamiliar became commonplace, many British Columbian settlers described their colonial work through a new and disappointing sense of tedium. These complaints focused on temporary tasks and ongoing conditions of labour in a place that could seem very distant from both metropolitan ideals and the imagined opportunities of British Columbia. For Edmund Verney, his mid-nineteenth-century position as a naval officer on the coast not only meant prestige and what he had hoped would be the glories of military life in a colony but also included tasks like painting the ship, which he deemed "a very great bore."[56] Robert Burnaby initially found work as a civil servant, during which time he described his days as filled with "all the Govt.

drudgery."[57] In early 1860, he began pursuing work as a trader, but then he complained about the boredom of that job too. "I am now 'doing business,'" he wrote his sister Harriet. Comparing this work with other, apparently more exciting, colonial opportunities, he explained that "doing business" meant to "sit at home and seli Blankets and other matters day after day: It is not so pleasant as roaming about and prospecting the country, and variety is out of the question."[58] After visiting "the diggings" on the Fraser River in 1860, Mary Hawks Moody wrote her mother about this fleeting experience with prospecting work, concluding: "Digging and washing out the Gold is really hard work, & *so monotonous.*"[59]

In the early provincial period, settlers continued to complain about work and its impact on their correspondence. Writing about his experiences in the early twentieth-century Kootenays, for example, Wilf Rowell described the realities of his work as exhausting, disappointing, overwhelming, and ultimately poor fodder for letters. In one case, he wrote his mother that lumber camp life was busy but tedious when he was occupied with uninteresting tasks: "This is an awfully short letter & without much news, but I have been busy all day mending & washing clothes."[60] Sometimes complaints were articulated in direct contrast to settlers' expectations or initial experiences. Shortly after her spring 1912 arrival in Windermere, Daisy Oxley Phillips claimed that she was "far too busy to be dull." By October, however, she was writing that her household work had quickly settled into an unvaried routine in the place she had initially described as astonishing. As she remarked, her sister might now understand her life in British Columbia as "dull with no amusements, only scenery and hard work!"[61]

In other cases, it was not hard work but rather its unexpected absence that settler correspondents represented as boring, uninteresting, and dissatisfying about their lives. Roger Hicks spent the spring of 1898 stuck in Glenora with a lack of safe, affordable, or viable routes onward to Teslin and the Klondike goldfields. Although trained as a physician, he was not licensed to practise medicine in British Columbia, and found little meaningful in how he spent his time awaiting his anticipated adventures. He wrote his daughters:

> There is little or nothing to do here as shooting is not to be had & the river is running like a mill-race & is much too muddy for fishing. One loafs around to other camps & has a yarn & a smoke ... & so the days go on, slowly ... This

> doing nothing is worse than the hardest work as one gets little to read & finds it difficult to pass the time. Unfortunately for Barker [his travelling companion] & me we cannot practice here as we are still in B. Columbia & one has to pass an exam in Victoria before being allowed to practice.[62]

Like other letter writers, Hicks represented his sense of having "nothing to do" as tedium, rather than implying that it might be a frightening or anxiety-producing threat to his well-being. This claim to boredom was especially tied to collisions of identity, expectation, and experience, situated in his inability to practise medicine and his inability to get to the goldfields – his undesired entrapment in a liminal space of non-productivity in British Columbia, as he framed it.

Other correspondents grumbled about the lack of work or activity too. In February 1864, with his ship *Grappler* undergoing repairs, Verney complained to his father: "You know how extremely irksome to me is inactivity, and I do much regret that I see no prospect of its speed[y] termination."[63] In this context, his miserable letters emphasized the isolation and tedium of his colonial life. Closing another letter a week after he began it, Verney wrote:

> February 21. Today is as wet as a day can be: the mail arrived this morning bringing neither letters nor news, not having corresponded with the steamer at Panama. Hence I have no news to send you except that I am well and that one of my ducks had her left foot bitten by a rat three or four evenings ago.[64]

Less wretchedly but similarly emphasizing an absence of activity, Tommy Norbury wrote his father in 1888, declaring that his new ranch on the upper Columbia Lake was "a very pretty place but [had] absolutely nothing to do."[65] This was not literally true, of course. Instead, such descriptions of boredom and frustration were rooted in the perceived lack of familiar pleasures, pastimes, and work, and the disappointment of initially enthusiastic expectations.

Indeed, correspondents often described their lives in British Columbia as boring because they were lonely or felt isolated. Writing from his farm near New Westminster in 1863, John Brough remarked to his sister, "I sometimes weary a little when I have no one with me," although he then added – reassuring, perhaps – "but it is wonderful how a person becomes accustomed to a hermit's life!"[66] Other letter writers expressed more frustration with and concern over their isolation from people deemed appropriately sociable. For example, colonial secretary Arthur Birch anticipated a "dreary" time over the winter of 1864, during which he would not be completely alone but would lack people whom he considered friendly and suitable acquaintances. He wrote to his brother John: "Everyone has now left us & Evans leaves me by this mail[.] I shall miss him terribly and look forward to a dreary winter – without a soul but the Governor to speak to."[67]

Writing from the Royal Engineers camp near New Westminster, Mary Hawks Moody expressed similar concerns about her family's colonial social world, which she portrayed as distant from metropolitan standards. In one letter to her mother, she worried about her husband, remarking that Richard was "very tired of the monotonous existence we lead here," and as a result had become "so 'low' about himself." The colony, she declared, was "a dully place for gentlemen" in the absence of respectable social engagements and entertainment.[68] Another of Moody's letters described those whom she called "home sick" soldiers in the Royal Engineers camp. These men "come in here," she wrote to her sister, "and tell me how dull it is, & that they have no 'home' no *young ladies* &c &c!"[69] In repeating such complaints, she again pointed to broader concerns about the absence of familiar and appropriate social experiences for settlers. Colonial commentators and administrators considered British Columbia's striking gender imbalance among its white settler population to be morally and politically unacceptable, and dangerous for its future.[70] But for these Royal Engineers men, Moody suggested, concerns about race, gender, sex, and heterosociability could be simultaneously anxiety-producing *and* dull.

There were exceptions to this pattern of complaint, and not all correspondents complained of boredom or loneliness all the time. In 1900, for example, Harold Nation wrote a cheery letter to his mother about visiting Cranbrook: "I am always full up with engagements before I've been in town a day so can't complain of being lonely."[71] However, when read in the larger context of Nation's correspondence, this sense of excitement stands out. His busy social life in Cranbrook was implicitly contrasted with his experiences living and working in nearby logging communities, where he frequently complained about a lack of respectable company.[72] Ultimately, whether with feigned or earnest happiness, or grim or worried complaints, letter writers came to frame the usual local conditions as boring or unsatisfying because they were distant from British norms or expectations of social life.

In addition to describing their lives in British Columbia as drearily uneventful, British settlers also commented on the increasing monotony of their correspondence and responded directly to relatives who criticized the absence of interesting detail in their letters over time. Because their first letters had been so focused on their fascination, the writers' turn toward banality made for a stark contrast; this was perhaps especially so when writers or readers had anticipated ongoing colonial adventure. Correspondents accounted for these epistolary changes by connecting them to the process of becoming familiar with and settled in place. Robert Burnaby's correspondence serves as an example of this. He arrived in Victoria on Christmas Day in 1858, and at first, wrote letters that were full of local detail, which he described with interest and likely anticipated his relatives would find interesting. He soon fell into complaints, however, and in March 1860, he wrote his sister Rose: "What can I tell you: so little now is our life diversified by any variety of incidents."[73] Two months later, he grumbled to his mother: "We have little to vary our dull times."[74] When his family remarked on the new banality of his letters, he responded by explaining the relationship between his new sense of daily tedium, his struggle to write interesting letters, and his process of settling down in British Columbia. In the letter that opened this book, he wrote to his brother Tom:

> Sally complains that my despatches are not so lively nor full of incident as formerly – As Lewin used to say "I'll tell you for why." Because we stagnate in a sort of monotonous round, and after describing what seemed new, and telling you all about our daily life and so forth, although doubtless one might hourly pick up phrases and anecdotes to amuse you hugely, one gets deadened by the common-place and has no heart to record what comes day after day and ever the same.[75]

Burnaby made similar complaints in a letter to his sister Harriet, describing his life in British Columbia and his surroundings as unbearably monotonous:

> I owe you one in answer to your last long letter and must rub and scrub up all the odds and ends of news that I can muster in order to make up a budget

> from this fag end of the Earth. After the first novelty is over ... we subside into a chronic state of rocks, pine trees and natives, and anything but a wooden street with plank sidewalks, and vast seas of mud beyond, a population with Yankee cut and Hebrew phiz, and restless mass of Miners always talking and thinking about diggings and nuggets, rockers and sluices, would now appear to us quite beside the order of things.[76]

In this letter, Burnaby referenced topics that he had once depicted with fascination in remarkable detail. Now, however, he framed the colonial landscape and built environment as monotonous, and the people whom he had initially described with close ethnographic attention largely faded into a normalized background that represented an unthreatening, too-familiar, uninteresting place.

Edmund Verney's correspondence offers another example of the relationship between monotony, despair, and settling down in the colony. When his naval assignment at Esquimalt ended in 1865, he might have expected to feel relief. For several years, his letters had been full of complaints. As he prepared to leave Vancouver Island, he reflected on the ways that he had frequently felt "alone" and "down" in his colonial life:

> Life in a colony has a tendency to drag one down, especially one living so much alone as I have; I am conscious of having fought against it, but I am also conscious of having given in: I trust never again to have to undergo such a test, and if I have not been very victorious, I have learnt much from failure.

As he packed and commenced his farewells, however, he complained that it was "horrid ... having to move," realizing to his surprise that "I am quite settled down for life, I find, although I was not aware of it."[77] Here, he continued to present his Vancouver Island years as frustrating and challenging, especially in his perceived isolation, but he also recognized that a sense of settlement had crept into his understanding of the place, and shaped his interpretation of his colonial life and his departure.

Overall, then, settlers depicted themselves as growing accustomed to new places and disappointing routines over time. Again and again, they used descriptions of boredom, both to explain a range of daily experiences and to render them unremarkable or uninteresting in family letters. These included complaints about work or its absence, the monotony of household tasks, the impossibility of respectable and recognizable social worlds, and the struggle to find new and interesting topics for correspondence. In the process, they translated the distances between expectation and experience, or initial fascination and growing knowledge, into a bored settler everyday. In turn, by producing and circulating common representations of settler lives, these affective descriptions formed a site in which British families developed, reinforced, and refigured their understandings of British Columbia as a familiar – or even too familiar – place.

Coda: On the Unremarkable and the Unremarked

Epistolary emotion was an important form of trans-imperial knowledge, which both reflected and shaped shared family understandings of a colonial place as vulnerable or safe, exciting or familiar. By detailing their own emotions and telling affective stories, British settlers did not offer abstracted representations of settler power but rather made claims about their lived experiences in British Columbia through felt accounts of their everyday place in colonial society.[78] While this is true of epistolary emotion in general, the particular nature of boredom and banality matters here. As literary scholar Patricia Spacks explains, boredom is a feeling with the distinct power to "trivialize the world." More specifically, she writes, boredom is "a historically locatable manifestation of trivialization," which "provides a paradigm of the ordinary and, examined, helps elucidate the gradual construction of ordinariness."[79] This worked in two interconnected ways in settler British Columbia. In their unremarkable descriptions of employment, entertainment, and daily routines, British settlers defined the boundaries and meanings of "ordinary" life in British Columbia, and communicated these understandings to distant family. In some cases, their epistolary claims to dullness held up metropolitan standards as idealized norms for social life, which they found to be impossible in British Columbia. More generally, these affective descriptions produced trans-imperial ideas that claimed individual and collective senses of belonging in British Columbia, and reinforced the possibility of feeling at home there.

At the same time that they constructed particular experiences as unremarkable, Britons' letters left other aspects of settler lives unremarked. For example, as they claimed boredom, these letters remained almost entirely silent on topics related to settler vulnerability or anxiety, fears of Indigenous violence, and indeed (aside from the very first descriptive letters) Indigenous people altogether. In so doing, letter writers defined the parameters of "ordinary" by largely disregarding many of the remarkable social, economic, cultural, political, and environmental changes that characterized early settler British Columbia – and, by extension, the topics that drive the scholarship on settler colonialism. I see their imperial boredom as a powerful example of what anthropologist Ann Laura Stoler has termed "dispositions of disregard," or colonizers' "contrived ignorance" and "studied inattentiveness" to the practices and implications of empire around them.[80] Epistolary claims to boredom or the unremarkable were political acts of narration and performances of affective power that erased the settler colonial process and trivialized its consequences. In turn, Britons' epistolary disregard reframed British Columbia as an unremarkable, normal, everyday settler home.

IN SUM, THE CHANGING CONTOURS of epistolary emotion shaped the production and circulation of British family knowledge about British Columbia. Correspondence was typically marked by a shift in affective tone over the course of a settler's time there. Early letters expressed wonder and fascination in relation to local environments and to Indigenous and Chinese people. These descriptions informed readers about a new place by defining difference as interesting and by emphasizing settler security and confidence. However, correspondents also claimed that they had "nothing to say" and "nothing to do." Some of these passages reflected generic conventions in nineteenth- and early twentieth-century British family letter writing, while increasingly others were directly connected to the specifics of settler lives in British Columbia. These could be the product of individually experienced tedium or a number of other factors: the challenge of filling regular letters, the problem of explaining diverging lives, and the desire to reassure relatives by focusing on safe banality. Whatever their underlying motivations or feelings, these changing affective claims were significant because they constituted an important path by which British families came to represent and understand British Columbia. In these descriptions, settlers turned away from the possibilities of fear, anxiety, or vulnerability. Instead, letters focused the attention of writers and readers on a powerful, trivializing assurance that the settler colonial order was unremarkable. This, in turn, reflected and sustained a wider politics of disregard that increasingly rendered Indigenous people as unremarked absence, settler lives as banal, and colonialism as "absolutely nothing" to write home about.

4

"A Dreadful Little Glutton"

Settler Food Practices and the Epistolary Everyday

On 5 September 1912, Daisy Oxley Phillips wrote to her sister Freda from Athalmer, British Columbia. She had written to her mother a few days earlier, and she would write again to Freda only two days later. In the context of a thriving epistolary relationship, this particular letter offered minutely detailed updates on her week as part of an ongoing narrative of her settlement in southeastern British Columbia. It remarked on a sty on her eyelid, the weather, her relationship with her husband, Jack, their clothing, their progress on house construction, and the family letters that she had recently received. It also discussed her brother-in-law's sudden death, about which she had just heard. And, in a long section in the middle of the letter, Phillips wrote about food. This paragraph read, in part:

> On Monday Mrs. Poett sent us some more vegetables. Jack took some of them over to our neighbours and Mr. Robinson gave him a prairie chicken. Jack began to pluck it at once. He took out all the easy feathers and said, "You can finish that tomorrow!" I began to finish it on Tuesday morning and it took me an hour to get all the small feathers off the wings that are no good as pipe cleaners and therefore not interesting! The next was to behead it so I got out Mrs. Beeton [*Mrs.* (Isabella) *Beeton's Book of Household Management*] and did that fairly successfully. Then, when it came to trussing, I bent it up à la picture in Mrs. B. and tied it round with string in two places. I covered him well with flour and put a lump of lard on his breast, and then put him in the oven and stoked the fire carefully for an hour. By that time he was lovely and brown, and with a cauliflower as vegetable we had the nicest dinner we have had so far in camp. Oh, we had stewed rhubarb last night and we had the bird warmed up in white sauce and mashed turnips. When I tell you I have only one saucepan and a frying pan in use I think I am a *very* clever cook! You will think I am a dreadful little glutton always telling you about food.[1]

Phillips was right: she was always writing about food. Situating food as a central part of her British Columbian life and letters, she regularly reported on her development as a cook, explained where she acquired foodstuffs, described meals, requested recipes and clarification about cooking techniques, and reflected on dishes that she missed from her English "home." Although her correspondence addressed a range of topics, she mentioned this subject in almost every letter she wrote from British Columbia.

Given her specific situation there, it is perhaps not surprising that Phillips wrote so extensively about food. In September 1912, she was a young middle-class English woman starting a marriage and establishing a household in an unfamiliar place. She and her husband, Jack, had been in the Windermere district of British Columbia for only about four and a half months, setting up an orchard on land they had purchased from the Columbia Valley Irrigated Fruit Lands Company. They could not afford household employees, and cooking became her responsibility – a significant part of her daily work, which in turn constituted a major topic for her very regular correspondence. Phillips framed cooking as interesting, challenging, and a useful epistolary subject for two reasons. First, she had little previous experience or personal knowledge of cooking and, to help, she used letters to draw on the expert advice of her mother and sister. Second, she learned to cook first in a tent, then in a barn, and finally in a rudimentary kitchen in a comparatively isolated settler community. As she explained, the skills and knowledge required in this context varied significantly from her metropolitan family's experiences.[2] In these ways, the frequent discussions of food in her letters both enabled and chronicled her work as she navigated a new home, familial role, and life in British Columbia.

While Phillips's circumstances were particular to her, the frequency with which she wrote about food was not. In addition to expressing boredom in British Columbia, settler correspondents increasingly turned toward banal description of their everyday lives. Discussions of food were a prevalent example of this. Between 1858 and 1914, the subject was regularly woven through the correspondence of men and women from dissimilar British backgrounds who undertook varied types of work in British Columbia, wrote to relatives regularly or rarely, and had diverse experiences with food. Sometimes they told worrisome stories about hunger or entertaining tales of cooking creativity, but more often, their letters included unremarkable lists of groceries and reported on recent meals. Overall, food was one of the most common subjects in archived British family letters from early settler British Columbia – a clear thread that ties together the sources at the heart of this book.

The scholarship on immigrant or imperial family letter writing has largely focused on genre and affect, similar to my approach in Chapter 2. Reading correspondence as a whole, these studies rarely extract a common, concrete epistolary topic to investigate. In contrast, this chapter begins from the premise that the specific content and widely shared topics of family correspondence merit investigation since common subjects did not appear in letters by accident. In this spirit, this chapter turns from epistolary emotion to the epistolary everyday, reading this correspondence for the contours and significance of food. Which settlers wrote about food and why? How did these correspondents describe food practices? How did they use discussions of food to explain their lives in British Columbia? How did their letters connect settler food practices and long-distance family relationships? And taken together, what do epistolary discussions of food reveal about family correspondence and the making of settler British Columbia?

Considering these questions, I examine settlers' representations of food in three interrelated stages: acquisition, cooking, and consumption. Through their descriptions of procuring, preparing, and eating food, correspondents illustrated the regional and changing meanings of labour, markets, environment, gender, class, and respectability in British Columbia. They also maintained and adapted trans-imperial family relationships by exchanging cooking advice, resources, and knowledge. Overall, their letters framed food as a central, revealing symbol of British Columbian difference, and a settler everyday defined in connection and communication with metropolitan families. At the same time, settlers' letters did this work while almost entirely disregarding Indigenous people. This is a remarkable silence, given Indigenous people's significance in settlers' lives in this period, and the dominance of Indigenous-settler relations in the scholarship. In the interplay between the everyday and its accompanying silences, the chapter argues, Britons' epistolary discussions of food helped to construct meanings for settler lives not in contrast to the denigrated practices of locally racialized "others" – the binary of colonial identities that is usually discussed in the literature – but in trans-imperial comparison to familiar metropolitan "others," whose supposedly civilized practices were simultaneously idealized, reworked, and rejected as possible in British Columbia. In this way, epistolary descriptions of food contributed to trans-imperial British family knowledge about British Columbia as a potential home by constructing shared understandings of a different but relatable everyday in which settlers belonged, while erasing Indigenous people's presence and competing claims to belonging.

In this analysis, I approach food as a particular kind of subject – concurrently essential and commonplace, symbolic and material – that settlers employed to explain everyday lives and family relationships. At their heart, food practices are bodily sustenance and performances of identity, in addition to products of power relations, cultural discourses, and individual preferences. Food's connection to identity is notably potent for migrants and travellers, since it can be imagined as a consumable connection with home – for Britons in the empire, an opportunity "to ingest England" from afar, in literary scholar John Plotz's framing.[3] These general conceptual points have informed scholarly studies of food and colonialism, which tend to focus on two issues: the consumption of colonial foodstuffs in the metropole, and the role of food in representing, policing, and challenging boundaries between European colonizers and racialized and Indigenous peoples in other imperial sites.[4] Here, I tackle a different matter, namely, the particular interplay between food and letters in shaping mobile and trans-imperial understandings of the settler everyday. Food was a marker of identity, home, and family. This symbolic resonance rendered it a powerful epistolary topic for settlers that could be used to evoke connections between writers and readers, to explain their diverging experiences, and in so doing, to negotiate changing meanings of self and relationship in a new place.

Through this discussion, I make a larger point about the particular power of the epistolary everyday as an important but under-examined form of British imperial knowledge. British settlers explained wider contexts and refracted broader colonial ideas through the routines and variations of their individual experience, with particular attention to their material, sensory, embodied, and affective forms. As mobile texts, their letters did not require pre-existing local knowledge to understand, but rather were intended to explain British Columbian circumstances to an audience unfamiliar with the place. The everyday – including but not limited to food – was key to this. Because it was generally shared but different in its specifics, the everyday served as a common referent point for letters' writers and recipients. By discussing subjects like food, separated relatives could compare their experiences, and in the process, construct shared understandings of a new place. This epistolary everyday centred settlers and excluded Indigenous people. In the process, it simultaneously worked to illustrate the parameters and contexts of settler lives, make them comprehensible in the metropole, and produce trans-imperial family knowledge about British Columbia that suggested it was an exclusive, safe, and normal home for Britons.

"To Keep the Larder Supplied": Food Acquisition as British Columbian Difference

In their family letters, a range of settlers regularly described how they produced, purchased, or otherwise procured food in British Columbia. As an example of the epistolary everyday, their discussions of food acquisition focused on a common task that was shared by letter writers and readers despite the distances between them. Letters from British Columbia depicted a diverse, patchwork system of food acquisition, generally emphasizing foods familiar to the metropole but procurement strategies that were markedly different from settlers' previous experiences or their families' norms. These were the aspects of everyday practice that settlers encountered with surprise, deemed interesting to relatives, or felt required explanation as peculiar to British Columbia. More specifically, letter writers complained about exorbitant prices and the limited availability of foodstuffs for purchase. They described hunting, fishing, and farming as important and affordable alternatives to settler markets, although ones that required local knowledge and new skills in order to be effective. By the turn of the twentieth century, they also used the post to acquire specific foods that they could not obtain locally, either ordering items from department stores or requesting them from relatives. Through these discussions, letters framed food acquisition in British Columbia as a telling point of daily difference from Britain that could reveal to distant relatives the regional, environmental, infrastructural, economic, and social context in which settlers lived.

The British metropole haunted settlers' epistolary descriptions of food acquisition. In the United Kingdom, people procured food in diverse ways shaped by class and location, but by the eighteenth century, almost every household bought some of its food, which could then be supplemented by family or small-scale local production.[5] While some households continued to produce their own foods, over the course of the nineteenth century metropolitan Britons became increasingly dependent on purchasing food that was processed and sold in expanding markets, as industrialization and urbanization wrought significant changes in daily life across the country. The growing large-scale production and long-distance commercial trade in foodstuffs were facilitated by expanding networks of railways and steamships and by improving technologies such as refrigeration and canning. Although individual experiences varied and the named recipients of letters may not have been personally responsible for household shopping, for many of these families, it was an accepted and expected practice to purchase foods.[6] While metropolitan relatives navigated this changing terrain, settlers in British Columbia generally engaged in a mixture of food acquisition strategies. Although the specifics again varied, letter writers typically described them as different from Britain and revealing of local circumstances.

When British Columbian letter writers wrote about purchasing food – the strategy most likely to be shared with metropolitan relatives – they focused on what they bought from other settlers, especially those who ran local stores. In practice, region mattered; urban residents were usually more dependent on purchasing food, while those in rural areas often drew on farming, hunting, fishing, and local trade to supplement their limited access to wider settler markets. Time mattered too. Over the period, settlers across the province purchased more and more of their food, but the possibility and affordability of doing so continued to depend on their proximity to transportation routes and urban markets. Within this general context, the topic appeared most frequently in correspondence as a way to explain what settlers deemed their frustratingly inadequate access to high-quality and affordable foods for purchase. These descriptions highlighted unfamiliar environmental, infrastructural, and economic conditions, and explained the nascent or non-existent state of local settler food production and trade networks. In 1864, for example, Welsh prospector John Davies explained to his wife and children that the Cariboo region had unreliable access to foods from California or Oregon, the main sources of foodstuffs on the settler market in this period: "The distance is so great and very difficult and every pound that comes here has to be packed in on the backs of mules for sixty miles which is the nearest point that can be reached by wagons."[7] Such passages used the limitations of food markets to evoke regional isolation within and beyond British Columbia, and to explain the apparent peculiarities of local lives that resulted from it.

In the mid-nineteenth century, rural and urban settlers also wrote worried or scandalized letters about the high food prices that resulted from these limited markets, which they compared unfavourably with British norms and British Columbia incomes. In early 1859, Mary Hawks Moody wrote her mother from Victoria, expressing her regret at not having packed "a good many little things," including food, when she moved from England with her husband's Royal Engineers detachment. "Groceries of *all kinds* I find we ought to have brought. Everything is so *dear* here," she wrote. She then listed grocery prices, punctuating some with exclamations: "Sago 1/lb! Barley 1/ – Candles 2/6!! *none* for less – Mutton 1/6 – Bread 4^{d} per lb."[8] In 1862, naval officer Edmund Verney likewise complained to his father from his base in Esquimalt: "I find myself a far poorer man than I was in England. I even contemplate having to sell my horse, as the price of food is so high."[9] Although Moody and Verney were unlikely to go unfed in their comparatively privileged positions, each supported by military officer salaries, their astonishment reflected a wider pattern of concern, as correspondents described colonial lives as remarkably expensive compared with metropolitan norms or expectations.

Over time, as trade and transportation networks developed, urban settlers gained more reliable access to groceries at prices that they deemed comparable with those in Britain.[10] As a result, by the late nineteenth and early twentieth centuries, rural settlers were the ones most likely to express concern about food costs, supply, and quality. In 1912, Jack and Daisy Oxley Phillips struggled with the high prices of foodstuffs for purchase in southeastern British Columbia, where a small number of shopkeepers monopolized the isolated settler market and, Daisy remarked, "made their fortunes before the railway" reached the region.[11] Like other settlers, she listed food prices in her letters, once explaining to her sister: "Our meat bill is about 7/- a week. I often wonder how much it ought to be, for two on a small income. I must ask Nellie."[12] Here, she imagined metropolitan prices as the comparative norm – what prices "ought to be" contrasted with her experiences in British Columbia.

As a result of these conditions, correspondents explained that they sometimes had to eat a monotonous diet of whatever was available and affordable. This could be, as Cariboo prospector and former London chemist Harry Guillod put it, "Beans and Bacon! Bacon and Beans!"[13]

Writing from Hope in the 1860s, Anglican minister David Pringle complained at length about the foods he could acquire, which he deemed inedible:

> Poor dear Louie [his wife] – she has been trying to disguise bacon (with 3 inches of fat and ½ an inch of meat) for the last week ... I cannot stomach it – and if it were not for a glass of porter in the day (3/a bottle) or some toddy at night I should be fit for nothing – This is not writing to make ourselves out martyrs – but it is fact.

This was a repulsive contrast with England, Pringle emphasized, shaped by the nascent nature of the local settler community, commerce, and production:

> We hav [*sic*] no butchers shop – our friend Charles has not received his sheep from Langley, and therefore we are reduced to fare ... wh[ich] in the height of summer makes my blood boil to be obliged to set it before my wife and children – let alone ones own repugnance to it ... every one must pay the penalty of inexperience & want of capital to meet the sudden rises in price of the necessaries of life.[14]

Pringle used such descriptions to illustrate settler life in a young colony, underscoring the personal impact of wider economic and social conditions to which he was unaccustomed.

While these letters complained about food in specific communities, individuals on the move described different challenges. Many settlers were peripatetic within British Columbia, moving regularly between job sites, for example. Their letters noted that they carried as many staples as they could, since they might not be able to access desirable, recognizable, or familiar food on the road. In April 1898, English physician Roger Hicks explained to his daughters that his group was travelling through the Stikine region toward the Klondike with "a sleigh loaded with 800 lbs of provisions" through "blinding" snow and "shriek[ing]" winds.[15] He later described arriving in Glenora with "60 lbs of bacon on [his] shoulder which had been rather too near the boilers [of a boat] & was inclined to melt a bit." He and his friend were also transporting "some half dozen sacks of flour, bacon, etc." Such descriptions emphasized the challenging physical labour and environmental conditions of life on the move, and highlighted the lack of reliable options for acquiring foods considered basic necessities. As Hicks noted, this remarkable load was both necessary and not enough. The police required prospectors to pack one thousand pounds of food "in order to prevent any subsequent famine in the land" – a task he claimed was "impossible."[16] Other correspondents on the move also referenced the possibility of food shortages due to poor supply. When Guillod's money and goods ran out along the Cariboo road, for instance, he wrote that he resorted to eating "flour and water cakes."[17] Though it is possible that letters' intended recipients had encountered food shortages as well, these descriptions framed settlers' experiences as remarkable illustrations of difficult and discomforting circumstances in British Columbia.

Some letter writers – both on the move and settled in place – explained to their relatives that it was essential to hunt and fish, as these offered alternative sources of food in areas with limited access to established agricultural industries, imported foods, and settler transportation lines. Tommy Norbury's letters offer one example. In 1888, the young remittance man – supported in British Columbia by remittances, or money sent from home – wrote from his newly established Kootenay ranch to thank his parents for a parcel. He reported: "The fishing things were all just what I wanted, & I made good use of them yest[erda]y, catching about 40 trout in Elk River." He then noted: "The gun is a thing everyone must have as nearly all the food in summer consists of duck and fish."[18] Although he emphasized kinds of game that were like those hunted in Britain and rarely mentioned other local animals, Norbury implicitly contrasted the province and metropole. As letter writers like him underscored, hunting and fishing were specialized, skilled pursuits in British Columbia, necessary for food acquisition rather than a class-defined leisure activity or sport, or comparatively regulated as in the United Kingdom.[19]

More specifically, Norbury explained to his parents that hunting was important because it was an indispensable alternative to expensive local settler markets. Shortly after his arrival, he sent his father a detailed budget that estimated he could live in the Kootenays for about $150 a year, as long as he did not drink alcohol or eat "luxuries such as beef in summer or tinned meats or fruits." He emphasized that this would be possible only because he would rely on "shooting and fishing."[20] Two years later, he responded to his father's suggested budget of £130, concluding that it would be sufficient for his needs. "One *can* live so very cheaply here although everything costs so much," he wrote. "There is no way of spending money except on grub, tobacco and clothing. The only 'pleasure' money one spends is on hunting and fishing materials which come to much the same as grub." Financially supported by his parents from afar, Norbury used these letters to list and justify his planned expenditures. Given that his parents expected him to account for their money and to spend it sensibly in support of his settlement, it is unsurprising that he acknowledged the high food costs – and then explained them away by emphasizing that hunting and fishing were necessary, responsible, and frugal activities in the Kootenays.[21]

At the same time, Norbury also remarked on the limitations of hunting and fishing, using these to explain local environmental conditions, the seasonal rhythms of settler life, and their impact on his budget and body. In April 1890, he explained to his father that spring was "the hardest time of year to keep the larder supplied." He had run out of sugar, while other foods were unavailable or problematic: "game is out of season," "beef won't keep," and the "few good duck around" were "here today & California tomorrow." He "live[d] principally on trout which sounds luxurious but one can get 'sated' on them sooner than anything."[22] Reports about food shortages caused family members to worry. In December 1887, Norbury responded to his relatives' concerns with thin reassurance: "You seem very afraid I don't get enough to eat. I get enough but I won't say that I couldn't do with some more."[23] On another occasion, he explained: "My belt has decreased 3 holes since arriving at Kootenay. At this rate my waist will be reduced to a minimum in about a year. 31 ½ at present."[24] Such passages described the impact of new conditions for settlers in British Columbia, including manual labour and an unreliable local food supply, which not only shaped daily experiences but also became imprinted onto bodies.

In addition to hunting, some settlers established small farms to supplement their diets. Although some metropolitan families did farm, the settlers in this book often had little experience with substantial food gardens or animal husbandry. They used letters to narrate their learning process as they gained farming skills and knowledge in unfamiliar conditions. David and Louie Pringle serve as one example. They were in Hope to establish an Anglican church in the 1860s, and undertook to produce their own food there in order to supplement the local options, which they deemed unsatisfactory, expensive, and unreliable. A significant portion of their correspondence was dedicated to explaining these efforts. In December 1860, shortly after her arrival in British Columbia, Louie Pringle wrote an optimistic letter to her sister-in-law explaining why she considered her new home bearable. She directly connected her belief in its potential livability with her and David's plans for producing food over time:

> You ask if I think "I can live here"? Certainly I do and very well too[,] another year we shall be much more comfortable than this, I am quite looking forward to the spring when we shall lay out our garden get some poultry, and *perhaps* a cow! Also a *pig* ... but we shan't be able to do all that in one year, I daresay the greater part must remain till next, poultry and vegetables are what we stand most in need of.[25]

The tone of David Pringle's letters was more frustrated than optimistic. He complained about the quality and variety of available foods, and considered farming a replacement for irredeemably bad colonial eating. In September 1861, for example, he explained that they had acquired thirty-five chickens and said: "I mean to make them *pay* so far as saving us buying the unwholesome beef wh[ich] has been sold here for long."[26] Though they approached the topic differently, both Pringles framed farming as essential for making Hope a livable and comfortable home because it would be a source of adequate, affordable, familiar, and otherwise unavailable foods.

The Pringles described their farming effort as a learning process. For instance, David described the 1862 purchase of a cow as an "important event with us." Even though she cost more than a cow would "at home," he deemed her critical as a rare source of milk. However, neither he nor Louie knew anything about raising dairy cows and, as he wrote, "we have had to cram up a good deal of knowledge, wh[ich] has yet to be *proved,* regarding milk, habits, and attention to calves – butter making &c."[27] His letters also revealed that farming did not guarantee a secure food source. Although his 1861 garden had been "something to be proud of," it did not work when he used the same techniques the following year: "This year they have had equal attention, but owing to scanty rains and my over laying it with a lot of manure which I got from a stable & kept through the winter without mixture with cooler materials, the soil has been overheated – this added to a pest of caterpillars, has settled our garden," meaning that "our summer crop is nil." In addition, despite their studious efforts, the cow turned out to be a "partial failure": "I was to have her after calving, wh[ich] she delayed till a week ago – She calved & the calf died the third night ... she wont give her milk, and I am now paying a man to remain here ($3 a day!), to see if he can bring her round."[28] These updates provided relatives with an ongoing narrative of food production (or its attempts), explaining farming as a point of local learning and difference that was important and valued but not secure. In the process, the Pringles outlined the risks, rhythms, challenges, and triumphs of a critical part of their new everyday in colonial Hope.

By the early twentieth century, the postal system supported settler food acquisition in addition to explaining the process. For example, Daisy Oxley Phillips used the Eaton's department store catalogue to order foods that she could not otherwise obtain in Athalmer. She explained to her sister in one case: "I don't suppose I shall ever taste fresh fish for years but we have ordered some tins of fresh herrings from Eaton's and they are very good with vinegar."[29] On another occasion, she described a new neighbour who was "horribly unhappy [in British Columbia] and does not like it a bit and begs her husband to go back." The state of local foods had sparked this despair:

> She ... evidently thought she was coming to Paradise! She thought there would be a lot of fruit and eggs and milk. Finding only tinned varieties has been too much for her and she is frightfully homesick. She is coming over here this afternoon and I am going to help her with a grocery list for Eaton's.[30]

Here, the post could be imagined as a treatment for homesickness, enabling Britons to obtain "home" foods and, in so doing, to contest the disappointing and unsettling differences encountered in British Columbia. In December 1912, Phillips also received a parcel from her mother containing mincemeat and Christmas pudding – special foods that directly evoked and connected her to an English home.[31] By using the post in this way, Phillips navigated regional conditions within British Columbia, supplemented local possibilities of food acquisition, and explained their impact on her everyday life for relatives whose strategies of procuring familiar foodstuffs differed significantly.

This patchwork system of food acquisition was a product of the state of transportation infrastructure, commercial networks, regional agriculture, and other industries in British Columbia, as well as settlers' ideas about appropriate sources of food, desirable foodstuffs, and reasonable budgets. Region and period shaped the acquisition of food too. Whatever their specific experiences, though, settler correspondents generally described this as an important and telling part of their everyday lives. It could illustrate their communities' isolation and limited local production, which resulted in high prices and the poor availability of familiar foods. Settlers also explained the necessity of hunting and fishing, the learning curve of farming, and the possibility of receiving food by post. Overall, their letters described food acquisition as a common task that was shared in its necessity but different in form between the United Kingdom and British Columbia. In particular, they represented food acquisition as British Columbian difference, highlighting unfamiliar experiences that contrasted with metropolitan practices. While these descriptions could be interesting in themselves to distant relatives, they also contributed to trans-imperial family understandings of everyday settler lives in the process.

"I Should Like Some of You to See Me Mixing the Bread": Cooking as British Columbian Difference and Family Relationship

While descriptions of food acquisition served as lenses into the environmental and economic conditions of settler lives, epistolary representations of cooking both reiterated these points and sought to explain how British Columbian expectations of gender, class, and work differed from metropolitan norms in the family. Men often used letters to explain that they had to cook in British Columbia; some described it as an abhorrent change in gender roles, while others represented it as respectable settler men's work. More generally, men and women detailed how local social and environmental circumstances pushed them to cultivate new and place-specific cooking skills, and used the post to solicit advice and "home" recipes from female relatives. They also shared their own advice and recipes, some translatable to a metropolitan context and others intended to contrast with British possibilities. Overall, letter writers framed cooking as a further explanation of British Columbian difference, and as a way to rework family relationships through changing configurations of expert knowledge and newly shared skills.

As with epistolary descriptions of food acquisition, British metropolitan expectations of cooking served as the spoken or implied contrast to settler experiences. Although some men prepared food in the United Kingdom in certain contexts (e.g., as professional chefs), the daily work of cooking was closely associated with women, whether family members or employees. For working-class women employed in domestic service, cooking could be both unpaid household work and paid labour. In addition, many of these metropolitan families expected food preparation to occur largely in indoor kitchens equipped with stoves and even running water.[32] Social, demographic, infrastructural, and environmental conditions in British Columbia prompted a different set of practices. Many settler men lived in households without women, especially in the mid-nineteenth century and in rural areas. For them, cooking typically formed part of what historian Adele Perry calls "white male homosocial culture" and work. Some settler households employed cooks or servants, often Chinese men, Indigenous women, or white women. However, unable to find, afford, or retain servants in British Columbia, a number of women from middle-class British backgrounds learned to cook too. This was a task that they had either not done before or not done without the labour and knowledge of female relatives and household employees.[33] In general, the settlers who wrote extensively about cooking were usually those who had not previously cooked, and who found themselves learning to do so in conditions that were markedly different from metropolitan kitchens. For them, the topic was revealing and symbolic of their British Columbian everyday, and especially its reconfigured expectations of gender, class, and work. Their letters drew on distinctions between settler and metropolitan practices in order to explain, and ultimately justify, their new routines, skills, and knowledge in this context.

In their family letters, many British men described developing at least some cooking skills in British Columbia, from baking bread over a campfire to making preserves from abundant wild berries.[34] Many used cooking as a way to explain the parameters of their everyday lives in homosocial communities or households without domestic servants. Writing to his daughter Josie, for example, Roger Hicks explained the camp cooking arrangements on his way to the Klondike in 1898, noting that each of the men in his party "take two days cooking at a time, so that we all have a share."[35] In so doing, settler men often tried to defend their participation in what their metropolitan relatives likely understood as (devalued) women's work. Sometimes, these correspondents explained the arrangements with embarrassment – a feeling they might have experienced or anticipated in their relatives' responses – as they acknowledged the revision of gendered divisions of labour in their British Columbian homes. In 1862,

Welsh prospector Morgan Lewis described his Cariboo household: "I am almost ashamed to tell you of our way of living ... I am one of four living in a plank house without one woman."[36] Because of what he framed as these unpleasant conditions, the four men shared tasks that his readers would have understood as women's work: cleaning, sewing, baking bread, and washing clothing. These common passages recognized the distinct differences between settler men's lives in British Columbia and their families' lives in Britain, and worked to explain their cooking as necessary, shared work in new homosocial living arrangements.

Unlike Lewis, some men cast cooking as a matter of pride and independence, and a new marker of settler masculinity in rural British Columbia. In their family letters, they emphasized how they learned to use local resources and cook creatively under all conditions. In one of his earliest letters from British Columbia, Tommy Norbury described his quick learning and readiness for new challenges. "I got on with the cooking part all right and made some very good dishes," he wrote, adding: "I made some good hashes but had not much to experiment on."[37] On his way to British Columbia in 1862, William Lomas kept a diary that addressed a metropolitan family audience. Here, he expressed enthusiasm about his new cooking skills, claiming to be "quite proud" of the men's ability to feed themselves. "We now make our own yeast bread, puddings etc," he wrote. "It is wonderful how we can do without the assistance of the ladies!! Don't be offended anyone."[38] In addition, men explained the impact of the local environment and infrastructure, asking relatives to visualize aspects of their cooking that differed from metropolitan kitchens. "Imagine cooking fritters and having to hold a handkerchief over the pan to keep the hail out," Harry Guillod directed his readers in one case.[39] In another instance, he described his travelling partner on the way to the Cariboo, explaining that "Mac" had cooked a strange meal in an open-air camp. He admired this work for its flexibility and creativity in difficult circumstances:

> Mac went to the stream with a big hook temporarily fixed to the end of a stick, and succeeded in a few minutes in spearing two small fish: these were forthwith consigned to a wonderful "billy" containing baconfat and the remains of a grouse; this was put on the fire with water and flour stirred in making "mush" which with the addition of a little sugar formed the old chap's decidedly original dinner; I might say, sumptuous, as there was fish, flesh, fowl and pudding.[40]

Such passages highlighted disjunctures between settler and metropolitan culinary worlds, shaped by the environment as well as different expectations of gendered work. These letters did not portray settler men's cooking as a poor translation of women's work, but rather as a performance of resourceful backwoods masculinity in a particular colonial context.

As letters explained, however, not all men were equally competent and keen about cooking. Although he reported that his camp members shared the task, Roger Hicks also told his daughter: "de Mattos may be a learned geologist, but he is no cook! Bread or puddings are quite beyond him & a pot of porridge is as much as he can rise to unless he has twelve hours preparation."[41] He still expected de Mattos to cook, though, and deemed his friend's failures a weakness worthy of critique in a context where men's cooking was both normal and essential. Other men insisted that they never became proficient at cooking, and altogether refused to embrace it as their responsibility. In September 1888, Tommy Norbury left his brother Billy alone at the Kootenay ranch and then worried in a letter: "I don't know how he'll get on, but he knows *how* to do all the cooking, but won't try it when I'm there, as he knows he has only got to do it badly & I shall have to do it."[42] When these men wrote their own letters, they framed cooking as a distasteful chore. Before his wife arrived in Hope, minister David Pringle complained about the "annoyances of fires & cookery & washing up," exclaiming: "What a blessing it w[oul]d be to live on air."[43] Correspondents also described the physiological consequences of occasional failed meals. Guillod mentioned ill-cooked beans that resulted in diarrheal attacks on the Cariboo trail, while Norbury once reported to his mother: "I made up my mind I would eat whatever I cooked, but I was extremely sorry I had made that resolve on my first attempt at baking, good old shoe leather couldn't have been tougher."[44] Individually and collectively, such descriptions highlighted the fact that cooking was new for settler men, and offered distant relatives accounts of their learning process.

Although most of these letters contrasted British Columbia with families' metropolitan norms, a few correspondents emphasized that the results of men's cooking were not so different from what was familiar and acceptable in Britain. Robert Burnaby underscored the quality of food that settler men could produce in colonial Victoria, for example. Describing one Masonic dinner cooked by a "chef" as a "great success," he stressed to his sister Harriet that "it would astonish you who fancy us poor fellows living in the wilds of the far-west to see the splendid turn out." He also described his "Bachelor Hall," where he lived with a man who was a "miracle in the cooking line," even suggesting that his food was perhaps better than what his family ate at home.[45] Burnaby did not mention whether he himself cooked; nonetheless, he sought to reassure his family about other men's cooking. In the process, he emphasized what he framed as the surprising quality of his life "in the wilds," providing his relatives with details by which to measure, compare, and understand his experiences as comfortable and perhaps even respectable, albeit in a colonial way. Overall, these men's descriptions of cooking explained local conditions relative to British experiences, and discussed differences between gendered divisions of labour in their metropolitan and settler households. Focusing on these points, their letters contributed to trans-imperial family knowledge about the environmental, demographic, and social contexts that shaped their daily lives in British Columbia.

Because so many British settlers learned to cook in British Columbia, food preparation also became a new site of shared knowledge between separated relatives, and letter writers used descriptions of cooking to recognize and negotiate changing family relationships in this context. For some men, learning to cook enabled them to assert a new form of expert knowledge that they claimed was shared with – or even superior to that of – their mothers and sisters. Writing from the ship to British Columbia, William Lomas already bragged: "I should like some of you to see me mixing the bread. You would be able to take lessons!"[46] Harry Guillod portrayed the pancake as a particularly colonial aspect of life that he and his brother had perfected on their way to the Cariboo. "George and I have turned into professed cooks, throwing a fritter or 'slap-jack' in firstrate style," he wrote in a travel diary addressed to his mother. "We'll show you how to cook pancakes when we come back."[47] In addition to such competitive exclamations, men situated cooking as a new topic of shared interest, understanding, and skill that connected them with female relatives. When Tommy Norbury's mother asked for information about a dish that he had mentioned, he responded with instructions: "Prairie chickens are generally cut in pieces fried with an onion, or else boiled & making a soup with potatoes & rice."[48] When he discovered a way to bake bread over the fire, Guillod wrote a detailed description of his technique.[49] Kootenay settler Harold Nation sent his recipe for Boston brown bread to his sister, including instructions that assumed a shared basic knowledge. "Mix as usual" and "bake as usual," he wrote vaguely.[50] Recipes could travel in the other direction too. In one case, Norbury requested that his family send a cookbook to facilitate "variation" in his cooking.[51] In these cases, settler men positioned newly shared interests and everyday knowledge as a potential point of connection with the women in their families, despite differences between their cooking experiences. They also used the post to expand their families' partially shared culinary worlds by exchanging recipes and advice.

Although most epistolary representations of settler cooking focused on men's experiences, some women wrote about food preparation in British Columbia too. The correspondence of Daisy Oxley Phillips provides one example. As the opening vignette in this chapter explained, cooking became a new responsibility for Phillips when she and her husband moved to Athalmer in 1912. Like many settler men, she too tracked her learning process in letters to her mother and sister. She understandably expressed less concern about the relationship between gender and cooking, though, and instead focused on how she could become a "clever" cook so far away from her more experienced female relatives and without servants. She used the post to request her family's advice, especially in producing meals that reminded her of "home." In one such case, she asked her sister Freda: "Ask Mother how to make the white sauce to put over cold fish, like we have on Sunday nights at home. Is it just melted butter with a little vinegar or has it the yolk of an egg in it as well?"[52] Struggling with limited supplies on another occasion, she sought her mother's advice on dessert recipes. "What about baked cake pudding? It is not called that in Mrs. Beeton," she wrote, asking: "Do you know the proportion of suet? I don't want puddings with more than one egg at present."[53]

Phillips also sent recipes to her mother and sister. Sometimes she described these as particularly Canadian, reflecting conditions, materials, and practices that differed from her distant family's. For example, in August 1912, she sent her mother a recipe for canning plums "in Canadian fashion," which she had learned from a neighbour: "You make a syrup of white sugar and water, 7 pints of sugar and 11 of water, I used. Prick the plums in one or two places, boil the syrup, put the fruit in for a few minutes, then put the fruit in the bottles and pour on the boiling syrup and seal quickly as possible." She then explained contrasts between the canning supplies used in England and British Columbia.[54] In addition to what she called this "Canadian" recipe, Phillips also mentioned or recommended dishes from specific cookbooks to which her family could refer. For example, she wrote to Freda in October 1912:

> I have not made bread yet, only baking powder bread and this is quite good if eaten fresh – see Mrs. Beeton and tell Dorrie Durrant to try it. Last night we had "dry curry and rice," followed by "baby carrots in sweet sauce" from the Mrs. Peel book [a cookbook by Dorothy (Mrs. C.S.) Peel], and then baked suet with apples inside.

She noted, however, that she "could not get the top" of the baked suet "sticky like ... we used to eat."[55] For separated relatives like the Oxley-Phillips family, shared recipes could evoke the possibility of shared eating experiences – a poignant point of material, sensory, and embodied connection. In addition, British recipes could symbolize a consumable connection to family and home from afar, and British Columbian recipes revealed details of the settler everyday in an accessible and translatable form across distance. However, this was always a partial and fragile connection too. Families may or may not have actually used the recipes. Settler cooks were disappointed when they could not replicate a dish quite how they remembered it. And British Columbian recipes highlighted diverging lives and new expert knowledge in the family as much as they suggested ongoing connections and shared experiences.

Taken together, epistolary representations of cooking contributed to family knowledge about the settler everyday as both different from and connected to metropolitan experiences. In men's letters especially, descriptions of food preparation emerge as one of the clearest points of contrast between everyday life in British Columbia and Britain. Men generally described experiences with cooking in order to justify its necessity and forms within the social and environmental contexts of settler British Columbia. In so doing, they explained new configurations and expectations of gender, class, and domestic labour. In addition, men's and women's letters linked the specific practices of cooking in British Columbia with metropolitan family knowledge and skills. As cooking became a new site of partially shared expertise between relatives, settlers used the post to draw on family advice and exchange resources, and adapt these to British Columbia. As well as being a defining marker of British Columbian difference, in other words, correspondents imagined cooking as a new point of potential, if tenuous, connection between men and women in the family, and between settlers, their metropolitan relatives, and their memories of British homes.

"A Scarcity of Plates": Eating as Settler Identity in Metropolitan Comparison

In addition to being necessary for survival, eating is a powerful symbolic act: the literal incorporation of food with all of its associated connections to identity.[56] So, what meanings did settlers ascribe to consuming British Columbian meals, and thus taking what they represented as local difference into the body? Building from discussions of food acquisition and cooking, letters often framed eating as a daily encounter with the unsuitability or impracticability of familiar dining practices in British Columbia. In this section, I consider three forms of this wider pattern: descriptions of eating in resource-extractive work camps, explanations of attempted but sometimes unsuccessful performances of respectable dining, especially in urban contexts, and yearning discussions of holiday meals far from family. While region and time period again shaped individual experiences, these letters generally described settler eating as oscillating between familiar and strange, civilized and rough. As they shifted between these framings, letter writers articulated meanings for everyday experiences and settler identities in British Columbia. They did so not in contrast to a racialized "other" who was differentiated and distanced in all ways, but in relation to a metropolitan "other" who was known and longed for, even as settlers recognized British or home eating as an impossibility in their circumstances in British Columbia.

British settler men engaged in manual labour wrote extensively about eating. In particular, they explained their lives as defined by a new hunger, which rendered large meals necessary and remarkable symbols of their bodily everyday in British Columbia. Understandably, settlers from sedentary backgrounds especially emphasized this point. For example, Harold Nation moved to the Kootenays after studying civil engineering in London.[57] When he found work in a logging camp, he wrote to his mother that he now had to eat "appalling quantities," declaring: "I feel so hungry after five hours steady work that I could eat a dozen rubber beef steaks."[58] This hunger, he wrote, turned camp meals into an urgent "scramble and gobble."[59] Wilf Rowell similarly worked in a Kootenay logging camp in the early twentieth century, and reported to his mother that he had "been eating like four mules" since he started the job.[60] These letter writers emphasized that food was both bodily sustenance and political in such a context. For many settlers, beans, bacon, and tea constituted a standard meal because they could be relatively easy and inexpensive to purchase. However, as Tommy Norbury complained from his ranch in 1889, these were "poor stuff to work on."[61] As such, the "food question" became "all important" in resource-extractive workplaces, as Nation reported to his mother in 1900.[62] Strikes frequently revolved around the quantity and quality of food. To emphasize this point, Nation explained in another letter that "it is rot not having plenty of grub when you are working very hard. In fact the food is the first thing the men kick about. They insist on good chuck and plenty of it."[63] Here, describing the importance of food highlighted the bodily conditions of these men's life and work in British Columbia, which could differ notably from their previous experiences and their families' practices.

Other letters actually listed dishes in workers' meals to illustrate further the remarkable quantity and urgency of their eating. Nation described one camp lunch to his sister: "Bean soup, Soda biscuits, Boiled dried Cod fish, cream sauce, Roast ribs of beef with roast potatoes, Boiled potatoes, Bread pudding, Vanilla sauce, and two pieces of apricot pie, Tea," adding for emphasis, "How's that for a light lunch? all down in 20 minutes."[64] Daisy Oxley Phillips visited a lumber camp near Athalmer in 1912, where she found a similar situation. She too highlighted the workers' capacity to eat, noting in a letter that one lunch contained "great dishes of meat stewed with potatoes, dishes of tomatoes, plum duff and open jam tarts; and tea." She also depicted a camp dining etiquette that eliminated the regulated progression of courses and what she understood as normal serving techniques. "You have it all on the same plate," she explained, "and just pick it out of the various dishes with your knife and fork."[65]

Whereas Phillips only made passing reference to it, Nation wrote extensively about the etiquette of camp dining, which he represented as a potential slip from civility toward scorned roughness. Disparaging the British Columbian working class of which he was now a part, he described his co-workers in the camp as "low beasts" who "eat like a pen full of hogs."[66] Again and again, he identified lumber camp eating as beastly and asserted a gentlemanly distance from others, even as he described himself engaging in similar practices. In so doing, he accounted for yet resisted the instability of class in British Columbia, as his middle-class upbringing and respectable aspirations were belied by camp life. However, Nation also wrote about the discomforting possibility that he had internalized these eating practices. When he visited the nearby town of Moyie in April 1901, he reported to his mother and sister that he ate with "a couple of gentlemen" from whom he had previously "held aloof" because he felt "so uncouth and dirty." He explained that he enjoyed the meal, but found the experience marked by difference. Dining was "awfully slow," he noted; "just fancy having to wait between the courses to have the plates changed! After ... the camp table it seemed interminable."[67] Later that year, Nation wrote about struggling with another town dinner, which posed a troubling material, bodily, and visual contrast to his new norm of what he called "more or less dirty surroundings." "My, how awkward I felt in manipulating the dainty silver and china," he wrote to his mother, "and my poor hands looked terrible against the tablecloth, being ingrained with pitch in every cracked place."[68] While the etiquette and material trappings of his town meals were more familiar to distant relatives, here Nation emphasized that they differed significantly from his now-normalized camp practice.

Other letter writers focused on different forms of dining, but similarly assessed their meanings in comparison to metropolitan experiences or family norms. For example, some settlers framed meals as reassuring, insistent evidence that middle-class British respectability could be upheld even as it was challenged by the British Columbian context. This was common in descriptions of special occasions such as the 1862 wedding between Arthur Bushby and Agnes Douglas, a major social event for Victoria's colonial elite. Writing to his mother about the wedding's "splendid breakfast," Robert Burnaby reported: "You would be astonished indeed to see how well they do those things in these wild parts, as good and as ornamental as you could see it done in London."[69] In 1859, Mary Hawks Moody described a meal that she had served on one of Judge Matthew Begbie's visits to her New Westminster home. Calling it a "civilized repast," she declared to her mother: "I really must tell you what a very good one we had, in order that you may see that in [*sic*] 'roughing it in the bush' is not such very hard work."[70] When the cook that Norbury hired for an 1897 Christmas dinner left without warning, one of his guests – "an excellent chef in disguise" – made a meal that he claimed "would have passed as good in civilization."[71] These comparisons to "civilized" British meals not only claimed continued respectability but also explicitly and implicitly assured distant family about settler lives in a place that by all accounts challenged metropolitan standards.

Settlers also claimed to maintain recognizable and respectable dining etiquette on an everyday basis. Daisy Oxley Phillips explained to her mother that her household regularly ate "dinner at seven" after "mak[ing] ourselves beautiful. It is so nice to use all our nice things, entrée dishes, etc." In contrast to her descriptions of single-plate eating in the lumber camp, Phillips underscored that she and her husband, Jack, ate with a tablecloth and changed plates between courses at home.[72] Vancouver Island farm labourer Leonard Witherby explicitly reassured his mother in 1899 that he was not "getting rough in any way" by explaining his daily eating habits and their material accompaniments. Although he wore "overalls & flannel shirts all day," he wrote, he always dressed in "other trousers & a decent coat" for dinner.[73] Such passages enabled relatives to assess settler practices, and specifically cast dining etiquette as a daily performance of respectability in British Columbia. Some settlers also used the postal system to acquire material items to assist with this. Shortly after arriving in Victoria in 1883, physician Charles Newcombe requested his wife, Marian, to send a parcel with "plate, cutlery, the best of the china & glass."[74] Norbury's mother posted a set of cutlery to him too, although when it arrived, he deemed it "altogether beyond the likes of the country" – a reminder of British Columbian difference even as he sought metropolitan familiarity.[75]

Other settlers suggested that it was possible to have "pleasant" experiences in British Columbia despite the absence of behaviour and materials that represented respectable metropolitan dining etiquette. In 1860, Louie Pringle described a party that she attended with her husband, David, in Hope. Writing to her sister-in-law Amy, she explained: "Dinner was at 4 P.M. it was a very good one The chief part cooked by Mrs C[harles] who has only a China Boy to assist her, of course we all waited on ourselves & there was a scarcity of plates & absence of table napkins but it was a very pleasant party not with standing."[76] The acceptance or normalization of such different forms of food preparation and consumption could help to make British Columbia seem more livable – even a home, for settlers – but this process could also represent a troubling incorporation of difference or a weakened connection to British family and values. Some responded to this tension by simultaneously claiming difference from and continued adherence to metropolitan norms. For example, Daisy Oxley

Phillips assured her sister Freda that it was possible to "[get] used to things" in British Columbia even as she continued to assert that she missed her mother's "excellent catering," the "nice food" of home, and familiar dining conditions "most awfully."[77]

Phillips was not alone in navigating the normalization of British Columbian eating and a continued idealization of metropolitan conventions by writing letters that simultaneously evoked connections to "home" and contained reminders of difference. Robert Burnaby's first meal in the colony was his 1858 Christmas dinner. Disembarking from the boat, he and his friends celebrated at Victoria's Hotel de France, in what he described as "a very decent comfortable restaurant, which if it were not of planks and generally of fragile character, would do very well in Les'ter Square or Soho." The men ate "good soup, salmon, boiled turkey, steaks, mutton, fried potatoes, apple fritters, rhubarb tart, apples, nuts, etc. lots of bitter beer, and *café noir* to wind up."[78] Here, Burnaby's assertions of metropolitan familiarity were fragile like the building – a shaky claim to connection elsewhere, inflected with the inescapable realization that 1858 Victoria was not actually like London's Leicester Square. Even as Burnaby described familiar holiday foods, in other words, Victoria occupied a narrow middle ground between civility and roughness; it was capable of tentative comparison to London, but in that comparison, there was always also the reminder of its distance.

Whether they complained about the absence of "nice food," delighted in a "civilized repast," or compared colonial and metropolitan restaurants, settlers ultimately recognized that they could not recreate the familial contexts that underpinned their attachment to certain kinds of eating. In practice, many metropolitan families did not often eat together. In working-class households, families typically ate few meals together, with many members eating at, or in transit to and from, work. In middle- and upper-class households, the adults likely dined together more often, but children generally ate different foods at separate times in the nursery. Boys were often sent to boarding schools too, and thus would have experienced a "family meal" only at holidays throughout much of their childhood. In short, the experience of a family meal consumed together was not ubiquitous in British society in the nineteenth and early twentieth centuries.[79] However, settler letter writers frequently idealized the notion of a family meal in the context of its impossibility in British Columbia. For example, Harry Guillod noted to his mother: "I often picture to myself what you are all doing at home; and many a time when I have been cold, hungry, wet and tired, my thoughts have centred on a quiet cup of tea at Paddington."[80] In such cases, in lieu of physical togetherness, settlers claimed that there was power in thinking about each other over meals that could not be shared, and described finding comfort in the idea that these thoughts could link people across distances.

Descriptions of Christmas dinners particularly drew on this imagery of the family meal and its ties of thought. By the nineteenth century, there was a common British romantic ideal of Christmas dinner as an act of family togetherness. Although not all families experienced this idealized formulation (let alone celebrated the holiday at all), it was ingrained in popular images and personal imaginations, and especially potent for those who found themselves far away.[81] Settlers used letters to negotiate their distance from home traditions at Christmas, and to assert their continued place at metropolitan family meals. Many reported relief and comfort that, as Robert Burnaby put it in 1860, "even so far away, the memory of Home customs, and jollifications is kept up all right well." Indeed, Burnaby was particularly insistent that he ate familiar Christmas meals, reporting that an 1861 hotel party was not one of "your wretched half-starved Colony affairs, but a real good dinner with mock turtle soup and delectable entrees, turkey, plum pudding and half and half." To similar ends, he described other Christmas dinners as "just like the Xmas dinner of old home" and "regular English fare, like our own Xmas dinner," concluding in one 1861 letter that "you can see we contrive to keep up the times and seasons, and to be as happy as we can be under our expatriation."[82]

Letter writers also used the holiday meal as a symbol, vehicle, and moment for claiming familial connection across space and time. As she prepared her Christmas dinner in 1912, Daisy Oxley Phillips described to her mother "trying to picture you all, eight hours in advance of us."[83] Naval officer Edmund Verney also incorporated the time difference into his reflections on the holiday meal, writing to his father on Christmas 1864: "With me it is 7 P.M. so now with you it is about 3 A.M., and you are all snoring in your beds, and trying to sleep off the effects of your heavy indigestible Christmas dinners."[84] Burnaby emphasized the reciprocity of family thoughts over Christmas dinner: "All our thoughts travelled home, you may well believe, and I pictured to myself your own happy circle, where I know I was well remembered and talked about."[85] Verney repeatedly made similar claims. In 1862, for example, he wrote to his father: "I shall be with you in thought ... on Christmas day, and I know that the toast of 'the absent ones' will be drunk thoughtfully and affectionately by you, as you and I, and Freddy, and Uncle and Aunt Fremantle drank it together last Christmas day." He then added that "wherever I may dine on that day I shall drink 'absent friends'" as well.[86] These passages asserted settlers' continued place at family meals, while signalling that they expected their relatives to work to maintain these affective connections of thought too.

Overall, British family letters explained eating in British Columbia as familiarity, difference, respectability, and roughness. This is apparent in their descriptions of labourers' unfamiliar eating habits, everyday performances of (or divergences from) respectable dining etiquette, and the emotional resonance of Christmas dinners far from "home." By discussing eating in this way, settlers positioned it as an experience that could represent their broader concerns about place, identity, and belonging. Letters served as mobile texts in which they could narrate and navigate these matters in relation to distant family. In this correspondence, descriptions of eating cast metropolitan counterparts as comparative "others," with settlers explaining their dining experiences as rooted in local conditions but given meaning in relation to British norms and family practices. Overall, settler letters framed eating as a symbolic performance of multiple, fragile, and aspirational iterations of British life, as they defined local differences, claimed familial connections, and negotiated meanings for settler identities by comparing metropolitan and British Columbian experiences with meals.

Coda: On the Politics of Indifference

In this chapter, I have read family correspondence along the grain, observing what letter writers actually discussed as they explained their everyday lives to distant relatives. The genesis of this approach lay in my realization that a remarkable proportion of British family letters from British Columbia engaged with the topic of food. As I traced patterns and variations in correspondents' representations of this common, concrete subject, it became clear that letters overwhelmingly focused on settlers' own experiences with obtaining, preparing, and consuming meals. This close attention to the personal everyday points to another striking issue: parallel descriptions of Indigenous food practices or those of non-Indigenous people of colour were extremely infrequent in this correspondence, whether as the primary subject or as a comparative counterpart to settler experiences. For example, Indigenous people were not identified in any of the letters about camp eating that I have located, despite their employment in the same industries.[87] In addition, many settlers bought game, fish, and other items from Indigenous people, but their archived letters almost never discussed this source of food despite its obvious difference from metropolitan experience and what I imagine as its potential interest to distant relatives on that basis.[88]

In a very rare deviation from this silence, Tommy Norbury sent his sister Nell a brief description of an 1888 New Year's meal that he shared with several Ktunaxa men in the Kootenay region. He remarked that the men "grabbed the beef in their hands and went at it like wild beasts and what they couldn't eat they put in their pouches."[89] Emphasizing hunger, speed, and an animalistic physicality, Norbury here mobilized imagery similar to that used by others to judge settler eating in logging camps. In so doing, he likewise used food to define the boundaries of civility and barbarity but embedded it in different discursive baggage about race, difference, and savagery.[90] Through its description and its relation to wider circulating ideas about race, this letter would likely have shaped or confirmed the Worcestershire Norbury family's understandings of Indigenous people. In this sense, the letter serves as an example of the epistolary production of trans-imperial family knowledge about British Columbia – but in focusing on Indigenous people, it was also a notable anomaly. Far more often, British letters about the everyday remained entirely silent on the subject of Indigenous people or other people of colour.

With this in mind, I see the epistolary everyday as another lens into the politics of disregard in family letters, as introduced in Chapter 3. While the construction of racialized difference has been widely and rightly understood as central to histories of settler colonialism and the British Empire, family letters – with few exceptions – largely took for granted its meanings rather than articulating them. Instead, letters focused again and again on explaining settlers' everyday experiences and connecting them to metropolitan families, while remaining silent on racialized difference or people of colour. This is not to suggest that Indigenous-settler relations or settler constructions of race were unimportant, or that the epistolary everyday merely distracted from this issue of "real" settler colonialism. Rather, it is to argue that what historians Jane

Burbank and Frederick Cooper term the imperial "politics of difference" was entwined with a politics of indifference.[91] In short, settler letters were indifferent to Indigenous people's presence, sovereignty, and claims to belonging. By ignoring these, trans-imperial discussions of settler food practices were able to "repackage" colonial places into something "deliciously familiar" for them and their families, in the words of literary scholar Annette Cozzi.[92] This mattered. As British people came to understand a familiar everyday in a once-unfamiliar place, they made feasible and imaginable long-term individual and collective belonging in British Columbia. Settler colonial projects depended on this construction of settler belonging, in inextricable combination with indifference, marginalization, and erasure of Indigenous people's prevailing belonging. In this way, the epistolary everyday was intimately interwoven with the settler project because it rendered British Columbia understandable to British families as a different but relatable and apparently unopposed home.

In sum, by examining correspondents' representations of one concrete subject, this chapter has examined the significance of the epistolary everyday in the entwined history of family letters and settler colonialism. Discussions of food participated in the larger epistolary production of trans-imperial family knowledge about British Columbia. For separated relatives, the everyday was a telling and powerful subject because it was partially shared, yet its specific forms in British Columbia required explanation. By discussing food, settler letter writers revealed and accounted for demographic, economic, environmental, and social differences between Britain and British Columbia. They explained that local infrastructure, industries, and markets shaped strategies of food acquisition. They described learning to cook, and justified their having to do so in British Columbia. And they portrayed their eating as significantly strange or partially familiar in relation to British practices. At the same time, settlers used the post to draw on relatives' cooking expertise and resources, and to connect with family through newly shared knowledge about food. Taken together, these discussions about food framed British Columbia as a place given meaning through comparison, communication, and connection to Britain, as settlers explained their everyday lives in relation to metropolitan relatives rather than in contrast to racialized "others" – the latter a topic almost entirely silenced in these letters. Through the epistolary everyday and its attendant erasures, these letters contributed to the sustenance of the settler colonial project. Ultimately, they facilitated personal and family knowledge of British Columbia as a different but legible, livable, and uncontested settler home – different from the metropole, but a possible home for British bodies and practices. Next, the final part of this book turns from the everyday and the unremarkable to family crises and silences, examining how ruptures along the faultlines of family also configured its relationships.

Part 3
Family Faultlines

5
"Irreparable Loss"
Family Rupture and Reconfiguration in Letters about Death

ON 16 JULY 1895, Julia Hyde Trutch died at home in Victoria, British Columbia.[1] Shortly afterwards, her sister-in-law Caroline Trutch O'Reilly or brother-in-law Peter O'Reilly sent a telegram from Victoria to notify John Trutch, her brother-in-law in England, who then informed others in the metropolitan branch of the family. By 20 July, the news had reached Emily Trutch Pinder White in Folkestone, on the English south coast. White then wrote a condolence letter to her brother, the widower and retired surveyor and politician Joseph Trutch, in Victoria. First tying her response to a wider network of communication and concern in the extended family, White explained how she had heard the news. Then, drawing on condolence conventions, she offered her "loving tender sympathy" for his "irreparable loss," reflected on memories of Julia, and expressed comfort that her sister-in-law would be buried "near [their] beloved Mother's tomb" in Victoria's Ross Bay Cemetery. Emphasizing spiritual comfort, she assured him that Julia was at "peace in the presence of our Saviour," and prayed that "His grace & strength" would help him to "bear this great sorrow." White also stressed the importance of emotional closeness and continued epistolary connection in a "sad sad time." "So far distant I am with you in spirit," she declared. "You must & will let us all share in striving to comfort you & love & care for you. Let me hear from you very soon I beg you."[2] In this way, White both used and explained the post as a vehicle for the extended Trutch family to mourn together, and to renew their commitments to each other in the wake of Julia's death.

Emily Trutch Pinder White's letter opens a window onto key patterns in a much larger body of family correspondence about death in the United Kingdom or British Columbia. It is only one of about two dozen archived letters written by the Trutch family (along with dozens from the Hyde family or friends) about Julia Hyde Trutch's death. In turn, the Trutch collection is one of more than twenty included in this book's research that include epistolary family responses to a death. This body of correspondence generally reflects the primary issues raised in White's letter: the emergence of extensive family communication after a death, the close adherence to condolence conventions, the evocation of emotional closeness and faith as forms of shared mourning that traversed distance, and the renewed promise of future letter writing. In addition, many letters trace relatives' efforts, sometimes conflict-ridden, to settle estates and make arrangements. This chapter investigates these common themes in order to understand how relatives responded to the rupture of death and reconfigured the surviving trans-imperial family in the wake of what White called "irreparable loss." What conventions shaped letters of notification and condolence as distinct sub-genres of correspondence? Through these conventions, how did letter writers represent, negotiate, and incorporate distance in family mourning? How did Britons use the post to navigate issues related to inheritance? And what do these patterns reveal about death and the epistolary remaking of relationships for trans-imperial families engaged with British Columbia?

The answers to these questions reveal a particular history of the epistolary family in a moment of rupture. Specific letter-writing conventions of notification and condolence enabled separated relatives to understand a death by connecting it to socially recognized codes of grief and comfort. When distance rendered physical interaction with the dead or other bereaved relatives impossible, Britons used the post to carve out shared epistolary spaces for collective family mourning. In addition, cases of tension or conflict about property show that correspondents also used correspondence to assert their interpretations of family membership and obligation while looking to advance their own interests. All of this could have material consequences for individuals and their lives in British Columbia. Thus, this chapter argues, correspondence about death remade trans-imperial families, as relatives enacted the changing emotions, responsibilities, and relationships that they understood to constitute family in a difficult moment.

Why does this matter? First, the importance of transnational forms of mourning in the late nineteenth and early twentieth centuries remains under-examined. Focusing largely on national or local scales, the existing scholarship on British death tends to emphasize discourses and practices of mourning that depended on physical proximity to the deceased and to other surviving relatives.[3] During this period, however, millions of Britons could not draw on proximity as they came to terms with a death, experienced grief and offered support, or conducted the business of inheritance across the empire and beyond. The post was therefore a critical tool for this work of mourning, as separated relatives translated expressions of grief and sympathy into epistolary form, and developed new social codes and strategies for responding to death at a distance. As this chapter shows, Britons' responses to death were not necessarily defined by proximity or confined by geopolitical borders in this period. British ways of death and mourning were not only products of local and national cultures, then, but also flexible, mobile, and border-crossing practices enacted by long-distance families.

This chapter also offers a new lens into the epistolary family. The existing scholarship on letter writing has paid comparatively little attention to the specific nature of letters about death, and has primarily focused on correspondence about everyday relationships and lives. Death, however, generated a body of correspondence that constitutes a notably distinct, diverse, and dense component of the epistolary archive, and that reveals how relatives negotiated relationships in the context of rupture or crisis. This correspondence is distinct in part because Britons tended to adhere strictly to separate sub-generic conventions when writing notifications or condolences about a death. Its diversity owes much to the fact that a wider range of relatives contacted one another after a death than usually wrote letters, and that they expressed more varied forms of relationship (including instances of explicit conflict) than are otherwise typically included in family collections. These letters perhaps cluster in the archive because they were more likely to be preserved, either for their emotional significance or because they served as evidence in settling contested estates. Overall, these letters were connected to the correspondence considered in the rest of this book, but they were also a discrete form. They were drawn into existence by death itself, and by a particular combination of duty, desire, or grief in this moment of familial change. And in that context, correspondents intended these letters to shape the direction of that change, whether by confirming and solidifying relationships, asserting individual material interests, or altering the boundaries of family altogether.

"I Am Obliged to Write": Conventions and Ideas about Death in Letters of Notification

Correspondence about death formed part of the wider family practice of letter writing, and drew on the general epistolary conventions discussed in previous chapters. At the same time, while discussions of other topics such as food were intermingled in letters without established form, correspondence about death not only focused on one subject but also broadly constituted a distinct sub-genre. Notification letters – letters that informed relatives about a death – reveal much about the conventions that made up this particular form of correspondence and their relationship to British ideas of dying. To a significant degree, such letters shared forms, content, and ideas, even as the specific circumstances of a death varied. These conventions enabled correspondents to explain individual loss by connecting it with a wider cultural system of dealing with death. In an emotionally intense moment, when finding the right words could feel both particularly important and particularly difficult, a clearly delineated epistolary etiquette offered letter writers a common social code through which to understand a death and express respect, grief, and support across distance.

In the nineteenth and early twentieth centuries, many Britons broadly shared a common understanding of what constituted a "good death." This was a death that occurred at home, with family nearby, and with time for the dying person and their relatives to prepare and support one another. In this idealized vision, a dying person expressed their resignation to death, affirmed their Christian faith, and bore any physical suffering with patience and fortitude – all actions seen as ensuring their salvation and eternal future. Proximity to the deathbed enabled relatives to nurse the dying person, to witness the death and understand its nature, and to comfort each other in shared grief and sympathy. However, while these ideals were widely shared, they were of course not uniformly experienced and were more complicated in practice. In general, broad discourses informed but did not override individuals' beliefs and emotions in specific circumstances. In addition, these were especially upper- and middle-class models of death, and working-class Britons could have distinct expectations and experiences. By the 1880s, elements of this good death had also begun to shift more generally as mortality rates and Evangelical fervour declined across the country. As a result, at the end of the nineteenth century, Britons were more likely to express concern about suffering or even avoid acknowledging that a death was imminent.[4] Despite these varied and changing discourses, however, the correspondents in this book typically represented death in ways that reflected the ideals of acceptance, patience, Christian faith, and familial support across the period.

For trans-imperial British families, the post was necessary for communicating about a death. Letters of notification were the essential first step, without which condolences, discussions of inheritance, and other related correspondence would not follow. Even as individual deaths and familial contexts differed, letters of notification were remarkably similar. Nearly all were written on mourning paper – black-edged stationery that signalled grief even before the words were read (see Figures 2 and 3). The letters themselves provided basic information about deaths, funerals, and burials. But they did more than simply inform relatives that a death had occurred; they also insistently represented these deaths as "good." Drawing on shared cultural ideas, letter writers invoked whatever forms of comfort were possible in the circumstances. This could include references to deceased persons' resignation, the final relief of their suffering, their bodies' peaceful appearance, or their demonstrated faith at the last. Often, letters also sought to translate final illnesses and deathbeds into epistolary form, providing vivid detail that recipients might have expected to witness if not for distance. The primary point of variance in notifications came near the end of the nineteenth century, when Britons were more likely to send the initial news by telegram rather than letter. Since they were brief, telegrams typically only included information like the time and place of death, and omitted longer descriptions of illness, references to comfort, or expressions of grief and support. In these cases, correspondents usually followed telegrams with longer letters that did include this material.[5] Whether or not a telegram was sent first, notification letters were shaped by common forms and adapted broad cultural ideas to explain individual deaths. Correspondents used these letters to reassure recipients of a good death as much as possible, and to express shared grief and sympathy that could not be demonstrated or conveyed in person.

Several examples help to illustrate these conventions and their limited variations in practice. In January 1894, George Kidner wrote to his daughter, Edith Kidner Langley, after the death of his wife in Market Lavington, Wiltshire, in southwestern England. Fifteen years earlier, Langley had married grocer John Gace Langley in England, and the couple had moved to Canada – first to Ontario, and then to British Columbia. In 1894, the

Langleys were living with two daughters in Mission in the Fraser Valley. Over the course of their separation, the extended Langley-Kidner family had maintained some correspondence. It was in this general context that Kidner wrote to inform Langley that her mother had died. His letter included typical features of the sub-genre, starting with its thick black borders and its first sentence, which together did the basic work of notification. "My dear Edith," it began. "It is in great sorrow of heart I am obliged to write to let you know dear Mama has fell asleep at ¼ to twelve last night." He then offered a narrative of his wife's final illness, which read in part:

> Her illness at first a fortnight ago was a severe attack of spasms. she got the better of that & had pains in her limbs. she doctored herself for that & got well for two or three days & that was a slight attack of Influenza & that was checked but it flew[?] to the lungs & also to her heart & when the doctor Mr Ambrose was called in he shook his head to this is a bad case & so it has turned out to be so.

He continued with a detailed description of the illness's advance and medical treatment, which Langley likely would have witnessed had she been nearby. He then described the death itself, emphasizing points of possible comfort for himself, his deceased wife, and his distant daughter. In particular, he focused on the quiet nature of the death, the idea that her bodily pain had been limited and was now over, his certainty of her future in heaven, and their shared faith at the end:

> She passed away at last very easy & very quiet. she had but very little accute [*sic*] suffering I am glad to say but extreme weekness [*sic*] & now my dear dear Edith she has gone to that rest where there is no pain or sorrow but everlasting praise to glory. she gave me & also the nurse testomony [*sic*] that she was happy while laying on the bed of sickness & death. I was staying with her while the nurse went down to tea. I asked her if she was happy. she was rather dosing & did not take any notice of what I said so I asked her again a little louder & she looked at me ... her eyes flashed up with great pleasure & her countenance was all aglow at the name of *Jesus.* it gave me much joy of heart.

Stressing how peaceful she appeared in death, Kidner then explained: "She looks beautiful ... she looks as if she was giving me one of her sweet smiles as I stooped down & kissed her cold face." After outlining these points of possible consolation, he then exclaimed on the fraught relationship between grief and comfort. "Oh dear Eadith [*sic*]," he wrote, "how I shall miss her but I could not wish her back knowing she is gone to a better home." Finally, he concluded by explaining how the surviving English relatives had responded by gathering and supporting each other. Although they had "not quite made up [their] mind as to where she will be burried [*sic*] & when," he wrote, Edith's brother Tom was "coming tonight to make arrangements," and her sister Althea was already in the family home and writing to her as well.[6] Overall, Kidner's letter offers a conventional example of notification, particularly in its detailed description of the illness and its religious and temporal claims to comfort in a good death.

Thomas Fawcett's correspondence from the deathbed of his wife, Jane, offers another conventional example of notification, and highlights in particular the Christian language and ideas that characterized many families' representations of a good death.[7] Between late 1863 and early 1864, Fawcett wrote several letters to his sisters-in-law in Britain, tracking Jane's ailing condition at home in Victoria. On 10 January 1864, he sent the formal notification of her death. Since he had written previously, he did not provide a detailed narrative of the illness as Kidner had done. Instead, he emphasized comfort in Christian faith – his own, and especially his deceased wife's – which he represented as defining a good death. "All is over!" he began. "Earth exchanged for Heaven – Suffering for Joy – The Cross, for The Crown." He emphasized that Jane had accepted her fate, expressed faith in Christ and salvation, and died peacefully in that assurance. "She had told me several times she was 'going home'!" he wrote, then underscored: "Her *last* words were 'Precious Saviour! Precious Saviour' and immediately *fell asleep in my arms*! By those who have been most with her, it has been said, that hers was 'A *glorious* death.'" In this letter, Fawcett provided his sister-in-law with information that she might have expected to witness had she been present, and even enclosed what he called a "sketch ... of the last hours" so that she could "derive comfort, and consolation from it." He also enclosed a photograph of Christ Church ("Seen from the bed room window during Jane Fawcett's illness"), a hymn, and a sermon. In addition, he passed on his wife's final message to her family in England, and emphasized that they had been in her thoughts despite the impossibility of their physical presence at her death.[8] Taken together, Fawcett's focus on Christian faith, Jane's resignation, and her connection to family highlighted critical, relevant elements that helped to define her death as good, or even "glorious," and rendered his letter another typical example of the form.

While Kidner and Fawcett produced letters of notification that observed widely shared conventions and ideas, other examples reflect the challenges when a specific death did not match idealized hopes or when a bereaved relative did not feel able to adhere to expected forms of communication. For example, detailed descriptions of illness and death were one of the most common features in this correspondence, and a key way to reassure relatives who could not be present at the deathbed. However, some letters suggest that this could be a particular point of difficulty too. For one, individual deaths often did not meet idealized expectations. Sometimes relatives had to come to terms with sudden or violent death that permitted neither final expressions of resignation and acceptance nor declarations that at least the deceased's protracted suffering had ended.[9] In addition, relatives on both ends of the correspondence could indicate that they found little consolation in the details. After his brother's death in Birmingham, for instance, judge Henry Crease requested his sister-in-law to "spare [herself] & [him] the painful details of the poor fellows last hours," arguing that "it can serve no good purpose to dwell."[10] After his wife's death in Victoria, Joseph Trutch claimed that he found it too emotionally difficult to contact his family about it at all, instead leaving other relatives to do the work of notification. After nearly a month, he wrote his brother John: "I ought to have written to you before but ... the fact is that my experience in witnessing the sufferings of my dear wife ... so upset me that I have not been fit for anything since ... I may not have the courage to [write to their sister Emily] – for I fear I am very weak and foolish."[11]

Other deviations from convention resulted from irregular correspondence or family conflict, which could delay or prevent notifications of a death, and either limit or expand the information included in letters.[12] For instance, if relatives had fallen out of touch, they might not be notified about a death in the family for a long time, or indeed at all. In one such case, settler Maurice Bellis wrote only to his mother after he moved to British Columbia, and when she died, he lost touch with his metropolitan family altogether. His friend in the Kootenays, Tommy Norbury, later explained to his own mother that Bellis had returned to England after a decade hoping to "make amends," but then found "at one blow that most of his relations [were] dead."[13] In other families, death provided the impetus to renew lapsed communication with distant relatives, or even to make epistolary contact for the first time. In these cases, letters of notification typically included a range of other news besides information about the death in question. In 1891, for example, J.B. McCleery wrote to inform his brother in Vancouver that his wife, Maggie, had died in Ireland. As did other notifications, he provided a narrative of her illness, medical treatment, and death. This was clearly a rare letter between the two men, though, and McCleery devoted a significant portion to updating his brother on the rest of the family. To this end, he wrote and underlined: "*I will give you the names of all the children and their ages. Lizze Margaret (Lizzie) Born 12 May 1879. Agnes Mary (Nannie) Born 2nd Sept 1881. Samuel Born 9 November 1883. Cathrine Jane (Jinny) Born 19 Oct 1885.*" He also included brief descriptions of the children, such as: "Jinny is a fine big lusty girl Samuel is light made but very lifey Nannie Samuel and Jinny are at school Lizzie is all the housekeeper I have now."[14] In these cases, notifications of death not only moved through an epistolary family network but also called it into existence, however temporarily.

Overall, letters of notification were shaped by a clear set of distinct epistolary conventions. At their heart, these letters were intended to enable separated relatives to understand a death together, despite physical distance. Correspondents sought to replicate (albeit in necessarily limited ways) the knowledge about a death that might have been gained in person if they were nearby. Most letters of notification focused on aspects of a death that could be imagined as comforting or positive, and correspondents typically deviated little from this form. When these norms were adjusted or ignored, correspondents usually ascribed the variation to their personal emotional distress or to the fact that they were resuming correspondence after a long silence. In general, though, these letters shared forms, content, and cultural understandings of death. By connecting individual grief with wider discourses, these conventions of notification thus offered relatives a clear etiquette for discussing death in a difficult moment across continued distances.

"How I Wish I Might Be Near": Condolence Letters and Family Mourning at a Distance

Like the letters of notification to which they responded, condolence letters constituted a distinct form of correspondence, one that was strongly shaped by specific epistolary conventions and ideas about death. They also played a particularly important role for separated relatives. Many of these families had already treated a member's migration as a kind of first death, understanding it as a final separation in the world of the living and anticipating reunion only in heaven. In some cases, they even drew on the conventions of condolence correspondence in order to comfort one another after a relative's departure.[15] This grief would only intensify in the event of actual deaths. While individuals could respond to a death in a range of ways on their own, the post offered separated family members the only possibility for creating and participating in a community of mourning across distances. Relatives used condolence letters to construct a shared epistolary space for mourning. Specifically, they evoked the possibility of emotional and epistolary closeness as a way for the long-distance family to grieve together. They reiterated the importance of connection in a moment of family rupture, recommitted to relationships, and produced a remarkably dense network of communication in the process. And in so doing, condolence letter writers worked to incorporate distance and the post into family mourning.

In nineteenth-century Britain, widely shared ideas about death and mourning emphasized the significance of physical closeness. According to common idealizations of the good death, surviving relatives could better understand a death if they were nearby. This meant they could draw on direct sensory knowledge by witnessing the death, viewing or touching the body, attending the funeral, observing the interment, and visiting the grave. This proximity would also enable them to engage with other relatives nearby, collectively working to come to terms with a death by sharing information and memories, exchanging affections, expressing mutual grief and support, fulfilling expected duties, or simply being present together.[16] Of course, physical closeness did not always result in mutual comfort or collective mourning; nonetheless, distance was frequently considered a problematic challenge in times of death. It made it impossible for distant relatives to be present at a death, for example, which in turn impeded their preparation for and understanding of it. Distance also tested Britons' ability to meet many expectations of familial duty and affect, including nursing the dying, receiving their final wishes, and caring for a grave. In this context, separated relatives turned to the post to create – or, at least, approximate – a shared space for grief and mourning.

Condolence letters were central to this. After receiving a letter of notification or otherwise hearing about a death, close relatives typically wrote long (or even multiple) letters of condolence, while extended family and friends sent shorter notes. Etiquette manuals framed condolence letter writing as "one of the most sacred duties" of those who could not offer sympathy in person, and it was considered very poor etiquette, though not unheard of, to fail to respond to a notification.[17] Condolences were addressed to the bereaved relative deemed closest to the deceased person, or more rarely, closest to the letter writer. Most often, recipients were the spouses, parents, or children of the deceased. Women wrote many of the condolences included in this chapter, although men also wrote when they were especially close to the deceased or to the recipient. This likely reflects a wider gendered practice of condolence letter writing.

In their content and form, condolence letters were similar in many ways to notifications. They too were written on mourning paper. The thickest black borders were usually reserved for letters written by the closest bereaved people immediately after a death, while thinner borders were generally used by acquaintances and more distant relatives, or after some time had passed. Some condolence letters included other topics, especially when they were written by irregular correspondents. However, most focused on the death itself, and primarily expressed grief and shared sympathy with the recipient. Significant deviation from condolence convention was rare since it risked disrespect or conflict in a moment of particular emotional intensity, whereas the use of familiar sentiments and conventional forms could help to express or provide comfort by connecting a specific death to wider social codes of mourning.

Within these broad parameters, condolence letters typically included several features that specifically engaged with distance and its place in family bereavement. In most cases, for instance, the opening sentence recorded how and when the writer heard about the death. These explanations illustrate how a death called on, or even called into being, family networks of communication. In a flurry of letter writing, extended families produced unusually dense collections of correspondence after a death, and moved information among relatives in ways shaped by location, technology, and interpersonal dynamics. As a large and comprehensive collection of one extended family's condolences, the Hyde-Trutch letters offer a clear case study. These reveal that the American Hyde family first received warnings of Julia Hyde Trutch's impending death in early July 1895 from a Seattle cousin, May Preston, who had been visiting her and her husband, Joseph, in Victoria. These were followed by notices of Julia's death in mid-July, mostly sent by Caroline Trutch O'Reilly, Joseph's sister and at that time his closest blood relative in Victoria. Either she or her husband, Peter, was also responsible for wiring John Trutch in England, who then notified other metropolitan members of the Trutch family. These people in turn spread the news to extended family in the Sudan, India, Europe, and elsewhere. Condolences moved in much the same way. Those closest to Joseph and Julia Hyde Trutch wired their immediate sympathy, followed by longer letters of condolence. Other relatives and friends only wrote letters. Some more distant acquaintances sent their sympathies by word of mouth until someone included them in a letter. This process took months; Joseph Trutch received condolence letters well into the autumn of 1895.

One letter highlights the uneven and fraught nature of this family network. Joseph's niece Grace Davey wrote him in mid-July 1895 from Datchet, then in Buckinghamshire, England. In an otherwise conventional condolence, Davey complained that she had heard of her aunt's imminent death only "by chance" when she contacted a relative about another matter. She explained: "I did feel very hurt that they should have known it all this time, Emily ... having heard from you about a fortnight ago, and it is not half the interest to her it is to me."[18] While the opening statements of condolences generally reveal how trans-imperial families moved information, with certain relatives serving as key nodes, Davey's letter underscores the fact that epistolary networks were also patchy, sensitive, and subject to coincidence.

After explaining how they had heard about a death, condolence letter writers then usually articulated an emotional response to the news. Some writers indicated that they had expected it, expressed diverse feelings such as regret or relief, or reflected on their own mortality with concern.[19] Most emphasized sadness and surprise, and suggested that this was an affective response that connected them with the recipient. Thus, Joseph's brother John Trutch wrote from England: "Although we had ... been prepared for this fatal termination of her illness, it nevertheless came as a great shock to us at the last. I grieve and sorrow with you, dear brother."[20] Another relative, Elizabeth Davey, connected Joseph's grief with her own past experiences of loss: "*I* have gone through it and know what a blow the loss of a loving companion makes."[21] These passages not only served as individual declarations of emotion but, stressing that neither relative was alone in their feelings, also suggested a collective affective response – a community of grief and mourning – that traversed distance and connected the family.

Condolence letter writers also explained that they desired to support distant relatives in their shared grief but were unable to provide types of mutual comfort or assistance that would have been possible and expected in person. Frustrated with what she could offer from afar as her aunt died, for example, Caroline Pinder Hare exclaimed in a letter to her uncle Joseph: "How I wish I might be near her as Aunt Carry is, and help you to nurse her, & sit and read to her."[22] Grace Davey similarly struggled with her inability to offer assistance in person, both at her aunt's deathbed and afterwards: "How I do wish I could have been of the slightest use to her or to you, during all that pain."[23] Another niece, Sarah Davey Ashley, accounted for a delay in her condolences: "I have waited a few days to write to you because I feel so helpless to offer you any comfort except my loving sympathy in your great sorrow."[24] Given the impossibility of providing help in person, relatives looked instead to foster forms of support that could traverse distance. In the letter that opened this chapter, for example, Emily Trutch Pinder White declared to her brother: "So far distant I am with you in spirit." Here, she resisted the barriers of physical distance and separation by evoking spiritual togetherness that could connect her with a grieving brother. Grace Davey claimed that she was moved emotionally, if not physically, by the literal mobility of letters, as she suggested that reading correspondence from her deceased aunt's home brought the news and her Victoria relatives "so much closer."[25] In such passages, correspondents cast distance as a challenge to family mourning, but indicated that letters and emotions could offer different kinds of closeness.

Ultimately, as they sought to express shared sympathy and grief, relatives framed condolence letters as both insufficient and indispensable for collective family mourning. Writing from the Sudan, Trutch's niece Fannie Harwood suggested: "There is such meager comfort in writing words. Still they offer me my means of expressing to you in sorrow, sympathy, and condolence."[26] His sister Emily Trutch Pinder White lamented that "words are so poor to convey to you how I feel for you," while his niece Beryl Ashley noted that "I cannot write all I feel about it," and his niece Grace Davey declared, "I wish I could write anything that would make you feel it less."[27] Another niece, Charlotte Ashley Brown, concluded her condolences thus: "I have not said half of what I meant to say in this letter, but I hope you will understand how much I really feel, although I am afraid I have expressed myself badly."[28] Niece Sarah Davey Ashley alluded to similar fears, though she emphasized not so much the inadequacy of words as their bluntness as tools for expressing respectful sympathy in a fraught emotional moment. She closed her letter by saying: "I must not write more[.] I am so afraid that in trying to write all I can that is loving and comforting that I might be only making you feel your trouble all the more."[29] In these statements, the family tried to express feelings and offer comfort in lieu of other forms of sympathy, but simultaneously recognized that they relied on words that might be insufficient or counterproductive as support from afar.

In addition to discussing familial emotion, letter writers focused on identifying points of possible comfort in the circumstances of a death. Relying on information in letters of notification, condolence letters similarly translated broad ideas of an idealized good death into epistolary form and in so doing, confirmed shared family understandings across distances. For example, drawing on conventional language, Grace Davey emphasized that "our great comfort must have been her perfect resignation" as she bore "all that pain ... so bravely." She also remarked that her aunt "must have been so wonderfully patient and resigned with all that terrible pain to bear," and concluded that "it seems as if no one could have borne it more sweetly."[30] Charlotte Ashley Brown explained that she had learned of her aunt's death from a letter from Caroline Trutch O'Reilly. This, she explained, "said that dear Aunt Julia's sufferings were terrible," but from its description, Brown concluded: "it was marvelous to see how she endured it all, with the greatest patience and resignation."[31] Numerous relatives also expressed comfort that Joseph had the O'Reillys nearby – a point that was not possible for many separated families.[32]

Like letters of notification, many condolences also made extensive reference to religious ideas as part of a good death, emphasizing that the dead were in heaven, released from temporal pains and worries, and expressing hope that faith would provide strength and support to the bereaved. For instance, John Trutch wrote to his brother:

> I pray God to strengthen & support you in this great affliction which He has seen fit to cast on you, & strength will come from Him, if you earnestly seek it through prayer; and later on full consolation; with comfort in the

assured belief that she died in entire trust & reliance in the merciful love of our blessed Redeemer.[33]

Similarly emphasizing a Christian good death, Joseph's niece Fannie Harwood suggested that the family "could not wish for a more divine passing away than hers. Her fervent faith, fortitude in suffering and thoughtfulness of others is most beautiful to know." Convinced of her aunt's good death, she even concluded: "She has taught me how to die – just going from this into a more beautiful life."[34] Caroline Pinder Hare wove together temporal and spiritual comfort, recognizing that the death left "a terrible blank" in her uncle's life but also reminding him that "hers is the gain as we are sure she is happy now and free from all her sufferings. Dear Uncle Joe you must not grieve *too* much as you know you have many left who love and care for you."[35] Here, she claimed comfort in Julia's salvation and in the family's continued "love and care" in life, despite their separation.

If a letter of notification did not include sufficient detail for such declarations of comfort, condolence letter writers might request more information, arguing that this would help them to come to terms with the loss and adequately participate in family mourning. More generally, writers typically closed condolence letters by committing to expanded or renewed correspondence with the bereaved – not only asking for information but also calling for more letters in general. To this end, Grave Davey ended her condolence letter by asking her uncle to "write us just a few words when you can, I should so like to hear from you."[36] Emily Trutch Pinder White similarly reminded her brother that the family relied on correspondence to "comfort ... & love & care" for him, and so he needed to write.[37] In this way, relatives emphasized the importance of letters for sharing grief in the immediate context of rupture, and for maintaining relationships and the family's future in its wake.

Finally, although this was a less common feature in condolence correspondence, the post could also be important for helping relatives address their distance from a burial and grave. Gravesites were imbued with special significance, serving both as a site for memory and grief and as a place for maintenance of relationship after death. Relatives were expected to visit and care for family graves, and they might even anticipate being buried together in a shared plot. In short, graves represented familial places on earth for eternity.[38] Recognizing this, Emily Trutch Pinder

White expressed particular comfort that Julia Hyde Trutch would be buried in the family plot in Victoria's Ross Bay Cemetery.[39] For most families, this kind of collectivity was not possible, however, and distant relatives could certainly not expect to carry out relationships and responsibilities at a grave in person. For them, correspondence offered a tool for discussing and reconfiguring their expectations. In many cases, family members, acquaintances, or strangers nearby arranged for burials and took care of graves on behalf of relatives who lived far away. These people often wrote letters explaining how they undertook this work, and even enclosed photographs or drawings in order to help relatives to picture a grave.[40]

In other cases, acquaintances used the post not only to provide information but also to solicit input or money for a grave. Thus, Kootenay resident Charles (Charlie or Charley) Edwards wrote Tommy Norbury, a former settler who had returned to Britain, when their mutual acquaintance Michael Phillipps died (Chapter 6). Providing details of the death, funeral, and burial, he asked Norbury to share the "particulars" with Phillipps's family in England, before writing:

> Will you tell Mrs. G [Augusta Phillipps Grasett, Phillipps's sister] that Alice [Phillipps's daughter] and I have decided not to put up a headstone to his memory yet, as no doubt she and the family would like to help. Alice intended to put one up herself, but I told her to wait until I heard from you – and further – [fellow settler] Tom McVittie and about a dozen others want to subscribe towards it, and with Alice and the children and what you can get from England will make a far nicer memorial than poor Alice's love offering.[41]

In this, Edwards used the post to offer Phillipps's distant relatives the opportunity to contribute to the headstone. At the same time, his description underscored the fact that it would not be a familial place for them. They had not witnessed the burial, they would not erect the stone, they would probably never see it, and the responsibility of maintenance would remain in the hands of people who – although they comprised Phillipps's family of marriage and friends – they had never met. Even as they could contribute to it by post, in other words, this would be a plot for his family of marriage in British Columbia, and the distances that had separated his family of origin in life would continue to separate them in death.

In sum, while people could respond to loss on their own in a range of ways, the post offered a critical medium for separated relatives to evoke a community of grief and participate in collective mourning. Again and again, Britons expressed concerns about how familial separation tested social ideals of mourning, and drew on similar language, content, and ideas in order to incorporate distance into the family grief. Among other strategies, they described shared feelings that connected relatives. They discussed the possibilities and limits of writing as a form of long-distance sympathy in lieu of other forms of mourning. They confirmed collective narratives of a death even though they had not witnessed it. They sent and received photographs of gravesites. And they reasserted their commitments to family and letter writing. Overall, Britons used condolence letters to represent the family as connected by shared emotions, knowledge, and the post itself during a moment of rupture. In these ways, condolences worked to produce a common epistolary space for family and mourning when the idealized practices enabled by physical proximity were impossible.

"Who Should Be Entitled to Benefit from a Man's Estate": Inheritance and Conflict

Epistolary responses to a death were not confined to emotional exchanges of grief or condolence. Correspondents also used the post to discuss issues related to inheritance, explain wills, transfer paperwork and property, and make other arrangements after a death. The outcome of these processes had material impacts on settlers' lives and their families' future engagement with British Columbia. However, relatives did not necessarily agree on what the result should be or how to reach it. In some cases, the distribution of family estates was relatively straightforward, but in many others, archived letters reveal friction and fractures. Indeed, more than any other occasion for writing, relatives were most likely to engage in explicit conflict in the wake of a death. They used letters to declare and defend their interpretations of family and property, reject others' positions, plead for support, and otherwise work to justify and obtain what they claimed was rightfully theirs. As this section argues, the post was an essential tool for these separated relatives who simultaneously sought to advance their own interests, navigate disagreements, and assert their understandings of family itself. Their correspondence underscores, in turn, the significance of property, individual interest, and conflict in reconfiguring epistolary family relationships after a death.

In the United Kingdom, colonial British Columbia, and the Canadian dominion, inheritance was administered either by the terms of a will or by intestacy laws if no legal will existed. In this period, wills usually focused on men's real and personal property. Married women were legally unable to hold and dispose of property before the Married Women's Property Acts (1870, 1881, and 1882 in the United Kingdom, and 1873 and 1887 in British Columbia). Common law and custom had long favoured patriarchal primogeniture, in which a man's real estate passed to his eldest son. This system had begun to break down in Britain in the early nineteenth century, when middle-class families especially began to distribute property at least somewhat more equally. In the 1860s, British Columbia politician Amor de Cosmos tried to abolish primogeniture as a legal principle in the colony, but it was not until 1872 that the province passed the Inheritance Act, which stipulated that estates would be distributed among all children unless a will stated otherwise. In addition to inheritance, surviving relatives also addressed a range of other issues after a death, including the settlement of debts, the distribution of life insurance money, and arrangements for the care of surviving children.[42]

All of these processes could reconfigure the trans-imperial family in addition to the loss of the deceased individual. When Marian Arnold Newcombe died after childbirth in Victoria in 1891, for example, her widower, Charles, sent their three eldest children to live with relatives in England.[43] Such arrangements could also have material consequences that directly or indirectly shaped Britons' settlement or future in British Columbia. For instance, the money that Jack and Daisy Oxley Phillips received from his English father's will in 1913 enabled them to hire a nurse to assist with the domestic labour required if they were to stay and settle in British Columbia's Windermere Valley.[44] Distance added a complicating element to these already challenging processes. Some settlers were able to travel "home" to Britain to complete paperwork or collect an inheritance, either remaining there or returning to British Columbia afterwards.[45] Metropolitan residents did not generally express an interest in travelling to British Columbia for similar purposes if a relative died there. In any case, travel remained difficult or expensive, and even those who might be able to afford it still hoped to avoid it by using the mail instead.[46]

Sometimes relatives made arrangements and exchanged paperwork or property through the post with little apparent difficulty. This may have been because they personally agreed on what should happen, felt that the will reflected their interests, or chose to acquiesce to the deceased's expressed wishes or legal processes.[47] In other cases, however, these arrangements caused or exacerbated family tension that is not otherwise apparent in archived correspondence. In cases of existing conflict, relatives often simply did not write to one another unless specific issues – such as the distribution of inheritance – required it. In other cases, new hostilities arose because of a will or death, perhaps compounded by the emotional intensity of the context, misunderstandings due to distance, or individuals' conflicting material interests. Whatever the reasons for tension, letters were the available tools for relatives to explain and engage in conflict at a distance. This correspondence reveals contested interpretations of family membership, relatives' obligations, and claims to property – all fraught issues that could be torn open by an estate and its settlement. Six examples of epistolary conflict illustrate the diverse ways that these points were manifested, and what they reveal about families.

The first reveals how epistolary explanations of conflict over estates could be shaped by existing family tensions and personal material circumstances. In February 1913, Windermere Valley settler Daisy Oxley Phillips reported to her sister that her father-in-law's affairs had still not been sorted out more than eight months after his death in England. She explained that her husband, Jack, struggled to settle the estate at a distance, and that his stepmother – or "that wretched woman," as Daisy called her – continued to hold "the lion's share of the money." Phillips's representation of her stepmother-in-law reflected two issues. First, it grew from pre-existing family hostilities. For several years, Jack had been estranged from his father, Thomas Edward Phillips. According to historical geographer Cole Harris, the elder Phillips began to drink heavily after his first wife's death, and then he married his housekeeper. The family objected to this second marriage as unrespectable, which likely informed Daisy's criticism of her stepmother-in-law. At the same time, her frustration was also rooted in material concerns. Asking her sister to keep the letter "quite entre you and Mother," Daisy explained that they needed to settle the estate because their finances were in "a tight corner at an awkward time." In early 1913, Jack and Daisy were grappling with the high price of their initial settlement in the Windermere Valley, where land had been more expensive and less fruitful than they had anticipated.[48] Overall, this letter explained a tension that likely would not have been apparent in the archive if not for distance. Its brief complaint revealed old family concerns about a marriage deemed unrespectable, and recent hostilities over the division of an estate between the deceased's child and his second wife. In so doing, it pointed to the potential limits of mutual support in a family when individual interests diverged, highlighted the potential challenges of settling estates at a distance, and underscored the material significance of inheritance for settlers' futures.

The second example illustrates how some correspondents used letters not only to explain conflict but also to actively engage in it in order to redefine family relationships and obligations after a death. Henry Crease was a prominent member of the settler elite. Between his arrival in Victoria in 1858 and his death in 1905, he worked as a lawyer, judge, politician, and attorney general. When his brother Edward died in Birmingham, England, he wrote to his widowed sister-in-law Rebecca. In some respects, this was a conventional condolence letter. Drawing on the language of religious solace, for example, he said that "it is a comfort to think that he is now at rest, having left this earth in the sure hope of a blessed Resurrection." He also explained that he had sent money to her in order to help with the funeral costs in his absence. However, he then deviated from these typical expressions of financial and affective support: "Before closing a correspondence, which only arose under the recent distressing circumstances, I think it right to tell you, that I am not in a position to extend to you any further assistance." He explained that his past support for his "poor brother" had been difficult because he also "assist[ed] so many others in the family," including his daughter and grandchildren, which meant that his "income [was] strained to the utmost." He concluded: "I am bound not to disguise from you the fact that you must not look to *me* for anything more."[49]

Although only a brief flash in the archive, this letter offers a lens into deeper tensions in the Crease family, which took a specific form after Edward's death, and which were otherwise not clearly apparent in their correspondence. Here, Crease rejected the idea that the money he sent for his brother's funeral signalled a commitment to his sister-in-law. Indeed, he refused any ongoing connection with her; by "closing a correspondence" that existed only because of the death, he essentially ended their relationship. His position was probably shaped by frustration with his siblings' prior requests for loans, and their ongoing conflict over the division of their mother's property.[50] As he suggested, he might have also felt unable to financially support an extended family, and certainly he acted to protect the material interests of his more immediate relatives and himself. By delineating these boundaries of support, he expressed a particular understanding of family. Specifically, he indicated strong responsibilities to assist relatives whom he considered closer, while he felt that Rebecca had a weak claim that had ended with Edward's death. For Henry Crease, in the context of existing familial tension, blood and proximity prevailed in defining relationship and obligation.

A third example elaborates on marital scandal and, in the absence of a will, its impact on the future of a widowed second wife who was rejected as a full family member by her deceased husband's blood relatives. William Henry Newcombe died in England in 1899, survived by a teenaged son from his first marriage and by his second wife and their seven-month-old infant. His brother Charles Newcombe, the Victoria physician and collector, received a number of letters after his death. These testify to two connected points. First, the Newcombes had largely fallen out of touch with William Henry before his death and did not know his wife (whom the letters never named). Second, they did not consider the widow an equal member of the family to whom they had affective or material responsibilities. Writing from Lincolnshire, England, Frank Newcombe explained that he had met his brother's widow for the first time at the funeral, where he also discovered that William Henry had left "no will – no insurance – and almost no money." Although he noted that he felt "sorry" for her because of this, Frank indicated no inclination or sense of obligation to provide support. "What they will do I cant think," he wrote. "We suggested lodgers."[51] Another letter reveals some reason for this. After William Henry's death, the family discovered that his second wife was his former servant. As with the Phillips family, this was something that the Newcombes saw as unrespectable. William Lister Newcombe condemned his son's "very shocking" and "grievous indiscretion in marrying his domestic," as well as his failure to provide for her by "neglecting to make a will, & his cruel folly in failing even to insure his life." However, he too concluded that he had no responsibility to assist her or compensate for his son's choices. "In my 83 year & in my precarious state of health," he wrote, "it is a cruel scandal that my few latter days should be that embittered by my eldest son's wicked folly!"[52]

In contrast, the Newcombe correspondents indicated that they felt a responsibility to look out for their teenaged nephew Harry, though they did not know him either. Charles Newcombe's sister suggested that "someone" in the family should visit the widow and "judge what manner of person she is." The purpose of such a visit would not be to determine whether they should support her, but rather to determine whether her stepson should "even for a time be left with her." Either way, this letter argued that the family should "keep an eye on Harry and be ready to help & also to look after him a bit."[53] In other words, these letters suggest that the Newcombes assumed that they did not owe their brother's widow and infant material or emotional support, but that they were at least somewhat concerned about their nephew from the first marriage. From their letters, it appears that they drew these boundaries around obligation because they viewed the second marriage as unrespectable, the widow primarily as a former servant and not worthy of family membership, and the late William Henry as an irresponsible husband for whose actions they had no responsibility. Overall, the Newcombe letters record tensions that emerged after a death, against a backdrop of a prior estrangement, and reveal shared ideas about the limits of family membership and obligation in these circumstances.

The fourth example reveals another family fracture related to a second marriage, exacerbated by the allocation of property after a death. John Morton had been one of the earliest settlers in what is currently Vancouver. He died in April 1912, survived by his second wife (Ruth Mount Morton), his adult children from his first marriage (Joseph Morton and Elizabeth [Lizzie] Morton Thornton), and grandchildren (Lizzie's children), all in British Columbia. In three letters written to his cousin Beaumont in Huddersfield, England, Joseph Morton explained his father's will and its implications for the family. From his perspective, because most of the estate had been left to Ruth, the will represented a shocking dereliction of his father's parental obligations, or even an inexplicable lack of care for his children. "When all is said and done," he asked in one letter, "who should be entitled to benefit from a man's estate more than his own children?" Joseph likely would not have articulated this expectation had the estate been left to him and his sister. But since it was not, he elaborated:

> No doubt it will astonish you that up to the day before Father died he had almost forgotten me in his Will [... and] he has left Lizzie in a very bad way

> as she is not to receive any money under his last Will until after the death of her Step-mother which of course I think you will agree with me is a gross shame. The Will came as a great surprise to me as I thought my Father cared better for us than to leave us in such a position.

Here, Morton equated fatherly "care" with inheritance. In contrast to wills that worked to "encircle" or draw together families after a death, Joseph Morton saw his father's as inexplicably driving a wedge through their family with its lack of care.[54]

Morton's letters also reveal that his father's will shattered his relationship with his stepmother. Initially, he explained, he strategically "kept up acquaintanceship with [his] Step-mother so as to get to know the facts as well as [he] could why Father did as he did." However, these efforts failed and from May 1913 to January 1914, he did "not ha[ve] any-thing to do with her." Although he claimed that he did not blame her for his "Father's doings," he cut off contact because of the will: "Knowing very well that I am not to blame[,] also I feel absolutely certain that Lizzie has not deserved such treatment[,] I am keeping away from her altogether." In September 1914, Morton reported that his stepmother had begun to avoid contact with him too:

> Although I have called to see her and tried to forget the past on account of her age etc. she has never returned the compliment and it was only just a little over a week ago that a party told us she had been over to see them but she never came around our way as I am aware of and the people in question only lived about five minutes walk from our house.[55]

Morton's letters not only described and accounted for the family fallout from his father's death but also advanced his particular interpretation of the will, his father's actions, and his stepmother's growing distance from him. Ruth Mount Morton presumably had other interpretations. By emphasizing his own story in these letters, though, Morton used the post to protest his circumstances, assert the righteousness of his expectations of parental duty, express anger at its denial, and ensure that his distant cousin understood his perspective.

The will continued to drive family conflict long after the archived letters ended, and was even contested in court in the 1930s.[56] Also in the 1930s, archivist James Skitt Matthews published a number of interviews with the Morton family in his history *Early Vancouver.* Here, Joseph added one point that had not emerged in his earlier letters. He argued that John Morton's fortune had initially come from the work of his first wife, Jane Ann Bailey Morton, who died after Joseph's birth in 1881. In this framing, Joseph insinuated that he was entitled to the estate not only because he was his father's child but also because it owed so much to his mother. In a postscript, Matthews noted that Joseph had died in the Asylum for the Insane in New Westminster in March 1933, shortly after he made this statement, and explained: "Joseph Morton has been well known to me for many years, and he has always labored until [*sic*] intense emotion when discussing the manner in which his father's estate was bequeathed, afterwards administered, and its present inaccessibility to him ... It was an obsession."[57] Overall, then, John Morton's death and will caused deep fractures in the family, with difficult consequences for his son and other relatives. Joseph used letters and later interviews to explain, defend, and protest his interpretation of the will, family roles, and parental duty.

In the previous cases, correspondents either described or concluded crises that arose after a death. In contrast, Ada Aspinall used the post in an active effort to alleviate what she perceived as the hostility of her letters' recipients (mostly her Vancouver cousin Michael Wilkinson) regarding the estate of their uncle, Sam Brighouse. Along with John Morton, Brighouse had been an early settler in the Vancouver area. In mid-1913, he died in England during a visit with his extended family. It then emerged that he had changed his will shortly before his death, leaving part of the estate to the metropolitan relatives. This conflicted with Michael Wilkinson's expectation that he would inherit the estate; indeed, he had initially moved from England to Vancouver on Brighouse's encouragement, with the understanding that he would become his uncle's primary heir. In the 1920s, he would contest the will in a case that ended with a Supreme Court of Canada ruling.[58] Before the conflict went to court, though, Aspinall tried to mitigate it through the post. Writing from Huddersfield and London, she sought to avoid blame, assert her interpretation of the situation, plead for forgiveness and understanding, and reassure her cousin of her commitment to his interests. In short, she tried to keep their relationship alive at least partly on her terms. In August 1913, for example, she wrote: "One thing, I wish to impress on you & that is *I have had nothing to do with the will making* it was compiled in London when I was in Yorkshire and I was doubly satisfied with uncle Sam's previous generosity & I wanted nothing more." As the months passed, she also railed against the lawyers hired to settle the estate. According to her, "Uncle Sam was dead against" lawyers, and she begged her cousin to "put [things] right" without "all money going in expenses." "I think it is shocking & quite against Uncle Sam's wishes, money going into their pockets," she wrote. In what she called a time of "great trouble" for the family, she insisted that she only wanted the relatives to remain on good terms – something that seemed increasingly unlikely as lawyers intervened.[59]

Most of Aspinall's letters went unanswered, which serves as a reminder that epistolary conflict could be carried out with both words and silence. At least, she interpreted her cousin's lack of response as anger, and begged for replies to alleviate her concerns about their relationship. "*No letter from you,* which has harmed me no end," she wrote in September 1913. "I hope you & the family are not thinking unkindly of me." Then she indicated that the English branch of the family was also embroiled in conflict, admitting that "the family here regard me as a *schemer* when I have had nothing to do with the matter." The next month, she wrote anxiously into the silence again, reiterating her innocence and commitment to Wilkinson's claims. "Why do you regard me like this? I am here & willing to do all I can for you in every way. I want *nothing*," she declared. Attempting to mend the relationship, she reiterated, "I did not know what the will was," and lamented that "if you only knew how *anxious* I am for your welfare in every way."[60] In the Brighouse example, hostility grew from the will itself. While there were undoubtedly other perspectives, Aspinall's letters track her efforts to make her own case to the Vancouver relatives, defend herself, and alleviate tension. In the process, her letters both reveal and participated in conflict, and indicate her strategies to maintain or mend family relationships in the context of significant rupture.

A final example of epistolary family conflict reveals a different relationship between inheritance and the post. Radcliffe Quine was a Manx ship's carpenter who moved to the United States in 1844, then to Vancouver Island in 1858. For decades, he maintained very limited contact with his brothers on the Isle of Man; he first wrote in 1861 from Victoria, then not again until 1878 from Seattle, after which he wrote more regularly.[61] These later letters both tracked and constituted a dispute that resulted directly from his failure to write while in British Columbia and Vancouver Island. The issue first surfaced when he received a letter from his brother John in mid-1878, in reply to one he had sent earlier in the year. The letter revealed that his brothers had had him declared legally dead, using his long silence in the colonies as evidence. In light of this, they claimed that the current correspondent was an imposter, not really Radcliffe. This unusual case highlights the importance of letters for continued long-distance relationships, and the potential consequences of not writing to family. After learning that he had been declared dead, Quine (or whoever he was) wrote again and again, attempting to prove his identity and attacking his brothers' actions. He provided details about his birth, migration, and life in British Columbia. He rejected their legal and moral right to "Coun[t him] as a ded man" without "the Least shadow of Proof" besides not having "Herd of [him] in 20 years." In addition, he claimed that he had in fact written to other relatives in that time. In the context of the accusations, his otherwise conventional signature – "I am your Brother Radcliffe Quine" – took on special resonance.[62]

For years, the Quines on the Isle of Man refused to believe or admit that the writer was Radcliffe, while he continued to insist that he was. While indicating the family's affective estrangement, the archived letters also suggest that this issue was rooted in the relatives' conflicting material interests. Specifically, Quine was persistent because he sought the inheritance that he believed had been left to him in his father's will years earlier. It is possible that his brothers' interests included maintaining their own shares of the family property, though this is not explicit in the archived letters. In any case, Quine acknowledged his almost total silence before 1878, but he claimed that he had sought the inheritance once previously. According to him, he had written to his sister (whose married name he had forgotten) in 1860 to request that she "get [his] legusay sent to [him] in Victoria." This had not been carried out, and he reported that he had instead received the response that "I shoudind get a farthing unless I came Home."[63] Since he had neither returned "Home" nor continued to write, there had been material consequences – the denial of his continued existence which meant in turn the denial of his claim. In the late 1870s and still living at a distance, he had no means other than the post to press his case. And so he wrote.

In letters to his brothers, Quine drew on a range of strategies in order to access the inheritance. In part, he tried to conduct the business of settling an estate. He requested a copy of the will, wrote to the High Bailiff in Douglas, Isle of Man, and even granted his brother a Power of Attorney in the vain hope that John would use it to send the money to his bank accounts in British Columbia. He also alternated between pleading with his brothers and censuring them. In one case, he explained that he had lost "6000" in eight years of "gould mining Claims" in British Columbia, and therefore desperately needed the money. He appealed to past relationships and continued family obligations, arguing that "when I was a boy I allwas attended too my Parents and likewas too yourself I acted Honourable and Faithfull too you." In turn, he implied, his brothers owed him honourable and faithful behaviour, both in believing him and in fulfilling what he thought was their father's intention. In other letters, though, he lashed out, arguing that John had "swindle[d him] out of [his] Legitimate writse," warning him to "be Carefull How [he] act[ed]," and declaring it "the moast Disgarsefull Pergeured swindling case that evere was Recourded in [his] Native Land."[64] Taken together, Quine's letters used various legal and emotional methods to try to compel action.

The resolution of Quine's claim is unclear, but the archived letters do reveal the contours of an epistolary conflict that lasted over seven years, and the consequences of an even longer absence of letters. In particular, they point to the siblings' different understandings of familial obligations, whether these involved writing regularly or acting "honourably," and underscore the challenges of trust and relationship at a distance, especially after a long and unexcused silence. Also underpinning the conflict were the brothers' competing individual interests in the family property. Overall, the letters reveal the potential material and affective consequences of not writing and not returning "home" – actions that severely undermined Quine's claim to family membership and inheritance. While I cannot say for certain whether the letter writer was indeed Radcliffe Quine or whether the brothers really believed him to be an imposter, the family's letters clearly indicate the essential yet inadequate nature of the post for separated relatives, whether for maintaining relationships, accessing an inheritance, or even proving one's identity. The post was the only tool Quine had for making a claim on the estate, but because he had not used it regularly in the past, his brothers had redefined the borders of family without him.

In sum, separated relatives used the post to explain, negotiate, and conduct the redistribution of property after a death. These arrangements shaped individual and family lives, for example, by enabling certain kinds of settlement in British Columbia or urging return migration to Britain.

To reach this outcome, however, many families engaged in temporary or protracted conflict through the post. In the case studies in this section, separated relatives used letters to assert their understandings of family membership and obligation, to advance or protect their interests, and to redefine relationships in rupture. In so doing, their correspondence reveals a history of the epistolary family that was fundamentally shaped by material concerns, individual interests, and conflict.

Coda: On Family Plots and the Politics of Imperial Grief

Lydeard St. Lawrence, Somerset

In 2009, I travelled from my home in London – a train and a bus, and then a long walk on a thin country road – to find a gravestone. In the churchyard, oak branches barely broke the early spring sun overhead, and only the bleating of sheep interrupted its deep quiet. The stone itself lay low in the grass, with letters that read: "Here rests the body of Sir Joseph William Trutch, a native of this county and 1st Lieut Governor of British Columbia, who died March 2nd 1904, aged 78 years." Here, Joseph Trutch is buried far from his wife Julia, in one final trans-imperial separation between Lydeard St. Lawrence and Victoria. But as I stood there, his grave felt far from British Columbia for other reasons too. In the United Kingdom, Trutch is but a colonial footnote – most associated with a settler colony that has been almost entirely forgotten in Britain's history of empire, and a settler dominion that is part of an imperial past imagined as largely past. At most, he was an official, the queen's representative in the most distant province of a former dominion. In Somerset, his last mark on the land is innocuous and unremarkable. A clichéd evocation of eternal peace, this plot is one of easy rest.

Unceded Musqueam, Squamish, and Tsleil-Waututh territories, Vancouver, British Columbia

In my present home in British Columbia, the land is heavy with a different emplotment of the past. Here, Joseph Trutch is primarily remembered in his role as colonial chief commissioner of lands and works in the 1860s, in which he led efforts to dispossess Indigenous peoples. Still etched into land-lines and policies, Trutch's colonial vision – rooted in the far end of nineteenth-century settler racism – laid the groundwork for the insistent denial of Aboriginal title and rights that continues to mark the province's relationship with Indigenous peoples today.[65] In what is currently known as Vancouver, Trutch Street runs through the heart of an affluent neighbourhood, Kitsilano, named in turn for the Sḵwx̱wú7mesh leader X̱ats'alanexw. Where Trutch and X̱ats'alanexw collide on unceded Indigenous territory, the politics of public remembrance are anything but innocuous or unremarkable. In the summer of 2012, shortly after I left England and returned to live in Vancouver, someone marked every Trutch Street sign with stickers that read: "Joseph Trutch was a racist bigot."[66] The city was swift to remove the stickers but traces remain, enduring reminders that both colonialism and resistance refuse erasure. Here, Trutch has come to symbolize the settler colonial project itself, and nobody can rest in peace.

To consider the death of Julia Hyde Trutch in 1895 – as this chapter has done in part – is to tell yet another story of the Trutches, one that recognizes the importance of family. Joseph Trutch's story is far from one of an individual who singlehandedly recrafted settler colonial land policy in the 1860s. In the mid-nineteenth century, the local settler elite included other members of his influential extended family: his wife Julia Hyde Trutch, his brother and colonial surveyor and engineer John Trutch, his sister-in-law Zoe Musgrave Trutch, his nephew and provincial surveyor William George Pinder, his sister Caroline Trutch O'Reilly, his brother-in-law and government official (including gold commissioner and Indian reserve commissioner) Peter O'Reilly, and Zoe's brother and colonial governor Anthony Musgrave. Beyond the borders of British Columbia, the family had a longer and wider history of imperial life and work too. This included military positions in South Asia and the Sudan, and roots in the Caribbean, where the family – former slave owners – had received compensation for their loss of property after the British emancipation of enslaved people in 1833.[67]

In focusing on Julia Hyde Trutch's death, and on British deaths more broadly, my intention in this chapter has not been to evoke sympathy or draw attention away from this imperial work and its impact on British Columbia. Instead, I have sought to consider how these Britons' powerful places in the settler project were interwoven with personal, affective, and trans-imperial iterations of family. For families like the Trutches, who have come to represent the violence of early settler British Columbia, what did their own death and mourning mean? Joseph Trutch's work in British Columbia was certainly rooted in settler colonial discourses on race, property, civilization, and sovereignty, but the family left this unremarked, instead looking toward other relationships, emotions, and concerns that required articulation. In their grief, we see the condensation of a dense network of family communication, with letters that throw into sharp relief the trans-imperial contours of what, from other sources, might otherwise seem like a local event for British Columbian settlers.[68] This correspondence both bemoaned and negotiated the distances that constituted family in an intense moment. And, in Trutch's case, it ultimately induced him to leave the British Columbia he had helped to build, in order to retire in Somerset closer to his metropolitan family.[69]

To examine epistolary discussions of death in this way is to tell a certain story about grief, family, and colonialism, which centres the bereavement of those who most benefited from the emergent settler structures in British Columbia. This focus replicates a prevailing epistolary silence about Indigenous people's deaths. On the one hand, we should not necessarily expect that Britons would have discussed Indigenous people in letters about their own relatives' deaths; at the very least, this would have usually been a jarring deviation from the conventional parameters and purposes of condolence letter writing. On the other hand, this silence also reflects wider patterns of settler disregard. As previous chapters have suggested, letters were shaped by settlers' powerful ability to normalize or look away from the human consequences of their lives and work in British Columbia. In this case, it is remarkable that, even as they were surrounded by devastating death rates and extensive mourning in Indigenous communities, these settlers again and again ignored the topic in their general correspondence. For many Britons in this period, Indigenous people's deaths were symptoms of a "dying race" destined to disappear, supposedly making way for a white society in its wake and thereby appearing to confirm the eliminationist goals at the centre of the settler colonial project. But in their family letters, these were also deaths that went without saying – in all of their pain, silenced as being expected and unremarkable.

In sum, focusing on what letter writers did say about death, this chapter has explored its contours and consequences for trans-imperial British families. A relative's death might have been felt or experienced as "irreparable loss," as Emily Trutch Pinder White described her sister-in-law's death in 1895.[70] But while it marked a rupture, it was not an ending for surviving relatives per se. The aftermath of deaths had material impacts, whether encouraging relatives to move or funding their future lives and work. Beyond this, letters about death sought to make sense of the separations that constituted families in a moment of change. In order to understand and respond to a distant death, correspondents drew on widely shared social conventions and ideas, and connected these to individual circumstances. The correspondence examined here has illustrated the power and flexibility of British ideas of death and mourning. In lieu of physical proximity, relatives produced epistolary spaces for shared family grief and sympathy, and negotiated or engaged in conflicts across distances. This, in turn, suggests the role of individual material concerns in defining the parameters of family obligation, emotion, and relationship. Overall, Britons used letters in order to reconfigure the family in a difficult moment and navigate the personal separations that enabled their continued engagement with British Columbia. In the process, these letters revealed both the tensions and the tenderness that characterized trans-imperial families. As explained next, so too did epistolary silence.

6

"Say Nothing"

Epistolary Gossip, Silence, and the Strategic Limits of Intimacy

AT FIRST, I HARDLY noticed him. Phillipps, or more often just *P.*, seemed barely a banal trace in the hundreds of family letters written by Kootenay settler Frederick Paget (Tommy) Norbury. But even in the quotidian threads of Norbury's correspondence, *P.* was there – a fleeting but insistent presence woven through his life again and again.

> Phillipps is off back again to Wild Horse tomorrow for about a fortnight.
> When P. comes back we are going to have a good turn hunting deer and bears.
> P's time of getting up is 5 oc. am.
> P. & I have been putting up a new stable.
> P. & I were away up a mountain prospecting for quartz.[1]

Frustrated by these fragmented edges of a life, uncertain even what to call him, I finally turned my attention to *P.* As I chased his evasive traces in and beyond Norbury's letters, they coagulated into an unexpected familial story. This chapter explores what it took to flesh out *P.* in the epistolary archive of late nineteenth-century British Columbia, and interrogates the significance of what I found: the English settler Michael Phillipps, his Ktunaxa (Indigenous) wife Rowena, their twelve children, and a trans-imperial web of simmering gossip and tenacious silence about the family. Despite correspondence and visits to England, Phillipps did not tell his metropolitan family of origin about his British Columbian family of marriage. Instead, he maintained decades of silence on the topic, broken only, albeit partially, by rumours spread outside his family. Extra-familial hints were then followed by years of persistent questions from his English relatives, his British Columbian friend's refusals to answer those questions, and a resulting trail of fragmented intimation communicated through the imperial post.

If, as historian Deborah Cohen argues, Victorian British families were "supposed to be transparent within" even as they kept secrets without, then the trans-imperial letters about the David-Phillipps marriage underscore that this was not always the case.[2] These letters call for an investigation of the place, function, and significance of secrecy maintained within a family but shared as gossip beyond its boundaries. Why was information about the marriage – locally prominent and publicly recognized – so persistently kept from Michael Phillipps's metropolitan family? Why did different correspondents understand the subject to be shareable, secret, scandalous, or commonplace knowledge? What do their intentionally uneven patterns of silence and talk reveal about family, letters, and settler colonialism? And what methodologies might help to trace the contours of epistolary gossip and silence?

Given what we know about common forms of settler colonial racialization and denigration of Indigenous people by the late nineteenth century, the most obvious interpretation of Phillipps's silence might be that he was ashamed of his family of marriage. I do not believe this. To conclude that it was ultimately about shame would be, at best, to partake in interpretive gossip that speculates on archival silence by filling it in with the most negative assumptions of colonial race-thinking. Instead, the evidence here suggests that his family of marriage constituted his most important personal relationships in adulthood – the people with whom he chose to spend and share his whole adult life. In this context, it is more likely that Phillipps was protecting them from the gossip and judgment of his distant family of origin, with whom he maintained connections but not necessarily intimate ones.

Working from this position, this chapter contends that silence, secrecy, and ignorance operated as significant epistolary strategies for maintaining trans-imperial relationships between relatives, especially in circumstances when colonial and metropolitan lives, and families of origin and marriage, seemed irreconcilable. The David-Phillipps marriage was deeply rooted in the Kootenay context, and its common sense there did not translate well to Britain. Thus, to speak of it across this distance would have meant to threaten Phillipps's relationships – both close and less close – that he sought to sustain. At the same time, the chapter demonstrates that extra-familial epistolary gossip could both uphold and threaten such familial silence, while gossipers' varied management of information reveals divergent ideas about race, gender, settler colonialism, and correspondence. Overall, the fragmented epistolary talk about the David-Phillipps relationship shows the clumsy, fraught, partial, and sometimes failed transmission of local colonial knowledge and personal experience across trans-imperial distances, and it underscores the limits of intimacy at the heart of family correspondence.

Although gossip and gossipers are often dismissed as unethical, petty, or indecent, I use these terms here not to pass moral judgment but rather to denote a specific kind of communication. Existing research has tended to focus on how public accusations, private rumours, and (especially sexual) scandal could be tools wielded against powerful individuals in settler colonial contexts.[3] As historian Luise White highlights, however, gossip is a diverse form of communication that builds relationships, produces knowledge, disciplines people, and asserts social values in a much broader sense too. Here, I build from her understanding of gossip as "talk about people when they are not present," which "reports behaviour" and "rests on evaluating reputations."[4] More specifically, I define epistolary gossip as talk that circulated in letters and focused on people other than the writer and intended readers. Whether shared in sensational detail or vague intimation, epistolary gossip was built on foundations of judgment that assessed other people's behaviour as unrespectable or problematic, unusual or shocking. The unwritten was always critical alongside the written; gossip was produced because of prevailing silences, and with the intention of interrupting them.

By examining the web of extra-familial epistolary gossip about the David-Phillipps marriage, this chapter aims to loosen one linchpin in the scholarship on colonial families: the dominance yet capaciousness of intimacy as a central analytical category. In recent years, scholars have turned to intimacy as a key framework through which to understand the trajectories, meanings, and significance of colonial formations. Drawing on analyses of intimacy, the literature on letter writing – like this book's earlier chapters – emphasizes the significance of affective claims to connection and shared knowledge for maintaining families separated by distance. While this work has been valuable, it has identified a staggeringly wide range of relationships, feelings, and behaviours as intimate. The term now serves as a euphemism for sex, a synonym for family, a form of imperial knowledge, or a category assumed but undefined.[5] The conflation of intimacy and family can be particularly problematic as, without precise investigation, it can imply that affective closeness or familiarity worked inevitably as defining features of familial relationships. As Chapter 5 demonstrated, families could be constituted by conflict as well as affection. In addition, a focus on intimacy risks obscuring other elements on which families depended, and it cannot capture the intentionally uneven ways in which relatives wielded familiarity, affection, or openness as epistolary strategies. For Phillipps, the function of correspondence might have been to maintain contact, or even basic familial decorum, but we should not assume that this was the same as intimacy. As this chapter suggests instead, family relationships could also be defined by and maintained due to the refusal of intimacy, crafted by strategic silence, and guarded through cultivated ignorance.

This chapter builds on the book's argument in three additional ways too. For one, the magnified focus on one case highlights the importance of regional distinctions. By tracing the chronologies and trajectories of settler colonialism in the Kootenays, it underscores that British Columbia was not a monolithic colonial site, something that is too often obscured when it is considered only from its southwestern corner. The uneven patterns of talk and silence in this case also point to the underexplored value of drawing families of origin and marriage into the same analytic frame. Both could hold salience for Britons in British Columbia, and an investigation of their relationships with one another – whether distant, close, carefully curated, or complexly fraught – can reveal much about the configurations, ideas, and practices of family as they were lived in and between colonial places. In particular, whereas most of this book has focused on white British families, this chapter connects them with the simultaneous history of interracial marriage. These two forms of colonial family are often studied as distinct or consecutive, but they were also relational and overlapped in important ways.

Finally, whereas both this book and the wider scholarship on family letter writing focus primarily on sources produced by relatives themselves, this chapter is rooted in a different methodology and set of sources. I made this decision by necessity; when I researched and wrote the chapter, no family correspondence to or from Michael Phillipps had been publicly archived and made available.[6] There might now be an exception, as the Ktunaxa Nation Council Archives has recently acquired a collection of Phillipps's records. A great-grandson of Michael and Rowena David Phillipps, Dave Brown, and his wife Pearl, donated the records in 2015 after a forest fire forced them to evacuate their home on the old family ranch. As explained in the archives's official press release, Michael and Rowena's descendants had cared for these records privately and attentively over the past century. When threatened with the fire, the Browns found that they "loaded these records into their car before they even packed their clothes," and so – knowing the value of the sources and "the magnitude of the responsibility" of looking after them – they decided to donate the materials to the Nation's archives. Their choice to do so underscores both that the family in British Columbia remains "deeply rooted in the fabric of the Ktunaxa Nation," as reported in the release, and that they understand the records' meaning and significance today as an Indigenous archive that belongs with the Nation rather than as settler records that belong in a colonial archive, as with the other letters in this book.[7]

The Phillipps family collection in the Nation's Archives had not yet been processed and opened for research when this chapter was completed. So, instead, I examine a silence that remains in the settler archive. Specifically, this chapter explores second- and third-hand discussions of the David-Phillipps family in the letters of other Britons, employing a kind of peripheral vision as methodology. Rather than looking directly at letters produced by the family, I consider the peripheral mentions of them in other correspondence in order to investigate what acquaintances said about them, how, and why. This methodology reveals a different pattern of communication. By uncovering new information, uneven tones, and silences, it makes visible a web of secrecy, privacy, and gossip that would not be apparent from a family's records alone and, in so doing, it exposes different epistolary strategies for maintaining relationships and shaping trans-imperial colonial knowledge. While historians recognize that archives are built on and through silence, it can be difficult to identify, let alone analyze.[8] Using a peripheral reading of the epistolary archive, I undertake to do just that here.

"The Pioneer of Pioneers": Telling Stories of Michael Phillipps

A conventional biography of Michael Phillipps would begin in the early 1840s, when he was born in Herefordshire, England, to Thomas and Penelope Biddulph Phillipps. His Rugby- and Cambridge-educated father was the vicar of Dewsall with Callow, and by the early 1860s, Michael was the eldest of five siblings living in the Dewsall vicarage with their parents. Soon afterwards, he left England, and with it his family of origin and his employment in the local ironworks.[9] Except for two later visits to England, he spent the rest of his life in the Kootenay region, in the southeastern corner of British Columbia, nestled between the Rocky Mountains and the international border with the United States. He first worked for the Hudson's Bay Company as a company clerk, and in 1866 married Rowena, the daughter of Ktunaxa Chief David of Tobacco Plains.[10] Three years later, he was fired by the Hudson's Bay Company.[11] In the years that followed, Rowena, Michael, and their children established a farm on the property that he pre-empted near her family and that later bordered her community's reserve. In addition to the farm, Phillipps pursued other work such as running a private trading post, prospecting, and building trails. He also served as magistrate, justice of the peace, and Indian Agent. Michael Phillipps died in 1916, survived by Rowena David Phillipps and eight of their children.[12]

After his death, public representations of Phillipps often framed him as a pioneering figure of local significance – in regional historian Naomi Miller's words, a "prominent Kootenay citizen."[13] Even in this brief biography, it is possible to see why. He has been commemorated as a man of firsts, said to be one of the first homesteaders in the region and the settler who discovered coal, built the first sawmill, ran the first commercial orchard, worked as the first Kootenay Indian Agent, and rode the first Canadian Pacific Railway train east.[14] In other words, he led or was involved with nearly all of the major political and economic developments in the Kootenays in the late nineteenth and early twentieth centuries. Thus, Michael Phillipps's life both represents and reveals much about a pivotal period in the extension of settler colonialism into southeastern British Columbia.

To date, however, most public settler histories of Phillipps have tended toward isolated individual biography or even hagiographic celebration of an exceptional settler. His Ktunaxa family, his fluency in the Ktunaxa language, and his close connections with the Tobacco Plains community are mentioned but remain marginal. Instead, he tends to be represented as a gritty pioneer who played a critical role in forging the region. In a particularly dramatic example, the Cranbrook *Daily Townsman* declared in 1973 that Michael Phillipps was "a legend," "the pioneer of pioneers," and "the type of character whom novels and TV westerns should be modeled after."[15] This is a quintessential case of a historical narrative inflected with what anthropologist Elizabeth Furniss has termed the "frontier complex." In both content and tone, such representations honour individual settlers (usually men) by emphasizing their "pioneering" enterprise and resolve. At the same time, they obscure political, economic, and social factors that made possible these settlers' lives and drove the larger colonial projects in which they participated.[16]

Historian Jean Barman reminds us that "how a trace is turned into a narrative gives the teller enormous power."[17] By spinning frayed archival threads into a story of settler colonialism and epistolary gossip, this chapter wields its interpretive power to reorient these existing narratives of Michael Phillipps in certain ways but not in others. For example, I acknowledge but largely re-inscribe the silences imposed on Ktunaxa people, especially women and children, by settler histories and archives. To be clear, it would be both possible and valuable to centre Rowena David Phillipps, her children, and her extended family and community in this story by asking different questions of different sources. Among many important contributions, such an approach would work to decentre British men and, in turn, help to reframe the academic histories of family and colonialism that are so often dominated by settler perspectives.[18] But I do not intend to speak for Rowena here, as the chapter is not rooted in the methodologies and relationships necessary for doing so. Instead, it maintains the book's analytical gaze on settlers' (and especially settler men's) trans-imperial networks. Even in this focus, though, there is an opportunity to reframe talk about the family on all sides. In the press release about the Ktunaxa Nation Council Archives's recent acquisition of the family's records, it is clear that descendants know, value, and are interested in different stories about Phillipps. Reflecting on what she called the "invaluable documents," Council employee Rosemary Phillips said:

> Exciting for me is to really get a sense of who this man – my great grandfather – whom I knew a little about, really was. There has been a bit of stigma that has cast a dark shadow on him but as the documents reveal their stories we can see that he really was a great man, humble, kind, and most of all not your typical Indian Agent.[19]

Although I focus on different records and perspectives here, I similarly seek to shed light on the family by investigating a remarkable silence in prevailing narratives about it. Considering his distant English family and their relationship to his life in British Columbia, the chapter tells a new history of Michael Phillipps – one that is simultaneously local and trans-imperial, and intimately interweaves epistolary talk and silence as they connected, and did not quite connect, the province and the metropole.

"A Very Great Objection": Informing Gossip and Settler Colonialism in the Kootenays

I first encountered Michael Phillipps in Tommy Norbury's family letters. Norbury was an English settler who arrived in the Kootenay region in 1887 as a remittance man supported by his relatives in Sherridge, Worcestershire. During his first months in British Columbia, he stayed with the David-Phillipps family at their Tobacco Plains farm. The two men had probably not met before, but their families of origin knew one another in England and Norbury arrived with "recommendations from Phillipps' sister, Mrs. Augusta Grassett." Norbury soon established his own farm nearby. Over the next decade, he became financially independent from his parents and a respected member of the local settler community, serving as government agent and special constable. He returned to England in 1899.[20]

Michael and Rowena David Phillipps had been married for more than two decades before Norbury's arrival. They already had nine children, the eldest of whom was twenty years old – the same age as Norbury. During these two decades, Phillipps had maintained some contact with his family of origin, including a recent visit to England during the winter of 1885–86.[21] However, the archival record suggests that Phillipps's English family did not know about his marriage until after Norbury's arrival in the Kootenays. The first archived epistolary mention of the topic – an observer's "objection" to the David-Phillipps family – reveals much about local configurations of settler colonialism at that time. At its heart, this first informing letter emerges from a late nineteenth-century turn toward the priorities of settler colonialism in the Kootenays, and reflects the changing but still contested settler attitudes toward marriages between Indigenous women and white men in this context.

The first word came from W. Henry Barnaby, a travel writer who knew the Norbury family. In September 1887, he sent a letter from Winnipeg to Tommy Norbury's father, Colonel Thomas Coningsby Norbury. This letter notified its readers about the David-Phillipps marriage, and explained how the information had travelled through a web of extra-familial communication within Canada. According to Barnaby, Norbury had met

Kootenay settler Colonel James Baker as he travelled toward his destination in British Columbia. In conversation, Baker discovered that Norbury planned to stay with Phillipps but did not know that Phillipps was married. Baker told Norbury about the marriage, then wrote Barnaby about this encounter. Barnaby, in turn, reported all of this to Norbury's father, writing in part:

> Colonel Baker told me Mr. Phillipps was a capital man in himself: well acquainted with the country: with a good holding – and a man who would show a young fellow how to work: *but* he said there was one and a very great objection, which I think I ought to mention to you, and I hope you will not think I am intruding in your affairs, but Colonel Baker said your son did not know it, so assume you do not either. Mr. Phillipps is married to an Indian S–w, and has a family by her – Colonel Baker said the eldest girl being 19 years old, and that none of the family except the Father could talk a word of English. I fear this will not be very comfortable for your son.[22]

Here, Barnaby acted as an informer in two senses – both providing information and denouncing – as he indicated what he believed to be the knowledge required for a metropolitan father to look out for the comfort, reputation, and well-being of a distant son.

But why was the David-Phillipps marriage a "very great objection" for Barnaby, imaginable as a potential point of discomfort or an important concern for the Norburys? Regional histories of settler colonialism provide essential context for making sense of this objection. In part, Barnaby's epistolary gossip reflected his place in a wider context of changing settler ideas about race and marriage in the late nineteenth century. Sexual or marital relationships between Indigenous women and non-Indigenous men had long been central to the politics of empire across the world.[23] In northern North America, such marriages – both à la façon du pays (in the custom of the country) and in the custom of Christian churches – had been fundamental to the operation of the fur-trade world.[24] The scholarship frames the second half of the nineteenth century as a period of decline in these marriages and their acceptability in the settler Canadian west. This was linked to an intensifying settler colonial project, which cast Indigenous peoples as obstacles for white settlers and Canadian sovereignty. As these priorities grew in significance, many settlers saw marriages with Indigenous women as threats to the possibility of a future white

Canada, and to white men's racial status and masculinity in particular. Though it was not made illegal in Canada, unlike in other imperial sites, such concerns fed a growing settler denigration of intermarriage or sex across racialized bounds. They also provided impetus for a wide range of political and legal state efforts to surveille, regulate, and intervene in the sexual and marriage practices of Indigenous people, especially women.[25]

While Barnaby's objections were linked to these changing discourses and growing criticism across the Canadian west, the David-Phillipps family also serves as a reminder that settler condemnations of intermarriage were powerful but did not entirely determine people's actions. Here, a straightforward narrative of fur-trade intimacy to settler denigration is important but insufficient to explain what was a more complex and enduring familial form. Some relationships between Indigenous women and settler men are well known for their influence in the second half of the nineteenth century, including several elite fur-trading families who became prominent "founding families" in Victoria.[26] The David-Phillipps relationship provides another example outside the city, characterized not only by the family's local prominence but also by its stability over five decades. Beyond these cases, it is likely that marriages between Indigenous women and non-Indigenous men remained a much more widespread practice in the early settler period than has been generally acknowledged.[27] The extent of such relationships can be difficult to assess, though, not least because colonial policies and social attitudes often obscured them in a "hazy" settler archive.[28] For example, under the Indian Act, women lost Indian status and were displaced from reserve communities if they married non-Indigenous men or men without Indian status.[29] Thus, women may not have been recognized as Indigenous in archived records such as censuses, but may instead have been identified – or have chosen to identify themselves – with their husbands' racial categories. Indeed, for many Indigenous people more generally, this could be a strategy to navigate and survive in a hostile settler society.[30] These relationships may also have been accepted in local contexts for much longer than general histories recognize, and certainly their practice and significance continued well after the years of fur-trade dominance. This was important for individuals, families, and communities at the time. But it also matters for us; unsettling the dominant narrative of declension and disappearance should change how we think about the history of race, gender, sexuality, and settler colonial British Columbia.

The David-Phillipps family and its relationship to these contested ideas about marriage must also be seen in relation to the particular local chronologies and configurations of settler colonialism in the Kootenays. Here, the shift between the fur economy and settler priorities began later than in southwestern British Columbia. When Michael Phillipps arrived in the 1860s, he was one of very few white newcomers in the region, and his work for the Hudson's Bay Company depended on close relationships with Indigenous people and a minimal settler presence. The 1880s and 1890s marked a turning point in relationships between the Ktunaxa and non-Indigenous people, as a mining boom sparked a rapid influx of settlers and industrial capital. This intensified conflict over competing claims to land, resources, and ways of life, and prompted the state to extend its reach further into the region.[31] At the same time, settlers and the state remained comparatively limited, local attitudes could change slowly, and Ktunaxa people continued to redefine the colonial project with their survival and resistance throughout this period and beyond.

Two visits by Indian reserve commissioner Peter O'Reilly serve as an example. O'Reilly travelled to the Kootenays in 1884 and 1887 in order to establish and adjust reserves for Indigenous people and make the rest of the territory available for white settlement. This was both in line with his mandate across the province and in response to growing settler interest in the region.[32] On these visits, however, he found Ktunaxa people who were unwilling to define and relinquish the land as he called for. In his December 1884 report, O'Reilly complained that Chief David had been "unreasonable in his demands ... claiming the whole country from the boundary line to the Columbia Lakes." In asserting this claim, O'Reilly noted, David demonstrated a close knowledge of Indigenous-state relations in the United States and on the Canadian Prairies:

> He repeatedly referred to the large reserves allotted by the United States Government to the Indians, containing millions of acres, and compared them with the small area he asked for. He also pointed out that the chiefs on American territory, only a few miles to the south, received an annual pension of $500.00 each; and he complained that the Kootenay Indians had received nothing at the hands of the Dominion Government, though the Crees, Blackfeet and Stoneys, on the other side of the mountains, had been furnished with stock, seeds, implements, and even rations.[33]

Noting but ignoring such arguments, O'Reilly set out three much smaller reserves by the end of his 1884 visit. As historical geographer Cole Harris observes, "almost none" of this reserve land was useful for cultivation or ranching.[34]

O'Reilly returned to the region in 1887 with F.G. Vernon and I.W. Powell in the context of ongoing Ktunaxa resistance to settlers, the reserve system, and state policy. The three commissioners added three small reserves in the hope, they wrote, of "allaying all feeling of dissatisfaction on the part of the Indians."[35] In the same year, in the wake of what Powell called "serious difficulties" in the region, the Department of Indian Affairs created the Kootenay Agency (spanning the territory of the Sinixt and Ktunaxa Nations) in another effort to advance state control and order. Michael Phillipps was appointed as the agency's first permanent Indian Agent, a position that he held between 1887 and 1893. Explaining his appointment, Powell praised Phillipps as "an old inhabitant of the district" who "speaks the Kootenay language fluently," and concluded that "if instructed to initiate and carry out some suggestions for utilizing the reserves, [he] will become most acceptable to the Indians, and a useful officer to the Department."[36] In practice, this meant that Phillipps's familial connections undoubtedly played a role in his appointment as Indian Agent, placing him in the important if complicated position of intermediary between the Ktunaxa people and the Canadian state.

These structural changes in Indigenous-state relations coincided with, and exacerbated, significant challenges in Ktunaxa life. Phillipps's annual agency reports reflected close knowledge of the Tobacco Plains community, and noted that they were particularly afflicted by the effects of colonialism. In his 1887 report, for example, he remarked that they

> suffered more from the loss of the buffalo than any other section of the tribe. They are unable to make money from the whites ... They have of late years been eating up their cattle and even cows, and now have little left. The failure of the surface berry crop will cause much suffering this year. They usually dry the berries for winter use.[37]

In 1914, members of the Tobacco Plains band spoke before the Royal Commission on Indian Affairs for the Province of British Columbia (also called the McKenna-McBride Commission). The commission had been called to investigate the allocation of reserves and resolve the so-called Indian land question in the province. In their evidence, witnesses from Tobacco Plains also provided clear, damning testimony regarding the impact of colonialism on their community during these years.[38]

The David-Phillipps family offers one window onto this regional history. The marriage began in the midst of the Kootenay fur-trade world in the 1860s, stretched through a period of major flux in the 1880s and 1890s, and well into the settler boom in the early years of the twentieth century. It was in 1887 – in the same year the Indian Agency was established – that Henry Barnaby described Michael Phillipps's marriage and his Ktunaxa-speaking family as "a very great objection." The information spread by Baker and Barnaby unsurprisingly provided no insight into the family's place in the Tobacco Plains Ktunaxa community, nor does it reveal what members of the family themselves thought or felt. It does, however, indicate that the family was locally remarkable, visible, and acknowledged by settlers. Barnaby's letter also suggests that, in the eyes of at least some settlers, relationships between Indigenous women and British men were becoming less normalized or accepted practice. The David-Phillipps family traversed hardening racialized boundaries in a turn toward settler colonial priorities, and Michael Phillipps troubled newly defined parameters of settler men's respectability in this context. For Barnaby, this was worthy of disapproval, and could affect Tommy Norbury by association. At the same time, Phillipps's marriage into the prominent David family clearly facilitated his local position as a colonial linchpin, skilled state representative, and influential settler. Overall, other settlers appear to have read his marital choice in complicated ways in a period of significant local change – neither entirely accepted nor entirely disparaged but rather simultaneously eliciting concern and criticism as well as garnering for him respect and power. However, though the David-Phillipps family was well known and important in the Kootenays, news of its existence would translate poorly across imperial distances for a metropolitan audience less familiar with long histories of colonial intermarriage and without any experience in the country.

"Excellent Description": Personal Experience, Colonial Knowledge, and Gossip with Authority

By exposing the marriage to a metropolitan readership, Barnaby's letter served as the catalyst for further questions and gossip. In the ensuing years, Tommy Norbury emerged as a key node in this network of talk, as he tried to manage trans-imperial knowledge production, transmission, and refusal. In response to his own family's inquiries in the wake of Barnaby's letter, he described the Indigenous family with whom he lived. As he did so, he moved between accounts of personal interactions and broad colonial tropes, filtered through claims that he both knew and did not know much about the David-Phillipps family. These letters were remarkable exceptions to prevailing epistolary silences about Indigenous peoples, and presented his experiences as both confirming and granting authority to the abstracted colonial ideas about race that were discussed in Chapter 3. In the process, his letters formed part of a wider circulation of settler knowledge about Indigenous people, which reinforced metropolitan fascination and anxiety about empire, and buttressed an enduring colonial common sense about race and difference.

In Norbury's first detailed epistolary discussion of the David-Phillipps family, he moved through a shifting kaleidoscope of limited knowledge, ethnographic description, the baggage of expectation, and personal encounter. On 13 November 1887, he responded to his parents' inquiries about Barnaby's information with a long letter about his everyday life and future plans in the Kootenays, before eventually acknowledging: "I suppose you are all rather anxious to learn about the Mrs. & fam. here." He then explained that he knew little, in part because of his inability to communicate verbally with them. As Barnaby had already reported, Ktunaxa was the household's language, and indeed, Norbury explained, "none of them can speak a single syllable of English." Nonetheless, this did not necessarily mean a complete lack of understanding or connection. "The boys often come out shooting with me & we get on capitally," Norbury continued. "I manage to make them understand anything I want with the aid of my Dictionary & signs."[39] He also set to work learning Ktunaxa, noting in another early letter: "I am getting on first rate with the Kootenay language."[40] In other words, while Barnaby had identified linguistic barriers as part of Norbury's expected discomfort, these did not necessarily equate to impenetrable boundaries in practice, nor did they mean that Norbury would insist on English as the only possible language of communication.

In his 13 November letter, Norbury also claimed that he knew little about the relationship because Phillipps had not explained it. He confirmed what Barnaby had already said, writing that he had learned about the marriage when he met Baker on his travels. "I first heard about it on the steamer coming up the Columbia when a man asked me where I was going & I told him to Mr. P.s.," he wrote. "He said it was a pity he had married a s–w. Of course I said yes it was, but at the same time I was a good bit taken aback." After this conversation, Norbury met Phillipps in the town of Kootenay, and anticipated that he would mention the family awaiting their arrival in Tobacco Plains. However, Norbury explained, Phillipps had maintained only resounding silence on the matter:

> I thought P. w[oul]d tell me that he was married directly, but no. I stayed as you know about 3 wks. at Kootenay with him & he always talked as if there was no one here; at last we made a start for Tobacco Plains. I thought at any rate he will tell me now, but he never said a word about her & never has yet. When we came into the house, she was sitting down, & the only introduction I had was from P. "Here's the woman," & that's all I know about it.

Indeed, he claimed, this left him uncertain about even the basic details. "I call her the Mrs. although P. has never told me that they are married," he wrote, adding later, "I believe they are legally married."[41] Norbury's letters imply that he expected an explanation of the relationship, while suggesting that race was a silencing factor. However, it is impossible to say whether his assumption was true. Phillipps might not have considered it remarkable at all, and his reticence could have been related to gender too: perhaps he did not say more because men did not necessarily talk about their wives or explain the legal status of their relationships in conversation with one another.[42]

In any case, Norbury used this first letter to talk against the silence, describing Rowena David Phillipps and her children. He first listed the children, including their English and "Indian" names (if he could remember them), ages, and, in some cases, brief descriptions.[43] He then focused on the family's dress, bodies, appearances, and daily activities. For example, he described (without ever naming) Rowena David Phillipps: "She is not bad looking but rather fat now, & dresses in a sort of cotton frock & a turban, very clean, & well mannered, and makes a capital wife, working well in the garden & house. She is of the Royal family, being the daughter of the Chief." Here, he largely reduced her to appearance, behaviour, and status defined by markers of gender and race. Similarly, as he moved beyond the children's names, Norbury focused on their physical appearance, dwelling on how he read their bodies and dress as simultaneously "Indian" and "white." "They all dress like white men," he wrote, "but have long black hair behind & they are only very little darker in colour."[44] On the one hand, in the absence of significant verbal communication, perhaps bodies and behaviour were Norbury's primary point of assessing and understanding the family.[45] On the other hand, his propensity to gaze on their bodies in this way and pass sweeping judgments in terms repeated in other settler records indicate the power of broadly shared discourses on race and difference.

In other letters, Norbury similarly drew on conventional settler ideas about Indigenous people, and rooted them in the authority of his own experiences. In one case, he responded to his sister Nelly's question with an intrusive description of the bodies and dress of the Indigenous women with whom he lived, even as he claimed that his knowledge was appropriately limited:

> I am told by as great an authority as Campbell that 5 yds of stuff makes a s–w a dress, so you may imagine there aren't many flounces &c. The stuff is generally a brilliant coloured cotton, quite thin, & I am told by the same authority but *of course* I don't know, that they wear *nothing underneath,* it must be rather chilly 40° below zero. They have a gaudy pockethand [blotted abbreviation, presumably handkerchief] tied round the head gipsy fashion and always wear a blanket over their shoulders. They of course all ride straddle legged with a blanket arranged in front of them to hide any little frills wh[ich] might be there.[46]

Here, he responded to his metropolitan family's curious interest in colonial description, while holding up women's dress as a marker of titillating and indecent difference. Using another settler man as an intermediary, he moved between personal knowledge and the knowledge that would not be respectable for him to know. Overall, the passage pointed to a wider set of representations that denigrated Indigenous women, both for nakedness and for clothing deemed gaudy or frivolous.[47] (Norbury's colonial gaze has become an enduring common sense that resonates into the present. On this letter's typescript copy in the archive, someone has handwritten at the bottom: "Excellent description of Kutenai women."[48])

Although his later correspondence largely avoided the topic in general, Norbury continued to provide his relatives with occasional and exceptional descriptions of Ktunaxa people that also reproduced wider colonial ideas about race, culture, and difference. In 1888, for example, he accused Rowena David Phillipps's brother of breaking into his house and stealing some items. In a letter about this incident, Norbury named him, unlike Rowena. However, this was not a description of a personal relationship between individuals. Rather, Norbury drew heavily on settler representations of Indigenous men as ungrateful and greedy, with common disregard for (European ideas of) personal property. He wrote: "I know the Indian who did it ... but can't prove it. he is an Indian I have always been good to[,] just like the ungrateful beasts, the more you give them, the more they want." Later in the same letter, Norbury indicated the potential consequences of settler accusations and collective racist stereotypes for Indigenous men. Although unable to prove his allegation, Norbury nonetheless told the priest "about the housebreaking," and as a result, "the priest ordered [him] to be flogged & he got it well, hurrah!"[49] In this description, Norbury contributed to a wider discourse that sought to legitimize colonial power by perpetuating and celebrating settler violence against Indigenous men.

In contrast, Norbury never provided similar embodied and behavioural descriptions of Phillipps or the other settler men he encountered in the Kootenays. He also did not articulate sweeping judgments of settler men as representatives of a general category of people. Instead, Phillipps primarily garnered a character reference, which underscored to the Norbury family that he was a suitable mentor and local connection. "He is an extremely nice man," Norbury wrote to his sister, bland in his brief reassurance, "and I get on with him very well."[50] In this way, his letters indicated that other settler men were not curiosities for him, nor were their bodies and dress apparently of much anticipated or expressed interest for his metropolitan relatives. This reflected a different silence and a different common-sense understanding, which normalized the place of white settler men in British Columbia, rendered them unremarkable, and cast them as individuals rather than representatives of a race.

Read alongside his sparse descriptions of settler men, Norbury's representations of Ktunaxa people provide a striking if not unexpected contrast. Like other British correspondents in British Columbia, he drew on a colonial toolkit of discourses about race, gender, and difference, producing descriptions of Indigenous people that were simultaneously abstracted from and supposedly corroborated by his personal experiences.[51]

His letters worked to produce and confirm trans-imperial British knowledge about Indigenous people and the local colonial project. These epistolary descriptions elaborated on common tropes, circulated them widely, granted them authority, and reinforced their place as commonsense knowledge and curious subjects in the metropole. The anticipated distant purchase of such racial discourses may or may not have underlain Phillipps's decision to say nothing about his marriage to his relatives in England. Either way, Norbury, like Barnaby, explicitly framed race as the primary factor in discussions of the David-Phillipps family – the issue that drove early trans-imperial questions, judgments, and descriptions. In the epistolary exchanges that followed, however, race would play a more complicated, role.

"Do Not Tell Anybody": Intimation, Refusal, and Uneven Epistolary Knowledge

Information about the David-Phillipps marriage did not remain solely within the Norbury family once it reached Britain, but instead travelled through a wider web of communication there. Michael Phillipps's sister, Augusta Phillipps Grasett, found out about the marriage shortly after Norbury's arrival in British Columbia. Given the timing and the two families' relationship, it is most likely that she heard the news from the Worcestershire Norburys after the latter received Barnaby's letter, although there is no concrete evidence of this in the archive. In any case, the Grasetts soon began to write to Tommy Norbury in order to request further information. Norbury tracked these letters and his responses in correspondence with his own family. Through these discussions, it is possible to trace an arc of gossip and silence about the David-Phillipps family. While Norbury answered his own relatives' questions, he refused to provide any specific details in correspondence with the Grasetts. In this way, his letters reveal the strategic and uneven work of secrecy and intimation – maintained by himself and by Michael Phillipps – as British Columbian correspondents sought to shape trans-imperial family relationships and colonial knowledge. Here, the performance of epistolary intimacy was clearly and intentionally limited, both within and beyond families.

As Chapter 2 explained, physical separation could be worrisome for relatives who wanted, expected, or sought close knowledge about one another, whether as a marker of affect or duty. The level of familial anxiety particularly spiked when separation was accompanied by reticent letters, or even no communication at all. In these circumstances, it was not unusual for distant relatives to use other forms of trans-imperial communication, well beyond the borders of family, in order to make inquiries.[52] In the absence of direct contact with family members, non-relatives could be called on to provide second-hand reassurance or information about settlers' health, well-being, or behaviour. In 1895, for example, Norbury received what he called a "'family enquiring' letter" from the brother of a British Columbian friend, Edmund Parker, who had apparently not written to his metropolitan relatives for over a year. As Norbury noted, he was "able to give ... a perfectly cheerful account of him."[53] Such letters serve as a reminder that trans-imperial correspondence was not limited to family. Rather, familial networks overlapped with extra-familial ones.

Norbury's letters from the Grasetts reflected this broader pattern with a focused and insistent intensity. By February 1888, he had received his first letter from "Mrs. G. & all the children, & what is worse, [she] wants to know if the rumour she has heard is true, that Mr. P. is married." As he noted to his brother Coni, "She wants an answer very much."[54] The Grasetts may also have written to Phillipps, but Norbury's letters suggest that this was unlikely. In any case, it is clear that Phillipps did not provide responses that satisfied their queries. Instead, for nearly four years, Augusta Phillipps Grasett continued to write to Norbury to request information. This was not merely a one-time check on a relative who had disappeared but rather an anxious campaign to understand a distant relationship in the context of an ongoing and increasingly obvious silence about the topic from Michael Phillipps himself.

In this yawning familial silence, Norbury must have seemed to Grasett like the best potential source of information. However, he would frustrate her over and over again, consistently refusing to provide the answers she sought. In February 1888, after receiving her first letter, he explained to his brother: "I have written to her & told her 'if Mr. P. has anything wh[ich] he does not want his family to know, I am not giving her anything' and that she had better write to him which she might have done instead of writing to ask me."[55] After receiving another letter, he noted: "This I shall not trouble to answer. I told her to ask her brother anything she wanted to know, & that is enough."[56] These refusals seemed, briefly, to discourage Augusta Phillipps Grasett. Later in 1888, Norbury wrote: "I have heard no more from Mrs. Grasett, so I suppose she did not fancy my answer to her question."[57] This was only a brief break, however, and in the years that followed, he continued to deny her persistent requests for information about her brother's British Columbian family. In July 1890, Norbury complained to his father that he had received yet another letter "from Mrs. Grasett on the old subject! When will she quit? I have not answered her last two & shan't answer this."[58]

According to Norbury's summary, Augusta Phillipps Grasett was first upset that she had not known about the marriage, but once she learned of it – apparently with no further details – she became concerned about what was not being said and why. The limits of her familiarity with her distant brother had become suddenly and starkly clear, but their reasons were not. What distant intimacies were intimated by Phillipps's silence? What did this mean for her own sense of connection or relationship with him? Did the marriage have implications for her brother's respectability in British Columbia, for hers in England, and indeed for that of the whole trans-imperial family? In one case, Norbury reported to his brother that "she says she is sure it can't be a nice person or P. w[oul]d have told her."[59] Later, he seems to have confirmed the marriage without any further information. She then responded to him with frustration: "I knew that my brother was married, but what I wanted to know was whether she was presentable." In this instance, she demanded his help in determining whether the English branch of the family should acknowledge her brother's marriage, and more broadly, what it might mean in a metropolitan context. If Phillipps's wife were "presentable," she suggested, "I would ask my brother if I sh[oul]d tell the family," but if she were a "common woman" and they had no children, "of course it is best to say nothing."[60] Three years later, she was still writing Norbury to ask, as he reported, whether her brother's wife "was fit to ask home to England!"[61]

These discussions suggest that information about the family had been rendered as only partial rumour in metropolitan conversations, with race unspoken and unspeakable even if it might have remained a blurred undercurrent. Barnaby's initial letter had explicitly explained that Rowena David Phillipps was an Indigenous woman – the very point that, for him, made the David-Phillipps family notable and objectionable. Norbury's detailed descriptions of the family were similarly focused on racialized difference. However, at least in Norbury's summaries, Augusta Phillipps Grasett's articulated anxieties seemed to rest most clearly on class or respectability, particularly in her opposition of "presentable" and "common." Indeed, Norbury repeatedly pointed to her ignorance of what he saw as the primary relevant information. In February 1888, he remarked to his brother that she did "not seem to know it is a s–w."[62] In a May 1891 letter to his father, he exclaimed that Grasett still did not know "the colour of the lady."[63] In such exchanges, networks of trans-imperial gossip not only constructed and transmitted knowledge but also revealed and sustained uneven forms of ignorance.

This insistence on secrecy was an intentional strategy for Norbury, as he framed race as the central factor in shaping his descriptions of the family for his own relatives and simultaneously as the central secret in his exchanges with the Grasetts. Initially, he sought to maintain Phillipps's silence in all of his correspondence, but when pressed, he was clearly willing to share particular information with his family. When they first learned of the relationship in the autumn of 1887, he responded to them: "I intended not to tell you the [*sic*] Mrs. & family but as you have found it out I will write & tell you all about it in my next. I have not time now." But he instructed them: "Do not tell *anybody* about it."[64] In this, he always actively sought to prevent the Grasetts from receiving the information. He emphasized the point again in his next letter. In a postscript to his first detailed description of the family, he reminded his readers not to tell others about "P. [*sic*] domestic affairs," noting that "he has never told me he does not want anyone to know but I know it is so."[65]

In truth, I do not know why Phillipps did not tell his family of origin because his reasons are elusive in the archive, as all silences are. I also do not know why Norbury sought to manage the information the way that he did. Given that Norbury's attitudes were more clearly articulated and archived, though, some more speculation on that front is possible. For example, it is plausible that he felt that the David-Phillipps family was strictly a British Columbian matter that would not translate well across trans-imperial distances. However, his willingness to answer his own family's questions (albeit with an insistence on their silence) suggests that these imagined boundaries of colonial knowledge could be rendered flexible and mobile in some circumstances. Perhaps, then, his strategic silences were performances of a polite masculinity, which manifested here in a refusal to intervene in the privacy of another man's family.[66] His adherence to this position was likely also rooted in the two men's particular relationship. Phillipps was both a settler-mentor and a local host to the young Norbury on his arrival, as well as an employer, partner, and friend in subsequent years. In this context, Norbury may have sought to maintain certain gendered, generational, and personal expectations of respectful silence by honouring the boundaries that Phillipps had established. Taking it upon himself to protect and partially replicate his friend's refusal to speak, Norbury seems to have (mostly) denied that Phillipps's family relationships were his business, and refused the role or responsibility of informer beyond the parameters of his own relatives. I suggest that this was about race – but not only about it.

Norbury's willingness to maintain secrets and his unwillingness to inform on Phillipps were reflected in another example of explicit self-censorship in his correspondence with the Grasetts. In October 1890, Phillipps was thrown from his horse and badly injured. Telling his own mother of the accident, Norbury added: "Of course do not mention this to anyone. I will write next mail to Mrs. Grasett."[67] Before Norbury could write the intended letter, however, Phillipps instructed him not to say anything. "He seems not to want his relations to know anything about it," he noted to his father the following month.[68] Then, in January 1891, Norbury received a letter from Augusta Phillipps Grasett. She had temporarily "dropped the old subject" of her brother's marriage, "but now wants to give me fits for not writing to tell her about her brother's accident." Norbury's English readers may have ignored his initial instructions "not [to] mention" the injuries to Phillipps's family, perhaps because they thought that the Grasetts should know or perhaps because their ability to talk together about relatives in British Columbia served to build metropolitan bonds that felt more immediate and important than Norbury's plea. It is also possible that Phillipps had recovered enough to write to his sister himself. In any case, Norbury sought to justify his decision to his mother, reminding her that, "as you know, he particularly asked me not to write, but he is just that sort of man."[69]

While Norbury tried (and failed) to impose a metropolitan silence about both the accident and the marriage, there seems to have been a significant difference in how he broached the subjects with Phillipps himself. According to Norbury's letters, the two men had a conversation about contacting the Grasetts about the accident, and Phillipps directly instructed him not to do so. In contrast, for several years Norbury tried not to mention the marriage or Augusta Phillipps Grasett's insistent and ongoing requests for information about it. For instance, he noted to his brother Coni in 1888: "I have not told P. she knows & don't think I shall."[70] Eventually, he could sustain this decision no longer. In the spring of 1891, with her concern about the accident assuaged, Augusta Phillipps Grasett returned to the topic of the marriage. Norbury explained to his father in early May: "I got another letter from Mrs. Grasett on the old subject." After more than three years of silence, Norbury finally decided to tell Michael Phillipps that his sister had been inquiring about the relationship. "P. did not know in the least how she had found out & I think rather naturally suspected I had told her," he explained. Phillipps's response was to do as Norbury had essentially already done – say nothing. As Norbury explained to his father, he translated those instructions into yet another refusal to Grasett: "I ... sent an ultimatum to the effect that I had asked Mr. Phillipps what he wished me to do on the subject & he replied 'Say nothing' and with that I intended to comply and hoped she w[oul]d not mention the subject to me again."[71] Norbury spoke volumes in this final refusal to speak. Phillipps knew that his sister knew, he reported. But Phillipps's own silence was replicated, reinforced, even strengthened in his response. *Say nothing.* More than any previous refusal to answer Grasett, this particular insistence on silence intimated that there was, indeed, something to be said.

The archival trail of questions, gossip, and refusals to answer fades away after the spring of 1891. The following year, Norbury wrote to his mother: "I have had no letter from Mrs. Grasett & don't count [on] one."[72] Although he maintained some postal contact with the Grasetts for several more years, he never again mentioned any requests for information on "the old subject." Indeed, by 1896, he had heard so little from them that he asked his mother "what has become of the Grasetts," and by his final years in British Columbia, only heard their news when he met up with "Old Phillipps" himself, who had continued to maintain contact with his English relatives.[73] From the archival record, it is unclear whether the Grasetts stopped writing to Norbury because they read between the lines, convinced Phillipps to tell them, found their answers another way, or simply gave up their quest. Whatever the reason, a four-year correspondence had made, moved, and maintained insistent silences among acquaintances and relatives, and then it slipped away into *nothing*.

Physical distances could sometimes protect families from the ramifications of a relative's actions, but the possibilities of epistolary silence and untruth – and the accompanying lack of familial knowledge – could be deeply worrying too. Metropolitan Britons sometimes turned to extra-familial networks of communication, which could enable them to find out information about their colonial relatives and even exert a kind of long-distance "moral control" over them, as historian David A. Gerber puts it.[74] However, discussions about the David-Phillipps family suggest that epistolary gossip did not necessarily work so neatly, as extra-familial networks could simultaneously break, extend, and complicate familial silence too. Taken together, the archived correspondence implies that Michael Phillipps maintained relationships with his family of origin despite, and perhaps because of, his refusal to explain his family of marriage. At the same time, Tommy Norbury's responses to Augusta Phillipps Grasett indicate how correspondents could seek to control gossip, knowledge, and ignorance between British Columbia and Britain, and point toward the wider strategic work of silence in shaping trans-imperial family relationships and knowledge about British Columbian lives.

Coda: On Last Words and Silence

When Michael Phillipps died in the Kootenays on 22 June 1916, Tommy Norbury once again emerged as a key node of trans-imperial communication about his old friend's life. Norbury had returned to England in 1899 and was then living at The Norrest, a farm near Malvern, Worcestershire. When he received word of Phillipps's death, he took on the role of sharing, translating, and commenting on information between the English Grasetts and his British Columbian acquaintances. On the evening of 23 June, he notified Augusta Phillipps Grasett of her brother's death. "My dear Mrs. Grasett," he wrote. "I have just received the enclosed from Charlie Edwards for which you are no doubt prepared but that still makes your loss no easier to bear." (There is no item enclosed in the archive, but it was presumably a telegram, given the timing.) Thus, he opened his letter in conventional terms, explaining how he had heard of the death and acknowledging her grief with words that might have been found in any condolence of the period, as explained in Chapter 5. He continued along the same lines:

> Though you and he had seen so little of each other all these years I know there existed an affection and love between you quite out of the common. Poor old Michael – a kinder hearted or more courageous man I never knew – he was absolutely fearless – neither flood, nor storm, nor wild beast ever perturbed him, but woe betide any man who ever crossed his path without good cause. Hot tempered but thoroughly just in every sense.

> I knew him so well and so many of my remembrances happy and otherwise are so closely associated with him. If ever a man knew what real rough life meant, he did – but with whatever people fate chose for his companions he always remained at all times a perfect English gentleman.
>
> I am so glad for you and for everyone connected either by relationship or friendship that Charlie E. was there to look after him when his time came to leave: he will doubtless write me full particulars which I will send you.[75]

Here, Norbury incorporated the standard components of the genre: he remarked on his relationship with Phillipps and reflected on fond memories of their lives together; he eulogized Phillipps as both a model British Columbian settler and "a perfect English gentleman"; he referred to a positive relationship between the distant siblings; he expressed comfort about the conditions of death; and he offered sympathy. Perhaps in keeping with the years of insistent silence and the conventional avoidance of controversy in condolence letters, Norbury implicitly referred to but never explicitly named Rowena or the children as Michael's "companions" in British Columbia.

Nearly a month later, Edwards wrote to Norbury. He began by thanking him for a letter, which had also enclosed a letter from Grasett. Similarly following convention, he offered a detailed description of "poor Michael's death" because Grasett "would probably like to hear some particulars." Unlike Norbury, though, Edwards emphasized the presence and significance of Phillipps's family of marriage at the deathbed:

> On June 21st I went over to see him and found him dying. I went off and brought the Dr. who told me there was no hope. I stayed all night and except Alice he knew no one. The Dr. came about 10.0 O'clock on the 22nd but he (M) died about half past twelve with his three daughters present. Alice, (dear girl) had been up with him for four or five days or nights and after his death simply went off her head, and I had an awful time with her, the only person round except the family, she would do nothing except for me.

Edwards then described Phillipps's burial in what he called "one of the prettiest little cemeteries one could find." The letter also discussed the will and arrangements for the headstone, and enclosed an obituary that he had written for a local newspaper.[76]

This letter was an ending – not only marking the death of Michael Phillipps but also being the last known, archived letter from British Columbia that talked about the David-Phillipps family. In some ways, it continued in the same vein as the earlier correspondence. It remained talk about the family that passed through intermediaries rather than talk among relatives themselves. In other ways, however, the letter differed from the others. It was not whispered rumour or abstracted colonial judgment. Instead, Edwards named Phillipps's daughter Alice, and recognized the family without dwelling on race and difference. He openly described the intimacy of a deathbed and the care of a family that remained distant and unknown to the metropolitan Grasetts. In so doing, he evoked a fraught and fragmented connection between Phillipps's families of origin and marriage, highlighting a moment of grief that they both shared and markedly did not share with one another. This was an ending that underscored, one more time, the sharp limits of intimacy for the trans-imperial family.

There is another final silence to note here too. Library and Archives Canada holds a copy of Edwards's letter, which was donated by a descendant of the family in England. One page has been extracted in the middle, leaving a section that now reads: "I wish you would tell Mrs. Grasett that (Page omitted – of a private nature only) not let R.L.T. near the house and asked me to sort out all papers and send to Galbraith only the papers necessary to probate the Will."[77] Considering the context of the rest of the letter, it seems likely that the excised discussion focused on the estate, but it is also possible that it related to family affairs more generally. In any case, it is an evocative archival silence that explicitly and intentionally intervenes in a story already built on secrecy, privacy, intimation, and fragmentation. In its refusal to reveal, it also seems a fitting, unresolved ending to a family history built from my own partial knowledge of a beguiling settler archive.

THIS CHAPTER BEGAN WITH a man whose life appeared splintered in someone else's correspondence, initials hardly breaking a prevailing silence. As historian Luise White reminds us: "Silence ... remains silence, powerful because it is not spoken, and cannot be pulled – or decoded – into speech. Silences do not necessarily lend themselves into the same straightforward interpretation that spoken words do; they require slower or looser analyses."[78] Here, I have considered what a "looser analysis" might mean in the face of epistolary silence. In the end, it took only a slight turn of the light – a new set of questions, a willingness to read peripherally in family records – to see the long archival shadows cast by Michael Phillipps and his family of marriage. These shadows tell a number of stories. They trace one family's complicated place among the hardening boundaries between Ktunaxa and settler life in a period of intensifying local colonialism. In the process, they highlight settlers' changing but still deeply contested ideas about race, gender, and marriage in a booming Kootenay region in the early settler period. In addition, epistolary gossip reveals the sometimes fraught relationships between families of origin and marriage, as these were constructed, cultivated, and negotiated by settlers seeking to navigate British Columbian and trans-imperial lives.

In so doing, the David-Phillipps story unsettles a too-easy equation between family correspondence and family intimacy. A close reading of the family's place in the epistolary archive reveals the critical role of strategic silence, cultivated ignorance, and gossip or intimation in shaping trans-imperial forms of colonial knowledge, and in reconfiguring personal relationships between British Columbia and Britain. Correspondents not only claimed connection and fashioned shared knowledge but also withheld details in specific instances, sustained long silences, and sought to manage or limit the spread of information. In some cases, silence could be seen as signalling failure or rupture in a family, while in other cases, it was wielded as an intentional and regular strategy to maintain relationships. Writing, in other words, did not always mean intimacy, connection, or closeness in a straightforward way, nor did silence necessarily break the family. Rather, talk and silence worked together to constitute familial relationships, colonial knowledge, and epistolary power.

In sum, the specific management of secrecy and gossip traced in this chapter reveals the gaps between local and metropolitan family lives, values, and expectations. Even as the details of silence can be elusive or invisible in the archive, the case study suggests that epistolary families were maintained by silence and the strategic limits of intimacy, as well as by words and claims to closeness, knowledge, and affective connection. Ultimately, the peripheral epistolary archive about the David-Phillipps marriage traces the parameters of family secrets that entwined individual relationships and broader settler colonial concerns. In so doing, it reveals how the threads of epistolary gossip and silence helped pull tighter the warp of family and weft of empire.

Conclusion

SINCE THE EARLY NINETEENTH century, the Murdoch family has travelled well-worn routes around the (now former) British imperial world, including and well beyond British Columbia. They have moved as sojourners and settlers, pursuing opportunities for education, work, adventure, comfort, love, and status. In the face of unsuccessful endeavours or unfulfilling jobs, they have packed up and started again elsewhere. Sometimes they have chosen unfamiliar destinations, but often they have followed in the footsteps of relatives who have moved before them. These trans-imperial trajectories began in the 1820s, when Henry Hunter Murdoch (senior) – born into a middle-class family of physicians and clergymen – left England and moved to Gibraltar.[1] There he operated a trading company in partnership with John Bowring, better known as a British intellectual, writer, and later Member of Parliament and governor of Hong Kong. In 1825, Henry married Mary Tapp, his second cousin, and she joined him at Gibraltar. When the firm Bowring and Murdoch failed the following year, the couple returned to England with their infant son Henry Hunter Murdoch (junior). Their growing family then spent the next several years moving around working-class East London, often several times a year, as they tried to recover from the heavy financial blow of business failure.

Henry Hunter Murdoch Jr. grew up during the family's insecure and transient years in London. He attended school until age thirteen, when he took up paid work to help support the family. After a decade as a junior clerk in London, he was offered a job in Calcutta with a textile import company, Ewing and Co. He accepted the position and set out for India in 1850. Around the same time, his brothers moved to South Asia and Australia, further extending the family across the empire. Within a few years, Henry Jr. had become a partner in Ewing and Co. Like many Britons in India, he spent the next fifteen years travelling back and forth between Calcutta and England, working in the former and maintaining a sense of the latter as home. Reflecting on this period, he later wrote: "I was obliged to live economically as owing to my father becoming paralyzed he and my mother and two sisters, were totally dependant [*sic*] on me, so I took no holidays, gave up my horses, and lived as closely as I could to my income."[2] Although the circumstances were specific to the family, this was also not an unusual arrangement for Anglo-Indians, who often reserved much of their income for distant relatives. This was certainly true for many members of the declining gentry and the aspiring middle classes (the Murdochs were among the latter), whose familial lifestyles and status in the metropole often depended on their profits from empire. At the same time, while Henry Jr. may have sacrificed expected luxuries, living "closely" to his income likely still involved conspicuous displays of imperial authority and middle-class respectability in Calcutta.[3] In any case, this arrangement did not negatively affect his financial security and future. Around 1865, he was able to return to England, having saved enough money to purchase Calverley Lodge in Tunbridge Wells, one heart of the Anglo-Indian repatriate community in Britain.[4] Three years later, he married Janet Ellis, and they raised six children while he painted watercolour landscapes and lived off his Ewing and Co. savings in semi-retirement in Tunbridge Wells.

Henry Jr.'s son Ellis Murdoch followed in his father's footsteps, albeit reluctantly. Born in Tunbridge Wells, he received an education at the Godalming public school, Charterhouse, with fees presumably paid by his father's financial success in India. On graduation, Ellis was pushed to enter the family business, and after a short period of training in Manchester, he moved to Calcutta to work for Ewing and Co. During a brief return to England in 1907, he met Katharine Marjorie Carruthers. Marjorie (as she was known) came from a family of newspaper editors in Inverness, and had already established herself as an imperial traveller and worker in her own right. She had read Classics at Oxford but, as a woman, had not been allowed to matriculate or graduate from the university, and Trinity College Dublin had awarded her degree instead. After completing university, she had taught English first in Egypt and then in Tunbridge Wells. Then she met Ellis, and having known him for perhaps as little as ten days, decided to board a ship to follow him back to India. They married on her arrival in Bombay and lived in Calcutta, where their first son was born. Ellis hated the work, however, and he and Marjorie did not want to settle in South Asia in the long term, so the family moved back to the Murdoch home base in Tunbridge Wells, where they lived on Henry Jr.'s estate and Ellis's own imperial profits, and where two more sons were born.

In 1913, when their youngest son, David, was only a year old, Ellis and Marjorie Carruthers Murdoch moved once more. This time, they looked west to the Okanagan region of British Columbia, where they hoped to find a permanent settler future for the family. In the early twentieth century, the Okanagan was booming with middle-class English migrants, promising families like the Murdochs – many of whom similarly hoped to retire from careers in India – a respectable settler home and a profitable, comfortable orcharding life.[5] Its general popularity as an English destination mattered, but the Murdochs' decision to move to the Okanagan was familial too. Marjorie's brother, Ted, had moved there from Inverness decades earlier when his mother's British Columbian cousin promised him work. In the intervening years, Ted had established himself as a successful local settler, heading major orcharding operations in the Kelowna area.[6] So Ellis, Marjorie, and their sons moved to Kelowna to settle near extended family. One daughter was born there, while Ellis worked for the insurance company Hewetson and Mantle. In 1920, they bought a twenty-acre farm in the nearby Okanagan Mission. This marked a striking shift for the family. As their son David later noted, Marjorie had an academic background and "had never kept house without help," while Ellis had experienced "no manual labour of any kind, and an adult life up to that time spent in office jobs."[7] The family struggled on the farm, but they persisted as the children grew up. David remembered, however, that even as his parents made a home in the Okanagan, they "tried hard to bring [the children] up to speak with a proper English accent or, as they would have put it, to save [them] from acquiring a Canadian accent."[8] In the early twentieth century, in other words, the Murdochs' imperial trajectories came to rest for a time in British Columbia, while England retained its power as an imagined home for the family.

This is a partial and gendered story of one family's mobility across the British imperial world and eventual settlement in British Columbia. Beyond the frayed edges of family memory, the Murdochs left only fleeting imprints in the archive. These suggest that, although they were never significant political or economic actors in any of these colonial places, they were nonetheless woven into the fabric of formal and informal empire. From Gibraltar to India, they contributed to the extension of British trade and economic power. They justified imperial rule in South Asia by repeating racializing arguments inflected with British jingoism, and participated in what might be understood as a civilizing mission of education in Egypt. In England, they brought imperial profits home to perform middle-class respectability, and they projected the confidence and promise of empire for other metropolitan Britons. In British Columbia, they became settler bodies on the ground, hoping to contribute to the creation of an English society there, and purchasing and occupying land on the unceded territory of the Syilx (Okanagan) people. In short, as they moved through these imperial circuits, the family helped to establish and sustain structures of inequality, dispossession, and British rule in diverse colonial places.

Read alongside other middle-class white British families, the Murdochs' story is unremarkable. In their multi-generational criss-crossed routes around the world, they travelled common paths of British migration for common reasons. For a century, the Murdochs, like many other such families, used mobility as an intentional strategy to protect or strengthen their economic position and social status. Again and again, they drew on the profits of empire to sustain the family, and always believed they could return "home" to the metropole when their endeavours succeeded or went awry. Britons looked to follow these paths of migration because they were convinced that colonial places afforded them opportunities, whether their families already had extensive histories of mobility or were contemplating a first move from the metropole. Indeed, the empire promised white Britons a wide range of privileges and possibilities withheld from others, including political power, legal rights, and sweeping social advantages. In this broader imperial context, settler colonies and dominions offered particular promises such as land, social mobility, more comfortable work, and a stable future in one place. Thus, although the Murdochs' experiences were specific to them, their story is also part of a much wider pattern of imperial possibility and mobility.[9] By the outbreak of the First World War, this kind of migration had brought many British families to the territory currently known as British Columbia, and, in turn, had brought an early settler British Columbia into the British Empire and the Canadian dominion.

Families like the Murdochs have formed the subject of this book. More specifically, the book has examined British families with members in British Columbia between 1858 and 1914 who maintained at least some epistolary contact with relatives in the United Kingdom. It has argued that their trans-imperial correspondence constituted a widely produced and circulated body of sources that both shaped and revealed the foundations of settler colonialism in British Columbia. In this pivotal period, the nascent settler society and its imagined future relied on British migration, which in turn necessitated individual settlers' temporary or permanent separation from extended relatives, if not also nuclear family. While some embraced this opportunity to cut ties, many other Britons wrote family letters in everyday separations and moments of crisis. In these letters, they mitigated and made sense of the personal distances integral to British Columbian lives, and shared information, materials, and emotions that sustained settlers' endeavours and constituted the trans-imperial family. At the same time, their correspondence was also an important medium that produced and transmitted family forms of colonial knowledge about British Columbia. Through emotional tones, common topics, and embedded silences, settlers focused on explaining their everyday lives. In the process, they almost entirely disregarded Indigenous people and non-Indigenous people of colour, as well as other challenges to white British settler claims to dominance and belonging. Ultimately, Britons used correspondence to rewrite British Columbia as an unremarkable settler home – at its heart, a familiar and familial place in the empire.

Through this argument, the book has generated new understandings of the history of the British Empire, British Columbia, and settler colonialism. In the British context, it has confirmed and extended the insights of the new imperial history scholarship by suggesting that family letters were a powerful way through which the empire came home to the metropole. Millions of people in the United Kingdom had relatives abroad in the long nineteenth century, and for many of them, the empire was not something irrelevant that existed beyond their attention and familiarity. Rather, through relatives' migrations and long-distance communications, the empire became woven into the fabric of the British family itself. While the post moved information and materials from all parts of the empire and beyond, it served as a particularly significant route by which metropolitan residents came to understand and connect with colonial sites like British Columbia, which were relatively seldom discussed in newspapers, fiction, political debates, or other representations of empire in the United Kingdom. It was specifically through family correspondence – produced by diverse people and widely circulated in personal networks – that British Columbia penetrated metropolitan Britons' daily lives and knowledge, and reconfigured the boundaries and forms of their relationships. We cannot fully understand the relationship between metropole and empire without engaging with family correspondence. These letters rendered colonial places like British Columbia not as a mere margin but as an intimate part of both family and empire at home.

In the British Columbian context, this book has focused on white Britons, a comparatively privileged group who were most involved in building the emergent settler order and who benefited most from it. On the one hand, this is not new; these people have long been the traditional subjects of history writing in Canada and elsewhere, and only relatively recently have scholars undertaken critical work to unsettle this dominance by centering the perspectives of Indigenous people, people of colour, and more marginalized white settlers. On the other hand, I contend, we have still not grappled with the affective and everyday configurations of white settler power in Canada, which should be understood as crucial and complicit in colonialism. Taking up this point, this book has urged an understanding of settler colonialism that takes seriously the power and consequences of the personal lives of British settlers. The settler colonial project was (and is) rooted in dispossession, race, inequality, and exclusion, but none of this was possible or sustainable in the late nineteenth or early twentieth centuries without these Britons' personal commitments to British Columbia as a conceivable and comfortable home.

In this spirit, my particular argument is rooted in British Columbia, but it speaks to wider patterns in the British Empire and illuminates something fundamental to the history of settler colonialism more broadly – namely, its trans-imperial and personal nature. Even so-called ordinary settlers should be understood as what, in another context, historian Mary Procida has called "active agents in imperial politics."[10] The existing scholarship most often explores settler colonialism through Indigenous-settler-state relations within the borders of a given place, often with particular attention to the state's most powerful representatives. In the nineteenth and early twentieth centuries, however, the proliferating but incipient settler colonial societies in the British Empire depended on significant numbers of white British people with individual and collective plans to leave former homes, experience separation from families, and settle for the long term. Without their work to translate broad settler colonial ideas into something unremarkable, personal, and everyday, these nascent political projects would have been neither thinkable nor enduring. In this book, I have asserted that the lives, families, and work of British settlers in early settler British Columbia must be considered in this light. These settlers' understandings of British Columbia informed their decisions to move and stay, and their lives there were shaped by their relationships to places and people beyond its borders. This was particularly true of their connections to Britain, which mattered as a political centre, a desired source of migration, a cultural referent point, and a familial home. A study of family correspondence is one way to approach this larger point. The post could facilitate Britons' initial migration to a settler colony, and once they were there, offered them an important medium through which to maintain family connections, explain their lives, and come to terms with a new home in conversation with elsewhere. In these ways, archived family letters shed light on a local and global history of settler colonialism, which recognizes settlers as people with longer and wider personal lives that they brought to bear on the colonial projects and places they built, with profound and long-lasting consequences.

To develop this discussion, I have engaged with the affective and mundane concerns that dominated British family letters, as well as the silences interwoven in these. In particular, I have noted that letter writers focused on their everyday lives and family relationships, and in the process almost entirely ignored Indigenous-settler relations, violence, land and immigration policy, and settler anxiety – the primary motors that drive the scholarship in British imperial history, settler colonial studies, and Canadian colonial historiography. My conclusion has been neither that these topics were unimportant because they were absent from letters, nor that these sources were unimportant because they did not discuss these topics; rather, they are significant as relative silences. Reading for content and absence, I first considered what Britons wrote in family letters, and then asked what could not be said or could go without saying. This approach has offered a critical new lens onto the social and everyday configurations of settler power, which were rooted in expressed concerns as well as in what was ignored, left unspoken, or intentionally muffled. Overall, the foundations of settler colonialism were laid in British Columbia because diverse British settlers came to understand it as an unremarkable place for themselves and their families, while normalizing or disregarding challenges to this understanding. Their trans-imperial correspondence supported and revealed this process as intimately personal, widely shared, and powerful.

This argument is based on my reading of family letters that descendants and others preserved with care, then donated to public repositories. While correspondents were diverse in many ways, the parameters of the study and the limitations of the archive mean that thousands of voices and letters – especially those of women, children, less powerful families, and non-British people – have not been included here. I also recognize that I have built this discussion on texts that were intended to be confined within limited circles of known people, and that the writers can no longer grant or refuse consent for my use of their letters beyond these boundaries. At the same time, I believe that we must examine the politics of personal relationships and interrogate the powerful assumptions embedded in privately expressed ideas in order to understand settler colonialism as a social formation. Seeking an ethical balance between these points, I have sought to develop an analysis of publicly available epistolary content and silence that does justice to their writers' complexity and humanity while recognizing their power, privilege, and impact in their historical contexts.[11] In this, my intention has not been to pass judgment, evoking either sympathy or disgust for Britons as individual imperial agents and settlers, but rather to understand them as people and families who played an important role during a formative period in British Columbia's history. Above all, my aim has been to dispel any sense of settler colonialism or British imperialism as unified and abstract projects of caricatured colonizers with singular aims to dominate, extract, dispossess, eliminate, and settle. A sustained reading of family letters has offered instead a more fractured, familiar, diffuse, and difficult colonial history embedded in a range of people's everyday concerns.

Through this approach, this book has traced a history of empire, migration, and settler colonialism that is rooted in the late nineteenth and early twentieth centuries but refuses any easy distance from the present. In shared and different ways, we all inherit the legacies of this history, which continues to have profound personal and structural impacts on the world in which we live today. Family is one thread that connects this past and present, shaping us whether its stories have been remembered, adapted, forgotten, erased, or stolen from descendants. In my case, the stories I know are intimately connected to the history in this book. In the years that followed their arrival in the Okanagan, the Murdochs remained settlers in British Columbia. I know this because David Carruthers Murdoch, the infant who arrived in Kelowna in 1913, was my maternal grandfather. He spent most of his adulthood in Vancouver, where my mother grew up. In turn, I was born and raised on W̲SÁNEC (Saanich) territory on southern Vancouver Island. Today, British Columbia feels like my home in part because the Murdochs believed it could be theirs in 1913. This remained true even during the four years when I lived in southern England, one of my ancestral homes and a place that never entirely came to feel like mine. In this sense, I am not only a historian in this project but also a descendant and direct beneficiary of its subjects.

At the same time, I am shaped by and responsible to other family stories too. In this same period, my father's family threaded across the Pacific world between Japan, Hawai'i, and the west coast of North America, travelling mostly well-established routes of Asian migration. I think that, like the Murdochs, they too moved in search of jobs, security, love, and adventure, and their migrations brought them to occupy Indigenous lands where they helped to make settler societies and economies work. But their stories were also configured by decades of racialized border control and state violence, the particular exploitation of their labour, and their political, legal, and social exclusion from full belonging in the aspiring "white men's countries" where they settled.[12] This book has centred people like the Murdochs, rather than other families – both like and unlike the Ishiguros – who were also significant in settler colonial histories even as they and their perspectives were rendered less visible in British sources and archives. In this sense, the long-nineteenth-century Murdoch and Ishiguro family stories have not only made me and shaped my place and home in the present; read together, they are also indelible reminders that the letters in this book were formed from both content and silence, reflecting a history of settler colonialism marked by the inextricable connections between migration and dispossession, privilege and marginalization, possibility and exclusion, the spoken and the unspoken.

Whatever our own family stories, the past remains embedded in our lives and built into the world around us. Indigenous people's resistance to colonialism builds on a continuous history since European people first arrived in their territories, and their active survival and sovereignty span millennia there. Within this much longer history, the legacies of the late nineteenth and early twentieth centuries loom especially large in the political, legal, economic, and social structures of Canada, still built on the aspirational foundations of a white settler dominion laid in these years. Between the mid-nineteenth and early twentieth centuries, the Indian Act, the reserve system, residential schools, and treaties (or their absence in much of British Columbia) were created, and settler colonial forms of social and economic inequality calcified along with patterns of settler disregard. Current debates over land claims, resource extraction, reconciliation, gendered and racialized violence, mass incarceration, poverty, child apprehension, and Indigenous-state relations grow from these origins. Today, any efforts to address what Emma Battell Lowman and Adam Barker have aptly termed the "settler problem" in Canada must contend with the structural and personal ways in which we live with the late nineteenth and early twentieth centuries in the present.[13]

This book urges our engagement with the history of empire, migration, and settler colonialism in this spirit. Embedded in family letters is the familiarity through which British settlers came to be at home in and with British Columbia, taking for granted their role, comfort, power, and belonging there. That so many settlers continue to be at home with Canada speaks to the enduring legacies of this history, as they leave the colonial order largely unrecognized, unremarked, and unchallenged in all its familiarity.[14] History offers the tools to uncover, understand, and ultimately unsettle this normal at its very roots. Taking up such tools, this book has sought to explain the formative years of settler colonial British Columbia in a new way. It has traced the contours of a trans-imperial and personal everyday at the heart of British settlers' relationship to this place. It has considered the significance of silence, indifference, and disregard. It has acknowledged the power of ordinary people. It has confronted the familiarity of this past. And in so doing, it has called us to render remarkable what goes without saying. What is it to be at home?

Notes

Introduction

1 Robert Burnaby to brother Tom, Victoria, 8 June 1860, in Anne Burnaby McLeod and Pixie McGeachie, eds., *Land of Promise: Robert Burnaby's Letters from Colonial British Columbia 1858–1863* (Burnaby: City of Burnaby, 2002), 143. All quotations from letters use the original or published spelling and emphasis, except when additions or clarifications are required for understanding.

2 This includes the separate colonies of Vancouver Island and British Columbia between 1858 and their amalgamation in 1866. Throughout this book, I denote the specific colonies when relevant, but for clarity and succinctness in general discussion, I also use the term "British Columbia" to refer broadly to the territory united under this name in 1866.

3 Emma Battell Lowman and Adam J. Barker, *Settler: Identity and Colonialism in 21st Century Canada* (Halifax: Fernwood, 2015). See also Patrick Wolfe, *Settler Colonialism and the Transformation of Anthropology: The Politics and Poetics of an Ethnographic Event* (London: Cassell, 1999); Caroline Elkins and Susan Pederson, eds., *Settler Colonialism in the Twentieth Century: Projects, Practices, Legacies* (New York: Routledge, 2005); Annie Coombes, ed., *Rethinking Settler Colonialism: History and Memory in Australia, Canada, Aotearoa New Zealand and South Africa* (Manchester: Manchester University Press, 2006); Patrick Wolfe, "Settler Colonialism and the Elimination of the Native," *Journal of Genocide Research* 8, 4 (2006): 387–409; Lisa Ford, *Settler Sovereignty: Jurisdiction and Indigenous People in America and Australia, 1788–1836* (Cambridge, MA: Harvard University Press, 2010); Tracey Banivanua Mar and Penelope Edmonds, eds., *Making Settler Colonial Space: Perspectives on Race, Place and Identity* (Basingstoke, UK: Palgrave Macmillan, 2010); Lorenzo Veracini, *Settler Colonialism: A Theoretical Overview* (Basingstoke, UK: Palgrave Macmillan, 2010); Scott Lauria Morgensen, *Spaces between Us: Queer Settler Colonialism and Indigenous Decolonization* (Minneapolis: University of Minnesota Press, 2011); and Edward Cavanagh, *Settler Colonialism and Land Rights in South Africa: Possession and Dispossession on the Orange River* (Basingstoke, UK: Palgrave Macmillan, 2013).

4 Key works on colonialism in early settler British Columbia include Adele Perry, *On the Edge of Empire: Gender, Race, and the Making of British Columbia, 1849–1871* (Toronto: University of Toronto Press, 2001); R. Cole Harris, *Making Native Space: Colonialism, Resistance, and Reserves in British Columbia* (Vancouver: UBC Press, 2002); R.W. Sandwell, *Contesting Rural Space: Land Policy and Practices of Resettlement on Saltspring Island, 1859–1891* (Montreal and Kingston: McGill-Queen's University Press, 2005); Renisa Mawani, *Colonial Proximities: Crossracial Encounters and Juridical Truths in British Columbia, 1871–1921* (Vancouver: UBC Press, 2009); Penelope Edmonds, *Urbanizing Frontiers:*

Indigenous Peoples and Settlers in 19th-Century Pacific Rim Cities (Vancouver: UBC Press, 2010); Jean Barman, *French Canadians, Furs, and Indigenous Women in the Pacific Northwest* (Vancouver: UBC Press, 2014); and Kenton Storey, *Settler Anxiety at the Outposts of Empire: Colonial Relations, Humanitarian Discourses, and the Imperial Press* (Vancouver: UBC Press, 2016). On the imbrication of settler colonialism with other forms of power and relationship in this context, see Adele Perry, *Colonial Relations: The Douglas-Connolly Family and the Nineteenth-Century Imperial World* (Cambridge: Cambridge University Press, 2015). With its focus on Indigenous-settler relations, this scholarship sits alongside research that centres on Indigenous people. For an overview of related work, see Susan Neylan, "Colonialism and Resettling British Columbia: Canadian Aboriginal Historiography, 1992–2012," and "Unsettling British Columbia: Canadian Aboriginal Historiography, 1992–2012," *History Compass* 11, 10 (2013): 833–58. On similar issues in Western Canada, see, for example, Lesley Erickson, *Westward Bound: Sex, Violence, the Law, and the Making of a Settler Society* (Vancouver: UBC Press, 2011); and Ryan C. Eyford, *White Settler Reserve: New Iceland and the Colonization of the Canadian West* (Vancouver: UBC Press, 2016).

5 Robert Burnaby to brother Tom, Victoria, 8 June 1860, in McLeod and McGeachie, *Land of Promise,* 143.

6 See Elizabeth Vibert, "Real Men Hunt Buffalo: Masculinity, Race and Class in British Fur Traders' Narratives," *Gender and History* 8, 1 (1996): 4–21; Jean Barman, "Taming Aboriginal Sexuality: Gender, Power, and Race in British Columbia, 1850–1900," *BC Studies* 115/116 (Autumn/Winter 1997/98): 237–66; Adele Perry, "From 'the Hot-Bed of Vice' to the 'Good and Well-Ordered Christian Home': First Nations Housing and Reform in Nineteenth-Century British Columbia," *Ethnohistory* 50, 4 (2003): 587–610; Paige Raibmon, "Living on Display: Colonial Visions of Aboriginal Domestic Spaces," *BC Studies* 140 (2003): 69–89; Paige Raibmon, *Authentic Indians: Episodes of Encounter from the Late-Nineteenth-Century Northwest Coast* (Durham, NC: Duke University Press, 2005); Paige Raibmon, "The Practice of Everyday Colonialism: Indigenous Women at Work in the Hop Fields and Tourist Industry of Puget Sound," *Labor* 3, 3 (Fall 2006): 45–49; John Sutton Lutz, *Makúk: A New History of Aboriginal-White Relations* (Vancouver: UBC Press, 2008), ch. 3; Emma LaRocque, *When the Other Is Me: Native Resistance Discourse, 1850–1990* (Winnipeg: University of Manitoba Press, 2010); Daniel Francis, *The Imaginary Indian: The Image of the Indian in Canadian Culture,* 2nd ed. (Vancouver: Arsenal Pulp Press, 2011); and Kim Anderson, *Recognition of Being: Reconstructing Native Womanhood,* 2nd ed. (Toronto: Women's Press, 2016), ch. 6.

7 The other was written five months later, and focused on a feast and dance near Hope. Robert Burnaby to mother, Victoria, 9 November 1860, in McLeod and McGeachie, *Land of Promise,* 151–152.

8 Robert Burnaby to mother and all, Victoria, 26 December 1858, in McLeod and McGeachie, ibid., 59.

9 Catherine Hall, *Civilising Subjects: Metropole and Colony in the English Imagination 1830–1867* (Chicago: University of Chicago Press, 2002), especially 14.

10 Esmé Cleall, Laura Ishiguro, and Emily J. Manktelow, "Imperial Relations: Histories of Family in the British Empire," *Journal of Colonialism and Commonwealth History* 14, 1 (Spring 2013). For some examples, see Ann Laura Stoler, *Carnal Knowledge and Imperial Power: Race and the Intimate in Colonial Rule* (Berkeley: University of California Press, 2002); Elizabeth Buettner, *Empire Families: Britons and Late Imperial India* (Oxford: Oxford University Press, 2004); Durba Ghosh, *Sex and the Family in Colonial India: The*

Making of Empire (Cambridge: Cambridge University Press, 2006); Sarah Carter, *The Importance of Being Monogamous: Marriage and Nation Building in Western Canada to 1915* (Edmonton: University of Alberta Press and Athabasca University Press, 2008); Tony Ballantyne and Antoinette Burton, eds., *Moving Subjects: Gender, Mobility, and Intimacy in an Age of Global Empire* (Urbana: University of Illinois Press, 2009); Anne F. Hyde, *Empires, Nations, and Families: A History of the North American West, 1800–1860* (Lincoln: University of Nebraska Press, 2011); Emma Rothschild, *The Inner Life of Empires: An Eighteenth-Century History* (Princeton, NJ: Princeton University Press, 2011); Esmé Cleall, *Missionary Discourses of Difference: Negotiating Otherness in the British Empire, 1840–1900* (Basingstoke, UK: Palgrave Macmillan, 2012); Angela Wanhalla, *Matters of the Heart: A History of Interracial Marriage in New Zealand* (Auckland: Auckland University Press, 2013); Emily J. Manktelow, *Missionary Families: Race, Gender and Generation on the Spiritual Frontier* (Manchester: Manchester University Press, 2013); and Jane McCabe, *Race, Tea and Colonial Resettlement: Imperial Families, Interrupted* (London: Bloomsbury, 2017).

11 For example, Kathryn Bridge, *Henry & Self: The Private Life of Sarah Crease 1826–1922* (Victoria: Sono Nis, 1996); Barman, "Taming Aboriginal Sexuality"; Perry, *On the Edge of Empire*; Chris Clarkson, *Domestic Reforms: Political Visions and Family Regulation in British Columbia, 1862–1940* (Vancouver: UBC Press, 2007); Richard Phillips, "Settler Colonialism and the Nuclear Family," *Canadian Geographer* 53, 2 (Summer 2009): 239–53; and Laura Ishiguro, "'Growing Up and Grown Up ... in Our Future City': Discourses of Childhood and Settler Futurity in Colonial British Columbia," *BC Studies* 190 (Summer 2016): 15–37. For a Canadian overview, see Cynthia R. Comacchio, *The Infinite Bonds of Family: Domesticity in Canada, 1850–1940* (Toronto: University of Toronto Press, 1999).

12 Exceptions include Jean Barman, *Sojourning Sisters: The Lives and Letters of Jessie and Annie McQueen* (Toronto: University of Toronto Press, 2003); and Perry, *Colonial Relations.*

13 Leonore Davidoff et al., *The Family Story: Blood, Contract and Intimacy, 1830–1960* (London: Longman, 1999); and Adele Perry, "The State of Empire: Reproducing Colonialism in British Columbia, 1849–1871," *Journal of Colonialism and Colonial History* 2, 2 (Fall 2001).

14 Perry, *Colonial Relations*, 7.

15 Among a large related body of work, see Linda Colley, "Britishness and Otherness: An Argument," *Journal of British Studies* 31, 4 (October 1992): 309–29; and Kate Darian-Smith, Patricia Grimshaw, and Stuart Macintyre, eds., *Britishness Abroad: Transnational Movements and Imperial Cultures* (Melbourne: Melbourne University Press, 2007). On the complications of identities within "Britishness," see, for example, Onni Gust, "Remembering and Forgetting the Scottish Highlands: Sir James Mackintosh and the Forging of a British Imperial Identity," *Journal of British Studies* 52, 3 (July 2013): 615–37. In the British Columbia context, I sometimes refer to these people in shorthand as settlers, but this should be read with the understanding that white Britons were not the only settlers there.

16 For a summary, see Davidoff et al., *The Family Story*, 123–27. See also Simon Szreter, *Fertility, Class and Gender in Britain 1860–1940* (Cambridge: Cambridge University Press, 1993); Leonore Davidoff and Catherine Hall, *Family Fortunes: Men and Women of the English Middle Class 1780–1850*, rev. ed. (London: Routledge, 2002); Leonore Davidoff, "The Legacy of the Nineteenth-Century Bourgeois Family and the Wool Merchant's

Son," *Transactions of the Royal Historical Society,* Sixth Series, 14 (2004): 25–46; and Robert Morris, *Men, Women and Property in England, 1780–1870: A Social and Economic History of Family Strategies amongst the Leeds Middle Class* (Cambridge: Cambridge University Press, 2005).

17 Davidoff et al., *The Family Story,* 116–23. See also John Burnett, *Destiny Obscure: Autobiographies of Childhood, Education and Family from the 1820s to the 1920s* (first published 1982; republished Abingdon, UK: Routledge, 2013); Julie-Marie Strange, *Fatherhood and the British Working Class, 1865–1914* (Cambridge: Cambridge University Press, 2015); and Nigel Goose and Katrina Honeyman, eds., *Childhood and Child Labour in Industrial England: Diversity and Agency, 1750–1914* (London: Routledge, 2016).

18 Davidoff et al., ibid., 114–16. See also Leonore Davidoff, *The Best Circles: Society, Etiquette and the Season* (London: Croon Helm, 1973).

19 For an overview, see Davidoff et al., *The Family Story;* and for a germinal text, Davidoff and Hall, *Family Fortunes.* For considerations of empire, see, for example, John Tosh, *Manliness and Masculinities in Nineteenth-Century Britain: Essays on Gender, Family and Empire* (Harlow, UK: Pearson Longman, 2005), chs. 8 and 9; and Margot Finn, "Family Formations: Anglo India and the Familial Proto-State," in *Structures and Transformations in Modern British History,* ed. David Feldman and Jon Lawrence (Cambridge: Cambridge University Press, 2011), 100–17. As reflected in note 10, above, there is also a large and rich scholarship on families in the British Empire, but this remains comparatively separate from the study of British families in the metropole.

20 Marjory Harper, *Adventurers and Exiles: The Great Scottish Exodus* (London: Profile, 2003), 2. See also Charlotte Erickson, *Leaving England: Essays on British Emigration in the Nineteenth Century* (Ithaca, NY: Cornell University Press, 1994); Angela McCarthy, ed., *A Global Clan: Scottish Migrant Networks and Identities since the Eighteenth Century* (London: Tauris, 2006); Buettner, *Empire Families;* Marjory Harper and Stephen Constantine, *Migration and Empire* (Oxford: Oxford University Press, 2010); Robert Bickers, ed., *Settlers and Expatriates: Britons Over the Seas* (Oxford: Oxford University Press, 2010); and Kent Fedorowich and Andrew Thompson, eds., *Empire, Migration and Identity in the British World* (Manchester: Manchester University Press, 2013).

21 For example, see Patrick A. Dunae, *Gentlemen Emigrants: From the British Public Schools to the Canadian Frontier* (Vancouver: Douglas and McIntyre, 1981); Jean Barman, "Ethnicity in the Pursuit of Status: British Middle and Upper-Class Emigration to British Columbia in the Late Nineteenth and Early Twentieth Centuries," *Canadian Ethnic Studies* 18, 1 (1986): 32–51; Lisa Chilton, *Agents of Empire: British Female Migration to Canada and Australia, 1860–1930* (Toronto: University of Toronto Press, 2007); Timothy S. Forest, "Highland Warriors or 'Scotch Coolies'? Hebridean Crofters in British Columbia, 1887–1893," *Pacific Northwest Quarterly* 102, 2 (2011): 79–90; Ellen Boucher, *Empire's Children: Child Emigration, Welfare, and the Decline of the British World, 1869–1967* (Cambridge: Cambridge University Press, 2014); and Elizabeth A. Scott, "'The Ill-Name of the Old Country': London's Assisted Emigrants, British Unemployment Policy, and Canadian Immigration Restriction, 1905–1910," *Journal of the Canadian Historical Association* 26, 1 (2015): 99–130.

22 Michael Anderson, "The Social Implications of Demographic Change," in *The Cambridge Social History of Britain,* vol. 2, *People and Their Environment,* ed. F.M.L. Thompson (Cambridge: Cambridge University Press, 1990), 9.

23 While more work remains to be done on the people of colour crewing on these ships, existing research includes David Chuenyan Lai, "From Downtown Slums to Suburban

Malls: Chinese Migration and Settlement in Canada," in *The Chinese Diaspora: Space, Place, Mobility, and Identity,* ed. Laurence J.C. Ma and Carolyn Cartier (Lanham, MD: Rowman and Littlefield, 2003), 311–12; Jean Barman and Bruce McIntyre Watson, *Leaving Paradise: Indigenous Hawaiians in the Pacific Northwest, 1787–1898* (Honolulu: University of Hawai'i Press, 2006); Matt K. Matsuda, *Pacific Worlds: A History of Seas, Peoples, and Cultures* (Cambridge: Cambridge University Press, 2012), 188; and David Igler, *The Great Ocean: Pacific Worlds from Captain Cook to the Gold Rush* (Oxford: Oxford University Press, 2013), 81.

24 Mackie, "The Colonization of Vancouver Island," 30 and 40; Richard Mackie, "The Colonization of Vancouver Island, 1849–1858," *BC Studies* 96 (Winter 1992/93): 3–40; Cole Harris, "Towards a Geography of White Power in the Cordilleran Fur Trade," *Canadian Geographer* 39, 2 (June 1995), especially 132; Jeremy Mouat, "Situating Vancouver Island in the British World, 1846–49," *BC Studies* 145 (Spring 2005): 5–30; and Perry, *Colonial Relations.*

25 Robert A.J. McDonald, *Making Vancouver: Class, Status, and Social Boundaries, 1863–1913* (Vancouver: UBC Press, 1996); Jason Patrick Bennett, "Apple of the Empire: Landscape and Imperial Identity in Turn-of-the-Century British Columbia," *Journal of the Canadian Historical Association* 9, 1 (1998): 63–92; Cole Harris, *The Resettlement of British Columbia: Essays on Colonialism and Geographical Change* (Vancouver: UBC Press, 1997), ch. 3 and 9, especially 252; and David Vogt and David Alexander Gamble, "'You Don't Suppose the Dominion Government Wants to Cheat the Indians?': The Grand Trunk Pacific Railway and the Fort George Reserve, 1908–12," *BC Studies* 166 (2010): 55–72.

26 For one overview, see Olive Patricia Dickason with David T. McNab, *Canada's First Nations: A History of Founding Peoples from Earliest Times,* 4th ed. (Don Mills, ON: Oxford University Press, 2009). A large field on British Columbia includes Harris, *Making Native Space,* pts. 2 and 3; Sarah de Leeuw, "'If Anything Is to Be Done with the Indian, We Must Catch Him Very Young': Colonial Constructions of Aboriginal Children and the Geographies of Indian Residential Schooling in British Columbia, Canada," *Children's Geographies* 7, 2 (2009): 123–40; Leslie A. Robertson with the Kwagu'l Gixsam Clan, *Standing Up with Ga'axsta'las: Jane Constance Cook and the Politics of Memory, Church, and Custom* (Vancouver: UBC Press, 2012); Megan Harvey, "Story People: Stó:lō-State Relations and Indigenous Literacies in British Columbia, 1864–1874," *Journal of the Canadian Historical Association* 24, 1 (2013): 51–88; and Sabina Trimble, "Storying Swí:lhcha: Place Making and Power at a Stó:lo Landmark," *BC Studies* 190 (2016): 39–66.

27 For one summary of this period, see Jean Barman, *West beyond the West: A History of British Columbia,* 3rd ed. (Toronto: University of Toronto Press, 2007), including demographic data on 64, 68, and 136. See also Perry, *On the Edge of Empire;* Cole Harris, "How Did Colonialism Dispossess? Comments from an Edge of Empire," *Annals of the Association of American Geographers* 94, 1 (2004): 165–82; Sandwell, *Contesting Rural Space;* Harris, *Making Native Space,* pt. 1; Edmonds, *Urbanizing Frontiers;* and Storey, *Settler Anxiety.*

28 T.W.C. Murdoch and Frederic Rogers to Herman Merivale, 24 November 1859, National Archives of the United Kingdom (NAUK), CO 305/12, 11630, 152–53, from *Colonial Despatches of Vancouver Island and British Columbia 1846–1871* digital archive, http://bcgenesis.uvic.ca/imageBrowser.htm?image=co_305_12_00155r.jpg.

29 Adele Perry, "Hardy Backwoodsmen, Wholesome Women, and Steady Families: Immigration and the Construction of a White Society in Colonial British Columbia, 1849–1871," *Histoire Sociale* 33, 66 (November 2000): 343–60; Perry, *On the Edge of Empire;*

Chilton, *Agents of Empire;* and Robert Hogg, *Men and Manliness on the Frontier: Queensland and British Columbia in the Mid-Nineteenth Century* (Basingstoke, UK: Palgrave Macmillan, 2012).

30 John Douglas Belshaw, *Becoming British Columbia: A Population History* (Vancouver: UBC Press, 2009), 42; and Robert Galois and Cole Harris, "Recalibrating Society: The Population Geography of British Columbia in 1881," *Canadian Geographer* 38, 1 (March 1994): 38–39 and 41–43. See also Perry, *On the Edge of Empire,* 13–14.

31 On this point in British Columbia and northwestern North American more broadly, see Raibmon, *Authentic Indians;* Andy Parnaby, "'The Best Men That Ever Worked the Lumber': Aboriginal Longshoremen on Burrard Inlet, BC, 1863–1939," *Canadian Historical Review* 87, 1 (2006): 53–78; Lutz, *Makúk;* Sherry Farrell Racette, "Nimble Fingers and Strong Backs: First Nations and Métis Women in Fur Trade and Rural Economies," in *Indigenous Women and Work: From Labor to Activism,* ed. Carol Williams (Champaign: University of Illinois Press, 2012), 148–62; and Mica Jorgenson, "'Into That Country to Work': Aboriginal Economic Activities during Barkerville's Gold Rush," *BC Studies* 185 (2015): 109–36.

32 Among a very large body of scholarship, see Crawford Kilian, *Go Do Some Great Thing: The Black Pioneers of British Columbia* (Vancouver: Douglas and McIntyre, 1978); Timothy J. Stanley, "'Chinamen, Wherever We Go': Chinese Nationalism and Guangdong Merchants in British Columbia, 1871–1911," *Canadian Historical Review* 77, 4 (1996): 475–503; Wade Compton, ed., *Bluesprint: Black British Columbian Literature and Orature* (Vancouver: Arsenal Pulp Press, 2001); Barman and Watson, *Leaving Paradise;* Enakshi Dua, "Exclusion through Inclusion: Female Asian Migration in the Making of Canada as a White Settler Nation," *Gender, Place and Culture* 14, 4 (2007): 445–66; Henry Yu, "Refracting Pacific Canada: Seeing Our Uncommon Past," *BC Studies* 156/157 (2007): 5–10; Mawani, *Colonial Proximities;* Nayan Shah, *Stranger Intimacy: Contesting Race, Sexuality and the Law in the North American West* (Berkeley: University of California Press, 2011); Andrea Geiger, *Subverting Exclusion: Transpacific Encounters with Race, Caste, and Borders, 1885–1928* (New Haven, CT: Yale University Press, 2011); Jean Barman, "Beyond Chinatown: Chinese Men and Indigenous Women in Early British Columbia," *BC Studies* 177 (2013): 39–64; Tzu-I Chung, "Kwong Lee & Company and Early Trans-Pacific Trade: From Canton, Hong Kong, to Victoria and Barkerville," *BC Studies* 185 (2015): 137–60; and Shelly Ikebuchi, *From Slave Girls to Salvation: Gender, Race, and Victoria's Chinese Rescue Home, 1886–1923* (Vancouver: UBC Press, 2015).

33 Ann Laura Stoler and Frederick Cooper, "Between Metropole and Colony: Rethinking a Research Agenda," in *Tensions of Empire: Colonial Cultures in a Bourgeois World,* ed. Frederick Cooper and Ann Laura Stoler (Berkeley: University of California Press, 1997), especially 4; Alan Lester, *Imperial Networks: Creating Identities in Nineteenth-Century South Africa and Britain* (London: Routledge, 2001); Tony Ballantyne, *Orientalism and Race: Aryanism in the British Empire* (Basingstoke, UK: Palgrave Macmillan, 2002); Zoë Laidlaw, *Colonial Connections 1815–45: Patronage, the Information Revolution and Colonial Government* (Manchester: Manchester University Press, 2005); Catherine Hall and Sonya O. Rose, eds., *At Home with the Empire: Metropolitan Culture and the Imperial World* (Cambridge: Cambridge University Press, 2006); and Tony Ballantyne, *Webs of Empire: Locating New Zealand's Colonial Past* (Wellington: Bridget Williams, 2012). See also Catherine Hall, ed., *Cultures of Empire, A Reader: Colonisers in Britain and the Empire in the Nineteenth and Twentieth Centuries* (Manchester: Manchester University Press, 2000); Hall, *Civilising Subjects;* Kathleen Wilson, ed., *A New Imperial History: Culture, Identity*

and Modernity in Britain and the Empire, 1660–1840 (Cambridge: Cambridge University Press, 2004); Stephen Howe, ed., *The New Imperial Histories Reader* (London: Routledge, 2009); and Antoinette Burton, *Empire in Question: Reading, Writing, and Teaching British Imperialism* (Durham, NC: Duke University Press, 2011). For an example that maintains a distinction between Britain and empire, see Bernard Porter, *The Absent-Minded Imperialists: What the British Really Thought about Empire* (Oxford: Oxford University Press, 2004).

34 See Adele Perry, "Canada and the Empires of the Past," *History Compass* 1, 1 (2003): 1–4; and Lisa Chilton, "Canada and the British Empire: A Review Essay," *Canadian Historical Review* 89, 1 (March 2008): 89–95. Since these, key work related to British Columbia includes Edmonds, *Urbanizing Frontiers;* Perry, *Colonial Relations;* and Storey, *Settler Anxiety.*

35 Penelope Edmonds, "'I Followed England Round the World': The Rise of Trans-Imperial Anglo-Saxon Exceptionalism, and the Spatial Narratives of Nineteenth-Century British Settler Colonies of the Pacific Rim," in *Re-orienting Whiteness,* ed. Leigh Boucher, Jane Carey, and Katherine Ellinghaus (New York: Palgrave Macmillan, 2009), 99–115; and Marilyn Lake and Henry Reynolds, *Drawing the Global Colour Line: White Men's Countries and the International Challenge of Racial Equality* (Cambridge: Cambridge University Press, 2008). See also James Belich, *Replenishing the Earth: The Settler Revolution and the Rise of the Anglo-World, 1783–1939* (Oxford: Oxford University Press, 2009); Cecilia Morgan, *Building Better Britains? Settler Societies in the British World, 1783–1920* (Toronto: University of Toronto Press, 2016); and Edward Cavanagh and Lorenzo Veracini, eds., *The Routledge Handbook on the History of Settler Colonialism* (New York: Routledge, 2017).

36 Perry, *Colonial Relations,* 263.

37 Wolfe, *Settler Colonialism and the Transformation of Anthropology,* 2.

38 Examples of published letters include *Charlotte Erickson, Invisible Immigrants: The Adaptation of English and Scottish Immigrants in Nineteenth-Century America* (Leicester: Leicester University Press, 1972); David Fitzpatrick, *Oceans of Consolation: Personal Accounts of Irish Migration to Australia* (Cork: Cork University Press, 1994); Judith Hudson Beattie and Helen M. Buss, eds., *Undelivered Letters to Hudson's Bay Company Men on the Northwest Coast of America, 1830–57* (Vancouver: UBC Press, 2003); Cecily Devereux and Kathleen Venema, eds., *Women Writing Home, 1700–1920: Female Correspondence across the British Empire,* vol. 3, Canada (London: Pickering and Chatto, 2006); and Charlotte J. Macdonald, ed., *Women Writing Home, 1700–1920: Female Correspondence across the British Empire,* vol. 5, *New Zealand* (London: Pickering and Chatto, 2006). My archival research on South Asia focused on large collections of correspondence written by fourteen extended British families, though examples from only four are cited in this book. For more on this research, see my dissertation, "Relative Distances: Family and Empire between Britain, British Columbia and India, 1858–1901" (PhD dissertation, University College London, 2011).

39 See David Vincent, *Literacy and Popular Culture: England 1750–1914* (Cambridge: Cambridge University Press, 1993), especially 23 and 30–32; Beattie and Buss, *Undelivered Letters;* and Susan Whyman, *The Pen and the People: English Letter Writers, 1660–1800* (Oxford: Oxford University Press, 2010).

40 See Carolyn Hamilton et al., eds., *Refiguring the Archive* (London: Kluwer, 2002); and Antoinette Burton, ed., *Archive Stories: Facts, Fictions, and the Writing of History* (Durham, NC: Duke University Press, 2005).

41 Among a large body of scholarship, see Rebecca Earle, ed., *Epistolary Selves: Letters and Letter-Writers, 1600–1945* (Aldershot, UK: Ashgate, 1999); Clare Brant, *Eighteenth-Century Letters and British Culture* (Basingstoke, UK: Palgrave Macmillan, 2006); Konstantin Dierks, *In My Power: Letter Writing and Communications in Early America* (Philadelphia: University of Pennsylvania Press, 2009); and Cassandra A. Good, *Founding Friendships: Friendships between Men and Women in the Early American Republic* (Oxford: Oxford University Press, 2015), ch. 5.

42 See Fitzpatrick, *Oceans of Consolation;* Erika Rappaport, "'The Bombay Debt': Letter Writing, Domestic Economies and Family Conflict in Colonial India," *Gender and History* 16, 2 (August 2004): 233–60; Bruce S. Elliott, David A. Gerber, and Suzanne M. Sinke, eds., *Letters across Borders: The Epistolary Practices of International Migrants* (Basingstoke, UK: Palgrave Macmillan, 2006); David A. Gerber, *Authors of Their Lives: The Personal Correspondence of British Immigrants to North America in the Nineteenth Century* (New York: New York University Press, 2006); Sarah M.S. Pearsall, *Atlantic Families: Lives and Letters in the Later Eighteenth Century* (Oxford: Oxford University Press, 2008); Charlotte Macdonald, "Intimacy of the Envelope: Fiction, Commerce, and Empire in the Correspondence of Friends Mary Taylor and Charlotte Brontë, c. 1845–55," in Ballantyne and Burton, *Moving Subjects;* Elizabeth Jane Errington, *Emigrant Worlds and Transatlantic Communities: Migration to Upper Canada in the First Half of the Nineteenth Century* (Kingston and Montreal: McGill-Queen's University Press, 2007), ch. 5; Megan Robertson, "Epistolary Memory: First World War Letters to British Columbia," *BC Studies* 182 (Summer 2014): 125–51; and Alexandra Lindgren-Gibson, "'I Wish I Could See You as Often as I Could See Your Letter': Imperial Anxieties and Working Class Family Life in the Raj," *Journal of Colonialism and Colonial History* 17, 3 (Winter 2016).

43 Barman, *Sojourning Sisters;* and Ryan C. Eyford, "'Close Together, though Miles and Miles Apart': Family, Distance, and Emotion in the Letters of the Taylor Sisters, 1881–1921," *Histoire Sociale* 47, 96 (2015): 67–86.

44 Ann Laura Stoler, *Along the Archival Grain: Epistemic Anxieties and Colonial Common Sense* (Princeton, NJ: Princeton University Press, 2009), especially 50; and Sharon Marcus, *Between Women: Friendship, Desire, and Marriage in Victorian England* (Princeton, NJ: Princeton University Press, 2007), especially 3 and 74–75.

45 Alan Conway, "Preface," in *The Welsh in America: Letters from the Immigrants* (Cardiff: University of Wales Press, 1961), unpaginated, quoted in Bill Jones, "Writing Back: Welsh Emigrants and Their Correspondence in the Nineteenth Century," *North American Journal of Welsh Studies* 5, 1 (Winter 2005): 27.

46 David Lambert and Alan Lester, eds., *Colonial Lives across the British Empire: Imperial Careering in the Long Nineteenth Century* (Cambridge: Cambridge University Press, 2006), 17.

47 Hall and Rose, *At Home with the Empire,* introduction, especially 2 and 22–25. See also Mark Rifkin, *Settler Common Sense: Queerness and Everyday Colonialism in the American Renaissance* (Minneapolis: University of Minnesota Press, 2014).

Chapter 1: "Bind the Empire Together"

1 Quoted in Mrs. Adrian [Rose] Porter, *The Life and Letters of Sir John Henniker Heaton* (London: John Lane, 1916), 177.

2 J. Henniker Heaton, "A Penny Post for the Empire," *The Nineteenth Century: A Monthly Review* 27, 160 (June 1890): 917.

3 For example, Miles Ogborn, *Indian Ink: Script and Print in the Making of the English East India Company* (Chicago: University of Chicago Press, 2007); Konstantin Dierks, *In My Power: Letter Writing and Communications in Early America* (Philadelphia: University of Pennsylvania Press, 2009); and Patrick Joyce, *The State of Freedom: A Social History of the British State Since 1800* (Cambridge: Cambridge University Press, 2013).

4 For an exception that considers personal uses of the postal system, though without attention to empire, see David A. Gerber, *Authors of Their Lives: The Personal Correspondence of British Immigrants to North America in the Nineteenth Century* (New York: New York University Press, 2006), ch. 4.

5 For an overview, see Michael Anderson, "The Social Implications of Demographic Change," in *The Cambridge Social History of Britain*, vol. 2, *People and Their Environment*, ed. F.M.L. Thompson (Cambridge: Cambridge University Press, 1990), 1–70; and Susie L. Steinbach, *Understanding the Victorians: Politics, Culture and Society in Nineteenth-Century Britain*, 2nd ed. (New York: Routledge, 2016).

6 Catherine J. Golden, *Posting It: The Victorian Revolution in Letter Writing* (Gainesville: University Press of Florida, 2009), ch. 1; and Joyce, *The State of Freedom*, 69–70.

7 See Howard Robinson, *Britain's Post Office: A History of Development from the Beginnings to the Present Day* (London: Oxford University Press, 1953); M.J. Daunton, *Royal Mail: The Post Office since 1840* (London: Athlone, 1985); C.R. Perry, *The Victorian Post Office: The Growth of a Bureaucracy* (London: Royal Historical Society, 1992); Christopher Browne, *Getting the Message: The Story of the British Post Office* (Stroud, UK: A. Sutton, 1993); Golden, *Posting It*; and Joyce, *The State of Freedom*.

8 Joyce, ibid., ch. 2.

9 Golden, *Posting It*, 74.

10 Joyce, *The State of Freedom*, 102–20 and 88–90.

11 Golden, *Posting It*, 196; and Joyce, ibid., 65, 68, and 88.

12 Joyce, ibid., 139–40; David Vincent, *Literacy and Popular Culture: England 1750–1914* (Cambridge: Cambridge University Press, 1993), including 47; and Golden, ibid., 68–69.

13 Golden, ibid.

14 For example, on American postal reforms, see Richard R. John, *Spreading the News: The American Postal System from Franklin to Morse* (Cambridge, MA: Harvard University Press, 1998); and David M. Henkin, *The Postal Age: The Emergence of Modern Communications in Nineteenth-Century America* (Chicago: University of Chicago Press, 2007).

15 Joyce, *The State of Freedom*, 124. See also Francis Lyall, *International Communications: The International Telecommunication Union and the Universal Postal Union* (Farnham, UK: Ashgate, 2011), ch. 7; and Douglas Howland, "An Alternative Mode of International Order: The International Administrative Union in the Nineteenth Century," *Review of International Studies* 41, 1 (January 2015): 161–83.

16 Robert M. Pike, "National Interest and Imperial Yearnings: Empire Communications and Canada's Role in Establishing the Imperial Penny Post," *Journal of Imperial and Commonwealth History* 26, 1 (1998): 45, n. 48. For an overview, see Howard Robinson, *Carrying British Mails Overseas* (London: G. Allen and Unwin, 1964).

17 A. Stanley Deaville, "The Colonial Postal Systems of Vancouver Island and British Columbia, 1849–1871," *British Columbia Historical Association Annual Report and Proceedings* 3 (1925): 45–53.

18 Arthur Kennedy, Victoria, 21 September 1864, in James E. Hendrickson, ed., *Journals of the Colonial Legislatures of the Colonies of Vancouver Island and British Columbia,*

1851–1871, vol. I (Victoria: Provincial Archives of British Columbia, 1980), 277–78. For examples, see Hendrickson, *Journals of the Colonial Legislatures:* 31 March 1864, 2 April 1864, and 20 July 1866, in vol. I, 123–24 and 224; 26 June 1861 and 8 October 1861, in vol. II, 281 and 317; 12 September 1864, in vol. III, 173; 4 May 1864 and 18 March 1871, in vol. IV, 241 and 169; and 27 April 1868, in vol. V, 149.

19 Deaville, "The Colonial Postal Systems," 53. See also James Douglas to Edward Bulwer Lytton, Victoria, 5 November 1858, NAUK, CO60/1, 535, from *Colonial Despatches*, http://bcgenesis.uvic.ca/getDoc.htm?id=B58016.scx.

20 Mary Hawks Moody to sister Emily, Victoria, 2 February [1859], British Columbia Archives (BCA), MS-1101, Mary Susanna (Hawks) Moody. Emphasis in original.

21 Henry Crease to parents, Victoria, 12 December 1859, BCA, MS-0055, Crease family, box 10, file 74; Charles Hayward, diary, Victoria, 29 May 1862, City of Victoria Archives (CVIC), PR-118, Charles Hayward, folder 3; and Arthur Kennedy, Victoria, 21 September 1864, in Hendrickson, *Journals of the Colonial Legislatures*, vol. I, 277–78.

22 Robert Burnaby to sister Victoria, 27 November 1859, in Anne Burnaby McLeod and Pixie McGeachie, eds., *Land of Promise: Robert Burnaby's Letters from Colonial British Columbia 1858–1863* (Burnaby: City of Burnaby, 2002), 125.

23 John Christie, diary, [n.p.], 28 July 1861, BCA, MS-0142, John Christie.

24 The postal system's changing state and regulations can be tracked between Canada, Postmaster General, *Canada Official Postal Guide: Comprising the Chief Regulations of the Post Office, Rates of Postage and Other Information, Together with an Alphabetical List of Post Offices in Canada* (Ottawa: Maclean, Roger, 1887) and (Ottawa: Government Printing Bureau, 1914). See also Pike, "National Interest," especially 26; and Chantal Amyot, Bianca Gendreau, and John Willis, *Special Delivery: Canada's Postal Heritage* (Hull, QC: Canadian Museum of Civilization, 2000).

25 Deaville, "Colonial Postal Systems," 56–58.

26 Canada, Postmaster General, *Official Postal Guide* (1887), lxiii.

27 Charles Newcombe to wife Marian, Victoria, 28 October 1883, BCA, MS-1077, Newcombe family, vol. 18, file 1.

28 For example, H. Kidner to daughter Edith Langley, West Lavington, 30 December 1891; and May Mann to cousin Edith Langley, London, 30 October 1907, University of British Columbia Rare Books and Special Collections (UBCSC), RBSC-ARC-1322, Langley family, box 1, files 1 and 2.

29 Leonard Witherby to father, Victoria, 7 May 1899, BCA, PR-1617, H. Leonard Witherby.

30 Thomas (Tommy) Norbury to mother, Fish Lakes, 18 May 1898, BCA, MS-0877, Norbury family, box 1, file 6. See also Cole Harris, "Moving Amid Mountains, 1870–1930," *BC Studies* 58 (Summer 1983): 3; Susan McLeod O'Reilly, *On Track: The Railway Mail Service in Canada* (Hull, QC: Canadian Museum of Civilization, 1992); Cole Harris, *The Resettlement of British Columbia: Essays on Colonialism and Geographical Change* (Vancouver: UBC Press, 1997), ch. 6; and Chantal Amyot and John Willis, *Country Post: Rural Postal Service in Canada, 1880–1945* (Gatineau, QC: Canadian Museum of Civilization, 2003).

31 Pike, "National Interest," 37. See also Gary B. Magee and Andrew S. Thompson, *Empire and Globalisation: Networks of People, Goods and Capital in the British World, c. 1850–1914* (Cambridge: Cambridge University Press, 2010), 83.

32 For example, mother to Philip Goepel, Barnsbury, 12 November 1875, City of Vancouver Archives (CVA), AM-23, Goepel family.

33 Leonard Witherby to father, Victoria, 7 May 1899, BCA, PR-1617, H. Leonard Witherby; and [Edward Lloyd] to Lloyd family, Vancouver, 24 June 1905, CVA, AM-875, Edward

Lloyd, reel M-104. See also J.H. Hamilton, "The 'All-Red Route,' 1893–1953: A History of the Trans-Pacific Mail Service between British Columbia, Australia, and New Zealand," *British Columbia Historical Quarterly* 20 (1956): 1–126; Robert E. Babe, *Telecommunications in Canada: Technology, Industry, and Government* (Toronto: University of Toronto Press, 1990), ch. 5; Robert W.D. Boyce, "Imperial Dreams and National Realities: Britain, Canada and the Struggle for a Pacific Telegraph Cable, 1879–1902," *English Historical Review* 115, 460 (February 2000): 39–70; and Frances M. Steel, "Via New Zealand around the World: The Union Steam Ship Company and the Trans-Pacific Mail Lines, 1880s–1910s," in *Coast to Coast: Case Histories of Modern Pacific Crossings*, ed. Prue Ahrens and Chris Dixon (Newcastle upon Tyne: Cambridge Scholars, 2010), 59–75.

34 Among others, see Mary Louise Pratt, *Imperial Eyes: Travel Writing and Transculturation* (London: Routledge, 1992); Antoinette Burton, *Dwelling in the Archive: Women Writing House, Home, and History in Late Colonial India* (Oxford: Oxford University Press, 2003); Julie F. Codell, ed., *Imperial Co-Histories: National Identities and the British and Colonial Press* (Madison, NJ: Fairleigh Dickinson University Press, 2003); Anna Johnston, *Missionary Writing and Empire, 1800–1860* (Cambridge: Cambridge University Press, 2003); Simon J. Potter, *News and the British World: The Emergence of an Imperial Press System, 1876–1922* (Oxford: Oxford University Press, 2003); Catherine Hall, *Macaulay and Son: Architects of Imperial Britain* (New Haven, CT: Yale University Press, 2012); Ogborn, *Indian Ink*; and Joyce, *The State of Freedom*, ch. 4.

35 Daniel R. Headrick, *The Tools of Empire: Technology and European Imperialism in the Nineteenth Century* (New York: Oxford University Press, 1981); and Pike, "National Interest," 39.

36 NAUK, CO 305, Colonial Office: Vancouver Island Original Correspondence, and CO 60, Colonial Office: British Columbia Original Correspondence, digitized by Colonial Despatches of Vancouver Island and British Columbia 1846–1871, University of Victoria., https://bcgenesis.uvic.ca/; Christopher Bracken, *The Potlatch Papers: A Colonial Case History* (Chicago: University of Chicago Press, 1997), especially 175; and Adele Perry, "The State of Empire: Reproducing Colonialism in British Columbia, 1849–1871," *Journal of Colonialism and Colonial History* 2, 2 (Fall 2001).

37 For one collection of letters that drove this regional economy, see UBCSC, RBSC-ARC-1702, Royal Fisk.

38 Asa Briggs, *Victorian Things* (Chicago: University of Chicago Press, 1989), ch. 9; Golden, *Posting It*, ch. 3 and 198; and Joyce, *The State of Freedom*, 75–82.

39 Examples include Library and Archives Canada (LAC), MG30 C165, Wilfred Bastyan Rowell, vol. 1 (standard notepaper); mother to Philip Dorset Goepel, Barnsbury, 12 November 1875, CVA, AM-23, Goepel family (personal letterhead); John Barnsley to father, Victoria, 13 July 1891, CVIC, PR-24, John Barnsley, box 36E3, file 1 (business letterhead); and E. Kidner to sister Edith, Putney, 24 April [1892], UBCSC, RBSC-ARC-1322, Langley family, box 1, file 1 (mourning stationery). Not all letters have been archived in (or only in) their original forms; see, for example, BCA, PR-1617, H. Leonard Witherby (copied letterbook); and BCA, MS-1151, Nation family (typescripts).

40 S. Bryant to son Cornelius, Holly Hall (Dudley), [?] 1859, BCA, MS-2819, Cornelius Bryant, box 1, file 1.

41 For typical examples, see UBCSC, RBSC-ARC-1322, Langley family, box 1.

42 Harold Nation to mother, Moyie, 27 August 1901, BCA, MS-1151, Nation family.

43 For an example of a typed letter, see Joseph Morton to cousin Beaumont, Vancouver, 6 January 1914, CVA, AM-860, Morton family, box 590-D-1, folder 14.

44 Alexander Papley to brothers and sisters, Nanaimo, 22 June 1867, BCA, PR-1509, Papley family; and the diversity of letters in Judith Hudson Beattie and Helen M. Buss, eds., *Undelivered Letters to Hudson's Bay Company Men on the Northwest Coast of America, 1830–57* (Vancouver: UBC Press, 2003).

45 Roger Hicks to daughters Flo, Pansie, and Josie, Stikine River, 3 April 1898, BCA, MS-2167, T. Roger C. Hays Hicks; and Leonard Witherby to mother, C.P. Railway, 15 April 1899, BCA, PR-1617, H. Leonard Witherby.

46 For examples of cross-hatched letters, see letters from Charlotte Barnes Trutch in UBCSC, RBSC-ARC-1561, Trutch family, box 1.

47 Mary Jane Matthews to son James and future daughter-in-law Maud, Rock Ferry, 27 December 1898, and Herbert Matthews to son James, Rock Ferry, [29] December 1898, CVA, AM-54-S11-3, Major Matthews, box 577-D-3, file 7.

48 George Robinson to son Ernest, Dudley, 3 January 1875, BCA, MS-2436, Victor Robinson.

49 Robert Burnaby to sister Rose, Victoria, 14 March 1860, in McLeod and McGeachie, *Land of Promise,* 137; and Roger Hicks to daughters, Stikine River, 18 May 1898, BCA, MS-2167, T. Roger C. Hays Hicks.

50 Harry Guillod in Dorothy Blakey Smith, ed., "Harry Guillod's Journal of a Trip to Cariboo, 1862," *British Columbia Historical Quarterly* 19, 3–4 (1955): 187–232; and Charles Hayward, diary, Victoria, 10 June 1862, CVIC, PR-118, Charles Hayward, folder 3.

51 John Brough to brother James, New Westminster, 16 April 1866, BCA, MS-2797, John Brough.

52 Tommy Norbury to father, Fish Lakes, 23 February 1895, BCA, MS-0877, Norbury family, box 1, file 10.

53 LAC, MG30 C165, Wilfred Bastyan Rowell, vol. 1. See also Beattie and Buss, *Undelivered Letters,* introduction.

54 John Brough to sister Catherine, Mary Hill, 24 December 1863, BCA, MS-2797, John Brough.

55 Tommy Norbury to brother Coningsby (Coni), Fort Steele, 9 December 1890, BCA, MS-0877, Norbury family, box 1, file 5.

56 Alexander David Pringle to wife Mary Louisa (Louie), Hope, 4 June 1860, BCA, MS-0369, Alexander David Pringle.

57 Tommy Norbury to brother Coni, Fort Steele, 9 December 1890, BCA, MS-0877, Norbury family, box 1, file 5; and Roger Hicks to daughters, Stikine River, 18 May 1898, BCA, MS-2167, T. Roger C. Hays Hicks.

58 Tommy Norbury to father, Fish Lakes, 7 February 1898, BCA, MS-0877, Norbury family, box 1, file 13.

59 Herbert Matthews to son James, Rock Ferry, 2 November 1898, CVA, AM-54-S11-3, Major Matthews, box 577-D-3, file 7.

60 Edmund Verney to father, New Westminster, 26 February 1865, in Allan Pritchard, ed., *Vancouver Island Letters of Edmund Hope Verney, 1862–65* (Vancouver: UBC Press, 1996), 248.

61 Samuel Beeman to sister Sarah, [n.p., Victoria?], 14 July 1868, BCA, MS-2073, Samuel O. Beeman, reel A01401. Emphasis in original.

62 Alan Conway, "Welsh Gold-Miners in British Columbia during the 1860s," *British Columbia Historical Quarterly* 21 (1958): 51–74; and William D. Jones, "'Going into Print':

Published Immigrant Letters, Webs of Personal Relations, and the Emergence of the Welsh Public Sphere," in *Letters across Borders: The Epistolary Practices of International Migrants,* ed. Bruce S. Elliott, David A. Gerber, and Suzanne M. Sinke (Basingstoke, UK: Palgrave Macmillan, 2006), 175–99.

63 David Pringle to wife Louie, Hope, 22 April 1860, BCA, MS-0369, Alexander David Pringle. Emphasis in original.

64 On similar conventions in the empire, see David Fitzpatrick, *Oceans of Consolation: Personal Accounts of Irish Migration to Australia* (Cork: Cork University Press, 1994), 19–28. On earlier periods, see Clare Brant, *Eighteenth-Century Letters and British Culture* (Basingstoke, UK: Palgrave Macmillan, 2006); Sarah M.S. Pearsall, *Atlantic Families: Lives and Letters in the Later Eighteenth Century* (Oxford: Oxford University Press, 2008); and James Daybell, *The Material Letter in Early Modern England: Manuscript Letters and the Culture and Practices of Letter-Writing, 1512–1635* (Basingstoke, UK: Palgrave Macmillan, 2012).

65 Eve Tavor Bannet, *Empire of Letters: Letter Manuals and Transatlantic Correspondence, 1688–1820* (Cambridge: Cambridge University Press, 2005); Deirdre M. Mahoney, "'More Than an Accomplishment': Advice on Letter-Writing for Nineteenth-Century American Women," *Huntington Library Quarterly* 66, 3/4 (2003): 411–23; and John T. Gage, "Vestiges of Letter-Writing in Composition Textbooks, 1850–1914," in *Letter-Writing Manuals and Instruction from Antiquity to the Present: Historical and Bibliographic Studies,* ed. Carol Poster and Linda C. Mitchell (Columbia: University of South Carolina Press, 2007), 200–29. For examples, see *How to Write: A Pocket Manual of Composition and Letter Writing* (London: William Horsell, 1857); *Chesterfield's Art of Letter-Writing Simplified: Being a Guide to Friendly, Affectionate, Polite and Business Correspondence* (London, ON: W. Bryce, 1886); and *Aids to Epistolary Correspondence, or, Familiar Directions for Writing Letters on Various Subjects: Also Rules of Punctuation* (Quebec: C. Darveau, 1887). See also Iowerth Lloyd to grandmother Nina Lloyd, Port Moody, 12 March 1912, CVA, AM-875, Edward Lloyd, reel M-104.

66 Liz Stanley, "The Epistolarium: On Theorizing Letters and Correspondences," *Auto/Biography* 12, 3 (2004): especially 217. See also David A. Gerber, "Epistolary Ethics: Personal Correspondence and the Culture of Emigration in the Nineteenth Century," *Journal of American Ethnic History* 19, 4 (Summer 2000): 5; Bill Jones, "Writing Back: Welsh Emigrants and Their Correspondence in the Nineteenth Century," *North American Journal of Welsh Studies* 5, 1 (Winter 2005): 45; and Elizabeth Jane Errington, "Webs of Affection and Obligation: Glimpse into Families and Nineteenth Century Transatlantic Communities," *Journal of the Canadian Historical Association* 19, 1 (2008): 8.

67 Lucy Mathias to cousin Charles Newcombe, Putney, 6 April 1899, BCA, MS-1077, Newcombe family, vol. 18, file 17. Emphasis in original.

68 Robert Burnaby to mother, Victoria, 23 December 1859; to sister Rose, Victoria, 6 January 1860; to sister Harriet, Victoria, 28 February 1860; and to brother Tom, Victoria, 8 June 1860, in McLeod and McGeachie, *Land of Promise,* 128, 130, 134, and 143.

69 Robert Burnaby to mother, Victoria, 6 October and 26 December 1861, in McLeod and McGeachie, *Land of Promise,* 164 and 166. Emphasis in original.

70 For example, Annie Deans to parents, [Victoria], 17 January 1853, BCA, PR-1540, Annie Deans; Radcliffe Quine to brother and sister, Victoria, 22 April 1861, CVA, AM-245, Quine family, box 514-G-3, folder 2; E.J. Newcombe to daughter-in-law Marian, Derby, 5 May 1885, BCA, MS-1077, Newcombe family, vol. 18, folder 3; Harold Nation to mother, Swansea (British Columbia), 29 October 1900, BCA, MS-1151, Nation family;

and John Gordon to brother, Belfast, 6 October 1911, New Westminster Archives (NWA), IH993.40, Official Administrator (New Westminster, BC).

71 John Brough to sister, New Westminster, 18 March 1862, BCA, MS-2797, John Brough.

72 See also Gerber, *Authors of Their Lives*, ch. 3; and Errington, "Webs of Affection and Obligation," 8.

73 Leonard Witherby to mother, Westholme, 15 May 1899, BCA, PR-1617, H. Leonard Witherby.

74 Roger Hicks to daughters Flo, Pansie, and Josie, Stikine River, 3 April 1898, BCA, MS-2167, T. Roger C. Hays Hicks.

75 For example, Mary Hawks Moody to mother, Hope, 15 August [n.y.], BCA, MS-1101, Mary Susanna (Hawks) Moody; and Tommy Norbury to mother, Kootenay, 21 July 1888, BCA, MS-0877, Norbury family, box 1, file 3.

76 Catherine Mittler Helmcken to son John, London, 7 August and 23 November 1866, BCA, MS-0505, Helmcken family, box 1, files 16 and 15; and Harold Nation to mother, Moyie, 8 April 1901, BCA, MS-1151, Nation family.

77 Tommy Norbury to father, Tobacco Plains, 13 November 1887, BCA, MS-0877, Norbury family, box 1, file 2.

78 Cornelius Bryant to parents, Nanaimo, [n.d., 1857?], CVA, AM-24, Cornelius Bryant, box 500-C-2, folder 1.

79 Pike, "National Interest," 44, n. 38; Margot C. Finn, "Colonial Gifts: Family Politics and the Exchange of Goods in British India, c. 1780–1820," *Modern Asian Studies* 40, 1 (February 2006): 203–31; Magee and Thompson, *Empire and Globalisation*, 97–105; and Joyce, *The State of Freedom*, 115.

80 Cornelius Bryant to parents, Nanaimo, [n.d., 1857?], CVA, AM-24, Cornelius Bryant, box 500-C-2, folder 1; David Pringle to wife Louie, Victoria, 10 December 1859, BCA, MS-0369, Alexander David Pringle; and Herbert Matthews to son James, Rock Ferry, 29 November and 3 December 1898, CVA, AM-54-S11-3, Major Matthews, box 577-D-3, file 7.

81 Harold Nation to mother, Moyie, 24 February 1901, BCA, MS-1151, Nation family.

82 Tommy Norbury to father, Tobacco Plains, 13 November 1887; Fort Steele, 13 July 1889; and [n.p.], 26 March 1897, BCA, MS-0877, Norbury family, box 1, files 2, 4, and 12.

83 Marilyn Lake and Henry Reynolds, *Drawing the Global Colour Line: White Men's Countries and the International Challenge of Racial Equality* (Cambridge: Cambridge University Press, 2008); Penelope Edmonds, "'I Followed England Round the World': The Rise of Trans-Imperial Anglo-Saxon Exceptionalism, and the Spatial Narratives of Nineteenth-Century British Settler Colonies of the Pacific Rim," in *Re-orienting Whiteness*, ed. Leigh Boucher, Jane Carey, and Katherine Ellinghaus (New York: Palgrave Macmillan, 2009), 99–115; and Laura Ishiguro, "'Growing Up and Grown Up ... in Our Future City': Discourses of Childhood and Settler Futurity in Colonial British Columbia," *BC Studies* 190 (Summer 2016): 15–37.

84 Adele Perry, *On the Edge of Empire: Gender, Race, and the Making of British Columbia, 1849–1871* (Toronto: University of Toronto Press, 2001), especially 13–14; and John Douglas Belshaw, *Becoming British Columbia: A Population History* (Vancouver: UBC Press, 2009), 36–46 and chs. 4 and 6.

85 See Joy Parr, *Labouring Children: British Immigrant Apprentices to Canada, 1869–1924* (Toronto: University of Toronto Press, 1980); Jason Patrick Bennett, "Apple of the

Empire: Landscape and Imperial Identity in Turn-of-the-Century British Columbia," *Journal of the Canadian Historical Association* 9, 1 (1998): 63–92; Perry, *On the Edge of Empire;* Lisa Chilton, *Agents of Empire: British Female Migration to Canada and Australia, 1860–1930* (Toronto: University of Toronto Press, 2007); Lisa Chilton, "Travelling Colonist: British Emigration and the Construction of Anglo-Canadian Privilege," in *Empire, Identity and Migration in the British World,* ed. Andrew S. Thompson and Kent Fedorowich (Manchester: Manchester University Press, 2013), 169–91; Ellen Boucher, *Empire's Children: Child Emigration, Welfare, and the Decline of the British World, 1869–1967* (Cambridge: Cambridge University Press, 2014); Elizabeth A. Scott, "'The Ill-Name of the Old Country': London's Assisted Emigrants, British Unemployment Policy, and Canadian Immigration Restriction, 1905–1910," *Journal of the Canadian Historical Association* 26, 1 (2015): 99–130; and the overview in Valerie Knowles, *Strangers at Our Gates: Canadian Immigration and Immigration Policy, 1540–2007,* rev. ed. (Toronto: Dundurn, 2007).

86 Arthur Birch, "Victorian Odyssey," BCA, MS-0061, Birch family, box 2, reel A00272; and Margaret A. Ormsby, "Moody, Richard Clement," *Dictionary of Canadian Biography Online,* vol. 11 (University of Toronto and Université Laval, 2000), http://www.biographi.ca/en/bio.php?id_nbr=5715.

87 John Christie, preface to diary, BCA, MS-0142, John Christie.

88 R. Cole Harris, "Introduction," in *Letters from Windermere 1912–1914,* ed. R. Cole Harris and Elizabeth Phillips (Vancouver: UBC Press, 1984), ix–xxii.

89 Daphne Sleigh, *The Man Who Saved Vancouver: Major James Skitt Matthews* (Surrey: Heritage House, 2008), chs. 1–3.

90 Richard Somerset Mackie, *Wilderness Profound: Victorian Life on the Gulf of Georgia* (Victoria: Sono Nis, 1995).

91 Heaton, "Penny Post for the Empire," 911.

92 Quoted in Pike, "National Interest," 29.

93 Cornelius Bryant to parents, Nanaimo, [n.d., 1857?], CVA, AM-24, Cornelius Bryant, box 500-C-2, folder 1; and fonds description, http://searcharchives.vancouver.ca/cornelius-bryant-fonds.

94 *Morton v. Brighouse,* [1927] SCR 118, 1927 CanLII 37 (SCC), http://canlii.ca/t/21v65.

95 Jessie Chambers, diary, 6 May 1891, BCA, MS-2166, Jessie Chambers.

96 David Carruthers Murdoch, recollections, author's private collection, 4; and W.R. Carruthers, "Edward Maurice Carruthers, J.P.," *Thirty-Second Report of the Okanagan Historical Society* (1968): 63–66.

97 See also Gerber, *Authors of Their Lives,* 185–86; and Magee and Thompson, *Empire and Globalisation,* 65 and 82–83.

98 Radcliffe Quine to brother and sister, Victoria, 22 April 1861, CVA, AM-245, Quine family, box 514-G-3, folder 2. See also David Pringle to father, Hope, 7 April 1860, BCA, MS-0369, Alexander David Pringle; and Tommy Norbury to mother, Tobacco Plains, 6 December 1887, BCA, MS-0877, Norbury family, box 1, file 2.

99 Charles Newcombe to wife Marian, Victoria, 17 and 28 October 1883, BCA, MS-1077, Newcombe family, vol. 18, file 1; and Kevin Neary, "Newcombe, Charles Frederic," *Dictionary of Canadian Biography Online,* vol. 15 (University of Toronto and Université Laval, 2000), http://www.biographi.ca/en/bio.php?id_nbr=8309.

100 David Pringle [to wife Louie], Victoria, 10 December 1859, BCA, MS-0369, Alexander David Pringle. See also Joe Harris to brother Alexander, quoted in Alexander Harris,

diary, BCA, MS-1463, Alexander Harris, reel A00674; William Arthur Lewis Deaville to parents, Victoria, 18 March 1898, BCA, MS-2044, Deaville family, box 1, file 1; and Jack Phillips to mother-in-law, Wilmer, 23 June 1912, in Harris and Phillips, *Letters from Windermere,* 45. On letters and chain migration more generally, see, for example, Dierks, *In My Power,* ch. 3; and Magee and Thompson, *Empire and Globalisation,* 82–85.

101 David Pringle [to wife Louie], Victoria, 10 December 1859, BCA, MS-0369, Alexander David Pringle.

102 For example, William Cleaver, letter of introduction for Frederick Dally's emigration to British Columbia, Wellingborough, 9 April 1862, BCA, MS-2443, Frederick Dally, file 4.

103 Tommy Norbury to father, Tobacco Plains, 13 November 1887, and Fish Lakes, 5 August 1892, BCA, MS-0877, Norbury family, box 1, files 2 and 7.

104 Preface (biography), 1, LAC, MG-30 C-165, Wilfred Bastyan Rowell, vol. 1, file 3.

105 This is rarely considered in the scholarship; for a brief discussion of discouraging emigration by post in the North American context, see Gerber, *Authors of Their Lives,* 184–85.

106 On travel guides, see Kenton Storey, *Settler Anxiety at the Outposts of Empire: Colonial Relations, Humanitarian Discourses, and the Imperial Press* (Vancouver: UBC Press, 2016).

107 Robert Burnaby to mother, Victoria, 22 January 1859, in McLeod and McGeachie, *Land of Promise,* 63.

108 Mary Hawks Moody to sister Emily, Victoria, 1 September 1859, BCA, MS-0060, Mary Susanna Moody.

109 John Brough to brother James, New Westminster, 16 April 1866, BCA, MS-2797, John Brough.

110 Alexander Papley to brothers and sisters, Nanaimo, 22 June 1867, BCA, PR-1509, Papley family.

111 For example, John Evans to children, Antler Creek, 3 May 1872; to son and daughter, Davis Creek, 9 October 1873; to daughter Mary Ellen, Van Winkle, 6 November 1875; and to son and daughter, Victoria, 31 December 1875, BCA, MS-2112, John Evans.

112 David Pringle to father, Hope, 7 April 1860, BCA, MS-0369, Alexander David Pringle.

113 Arthur Birch to brother John, New Westminster, 7 May 1864, BCA, MS-0061, Birch family, box 1, file 2, reel A00272.

114 Harold Nation to mother, [n.p.], 29 October 1900, BCA, MS-1151, Nation family.

115 Alexander Papley to brothers and sisters, Nanaimo, 22 June 1867, BCA, PR-1509, Papley family.

116 William Jones to parents, Victoria, 28 July 1862, published in the Merthyr *Telegraph,* 4 October 1862, in Conway, "Welsh Gold-Miners in British Columbia," 61. See also prospector to wife and children, Victoria, 23 July 1862, published in the Merthyr *Telegraph,* 13 September 1862, in Conway, ibid., 60.

117 Roger Hicks to daughters, Stikine River, 18 May 1898, BCA, MS-2167, T. Roger C. Hays Hicks.

118 Jack Phillips to mother-in-law, Invermere, 20 April 1912, in Harris and Phillips, *Letters from Windermere,* 10.

119 Harold Nation to [?], Swansea [British Columbia], 2 September 1900, BCA, MS-1151, Nation family.

120 On mail recovered from wrecked ships, see Mary Hawks Moody to mother, New Westminster, 30 January [n.y.], BCA, MS-1101, Mary Susanna (Hawks) Moody; David

Pringle to father, Victoria, 10 January 1860, BCA, MS-0369, Alexander David Pringle; Charles Hayward, diary, Victoria, 14 August 1862, CVIC, PR–118, Charles Hayward, folder 3; and Arthur Nonus Birch to brother John Birch, New Westminster, 15 May 1866, BCA, MS-0061, Birch family, box 1, file 2, reel A00272. On undelivered letters, see Beattie and Buss, *Undelivered Letters.* For one collection of letters that have been archived precisely because they were not delivered to their recipient, see LAC, MG30 C165, Wilfred Bastyan Rowell, vol. 1, file 1.

Chapter 2: "Affection Can Overstep Distance"

Acknowledgments: A small section of this chapter appeared in Laura Ishiguro, "Material Girls: Daughters, Dress and Distance in the Trans-Imperial Family," in *Colonial Girlhood in Literature, Culture and History, 1840-1950,* ed. Kristine Moruzi and Michelle J. Smith (Basingstoke: Palgrave Macmillan, 2014). Reproduced with permission of Palgrave Macmillan.

1 Robert Burnaby to mother, Queenborough [*sic,* New Westminster], 10 March 1859, in Anne Burnaby McLeod and Pixie McGeachie, eds., *Land of Promise: Robert Burnaby's Letters from Colonial British Columbia 1858–1863* (Burnaby: City of Burnaby, 2002), 71.

2 On British Columbia, for example, see Adele Perry, *On the Edge of Empire: Gender, Race, and the Making of British Columbia, 1849–1871* (Toronto: University of Toronto Press, 2001); Jean Barman, "Taming Aboriginal Sexuality: Gender, Power, and Race in British Columbia, 1850–1900," *BC Studies* 115/116 (Autumn/Winter 1997/98): 237–66; and Richard Phillips, "Settler Colonialism and the Nuclear Family," *Canadian Geographer* 53, 2 (Summer 2009): 239–53.

3 Key works on metropolitan Britain include Leonore Davidoff and Catherine Hall, *Family Fortunes: Men and Women of the English Middle Class 1780–1850,* rev. ed. (London: Routledge, 2002); Trev Lynn Broughton and Helen Rogers, eds., *Gender and Fatherhood in the Nineteenth Century* (Basingstoke, UK: Palgrave Macmillan, 2007); Leonore Davidoff, *Thicker Than Water: Siblings and Their Relations, 1780–1920* (Oxford: Oxford University Press, 2012); and Julie-Marie Strange, *Fatherhood and the British Working Class, 1865–1914* (Cambridge: Cambridge University Press, 2015).

4 Exceptions that situate imperial distances as part of British family life include Elizabeth Buettner, *Empire Families: Britons and Late Imperial India* (Oxford: Oxford University Press, 2004); Margot Finn, "Colonial Gifts: Family Politics and the Exchange of Goods in British India, c. 1780–1820," *Modern Asian Studies* 40, 1 (February 2006): 203–31; and Margot C. Finn, "Family Formations: Anglo India and the Familial Proto-State," in *Structures and Transformations in Modern British History,* eds. David Feldman and Jon Lawrence (Cambridge: Cambridge University Press, 2011), 100–17.

5 Leonore Davidoff et al., *The Family Story: Blood, Contract and Intimacy, 1830–1960* (London: Longman, 1999).

6 For example, David A. Gerber, *Authors of Their Lives: The Personal Correspondence of British Immigrants to North America in the Nineteenth Century* (New York: New York University Press, 2006); Sarah M.S. Pearsall, *Atlantic Families: Lives and Letters in the Later Eighteenth Century* (Oxford: Oxford University Press, 2008); and Elizabeth Jane Errington, "Webs of Affection and Obligation: Glimpse into Families and Nineteenth Century Transatlantic Communities," *Journal of the Canadian Historical Association* 19, 1 (2008): 1–26.

7 For example, Leonore Davidoff, *Worlds Between: Historical Perspectives on Gender and Class* (New York: Routledge, 1995); John R. Gillis, *A World of Their Own Making: Myth, Ritual, and the Quest for Family Values* (Cambridge, MA: Harvard University Press, 1997); Valerie Sanders, *The Brother-Sister Culture in Nineteenth-Century Literature: From Austen to Woolf* (Basingstoke, UK: Palgrave Macmillan, 2002); Eleanor Gordon and Gwyneth Nair, *Public Lives: Women, Family and Society in Victorian Britain* (New Haven, CT: Yale University Press, 2003); John Tosh, *A Man's Place: Masculinity and the Middle-Class Home in Victorian England* (New Haven, CT: Yale University Press, 2007); Claudia Nelson, *Family Ties in Victorian England* (Westport, CT: Praeger, 2007); Broughton and Rogers, *Gender and Fatherhood*; and Davidoff, *Thicker Than Water.*

8 Arthur Wentworth Hamilton Eaton, *Good Form: Letter-Writing, Its Ethics and Etiquette, with Remarks on the Proper Use of Monograms, Crests and Seals* (New York: Frederick A. Stokes, 1894), epigraph; and *Aids to Epistolary Correspondence, or, Familiar Directions for Writing Letters on Various Subjects: Also Rules of Punctuation* (Quebec: C. Darveau, 1887), 4.

9 Edward Cridge to wife Mary, South Kensington, 11 August 1876, CVIC, PR-76, Cridge family, box 26A5, file 5.

10 Sarah Lindley Crease to son Lindley, Victoria, 25 August 1878, BCA, MS-0055, Crease family, box 11, file 1.

11 James Douglas to daughter Martha, [Victoria], 10 December 1872, in W. Kaye Lamb, "Letters to Martha," *British Columbia Historical Quarterly* 1 (January 1937): 37. While Douglas worked as an agent of the British colonial state and had personal connections to the British Isles, he and his family were also racialized as non-white (Black and Indigenous) during their lifetimes, unlike other correspondents in this book. This position and family history both highlights and troubles the book's capacious definition of "Britishness." See Adele Perry, *Colonial Relations: The Douglas-Connolly Family and the Nineteenth-Century Imperial World* (Cambridge: Cambridge University Press, 2015).

12 Mary Hawks Moody to mother, Victoria, 21 March 1859, BCA, MS-0060, Mary Susanna Moody.

13 Daisy Oxley Phillips to sister Freda, Athalmer, 2 February 1913, 5 December 1912, 21 February 1913, and 7 September 1912, in R. Cole Harris and Elizabeth Phillips, eds., *Letters from Windermere, 1912–1914* (Vancouver: UBC Press, 1984), 153, 128, 161, and 91.

14 Henry Crease to wife Sarah, Victoria, 12 April 1859, BCA, MS-2879, Crease family, box 68, file 27, reel A1839. Emphasis in original.

15 Sarah Lindley Crease to father, New Westminster, 17 January 1864, BCA, MS-0055, Crease family, box 11, file 1. Emphasis in original.

16 Leonard Witherby to father, Victoria, 23 April 1899, BCA, PR-1617, H. Leonard Witherby; and Nellie Cridge to father, Hastings, England, 25 July 1895, CVIC, PR-76, Cridge family, file 5.

17 Lucy Mathias to cousin Charles Newcombe, Putney, 6 April 1899, BCA, MS-1077, Newcombe Family, vol. 18, file 17. Emphasis in original.

18 Tommy Norbury to [parents], Fish Lakes, 25 August 1898, BCA, MS-0877, Norbury family, box 1, file 13.

19 Herbert Matthews to son James, Rock Ferry, 22 November 1898, CVA, AM-54-S11-3, Major Matthews, box 577-D-3, file 7.

20 Daisy Oxley Phillips to sister Freda, [Athalmer], 5 December 1912, in Harris and Phillips, *Letters from Windermere,* 127.

21 For example, letters in BCA, MS-2047, Thomas Porter; and PR-1509, Papley family.

22 John Brough to sister Catherine, Mary Hill, 24 December 1863, BCA, MS-2797, John Brough.

23 Tommy Norbury to mother, Fish Lakes, 4 May 1895, BCA, MS-0877, Norbury family, box 1, file 10; and John Christie, diary entry, 28 July 1861, BCA, MS-0142, John Christie.

24 Catherine Mittler Helmcken to son John, Whitechapel, 7 August 1866, BCA, MC-0505, Helmcken family, box 1, file 16.

25 Mary Hawks Moody to sister Emily, Victoria, Good Friday [1859], BCA, MS-0060, Mary Susanna Moody. Emphasis in original.

26 Caroline Robinson to son Ernest, Leamington, 27 August 1876, BCA, MS-2436, Victor Robinson. Emphasis in original.

27 Arthur Birch to brother John, New Westminster, 11 June 1864, BCA, MS-0061, Birch family, box 1, folder 2, reel A00272. See also James Douglas's advice to his daughter Martha. Lamb, "Letters to Martha," 37; and Radcliffe Quine to brother and sister, Victoria, 22 April 1861, CVA, AM-245, Quine family, box 514-G-3, folder 2.

28 Lucy Mathias to cousin Charles Newcombe, Putney, 6 April 1899, BCA, MS-1077, Newcombe family, folder 17, reel A01754.

29 For example, James Douglas to daughter Martha, [Victoria], 26 November 1872, in Lamb, "Letters to Martha," 38.

30 Mary Hawks Moody to sister Emily, Victoria, 7 April [1859], BCA, MS-1101, Mary Susanna (Hawks) Moody.

31 Leonard Witherby to mother, CP Railway, 15 April 1899, BCA, PR-1617, H. Leonard Witherby.

32 Daisy Oxley Phillips to [sister Freda], Athalmer, 8 June 1913, in Harris and Phillips, *Letters from Windermere,* 183.

33 Radcliffe Quine to brother and sister, Victoria, 22 April 1861, CVA, AM-245, Quine family, box 514-G-3, folder 2.

34 On Evans, see Robie L. Reid, "Captain Evans of Cariboo," *British Columbia Historical Quarterly* 2, 4 (1938): 233–46; and on Welsh miners in British Columbia, see Alan Conway, "Welsh Gold-Miners in British Columbia during the 1860s," *British Columbia Historical Quarterly* 21 (1958): 51–74.

35 John Evans to son and daughter, Davis Creek, 9 October 1873, BCA, MS-2112, John Evans.

36 John Evans to daughter Mary Ellen, Van Winkle, 6 November 1875, BCA, MS-2112, John Evans.

37 John Evans to son and daughter, Victoria, 31 December 1875, BCA, MS-2112, John Evans.

38 Robert Burnaby to mother, Queenborough [*sic,* New Westminster], 10 March 1859, in McLeod and McGeachie, *Land of Promise,* 71.

39 Edward Lloyd to [parents], telegram, Vancouver, 24 June 1905; to father, Steveston, 15 August 1905, including enclosed clipping; and to father, Vancouver, 26 September 1905, CVA, AM-875, Edward Lloyd, reel M104.

40 Catherine Mittler Helmcken to son John, Whitechapel, 23 November 1866, BCA, MS-0505, Helmcken family, vol. 1, file 15.

41 Wilf Rowell to mother, Fairmont Springs, 10 November 1905 and 2 December 1905; and to sister Ellen, Sheep Creek, 6 January 1906, LAC, MG30 C165, Wilfred Bastyan Rowell, vol. 1, file 1.

42 For example, Catherine Mittler Helmcken to son John, Whitechapel, 7 August 1866, BCA, MS-0505, Helmcken family, box 1, file 15; and Mary Hawks Moody to mother,

Victoria, 6 May 1859, BCA, MS-1101, Mary Susanna (Hawks) Moody. See also Nicole Hudgins, "A Historical Approach to Family Photography: Class and Individuality in Manchester and Lille, 1850–1914," *Journal of Social History* 43, 3 (Spring 2010): 559–86.

43 Daisy Oxley Phillips to sister Freda, Athalmer, 7 September 1912, in Harris and Phillips, *Letters from Windermere,* 88.

44 John Bayley to sister Carrie, Curragh Camp, 2 September [1874], BCA, PR-1616, Felicite Caroline (Bayley) Wolfenden.

45 John Evans to daughter Mary Ellen, Van Winkle, 6 November 1875, BCA, MS-2112, John Evans. Emphasis in original.

46 John Evans to son and daughter, Davis Creek, 9 October 1873, BCA, MS-2112, John Evans.

47 John Evans to son and daughter, Victoria, 31 December 1875, BCA, MS-2112, John Evans.

48 John Evans to daughter Mary Ellen, Van Winkle, 6 November 1875, and to son and daughter, Victoria, 31 December 1875, BCA, MS-2112, John Evans.

49 For example, Herbert Matthews to son James, Rock Ferry, 22 November 1898, CVA, AM-54-S11-3, Major Matthews, box 577-D-3, file 7.

50 Emily Trutch Pinder White to sister-in-law Zoe, [Sidhbari?, India] 1 April 1871, BCA, MS-2897, Trutch family, box 10, file 12, reel A01952.

51 Catherine Mittler Helmcken to daughter-in-law Cecilia, London, 12 April 1853, BCA, MS-0505, Helmcken family, vol. 14, file 2.

52 Henry Hawkins to brother Alben, Tottenham, 16 February 1879, BCA, MS-0441, Alben Hawkins, box 1, file 2. Also [?] Mawson Rattenbury to son Francis, Headingley, 13 May 1898, CVIC, PR-35, Rattenbury family, box 27D10, file 8.

53 Caroline Robinson to son Ernest, Leamington, 27 August 1876, BCA, MS-2436, Victor Robinson.

54 Jane Murie Peebles Leighton to future daughter-in-law Angusta Grant, Aberdeen, 2 February 1886, NWA, IH2007.151F.2 (1/2), Peebles family, box 1.

55 John Bayley to sister Carrie, Dublin, 19 June 1874, BCA, PR-1616, Felicite Caroline (Bayley) Wolfenden.

56 John Bayley to sister Carrie, Curragh Camp, 2 September [1874], BCA, PR-1616, Felicite Caroline (Bayley) Wolfenden.

57 Cissie Bayley to sister-in-law Carrie, New Brompton, 13 April 1875, BCA, PR-1616, Felicite Caroline (Bayley) Wolfenden.

58 For example, Charles Newcombe to father, Inverness, Hertford, and London, 1890s–1900s, BCA, MS-1077, Newcombe family, vol. 18, file 5, reel A01754; and Lindley Crease to mother, Ramsgate, ca. 1880s, and Arthur Crease to mother, Haileybury, ca. 1890s, BCA, MS-2879, Crease family, vol. 68, file 28, and vol. 69, file 1, reel A01839. See also Kathryn Anne Bridge, "Being Young in the Country: Settler Children and Childhood in British Columbia and Alberta, 1860–1925" (PhD dissertation, University of Victoria, 2012); and Erin Millions, "'By Education and Conduct': Educating Trans-Imperial Indigenous Fur-Trade Children in the Hudson's Bay Company Territories and the British Empire, 1820s to 1870s" (PhD dissertation, University of Manitoba, 2017).

59 For example, George Robinson to granddaughter Florence, Hastings, 20 October 1889, BCA, MS-2436, Victor Robinson; and Iowerth Lloyd to grandmother, Port Moody, 1 March 1912, CVA, AM-875, Edward Lloyd, reel M104.

60 Mary Hawks Moody to mother, New Westminster, 12 September [1861], BCA, MS-0060, Mary Susanna Moody.

61 Mary Hawks Moody to mother, Victoria, 6 May 1859, BCA, MS-1101, Mary Susanna (Hawks) Moody.

62 For example, Mary Hawks Moody to mother, New Westminster, 14 November [1861], BCA, MS-0060, Mary Susanna Moody; and 11 August [1861 or 1862] and 30 January [1863], BCA, MS-1101, Mary Susanna (Hawks) Moody.

63 However, by exploring relationships between women, Sharon Marcus fundamentally challenges an easy equation of heterosexuality and marriage during the period. Sharon Marcus, *Between Women: Friendship, Desire, and Marriage in Victorian England* (Princeton, NJ: Princeton University Press, 2007), pt. 3.

64 For one overview, see Jennifer Phegley, *Courtship and Marriage in Victorian England* (Santa Barbara, CA: Praeger, 2012).

65 Leonore Davidoff, "'Close Marriage' in the Nineteenth and Twentieth Century Middle Strata," in *Kinship Matters,* ed. Fatemeh Ebtehaj, Bridget Lindley, and Martin Richards, (Cambridge: Hart, 2006), 19–45.

66 Daphne Sleigh, *The Man Who Saved Vancouver: Major James Skitt Matthews* (Surrey: Heritage House, 2008), 36.

67 Catherine Mittler Helmcken to unspecified, London, 6 July 1852, BCA, MS-0505, Helmcken family, vol. 14, file 2; and Perry, *Colonial Relations,* 220.

68 George Robinson to son Ernest, Dudley, 3 January 1875, BCA, MS-2436, Victor Robinson.

69 Harold Nation to mother, Moyie, 8 December 1901, BCA, MS-1151, Nation family.

70 Tommy Norbury to mother, Tobacco Plains, 6 December 1887, BCA, MS-0877, Norbury family, box 1, file 2. In a different tone, see Edmund Verney to father, New Westminster, 26 February 1865, in Allan Pritchard, ed., *Vancouver Island Letters of Edmund Hope Verney, 1862–65* (Vancouver: UBC Press, 1996), 248–49.

71 John Bayley to sister Carrie, Dublin, 19 June 1874, BCA, PR-1616, Felicite Caroline (Bayley) Wolfenden.

72 Ibid.

73 John Bayley to sister Carrie, Chatham, 17 August 1873, BCA, PR-1616, Felicite Caroline (Bayley) Wolfenden.

74 Marriage between Felicite Caroline Bayley and Richard Wolfenden, Nanaimo, 12 September 1879, BCA, registration 1879-09-092583, reel B11380.

75 Jane Murie Peebles Leighton to future daughter-in-law Angusta Grant, Aberdeen, 2 February 1886, NWA, IH2007.151F.2 (1/2), Peebles family, box 1.

76 Sleigh, *The Man Who Saved Vancouver,* 30–36.

77 Herbert Matthews to son James, Rock Ferry, 22 November and 7 December 1898, CVA, AM-54-S11-3, Major Matthews, box 577-D-3, file 7. Also Mary Jane Matthews to son James, Rock Ferry, 9 December 1898, in the same collection.

78 Herbert Matthews to son James, Rock Ferry, 17 December 1898; and Mary Jane Matthews to son James, Rock Ferry, n.d. [December 1898], CVA, AM-54-S11-3, Major Matthews, box 577-D-3, file 7.

79 Herbert Matthews to son James, Rock Ferry, 22 November and 31 and 17 December 1898, CVA, AM-54-S11-3, Major Matthews, box 577-D-3, file 7. Also Herbert Matthews to son James, Rock Ferry, 27 December 1898; and Mary Jane Matthews to son James, Rock Ferry, 9 December 1898, in the same collection.

80 Herbert Matthews to son James, Rock Ferry, 22 November 1898 and 31, 3, and 17 December 1898, CVA, AM-54-S11-3, Major Matthews, box 577-D-3, file 7. Emphasis in original.

81 Herbert Matthews to son James, Rock Ferry, 29 November 1898, CVA, AM-54-S11-3, Major Matthews, box 577-D-3, file 7. See also Herbert Matthews to son James, Rock Ferry, 2 and 17 December 1898, and Mary Jane Matthews to son James, Rock Ferry, 9 December 1898.

82 Herbert Matthews to son James, Rock Ferry, 7 December 1898; and Mary Jane Matthews to son James, Rock Ferry, 9 December 1898, CVA, AM-54-S11-3, Major Matthews, box 577-D-3, file 7.

Chapter 3: "Absolutely Nothing Going On"

1 Tommy Norbury to brother Coni, Fort Steele, 29 July 1889, BCA, MS-0877, Norbury family, box 1, file 4.

2 See Nicole Eustace et al., "AHR Conversation: The Historical Study of Emotions," *American Historical Review* 117, 5 (December 2012): 1487–1531.

3 Ann Laura Stoler, "Tense and Tender Ties: The Politics of Comparison in North American History and (Post) Colonial Studies," *Journal of American History* 88, 3 (December 2001): 829–65. For a wider reflection, see Catherine Hall, "Commentary," in *Haunted by Empire: Geographies of Intimacy in North American History*, ed. Ann Laura Stoler (Durham, NC: Duke University Press, 2006), 452–68. See also David Arnold, "Deathscapes: India in an Age of Romanticism and Empire, 1800–1856," *Nineteenth-Century Contexts* 26, 4 (2004): 339–53; Christopher Herbert, *War of No Pity: The Indian Mutiny and Victorian Trauma* (Princeton, NJ: Princeton University Press, 2008); James Beattie, *Empire and Environmental Anxiety: Health, Science, Art and Conservation in South Asia and Australasia, 1800–1920* (Basingstoke, UK: Palgrave Macmillan, 2011); James Epstein, *Scandal of Colonial Rule: Power and Subversion in the British Atlantic during the Age of Revolution* (Cambridge: Cambridge University Press, 2012); Kim Wagner, "'Treading Upon Fires': The 'Mutiny'-Motif and Colonial Anxieties in British India," *Past and Present* 218, 1 (2013): 159–97, especially 160; and Robert Peckham, ed., *Empires of Panic: Epidemics and Colonial Anxieties* (Hong Kong: Hong Kong University Press, 2015).

4 Lorenzo Veracini, *Settler Colonialism: A Theoretical Overview* (Basingstoke, UK: Palgrave Macmillan, 2010), 81.

5 Kenton Storey, *Settler Anxiety at the Outposts of Empire: Colonial Relations, Humanitarian Discourses, and the Imperial Press* (Vancouver: UBC Press, 2016).

6 "Survivance" is Anishnaabe scholar Gerald Vizenor's term, denoting Indigenous people's active presence beyond mere survival. See Gerald Vizenor, ed., *Survivance: Narratives of Native Presence* (Lincoln: University of Nebraska Press, 2008).

7 David Pringle to father, Hope, 7 April 1860, BCA, MS-0369, Alexander David Pringle.

8 For an expanded discussion of similar themes, see J.I. Little, "West Coast Picturesque: Class, Gender, and Race in a British Colonial Landscape, 1858–71," *Journal of Canadian Studies/Revue d'Etudes Canadiennes* 41, 2 (Spring 2007): 5–41.

9 Among the families investigated in this book, examples of these men include Henry Crease, Charles Hayward, Charles Newcombe, and David Pringle.

10 Charles Newcombe to wife Marian, Victoria, 5 October 1883, BCA, MS-1077, Newcombe family, vol. 18, file 1.

11 Edmund Hope Verney to father, Esquimalt, 15 May 1862, in Allan Pritchard, ed., *Vancouver Island Letters of Edmund Hope Verney, 1862–65* (Vancouver: UBC Press, 1996), 61–63.

12 Edmund Hope Verney to father, Esquimalt, 25 May 1862, in Pritchard, *Vancouver Island Letters*, 63. For examples of sketches, see Tommy Norbury, undated drawings titled

"View looking south from visitor's house" and "View looking north," and sketched map of Kootenay River and Tobacco Plains area, BCA, MS-0877, Norbury family, box 1, file 1.

13 Leonard Witherby to father, Victoria, 23 April 1899, BCA, PR-1617, H. Leonard Witherby; and the Canadian Expeditionary Force soldier detail for Driver Henry Leonard Witherby, *Canadian Great War Project* database, http://canadiangreatwarproject.com/searches/soldierDetail.asp?ID=141110, compiled from LAC, RG-150, CEF Personnel Files.

14 Daisy Oxley Phillips to mother, Invermere, 20 April 1912, in R. Cole Harris and Elizabeth Phillips, eds., *Letters from Windermere, 1912–1914* (Vancouver: UBC Press, 1984), 8–9.

15 Charles Newcombe to wife Marian, Victoria, 8 October 1883, BCA, MS-1077, Newcombe family, vol. 18, file 1.

16 Tommy Norbury to mother, Tobacco Plains, 6 December 1887, BCA, MS-0877, Norbury family, box 1, file 2.

17 Little, "West Coast Picturesque," 25–31. See also Daniel Francis, *The Imaginary Indian: The Image of the Indian in Canadian Culture,* 2nd ed. (Vancouver: Arsenal Pulp Press, 2011); Elizabeth Vibert, *Traders' Tales: Narratives of Cultural Encounters in the Columbia Plateau, 1807–1846* (Norman: University of Oklahoma Press, 1997); and John Sutton Lutz, *Makúk: A New History of Aboriginal-White Relations* (Vancouver: UBC Press, 2008), ch. 3.

18 Edmund Hope Verney to father, Esquimalt, 15 May 1862, in Pritchard, *Vancouver Island Letters,* 62.

19 Leonard Witherby to mother, C.P. Railway, 15 April 1899, BCA, PR-1617, Leonard Witherby.

20 Leonard Witherby to father, Victoria, 23 April 1899, BCA, PR-1617, Leonard Witherby.

21 Charles Newcombe to wife Marian, Victoria, 5 October 1883, BCA, MS-1077, Newcombe family, vol. 18, file 1.

22 Arthur Birch to brother John, [Victoria], 11 June 1864, BCA, MS-0061, Birch family, reel A00272.

23 Billy Norbury to mother, [n.p.], 29 June 1889, BCA, MS-0877, Norbury family, box 1, file 16.

24 Tommy Norbury to mother, Fort Steele, 2 November 1889, BCA, MS-0877, Norbury family, box 1, file 4.

25 Tommy Norbury to brother Coni, Fort Steele, 9 December 1890, BCA, MS-0877, Norbury family, box 1, file 5.

26 Mary Hawks Moody to sister Emily, New Westminster, 15 October 1860, and Mary Moody to mother, New Westminster, 7 November [1859], BCA, MS-1101, Mary Susanna (Hawks) Moody. In the same collection, see also Mary Hawks Moody to sister Emily, Victoria, 7 April [1859]; and to mother, New Westminster, 28 June 1860.

27 Mary Hawks Moody to mother, Victoria, 18 February 1859, BCA, MS-0060, Mary Susanna Moody.

28 Edmund Hope Verney to father, Esquimalt, 23 January 1864, in Pritchard, *Vancouver Island Letters,* 187.

29 John Brough to brother James, New Westminster, 16 April 1866, BCA, MS-2797, John Brough.

30 John Morton to wife Ruth, Vancouver, 2 August 1890, CVA, AM-860, Morton family, box 590-D-1, file 14.

31 Roger Hicks to daughters, Stikine River, 18 May 1898, 3 June entry, BCA, MS-2167, T. Roger C. Hays Hicks.

32 Tommy Norbury to sister Florence, Golden City, 4 September 1887, BCA, MS-0877, Norbury family, box 1, file 2.
33 See also William Merrill Decker, *Epistolary Practices: Letter Writing in America before Telecommunications* (Chapel Hill: University of North Carolina Press, 1998), 19.
34 Catherine Mittler Helmcken to daughter-in-law Cecilia Douglas Helmcken, London, 12 April 1853, BCA, MS-0505, Helmcken family, vol. 14, file 2.
35 George Robinson to son Ernest Robinson, Dudley, 3 January 1875, BCA, MS-2436, Victor Robinson.
36 Herbert Matthews to son James Skitt Matthews, Rock Ferry, 14 January 1899, CVA, AM-54-S11-3, Major Matthews, box 577-D-3, file 8.
37 Alexander Rose to brother James Rose, Nairn, 9 April 1850, in Judith Hudson Beattie and Helen M. Buss, eds., *Undelivered Letters to Hudson's Bay Company Men on the Northwest Coast of America, 1830–57* (Vancouver: UBC Press, 2003), 354–55.
38 Robert Wilson to brother James Wilson, York Factory, 7 July 1833, in ibid., 45.
39 Elizabeth Carrack to son William Carrack, London, 7 March 1844, in ibid., 185.
40 Susannah Wallis [?] to brother Charles Wallis, Bromley, 17–19 September 1847, in ibid., 220.
41 Will A. Nicholls to brother Robert Nicholls, Penryn, 13 May 1832, in ibid., 24.
42 W. Lawrence Beynon to mother, Gilgit, 9 September 1895, British Library (BL), India Office Private Papers, Mss Eur D830, Maj.-Gen. Sir William George Lawrence Beynon, file 25.
43 W. Lawrence Beynon to mother, Almora, 17 November 1896, BL, India Office Private Papers, Mss Eur D830, Lawrence Beynon, file 25.
44 Franklin Kendall to mother, Bombay, 16 May 1858, BL, India Office Private Papers, Eur Photo Eur 60, Franklin Richardson Kendall, file 2.
45 Alexander (Allie) Beveridge to sister Phemie, Poona [Pune], 9 October [1868 or 1869]; to mother Jemima, Mean Meer [Mian Mir], 7 December 1868; and to sister Phemie, Rawal Pindee [Rawalpindi], 12 March 1869, BL, India Office Private Papers, Mss Eur C176, Henry and Annette Akroyd Beveridge, file 152.
46 Pollie Keen to mother, Sialkot, 19 January 1890, BL, India Office Private Papers, Mss Eur F528, Mary Caroline (Pollie) Holloway Keen, file 8.
47 Faithy to brother Jonathan Buck, [Ireland], 1 March [1848], in Beattie and Buss, *Undelivered Letters,* 205.
48 Edmund Hope Verney to father, Esquimalt, 21 May 1865, in Pritchard, *Vancouver Island Letters,* 260.
49 Robert Burnaby to sister Sally, Victoria, 27 November 1859, in Anne Burnaby McLeod and Pixie McGeachie, eds., *Land of Promise: Robert Burnaby's Letters from Colonial British Columbia 1858–1863* (Burnaby: City of Burnaby, 2002), 125.
50 See also David A. Gerber, "Epistolary Masquerades: Acts of Deceiving and Withholding in Immigrant Letters," in *Letters across Borders: The Epistolary Practices of International Migrants,* ed. Bruce S. Elliott, David A. Gerber, and Suzanne M. Sinke (Basingstoke, UK: Palgrave Macmillan, 2006), 141–57.
51 Lucy Mathias to cousin Charles Newcombe, Ealing, [n.d.], BCA, MS-1077, Newcombe Family, vol. 18, file 17.
52 Mary Hawks Moody to mother, Victoria, 21 March [1859], BCA, MS-0060, Mary Susanna Moody. Emphasis in original.
53 Edmund Hope Verney to father, Esquimalt Harbour, 16 June 1862, in Pritchard, *Vancouver Island Letters,* 69.

54 Patricia Meyer Spacks, *Boredom: The Literary History of a State of Mind* (Chicago: University of Chicago Press, 1995), 9–24; and Elizabeth S. Goodstein, *Experience without Qualities: Boredom and Modernity* (Stanford, CA: Stanford University Press, 2005).
55 Jeffrey Auerbach, "Imperial Boredom," *Common Knowledge* 11, 2 (Spring 2005): 283–305; and Onni Gust, "'The Perilous Territory of Not Belonging': Exile and Empire in Sir James Mackintosh's Letters from Bombay, c. 1804–1811," *History Workshop Journal*, 86, 1 (October 2018): 22–43. https://doi.org/10.1093/hwj/dby013.
56 Edmund Hope Verney to father, Esquimalt, 1 June 1862, in Pritchard, *Vancouver Island Letters*, 69.
57 Robert Burnaby to brother Tom, Victoria, 21 July 1859, in McLeod and McGeachie, *Land of Promise*, 101.
58 Robert Burnaby to sister Harriet, Victoria, 28 February 1860, in McLeod and McGeachie, *Land of Promise*, 135.
59 Mary Hawks Moody to mother, Hope, 29 August 1860, BCA, MS-1101, Mary Susanna (Hawks) Moody. Emphasis in original.
60 Wilf Rowell to mother, Fort Steele, 11 February 1906, LAC, MG30 C165, Wilfred Bastyan Rowell, vol. 1, file 1.
61 Daisy Oxley Phillips to sister Freda, Wilmer, 14 June 1912, and Athalmer, 1 October 1912, in Harris and Phillips, *Letters from Windermere*, 43 and 102.
62 Roger Hicks to daughters, Stikine River, 18 May 1898, BCA, MS-2167, T. Roger C. Hays Hicks.
63 Edmund Hope Verney to father, Esquimalt, 7 February 1864, in Pritchard, *Vancouver Island Letters*, 191.
64 Edmund Hope Verney to father, Esquimalt, 15 February 1864, in ibid., 192–93.
65 Tommy Norbury to father, Columbia Lakes, 2 August 1888, BCA, MS-0877, Norbury family, box 1, file 3.
66 John Brough to sister Catherine, New Westminster, 24 December 1863, BCA, MS-2797, John Brough.
67 Arthur Birch to brother John, New Westminster, 15 November [1864?], BCA, MS-0061, Birch family, reel A00272.
68 Mary Hawks Moody to mother, New Westminster, 24 November 1862, BCA, MS-1101, Mary Susanna (Hawks) Moody.
69 Mary Hawks Moody to sister Emily, [n.p., late 1859?], BCA, MS-1101, Mary Susanna (Hawks) Moody. Emphasis in original.
70 Adele Perry, *On the Edge of Empire: Gender, Race, and the Making of British Columbia, 1849–1871* (Toronto: University of Toronto Press, 2001), ch. 6; and Laura Ishiguro, "Growing Up and Grown Up ... in Our Future City': Discourses of Childhood and Settler Futurity in Colonial British Columbia," *BC Studies* 190 (Summer 2016): 22–29.
71 Harold Nation to mother, Cranbrook, 13 December 1900, BCA, MS-1151, Nation family.
72 For example, Harold Nation to sister, in camp via Moyie, 24 March 1901, BCA, MS-1151, Nation family.
73 Robert Burnaby to sister Rose, Victoria, 14 March 1860, in McLeod and McGeachie, *Land of Promise*, 137.
74 Robert Burnaby to mother, Victoria, 10 May 1860, in ibid., 141.
75 Robert Burnaby to brother Tom, Victoria, 8 June 1860, in ibid., 143.
76 Robert Burnaby to sister Harriet, Victoria, 28 February 1860, in ibid., 134.

77 Edmund Hope Verney to father, Esquimalt, 6 and 7 May 1865, in Pritchard, *Vancouver Island Letters,* 259–260.

78 Here, I see epistolary emotion functioning as what, in a different context, Ann Cvetkovich calls an "affective register" that translates and redirects attention from the wider political, economic, and social "problems" that actually cause the feeling. Ann Cvetkovich, *Depression: A Public Feeling* (Durham, NC: Duke University Press, 2012), especially 11–12.

79 Spacks, *Boredom,* 13, 25, and 27.

80 Ann Laura Stoler, *Along the Archival Grain: Epistemic Anxieties and Colonial Common Sense* (Princeton, NJ: Princeton University Press, 2009), 247 and 51.

Chapter 4: "A Dreadful Little Glutton"

Acknowledgment: Part of this chapter was previously published as Laura Ishiguro, "'A Dreadful Little Glutton Always Telling You About Food': The Epistolary Everyday and the Making of Settler Colonial British Columbia," *Canadian Historical Review* 99, 2 (June 2018): 258–83. Reprinted with permission from University of Toronto Press, https://www.utpjournals.press/doi/abs/10.3138/chr.99.2.04. Copyright University of Toronto Press.

1 Daisy Oxley Phillips to sister Freda, Athalmer, 5 September 1912, in R. Cole Harris and Elizabeth Phillips, eds., *Letters from Windermere, 1912–1914* (Vancouver: UBC Press, 1984), 84–85. Emphasis in original.

2 See R. Cole Harris, "Introduction," in ibid., xi–xiii and xvii–xviii.

3 John Plotz, *Portable Property: Victorian Culture on the Move* (Princeton, NJ: Princeton University Press, 2008), 45; and Anne J. Kershen, ed., *Food in the Migrant Experience* (Aldershot, UK: Ashgate, 2002). For an overview of the conceptual scholarship on food, see Warren Belasco, *Food: The Key Concepts* (Oxford: Berg, 2008). For a discussion of food in Canadian history, see Franca Iacovetta, Valerie J. Korinek, and Marlene Epp, eds., *Edible Histories Cultural Politics: Towards a Canadian Food History* (Toronto: University of Toronto Press, 2012).

4 On the first point, Sidney W. Mintz, *Sweetness and Power: The Place of Sugar in Modern History* (New York: Viking, 1985); Woodruff D. Smith, "Complications of the Commonplace: Tea, Sugar, and Imperialism," *Journal of Interdisciplinary History* 23, 2 (1992): 259–78; Susan Zlotnick, "Domesticating Imperialism: Curry and Cookbooks in Victorian England," *Frontiers: A Journal of Women Studies* 16, 2/3 (1996): 51–68; James Walvin, *Fruits of Empire: Exotic Produce and British Taste, 1660–1800* (Basingstoke, UK: Macmillan, 1997); and Troy Bickham, "Eating the Empire: Intersections of Food, Cookery and Imperialism in Eighteenth-Century Britain," *Past and Present* 198, 1 (2008): 71–109. On the second point, Elizabeth Vibert, "The Contours of Everyday Life: Food and Identity in the Plateau Fur Trade," in *Gathering Places: Aboriginal and Fur Trade Histories,* ed. Carolyn Podruchny and Laura Peers (Vancouver: UBC Press, 2010), 119–48; Coll Thrush, "Vancouver the Cannibal: Cuisine, Encounter, and the Dilemma of Difference on the Northwest Coast, 1774–1808," *Ethnohistory* 58, 1 (2011): 1–35; Cecilia Leong-Salobir, *Food Culture in Colonial Asia: A Taste of Empire* (New York: Routledge, 2011); Alison Norman, "'Fit for the Table of the Most Fastidious Epicure': Culinary Colonialism in the Upper Canadian Contact Zone," in Iacovetta, Korinek, and Epp, *Edible Histories Cultural Politics,* 31–51; and Rebecca Earle, *The Body of the Conquistador: Food, Race and the Colonial Experience in Spanish America, 1492–1700* (Cambridge: Cambridge University Press, 2012).

5 Bickham, "Eating the Empire," 73.

6 For overviews, see John Burnett, *Plenty and Want: A Social History of Food in England from 1815 to the Present Day* (London: Thomas Nelson, 1966); Jack Goody, *Cooking, Cuisine and Class* (Cambridge: Cambridge University Press, 1982); Stephen Mennell, *All Manners of Food: Eating and Taste in England and France from the Middle Ages to the Present* (Oxford: Basil Blackwell, 1985); and Andrea Broomfield, *Food and Cooking in Victorian England: A History* (London: Praeger, 2007).

7 John Davies to wife and children, Williams Creek, 17 July 1864, published in *Y Gwladgarwr,* 5 November 1864, republished in Alan Conway, "Welsh Gold-Miners in British Columbia during the 1860s," *British Columbia Historical Quarterly* 21 (1958): 71. See also Radcliffe Quine to brother and sister, Victoria, 22 April 1861, CVA, AM-245, Quine family, box 514-G-3, folder 2.

8 Mary Hawks Moody to mother, Victoria, 23 February [1859], BCA, MS-1101, Mary Susanna (Hawks) Moody. Emphasis in original.

9 Edmund Verney to father, Esquimalt, 17 July 1862, in Allan Pritchard, ed., *Vancouver Island Letters of Edmund Hope Verney, 1862–65* (Vancouver: UBC Press, 1996), 73–74.

10 William Arthur Lewis Deaville to parents, Victoria, 18 March 1898, BCA, MS-2044, Deaville family, file 1, box 1.

11 Daisy Oxley Phillips to mother, Athalmer, 8 November 1912, in Harris and Phillips, *Letters from Windermere,* 120.

12 Daisy Oxley Phillips to sister Freda, Athalmer, 4 April 1913, in ibid. 171.

13 Harry Guillod, in Dorothy Blakey Smith, ed., "Harry Guillod's Journal of a Trip to Cariboo, 1862," *British Columbia Historical Quarterly* 19, 3–4 (1955): 208–9.

14 David Pringle to father, Hope, 9 July 1862, BCA, MS-0369, Alexander David Pringle.

15 Roger Hicks to daughters, Boundary Camp, 3 April 1898, BCA, MS-2167, T. Roger C. Hays Hicks.

16 Roger Hicks to daughters, Stikine River, 18 May 1898, BCA, MS-2167, T. Roger C. Hays Hicks.

17 Harry Guillod, in Smith, "Journal of a Trip to Cariboo," 224.

18 Tommy Norbury to mother, Valentine Ranche, 2 August 1888, BCA, MS-0877, Norbury family, box 1, file 3.

19 See Tina Loo, *States of Nature: Conserving Canada's Wildlife in the Twentieth Century* (Vancouver: UBC Press, 2006), ch. 1; Rob Boddice, "Manliness and the 'Morality of Field Sports': E.A. Freeman and Anthony Trollope, 1869–71," *Historian* 70 (2008): 1–29; Mike Huggins, "Sport and the British Upper Classes c. 1500–2000: A Historiographic Overview," *Sport in History* 28, 3 (2008): 364–88; and Peter Bartrip, "Food for the Body and Food for the Mind: The Regulation of Freshwater Fisheries in the 1870s," *Victorian Studies* 28, 2 (1985): 285–304. Some people in Britain did hunt for food, but under different legal, social, and environmental conditions. See Harvey Osborne and Michael Winstanley, "Rural and Urban Poaching in Victorian England," *Rural History* 17, 2 (2006): 187–212.

20 Tommy Norbury to father, Tobacco Plains, 13 November 1887, BCA, MS-0877, Norbury family, box 1, file 2.

21 Tommy Norbury to father, Tobacco Plains, 6 March 1889, BCA, MS-0877, Norbury family, box 1, file 4. Emphasis in original.

22 Tommy Norbury to father, Fort Steele, 14 April 1890, BCA, MS-0877, Norbury family, box 1, file 5.

23 Tommy Norbury to mother, Tobacco Plains, 6 December 1887, BCA, MS-0877, Norbury family, box 1, file 2.
24 Tommy Norbury to father, Tobacco Plains, 13 November 1887, BCA, MS-0877, Norbury family, box 1, file 2.
25 Louie Pringle to sister-in-law Amy, Hope, 16 December 1860, BCA, MS-0369, Alexander David Pringle. Emphasis in original.
26 David Pringle to Mrs. Pringle, Hope, 14 September 1861, BCA, MS-0369, Alexander David Pringle. Emphasis in original.
27 David Pringle to father, Hope, 31 May 1862, BCA, MS-0369, Alexander David Pringle. Emphasis in original.
28 David Pringle to father, Hope, 9 July 1862, BCA, MS-0369, Alexander David Pringle.
29 Daisy Oxley Phillips to sister Freda, Athalmer, 5 September 1912, in Harris and Phillips, *Letters from Windermere,* 85.
30 Daisy Oxley Phillips to sister Freda, Athalmer, 7 August 1912, in ibid., 76.
31 Daisy Oxley Phillips to mother, [Athalmer?], 10 December 1912, in ibid., 134.
32 For an overview, see Broomfield, *Food and Cooking,* especially ch. 1.
33 Adele Perry, *On the Edge of Empire: Gender, Race, and the Making of British Columbia, 1849–1871* (Toronto: University of Toronto Press, 2001), especially 25–28 and 151; and Robert Hogg, *Men and Manliness on the Frontier: Queensland and British Columbia in the Mid-Nineteenth Century* (Basingstoke, UK: Palgrave Macmillan, 2012), especially 113.
34 Harry Guillod, in Smith, "Journal of a Trip to Cariboo," 206; Robert Burnaby to mother and sisters, Burrards Inlet [*sic*], 31 August 1859, in Anne Burnaby McLeod and Pixie McGeachie, eds., *Land of Promise: Robert Burnaby's Letters from Colonial British Columbia 1858–1863* (Burnaby: City of Burnaby, 2002), 112; and Edmund Verney to father, Esquimalt, 25 May 1862, in Pritchard, *Vancouver Island Letters,* 63.
35 Roger Hicks to daughter Josie, Glenora, 12 June 1898, BCA, MS-2167, T. Roger C. Hays Hicks.
36 Morgan Lewis to Rev. D.R. Lewis, New Westminster, 29 October 1862, published in *Seren Cymru,* 23 January 1863, republished in Conway, "Welsh Gold-Miners in British Columbia," 65.
37 Tommy Norbury to mother, Tobacco Plains, 6 December 1887, BCA, MS-0877, Norbury family, box 1, file 2.
38 William Henry Lomas, diary, 24 August 1862, BCA, MS-1236, Lomas family.
39 Harry Guillod, in Smith, "Journal of a Trip to Cariboo," 210.
40 Ibid., 221.
41 Roger Hicks to daughter Josie, Glenora, 12 June 1898, BCA, MS-2167, T. Roger C. Hays Hicks.
42 Tommy Norbury to brother Coni, Tobacco Plains, 24 September 1888, BCA, MS-0877, Norbury family, box 1, file 3. Emphasis in original.
43 David Pringle to father, Hope, 7 April 1860, BCA, MS-0369, Alexander David Pringle. See also Perry, *On the Edge of Empire,* 25.
44 Harry Guillod, in Smith, "Journal of a Trip to Cariboo," 209; and Tommy Norbury to mother, Tobacco Plains, 6 December 1887, BCA, MS-0877, Norbury family, box 1, file 2.
45 Robert Burnaby to sister Harriet, Victoria, 26 January 1861, in McLeod and McGeachie, *Land of Promise,* 158.

46 William Henry Lomas, diary, 18 August 1862, BCA, MS-1236, Lomas family.
47 Harry Guillod, in Smith, "Journal of a Trip to Cariboo," 206.
48 Tommy Norbury to brother Coni Norbury, Tobacco Plains, 24 September 1888, BCA, MS-0877, Norbury family, box 1, file 3.
49 Harry Guillod, in Smith, "Journal of a Trip to Cariboo," 206.
50 Harold Nation to sister, Moyie, 24 March 1901, BCA, MS-1151, Nation family.
51 Tommy Norbury to father, Tobacco Plains, 13 November 1887, BCA, MS-0877, Norbury family, box 1, file 2.
52 Daisy Oxley Phillips to sister Freda, Athalmer, 5 September 1912, in Harris and Phillips, *Letters from Windermere,* 85.
53 Daisy Oxley Phillips to mother, Athalmer, 15 October 1912, in ibid., 108.
54 Daisy Oxley Phillips to mother, Athalmer, 30 August 1912, in ibid., 82.
55 Daisy Oxley Phillips to sister Freda, Athalmer, 20 October 1912, in ibid., 111.
56 Claude Fischler, "Food, Self and Identity," *Social Science Information/Information Sur les Sciences Sociales* 27, 2 (June 1988): 275–92.
57 Fonds description, Fort Steele Heritage Town Archives (FSHTA), MS 30, Nation family, *Memory BC* database, https://www.memorybc.ca/nation-family-fonds.
58 Harold Nation to mother, in camp, Moyie, 5 May 1901, BCA, MS-1151, Nation family.
59 Harold Nation to mother and sister, in camp, Moyie, 17 April 1901, BCA, MS-1151, Nation family.
60 Wilf Rowell to mother, Fairmont Springs, 10 November 1905, LAC, MG30 C165, Wilfred Bastyan Rowell, vol. 1, file 1.
61 Tommy Norbury to mother, Fort Steele, 2 November 1889, BCA, MS-0877, Norbury family, box 1, file 4.
62 Harold Nation to mother, Moyie, 29 November 1900, BCA, MS-1151, Nation family.
63 Harold Nation to mother, Moyie, 8 April 1901, BCA, MS-1151, Nation family.
64 Harold Nation to sister, Moyie, [spring 1901], BCA, MS-1151, Nation family.
65 Daisy Oxley Phillips to mother, near Toby Creek, 24 April 1912, in Harris and Phillips, *Letters from Windermere,* 12.
66 Harold Nation to mother, 5 May 1901, and to sister Belle, 24 November 1901, BCA, MS-1151, Nation family.
67 Harold Nation to mother and sister, Moyie, 17 April 1901, BCA, MS-1151, Nation family.
68 Harold Nation to mother, [n.p.], 31 December 1901, BCA, MS-1151, Nation family.
69 Robert Burnaby to mother, Victoria, 22 May 1862, in McLeod and McGeachie, *Land of Promise,* 169.
70 Mary Hawks Moody to mother, New Westminster, 7 November [1859], BCA, MS-1101, Mary Susanna (Hawks) Moody.
71 Tommy Norbury to mother, Fort Steele, 26 December 1897, BCA, MS-0877, Norbury family, box 1, file 12.
72 Daisy Oxley Phillips to mother, Athalmer, 15 October 1912, in Harris and Phillips, *Letters from Windermere,* 108–9.
73 Leonard Witherby to mother, Westholme, 23 May 1899, BCA, PR-1617, H. Leonard Witherby.
74 Charles Newcombe to wife Marian, Victoria, 11 October 1883, BCA, MS-1077, Newcombe family, vol. 18, file 1.
75 Tommy Norbury to mother, Valentine Ranche, 2 August 1888, BCA, MS-0877, Norbury family, box 1, file 3.

76 Louie Pringle to sister-in-law Amy, Hope, 16 December 1860, BCA, MS-0369, Alexander David Pringle.
77 Daisy Oxley Phillips to sister Freda, Athalmer, 5 September 1912, in Harris and Phillips, *Letters from Windermere,* 85.
78 Robert Burnaby to mother and "all," Victoria, 26 December 1858, in McLeod and McGeachie, *Land of Promise,* 59. Emphasis in original.
79 Alex McIntosh, "The Family Meal and its Significance in Global Times," in *Food in Global History,* ed. Raymond Grew (Oxford: Westview, 1999), 220 and 222; Kate Colquhoun, *Taste: The Story of Britain through Its Cooking* (London: Bloomsbury, 2007), 288–89; and Valerie Mars, "Parsimony amid Plenty: Views from Victorian Didactic Works on Food for Nursery Children," in *Food, Culture and History,* vol. 1, ed. Gerald Mars and Valerie Mars (London: London Food Seminar, 1993), 155.
80 Harry Guillod, in Smith, "Journal of a Trip to Cariboo," 196.
81 See Bruce David Forbes, *Christmas: A Candid History* (Berkeley: University of California Press, 2007); Elizabeth Hafkin Pleck, *Celebrating the Family: Ethnicity, Consumer Culture, and Family Rituals* (Cambridge, MA: Harvard University Press, 2000); Broomfield, *Food and Cooking,* ch. 8; and Kaori O'Connor, "The King's Christmas Pudding: Globalization, Recipes, and the Commodities of Empire," *Journal of Global History* 4, 1 (2009): 127–55.
82 Robert Burnaby to sister Rose, Victoria, 6 January 1860, and to mother, Victoria, 26 December 1861, in McLeod and McGeachie, *Land of Promise,* 130 and 165.
83 Daisy Oxley Phillips to mother, Athalmer, 25 December 1912, in Harris and Phillips, *Letters from Windermere,* 142.
84 Edmund Verney to father, Esquimalt, 25 December 1864, in Pritchard, *Vancouver Island Letters,* 238.
85 Robert Burnaby to mother and "all," Victoria, 26 December 1858, in McLeod and McGeachie, *Land of Promise,* 58.
86 Edmund Verney to father, Esquimalt, 8 December 1862, in Pritchard, *Vancouver Island Letters,* 108.
87 See John Sutton Lutz, *Makúk: A New History of Aboriginal-White Relations* (Vancouver: UBC Press, 2008), ch. 7; Susan Roy and Ruth Taylor, "'We Were Real Skookum Women': The shíshálh Economy and the Logging Industry on the Pacific Northwest Coast," in *Indigenous Women and Work: From Labor to Activism,* ed. Carol Williams (Urbana: University of Illinois Press, 2012), 104–19; and Charles R. Menzies and Caroline F. Butler, "Working in the Woods: Tsimshian Resource Workers and the Forest Industry of British Columbia," *American Indian Quarterly* 25, 3 (2001): 409–30.
88 Rare exceptions include James Bell to brother John Thomson, San Francisco, 27 February 1859, in Willard E. Ireland, ed., "Gold-Rush Days in Victoria, 1858–1859," *British Columbia Historical Quarterly* 12, 3 (July 1948): 239; and Harold Nation to mother, Cranbrook, 23 September 1900, BCA, MS-1151, Nation family.
89 Tommy Norbury to sister Nell, Tobacco Plains, 6 January 1888, BCA, MS-0877, Norbury family, file 3, box 1.
90 On food, race, and Canadian settler colonialism through other kinds of primary sources, see Vibert, "Contours of Everyday Life"; James Daschuk, *Clearing the Plains: Disease, Politics of Starvation, and the Loss of Aboriginal Life* (Regina: University of Regina Press, 2013); and Ian Mosby, "Administering Colonial Science: Nutrition Research and Human Biomedical Experimentation in Aboriginal Communities and Residential Schools, 1942–1952," *Histoire Sociale/Social History* 46, 91 (May 2013): 145–72.

91 Jane Burbank and Frederick Cooper, *Empires in World History: Power and the Politics of Difference* (Princeton, NJ: Princeton University Press, 2010).
92 Annette Cozzi, *The Discourses of Food in Nineteenth-Century British Fiction* (Basingstoke, UK: Palgrave Macmillan, 2010), 7.

Chapter 5: "Irreparable Loss"

Acknowledgment: Part of this chapter draws from an earlier version published as Laura Ishiguro, "'How I Wish I Might Be Near': Distance and the Epistolary Family in Late-Nineteenth-Century Condolence Letters," in *Within and Without the Nation: Canadian History as Transnational History*, ed. Adele Perry, Karen Dubinsky, and Henry Yu (Toronto: University of Toronto Press, 2015). Reprinted with permission from University of Toronto Press. Copyright University of Toronto Press.

1 Death registration 1895-09-009846, Julia Trutch, BCA. See also Peter O'Reilly, diaries and papers, 1895, BCA, MS-2894, O'Reilly family, box 3, files 5 and 20, reels A01911 and A01912; and Ishiguro, "How I Wish I Might Be Near," 212–27.
2 Emily Trutch Pinder White to brother Joseph, Folkestone, 20 July 1895, BCA, MS-2897, Trutch family, box 3, file 54, reel A01949.
3 On Britain, see, for example, Esther Schor, *Bearing the Dead: The British Culture of Mourning from the Enlightenment to Victoria* (Princeton, NJ: Princeton University Press, 1994); Pat Jalland, *Death in the Victorian Family* (Oxford: Oxford University Press, 1996); Sarah Tarlow, "Landscapes of Memory: The Nineteenth-Century Garden Cemetery," *European Journal of Archaeology* 3, 2 (2000): 217–39; Ruth Richardson, *Death, Dissection and the Destitute,* 2nd ed. (London: Phoenix, 2001); Julie-Marie Strange, *Death, Grief and Poverty, 1870–1914* (Cambridge: Cambridge University Press, 2005); Deborah Lutz, "The Dead Still among Us: Victorian Secular Relics, Hair Jewelry, and Death Culture," *Victorian Literature and Culture* 39, 1 (March 2011): 127–42; and Pat Jalland, "Bereavement in the English Family 1850–1980: Exploring Change over Time," *Family Science* 4, 1 (2013): 4–11. On empire, see, for example, David Arnold, "Deathscapes: India in an Age of Romanticism and Empire, 1800–1856," *Nineteenth-Century Contexts* 26, 4 (2004): 339–53; Elizabeth Buettner, "Cemeteries, Public Memory, and Raj Nostalgia in Postcolonial Britain and India," *History and Memory* 18, 1 (Spring/Summer 2006): 5–42; Trev Lynn Broughton, "The *Bengal Obituary:* Reading and Writing Calcutta Graves in the Mid Nineteenth Century," *Journal of Victorian Culture* 15, 1 (April 2010): 39–59; and Lydia Murdoch, "'Supressed Grief': Mourning the Death of British Children and the Memory of the 1857 Indian Rebellion," *Journal of British Studies* 51, 2 (April 2012): 364–92. An exception that considers trans-imperial responses to death is Andrew Prescott Keating, "The Empire of the Dead: British Burial Abroad and the Formation of National Identity" (PhD dissertation, University of California, Berkeley, 2011).
4 For a concise overview, see Pat Jalland, "Victorian Death and its Decline: 1850-1918," in *Death in England: An Illustrated History,* ed. Peter C. Jupp and Clare Gittings (Manchester: Manchester University Press, 1999), 230–55. See also John Morley, *Death, Heaven and the Victorians* (Pittsburgh: University of Pittsburgh Press, 1971); James Stevens Curl, *The Victorian Celebration of Death* (Newton Abbot, UK: David and Charles, 1972); Jalland, *Death in the Victorian Family,* especially 26; Schor, *Bearing the Dead;* Terri Renee Sabatos, "Images of Death and Domesticity in Victorian Britain" (PhD dissertation, Indiana University, 2001); and Sonia A. Bedikian, "The Death of Mourning: From Victorian Crepe to the Little Black Dress," *Omega: Journal of Death and Dying* 57, 1

(2008): 35–52. On poverty and working-class experiences of death, see Strange, *Death, Grief and Poverty;* and Richardson, *Death, Dissection and the Destitute.*

5 For example, C.M. Edwards to Tommy Norbury, Baynes Lake, 19 July 1916, LAC, MG29 C22, Michael Phillipps.

6 George Kidner to daughter Edith Kidner Langley, Market Lavington, 24 January 1894, UBCSC, RBSC-ARC-1322, Langley family, box 1, file 1. I have added punctuation for clarity. Emphasis in original. See also P. Moore to sister, New Westminster, 21 December 1870, NWA, discrete item collection, 144.

7 In my research for this book, I have not located any notifications or condolences that drew on religious traditions other than Christianity, although some British families engaged with British Columbia would have written these. In the closest exception, Sarah Lindley Crease expressed concerns about her father's atheism as he died. Sarah Lindley Crease to father, New Westminster, 17 January 1864, BCA, MS-0055, Crease family, box 11, file 1. On religion, see Michael Wheeler, *Heaven, Hell, and the Victorians* (Cambridge: Cambridge University Press, 1994); and Lynne Marks, *Infidels and the Damn Churches: Irreligion and Religion in Settler British Columbia* (Vancouver: UBC Press, 2017).

8 Thomas Fawcett to sister-in-law, Victoria, 10 January 1864, BCA, MS-1963, Jane Fawcett, reel A1358. Emphasis in original.

9 Daisy Oxley Phillips to mother, Athalmer, 15 August 1912, in R. Cole Harris and Elizabeth Phillips, eds., *Letters from Windermere, 1912–1914* (Vancouver: UBC Press, 1984), 79.

10 Henry Crease to sister-in-law Rebecca, [n.p.], 2 February [n.y.], BCA, MS-0055, Crease family, box 1, file 3.

11 Joseph Trutch to brother John, Victoria, 11 August 1895, UBCSC, RBSC-ARC-1561, Trutch family, box 1, file 58.

12 Frank Newcombe to brother Charles, Ancaster, 12 January 1899, BCA, MS-1077, Newcombe family, vol. 18, file 12, reel A01754; and Daisy Oxley Phillips to mother, Athalmer, 12 September 1912, in Harris and Phillips, *Letters from Windermere,* 94.

13 Tommy Norbury to mother, Fort Steele, 17 May 1896, BCA, MS-0877, Norbury family, box 1, file 11.

14 J.B. McCleery to brother [Fitzgerald?], Clea Lough, 14 January 1891, CVA, AM-114, McCleery family, box 511-F-1, folder 1. See also James Porter to sister-in-law, Victoria, 10 March 1859, BCA, MS-2047, Thomas Porter; and Henry Hawkins to brother Alben, Tottenham, 16 February 1879, BCA, MS-0441, Alben Hawkins, box 1, file 2.

15 For instance, Elizabeth Trutch to Charlotte Hannah Barnes Trutch, [?], 4 August 1849, BCA, MS-2897, Trutch family, box 1, file 4, reel A01947.

16 Jalland, *Death in the Victorian Family,* 307.

17 *Chesterfield's Art of Letter-Writing Simplified: Being a Guide to Friendly, Affectionate, Polite and Business Correspondence* (London, ON: W. Bryce, 1886), 46; and Catherine Mittler Helmcken to son John, London, 7 August 1866, BCA, MS-0505, Helmcken family, box 1, file 16.

18 Grace Davey to uncle Joseph, Datchet, 17 July 1895, BCA, MS-2897, Trutch family, box 2, file 23, reel A01948.

19 For example, Edmund Verney to father, Esquimalt, 27 June 1862; Metlakatlah, 29 October 1863; and Bella-Coula [*sic*], 13 July 1864, in Allan Pritchard, ed., *Vancouver Island Letters of Edmund Hope Verney, 1862–65* (Vancouver: UBC Press, 1996), 70, 178, 180, and 219.

20 John Trutch to brother Joseph, Percy Lodge, 19 July 1895, BCA, MS-2897, Trutch family, box 3, file 47, reel A01948.

21 Elizabeth Davey to Joseph Trutch, Folkestone, 25 July 1895, BCA, MS-2897, Trutch family, box 2, file 25, reel A01948. Emphasis in original.

22 Caroline Pinder Hare to uncle Joseph, 18 July 1895, BCA, MS-2897, Trutch family, box 3, file 10, reel A01948.

23 Grace Davey to uncle Joseph, Datchet, 18 July 1895, BCA, MS-2897, Trutch family, box 2, file 23, reel A01948.

24 Sarah Davey Ashley to uncle Joseph, Percy Lodge, [?] 1895, BCA, MS-2897, Trutch family, box 2, file 9, reel A01948.

25 BCA, MS-2897, Trutch family: Emily Trutch Pinder White to brother Joseph, Folkestone, 20 July 1895, box 3, file 54, reel A01949; and Grace Davey to uncle Joseph, Datchet, 7 August 1895, box 2, file 23, reel A01948.

26 Fannie Harwood to uncle Joseph, Soudan, 10 August 1895, BCA, MS-2897, Trutch family, box 3, file 8, reel A01948.

27 BCA, MS-2897, Trutch family: Emily Trutch Pinder White to brother Joseph, Folkestone, 15 July 1895, box 3, file 54, reel A01949; Beryl Ashley to uncle Joseph, Folkestone, 2 August 1895, box 2, file 8, reel A01948; and Grace Davey to uncle Joseph, Datchet, 7 August 1895, box 2, file 23, reel A01948.

28 Charlotte Ashley Brown to uncle Joseph, Woodbridge, 1 August 1895, BCA, MS-2897, Trutch family, box 2, file 15, reel A01948.

29 Sarah Davey Ashley to uncle Joseph, Percy Lodge, [?] 1895, BCA, MS-2897, Trutch family, box 2, file 9, reel A01948.

30 Grace Davey to uncle Joseph, Datchet, 17 and 18 July 1895, BCA, MS-2897, Trutch family, box 2, file 23, reel A01948.

31 Charlotte Ashley Brown to uncle Joseph, Woodbridge, 1 August 1895, BCA, MS-2897, Trutch family, box 2, file 15, reel A01948.

32 BCA, MS-2897, Trutch family, reel A01948: H.C. Trutch to Joseph, Hornsey, [?] 1895, box 3, file 46; John Trutch to brother Joseph, Clawton, 5 August 1895, box 3, file 47; and Sarah Davey Ashley to uncle Joseph, [?] 1895, Percy Lodge, box 2, file 9.

33 John Trutch to brother Joseph, Percy Lodge, 19 July 1895, BCA, MS-2897, Trutch family, box 3, file 47, reel A01948.

34 Fannie Harwood to uncle Joseph, Soudan, 10 August 1895, BCA, MS-2897, Trutch family, box 3, file 10, reel A01948.

35 Caroline Pinder Hare to uncle Joseph, Folkstone, 20 July 1895, BCA, MS-2897, Trutch family, box 3, file 8, reel A01948. Emphasis in original.

36 Grace Davey to uncle Joseph, Datchet, 18 July 1895, BCA, MS-2897, Trutch family, box 2, file 23, reel A01948.

37 Emily Trutch Pinder White to brother Joseph, Folkestone, 20 July 1895, BCA, MS-2897, Trutch family, box 3, file 54, reel A01949.

38 See K.D.M. Snell, "Gravestones, Belonging and Local Attachment in England 1700–2000," *Past and Present* 179, 1 (May 2003): 97–134; and Karen Wilson Baptist, "Diaspora: Death without a Landscape," *Mortality* 15, 4 (2010): 294–307.

39 Emily Trutch Pinder White to brother Joseph, Folkestone, 20 July 1895, BCA, MS-2897, Trutch family, box 3, file 54, reel A01949.

40 Ada Aspinall to aunt Hannah, Huddersfield, 26 August 1913; and to cousins Michael and Jeannie Wilkinson, London, 5 August 1913, CVA, AM-111, Sam Brighouse, box

511-E-1, folder 3; and Daisy Oxley Phillips to sister Freda, Athalmer, 19 May 1914, and Windermere, 15 November 1914, in Harris and Phillips, *Letters from Windermere,* 209 and 226.

41 C.M. Edwards to Tommy Norbury, Baynes Lake, 19 July 1916, LAC, MG29 C22, Michael Phillipps.

42 Leonore Davidoff and Catherine Hall, *Family Fortunes: Men and Women of the English Middle Class 1780–1850,* rev. ed. (London: Routledge, 2002), 205–6; Jalland, *Death in the Victorian Family,* 224–25 and 295; Chris Clarkson, *Domestic Reforms: Political Visions and Family Regulation in British Columbia, 1862–1940* (Vancouver: UBC Press, 2007), 38–54 and 95–98; Mary Beth Combs, "'A Measure of Legal Independence': The 1870 Married Women's Property Act and the Portfolio Allocations of British Wives," *Journal of Economic History* 65, 4 (December 2005): 1028–57; Mary Beth Combs, "Cui Bono? The 1870 British Married Women's Property Act, Bargaining Power, and the Distribution of Resources within Marriage," *Feminist Economics* 12, 1–2 (2006): 51–83; and Mary Beth Combs, "'Concealing Him from Creditors': How Couples Contributed to the Passage of the 1870 Married Women's Property Act," in *Married Women and the Law: Coverture in England and the Common Law World,* ed. Tim Stretton and Krista J. Kesselring (Montreal and Kingston: McGill-Queen's University Press, 2013), 217–39. On the complexity of family strategies in relation to these structures, albeit in Montreal, see Bettina Bradbury, *Wife to Widow: Lives, Laws, and Politics in Nineteenth-Century Montreal* (Vancouver: UBC Press, 2011).

43 Kevin Neary, "Newcombe, Charles Frederic," in *Dictionary of Canadian Biography Online,* vol. 15 (University of Toronto and Université Laval, 2000), http://www.biographi.ca/en/bio.php?id_nbr=8309; and John Dixon to C.F. Newcombe, Inveran, 28 February 1891 and 30 September 1891, BCA, MS-1077, Newcombe family, vol. 18, file 22. See also William Hugh Wood to father, Derbyshire, 29 June 1880, CVA, AM-114, McCleery family, box 511-F-2, folder 1.

44 Daisy Oxley Phillips to sister Freda, Athalmer, 9 March 1913, in Harris and Phillips, *Letters from Windermere,* 166.

45 For example, Edward Lloyd to mother, Vancouver, 6 April 1905, CVA, AM-875, Edward Lloyd, reel M-104.

46 For example, Daisy Oxley Phillips to sister Freda, Athalmer, 7 September 1912 and 5 September 1912, in Harris and Phillips, *Letters from Windermere,* 91 and 85.

47 For example, John Barnsley to father, Victoria, 13 July 1891, CVIC, PR-24, John Barnsley, box 36E3, file 1.

48 Harris, "Introduction," and Daisy Oxley Phillips to sister Freda, Athalmer, 11 February 1913, in Harris and Phillips, *Letters from Windermere,* xi and 157.

49 Henry Crease to sister-in-law Rebecca, [n.p.], 2 February [n.y.], BCA, MS-0055, Crease family, box 1, file 3. Emphasis in original.

50 Gordon R. Elliott, "Henry P. Pellew Crease: Confederation or No Confederation," *BC Studies* 12 (Winter 1971–72): 70–71.

51 Frank Newcombe to brother Charles, Ancaster, 31 October 1899, BCA, MS-1077, Newcombe family, vol. 18, file 12, reel A01754.

52 William Lister Newcombe to son Frank (enclosed in letter to Charles), Boscombe, 31 October 1899, BCA, MS-1077, Newcombe family, vol. 18, file 12, reel A01754.

53 A.L. Newcombe to brother Charles, Winslow, 26 October 1899, BCA, MS-1077, Newcombe family, vol. 18, file 13, reel A01754.

54 Joseph Morton to cousin Beaumont, Vancouver, 22 January 1913 and 6 January 1914, CVA, AM-860, Morton family, box 590-D-1, folder 14; Robert Morris, *Men, Women and Property in England, 1780–1870: A Social and Economic History of Family Strategies amongst the Leeds Middle Class* (Cambridge: Cambridge University Press, 2005), 100; and Margot Finn, "Family Formations: Anglo India and the Familial Proto-State," in *Structures and Transformations in Modern British History,* ed. David Feldman and Jon Lawrence (Cambridge: Cambridge University Press, 2011), 111.

55 Joseph Morton to cousin Beaumont, Vancouver, 6 January and 7 September 1914, CVA, AM-860, Morton family, box 590-D-1, folder 14.

56 "Morton Will Case Settled," *Province,* 6 June 1934, in Major James Skitt Matthews, *Early Vancouver,* vol. 2 (first published 1933; Vancouver: City of Vancouver, 2011), 97, http://former.vancouver.ca/ctyclerk/archives/digitized/EarlyVan/DownloadPDF/MatthewsEarlyVancouverVol2_FullVersionPDF-A.pdf.

57 Matthews, *Early Vancouver,* vol. 2, 109.

58 *Morton v. Brighouse and Moxon,* Court of Appeal, in E.C. Senkler, *The British Columbia Reports being Reports of Cases Determined in the Court of Appeal, Supreme and County Courts and in Admiralty, with a Table of the Cases Argued, a Table of the Cases Cited, and a Digest of the Principal Matters Reported under the Authority of the Law Society of British Columbia,* vol. 36 (Victoria: Colonist Printing and Publishing, 1926), 231–37; *Morton v. Brighouse,* [1927] SCR 118, 1927 CanLII 37 (SCC), http://canlii.ca/t/21v65; and *Brighouse v. Morton,* [1929] SCR 512, 1929 CanLII 27 (SCC), http://canlii.ca/t/21v1h.

59 Ada Aspinwall to cousins Michael and Jeannie Wilkinson, London, 5 August 1913; to cousin Michael Wilkinson, London, 15 November 1913; to cousins Michael and Jeannie Wilkinson, London, 1 December 1913; and to aunt Hannah, Huddersfield, 26 August 1913, CVA, AM-111, Sam Brighouse, box 511-E-1, folder 3. Emphasis in original.

60 Ada Aspinall to cousin Michael Wilkinson, Huddersfield, 4 September 1913; and to cousins Michael and Jeannie Wilkinson, Huddersfield, 15 October 1913, CVA, AM-111, Sam Brighouse, box 511-E-1, folder 3. Emphasis in original.

61 See also David A. Gerber, "Epistolary Masquerades: Acts of Deceiving and Withholding in Immigrant Letters," in *Letters across Borders: The Epistolary Practices of International Migrants,* ed. Bruce S. Elliott, David A. Gerber, and Suzanne M. Sinke (Basingstoke, UK: Palgrave Macmillan, 2006), 153–54; and Charlotte Erickson, *Invisible Immigrants: The Adaptation of English and Scottish Immigrants in Nineteenth-Century America* (Leicester: Leicester University Press, 1972), 467–69.

62 Radcliffe Quine to brother John and sister, Seattle, 12 August and 2 June 1878; to brother Francis and sister-in-law Maria, Seattle, 29 September 1881; and to brother John, wife, and family, Seattle, 3 July 1879, CVA, AM-245, Quine family, box 514-G-3, folder 2.

63 Radcliffe Quine to brother John and sister, Seattle, 12 August 1878; and to brother Francis and sister-in-law Maria, Seattle, 29 September 1881, CVA, AM-245, Quine family, box 514-G-3, folder 2.

64 Radcliffe Quine to brother John and sister, Seattle, 3 October 1878; to brother Francis and sister-in-law Maria, Seattle, 1 July [1882?]; to brother Francis and sister-in-law, Seattle, 26 March 1882; to brother John, wife, and family, Seattle, 3 July 1879; to brother John, Seattle, 1 December 1879; to brother John and sister, Seattle, 12 August 1878; and to brother John and family, Seattle, 25 January [1882?], CVA, AM-245, Quine family, box 514-G-3, folder 2.

65 R. Cole Harris, *Making Native Space: Colonialism, Resistance, and Reserves in British Columbia* (Vancouver: UBC Press, 2002), ch. 3.

66 "Sticker Campaign Targets 'Racist' B.C. Lieutenant-Governor," CBC News, 14 August 2012, http://www.cbc.ca/news/canada/british-columbia/sticker-campaign-targets-racist-b-c-lieutenant-governor-1.1205660. In 2017, the University of Victoria responded to a long-standing student-led campaign with the decision to rename a residence building formerly commemorating Trutch. See Liam Britten, "UVic to Rename Trutch Building Because of Colonial Politician's Racist Legacy," CBC News, 6 June 2017, http://www.cbc.ca/news/canada/british-columbia/uvic-trutch-joseph-1.4147789. More recently, there has been a movement to change the name of Victoria's Trutch Street. See Deborah Wilson, "Change Urged to Victoria Street Named for 'Racist' Figure," CBC News, 16 January 2018, http://www.cbc.ca/news/canada/british-columbia/trutch-bc-street-name-change-racism-indigenous-1.4489550.

67 See marriage between William George Pinder and Annie Marie Heurielle Devereux, Victoria, 3 January 1877, BCA, registration 1877-09-001296, reel B11367; Trutch and Musgrave family entries in the Legacies of British Slave-Ownership database, University College London, https://www.ucl.ac.uk/lbs/; and, for context, Catherine Hall et al., *Legacies of British Slave-ownership: Colonial Slavery and the Formation of Victorian Britain* (Cambridge: Cambridge University Press, 2014).

68 *British Colonist,* 17 July 1895, 5 and 8; 18 July 1895, 5 and 8; and 19 July 1895, 5.

69 Joseph Trutch to brother John, Victoria, 11 August 1895, UBCSC, RBSC-ARC-1561, Trutch family, box 1, file 58; and List of Articles at Fairfield to be Packed and Sent to England if Required, 1896, BCA, MS-2897, Trutch family, box 9, file 10, reel A01952.

70 Emily Trutch Pinder White to brother Joseph, Folkestone, 20 July 1895, BCA, MS-2897, Trutch family, box 3, file 54, reel A01949.

Chapter 6: "Say Nothing"

1 BCA, MS-0877, Norbury family, box 1: Tommy Norbury, undated letter fragment, probably to a sibling, page beginning "is not anywhere near it," file 1; undated letter fragment, probably to a sibling, page beginning "We have to send up to Wild Horse," file 1; to sister Betty, Cranbrook, 30 October 1887, file 2; to mother, Tobacco Plains, 6 December 1887, file 2; and to brother Coni, Tobacco Plains, 24 September 1888, file 3.

2 Deborah Cohen, *Family Secrets: Living with Shame from the Victorians to the Present Day* (London: Viking, 2013), xiv.

3 For example, Adele Perry, "The Autocracy of Love and the Legitimacy of Empire: Intimacy, Power and Scandal in Nineteenth-Century Metlakahtlah," *Gender and History* 16, 2 (August 2004): 261–88; Kirsten McKenzie, *Scandal in the Colonies: Sydney and Cape Town, 1820–1850* (Melbourne: Melbourne University Press, 2004); and Angela Wanhalla, "The 'Bickerings' of the 'Mangungu Brethren': Talk, Tales and Rumour in Early New Zealand," *Journal of New Zealand Studies* 12 (2011): 13–28.

4 Luise White, *Speaking with Vampires: Rumor and History in Colonial Africa* (Berkeley: University of California Press, 2000), 60.

5 For two useful and very different discussions of colonial intimacy as an analytical category, see Tony Ballantyne, "Strategic Intimacies: Knowledge and Colonization in Southern New Zealand," *Journal of New Zealand Studies* 14 (2013): 4–18; and Lynn Zastoupil, "Intimacy and Colonial Knowledge," *Journal of Colonialism and Colonial History* 3, 2 (Fall 2002), https://doi.org/10.1353/cch.2002.0053.

6 The sources used here indicate that Phillipps did write to his metropolitan family. Both the Fort Steele Heritage Town Archives and Library and Archives Canada hold related records, but despite beguiling archival descriptions, neither contains family correspondence. See FSHTA, MS-3, Michael Phillipps; and LAC, MG29 C22, Michael Phillipps.

7 Margaret Teneese, "Michael Phillipps' Original Records Donated to the Ktunaxa Nation Council Archives," *NationTalk*, 25 November 2015, http://nationtalk.ca/story/michael-phillipps-original-records-donated-to-the-ktunaxa-nation-council-archives.

8 Michel-Rolph Trouillot, *Silencing the Past: Power and the Production of History* (Boston: Beacon, 1995).

9 The most specific birthdate in the archival record (29 September 1840) is in a memorandum providing personal information for Phillipps's employment as an Indian Agent. See correspondence regarding Indian matters and the appointment of Michael Phillipps [sic] as agent for the Kootenay Agency, 13 June 1890, LAC, RG 10, Indian Affairs, vol. 3719, file 22673, reel C10126. See also Naomi Miller, "Michael Phillipps: Prominent Kootenay Citizen," in *The Forgotten Side of the Border: British Columbia's Elk Valley and Crowsnest Pass,* ed. Wayne Norton and Naomi Miller (Kamloops: Plateau, 1998), 29; marriage registration, Thomas Phillipps and Penelope Biddulph, September 1838, St. Martin in the Fields, Civil Registration Index for England and Wales, vol. 1, p. 125, via FreeBMD, https://www.freebmd.org.uk; Record of Institution of Rev. Thomas Phillipps M.A. to vicarage of Dewsall, 2 May 1838, Herefordshire Archive and Records Centre, K98/8, catalogued in NAUK database; and household of Thomas Phillipps, Dewsall, NAUK, RG9/1816, Census Returns of England and Wales, 1861, via Ancestry, https://www.ancestry.co.uk. Early on, I was directed to clues about Phillipps's family of origin by Christopher Richards's compilation of genealogical research on "Richards of Wexford and Other Families," Rootsweb, http://homepages.rootsweb.ancestry.com/~cmricha/fam5391.html.

10 Miller, ibid., 31.

11 Biographical sheet, Michael Phillipps, Hudson's Bay Company Archives (HBCA), https://www.gov.mb.ca/chc/archives/hbca/biographical/p/phillips_michael.pdf.

12 Miller, "Michael Phillipps," 31–38; crown grant, Michael Phillipps, East Kootenay, 1 August 1892, BCA, GR-3097, Crown Land Grants, vol. 0055, no. 4221, reel B14232; records for the Rock Shaft Company, Wild Horse Creek, FSHTA, MS-3, Michael Phillipps; and death registration, Michael Phillipps, 22 June 1916, BCA, 1916-09-184035.

13 Miller, ibid., 29.

14 G.P.V. Akrigg and Helen Akrigg, "Phillipps Creek," in *British Columbia Place Names,* 3rd ed. (Vancouver: UBC Press, 1997), 207; Olga Weydemeyer Johnson, ed., *The Story of the Tobacco Plains Country: The Autobiography of a Community* (Rexford, MT: Pioneers of the Tobacco Plains Country, 1950), 56; "Fruitlands' Orchards – M. Phillipps Gives Some Facts Regarding This Promising Section," Cranbrook *Herald,* 18 April 1912, in Columbia Basin Institute (CBI), 0052.0494, https://basininstitute.org/search/details.html?id=26993#.W0GsUSen-Ul; Miller, ibid., 32–37; and Michael Phillipps, "Winter Trip on the C.P.R.," LAC, MG29 C22, Michael Phillipps.

15 "Michael Phillipps' House – Shades of the Colorful Past Cast Their Shadow," Cranbrook *Daily Townsman,* 6 September 1973, in CBI, 0052.0372, https://basininstitute.org/search/details.html?id=26871#.W0GsfCen-Ul. For an exception, with a brief discussion of Norbury's letters about the family, see Jean Barman, *Sojourning Sisters: The Lives and Letters of Jessie and Annie McQueen* (Toronto: University of Toronto Press, 2003), 171–73.

16 Elizabeth Furniss, *The Burden of History: Colonialism and the Frontier Myth in a Rural Canadian Community* (Vancouver: UBC Press, 1999), 69–70 and 16–22.

17 Barman, *Sojourning Sisters,* 3. This chapter takes particular inspiration from Clare Anderson's compelling approach to trace-based colonial biographies. See Clare Anderson, *Subaltern Lives: Biographies of Colonialism in the Indian Ocean World, 1790–1920* (Cambridge: Cambridge University Press, 2012).

18 Although it is not primarily about the David-Phillipps family, Barman's discussion of Sophie Morigeau does some of this work in its treatment of Susan Phillipps's recollections. See Jean Barman, "Sophie Morigeau: Free Trader, Free Woman," in *Recollecting: Lives of Aboriginal Women of the Canadian Northwest and Borderlands,* ed. Sarah Carter and Patricia McCormack (Edmonton: Athabasca University Press, 2011), 189–92.

19 Quoted in Teneese, "Michael Phillipps' Original Records Donated."

20 Miller, "Michael Phillipps'," 33; and BCA, MS-0877, Norbury family. Norbury was born in 1867, well after Phillipps had left England; see information on Norbury, box 2, file 5. Letters throughout the collection make it clear that the Norburys knew various members of the Grasett family. Examples include Tommy Norbury to father, Tobacco Plains, 13 November 1887, box 1, file 2; to brother Coni, Tobacco Plains, 24 September 1888, box 1, file 3; to mother, Fort Steele, 10 October 1888, box 1, file 3; to father, Fort Steele, 21 July 1890, box 1, file 5; and to mother, Fort Steele, 9 December 1891, box 1, file 6. These sources spell Grasett in different ways. Outside of direct quotations, I have standardized it to the spelling used in the UK census returns, including household of Edward Grasett, Herefordshire, Census Returns of England and Wales, 1891, RG12, NAUK, via *Ancestry,* https://www.ancestry.co.uk.

21 Michael Phillipps, "Winter Trip on the C.P.R.," LAC, MG29 C22, Michael Phillipps.

22 W. Henry Barnaby to Thomas Coningsby Norbury, Winnipeg, 14 September 1887, BCA, MS-0877, Norbury family, box 1, file 2. Barnaby uses a sexist and racist term to refer to Rowena David Phillipps here. This word also appears in several other passages quoted in this chapter. It was a common English settler term to denote Indigenous women in this period, but it is no longer in acceptable common usage. I have chosen to abbreviate the word throughout the chapter. Emphasis in original.

23 Philippa Levine, "Sexuality, Gender, and Empire," in *Gender and Empire,* ed. Philippa Levine (Oxford: Oxford University Press, 2004), 134–55; and Esmé Cleall, Laura Ishiguro, and Emily J. Manktelow, "Imperial Relations: Histories of Family in the British Empire," *Journal of Colonialism and Colonial History* 14, 1 (Spring 2013), https://doi.org/10.1353/cch.2013.0006. Among a large field, studies of interracial families and empire include Durba Ghosh, *Sex and the Family in Colonial India: The Making of Empire* (Cambridge: Cambridge University Press, 2006); Angela Wanhalla, *Matters of the Heart: A History of Interracial Marriage in New Zealand* (Auckland: Auckland University Press, 2013); Pernille Ipsen, *Daughters of the Trade: Atlantic Slavers and Interracial Marriage on the Gold Coast* (Philadelphia: University of Pennsylvania Press, 2015); Carina E. Ray, *Crossing the Color Line: Race, Sex, and the Contested Politics of Colonialism in Ghana* (Athens: Ohio University Press, 2015); and Jane McCabe, *Race, Tea and Colonial Resettlement: Imperial Families, Interrupted* (London: Bloomsbury, 2017).

24 Sylvia Van Kirk, *Many Tender Ties: Women in Fur-Trade Society in Western Canada, 1670–1870* (Winnipeg: Watson and Dwyer, 1980); Jennifer S.H. Brown, *Strangers in Blood: Fur Trade Company Families in Indian Country* (Vancouver: UBC Press, 1980);

Adele Perry, *On the Edge of Empire: Gender, Race, and the Making of British Columbia, 1849–1871* (Toronto: University of Toronto Press, 2001); and Jean Barman, *French Canadians, Furs, and Indigenous Women in the Making of the Pacific Northwest* (Vancouver: UBC Press, 2014).

25 Jean Barman, "Taming Aboriginal Sexuality: Gender, Power, and Race in British Columbia, 1850–1900," *BC Studies* 115/116 (Autumn/Winter 1997/98): 237–66; Sylvia Van Kirk, "From 'Marrying-In' to 'Marrying-Out': Changing Patterns of Aboriginal/Non-Aboriginal Marriage in Colonial Canada," *Frontiers: A Journal of Women Studies* 23, 3 (2002): 1–11; Jay Nelson, "'A Strange Revolution in the Manners of the Country': Aboriginal-Settler Intermarriage in Nineteenth-Century British Columbia," in *Regulating Lives: Historical Essays on the State, Society, the Individual, and the Law,* ed. John McLaren, Robert Menzies, and Dorothy E. Chunn (Vancouver: UBC Press, 2002), 23–62; Victoria Freeman, "Attitudes toward 'Miscegenation' in Canada, the United States, New Zealand, and Australia, 1860–1914," *Native Studies Review* 16, 1 (2005): 41–69; Angela Wanhalla, "Women 'Living across the Line': Intermarriage on the Canadian Prairies and in Southern New Zealand, 1870–1900," *Ethnohistory* 55, 1 (Winter 2008): 29–49; Sarah Carter, *The Importance of Being Monogamous: Marriage and Nation Building in Western Canada to 1915* (Edmonton: University of Alberta Press and Athabasca University Press, 2008); and Angela Wanhalla, "Rethinking 'Squaw Men' and 'Pakeha-Maori': Legislating White Masculinity in New Zealand and Canada, 1840–1900," in *Re-Orienting Whiteness,* ed. Leigh Boucher, Jane Carey, and Katherine Ellinghaus (New York: Palgrave Macmillan, 2009), 219–34. Cecilia Morgan demonstrates that these broader ideas shaped, in different ways, relationships between Indigenous men and non-Indigenous women. See "Creating Interracial Intimacies: British North America, Canada, and the Transatlantic World, 1830–1914," *Journal of the Canadian Historical Association* 19, 2 (2008): 76–105.

26 Sylvia Van Kirk, "Tracing the Fortunes of Five Founding Families of Victoria," *BC Studies* 115/116 (Winter 1997/98): 149–80; and Adele Perry, *Colonial Relations: The Douglas-Connolly Family and the Nineteenth-Century Imperial World* (Cambridge: Cambridge University Press, 2015).

27 A recent exception is Krista Barclay, "From Rupert's Land to Canada West: Hudson's Bay Company Families and Representations of Indigeneity in Small-Town Ontario, 1840–1980," *Journal of the Canadian Historical Association* 26, 1 (2015): 67–97.

28 Will Jackson discusses a similar "archival haze" that both reveals and obscures the social practices of a wide diversity of interracial relationships in early twentieth-century Natal, albeit in different legal and social circumstances. See Will Jackson, "Not Seeking Certain Proof: Interracial Sex and Archival Haze in High-Imperial Natal," in *Subverting Empire: Deviance and Disorder in the British Colonial World,* ed. Will Jackson and Emily J. Manktelow (Basingstoke, UK: Palgrave Macmillan, 2015), 185–204.

29 Van Kirk, "From 'Marrying-In' to 'Marrying-Out,'" 1; and Robin Jarvis Brownlie, "Intimate Surveillance: Indian Affairs, Colonization, and the Regulation of Aboriginal Women's Sexuality," in *Contact Zones: Aboriginal and Settler Women in Canada's Colonial Past,* ed. Katie Pickles and Myra Rutherdale (Vancouver: UBC Press, 2005), 170–71.

30 On Indigenous women's shifting strategies in this context, see, for example, Van Kirk, "Tracing the Fortunes"; and Nadine Schuurman, "Contesting Patriarchies: Nlha7pamux and Stl'atl'imx Women and Colonialism in Nineteenth-Century British Columbia," *Gender, Place and Culture* 5, 2 (1998): 141–58.

31 Jeremy Mouat, *Roaring Days: Rossland's Mines and the History of Mining in British Columbia* (Vancouver: UBC Press, 1995); R. Cole Harris, *The Resettlement of British Columbia: Essays on Colonialism and Geographical Change* (Vancouver: UBC Press, 1997), ch. 7; Leslie Robertson, *Imagining Difference: Legend, Curse, and Spectacle in a Canadian Mining Town* (Vancouver: UBC Press, 2005); and Myler Wilkinson and Duff Sutherland, "'From Our Side We Will be Good Neighbour[s] to Them': Doukhobor-Sinixt Relations at the Confluence of the Kootenay and Columbia Rivers in the Early Twentieth Century," *BC Studies* 174 (Summer 2012): 33–59.

32 R. Cole Harris, *Making Native Space: Colonialism, Resistance, and Reserves in British Columbia* (Vancouver: UBC Press, 2002), 7.

33 Peter O'Reilly, Reserve Commissioner Report, in Canada, Department of Indian Affairs, *Annual Report,* 1884, lxxiii. See also Johnson, *The Story of the Tobacco Plains Country,* 54–55.

34 Harris, *Making Native Space,* 210. Phillipps may have served as a Ktunaxa interpreter for O'Reilly. See O'Reilly, ibid.; and Miller, "Michael Phillipps," 32.

35 Peter O'Reilly, Reserve Commissioner Report, in Canada, Department of Indian Affairs, *Annual Report,* 1887, 154. See also Harris, ibid., 191 and 210–11.

36 I.W. Powell, Indian Superintendent Report, British Columbia, in Canada, Department of Indian Affairs, *Annual Report,* 1887, 131–33. This is detailed further in correspondence regarding Indian matters and the appointment of Michael Phillips [sic] as agent for the Kootenay Agency, LAC, RG-10, Indian Affairs, vol. 3719, file 22673, reel C10126.

37 Michael Phillipps, Indian Agent Report, Kootenay Agency, in Canada, Department of Indian Affairs, *Annual Report,* 1887, 123. See also Michael Phillipps, Indian Agent Report, Kootenay Agency, in Canada, Department of Indian Affairs, *Annual Report,* 1888, 115, and 1890, 193.

38 Canada, Royal Commission on Indian Affairs for the Province of British Columbia, *Agency Testimonies,* Meeting with the Tobacco Plains Tribe or Band of Indians, 17 September 1914, 30–46, via Union of British Columbia Indian Chiefs, Digital Collections, http://gsdl.ubcic.bc.ca/.

39 Tommy Norbury to father, Tobacco Plains, 13 November 1887, BCA, MS-0877, Norbury family, box 1, file 2.

40 Tommy Norbury to sister Betty, Cranbrook, 30 October 1887, BCA, MS-0877, Norbury family, box 1, file 2.

41 Tommy Norbury to father, Tobacco Plains, 13 November 1887, BCA, MS-0877, Norbury family, box 1, file 2.

42 Thanks to Paige Raibmon for this point.

43 Tommy Norbury to father, Tobacco Plains, 13 November 1887, BCA, MS-0877, Norbury family, box 1, file 2. The 1891 Canadian census return lists Michael, Robina [sic], and ten children living in the Phillipps household: William (21), Robina (19), Reginald (17), Michael (15), John (14), Philip (11), Susan (10), Maude (9), Jane (3), and Alice (8 months). Family 112, Upper Kootenai, Yale, British Columbia, LAC, RG 31, Census of Canada, 1891, reel T6292, p. 12, digitized as image 30953_148094–00514, http://www.bac-lac.gc.ca/eng/census/1891/Pages/item.aspx?itemid=91120.

44 Tommy Norbury to father, Tobacco Plains, 13 November 1887, BCA, MS-0877, Norbury family, box 1, file 2.

45 Thanks to Devin Eeg for a question that pushed me on this point.

46 Undated and unaddressed letter fragment, Tommy Norbury to parent(s), page beginning "If Bill is coming," BCA, MS-0877, Norbury family, box 1, file 1. Emphasis in original.

47 See Paige Raibmon, "The Practice of Everyday Colonialism: Indigenous Women at Work in the Hop Fields and Tourist Industry of Puget Sound," *Labor* 3, 3 (Fall 2006), especially 45–49; Peggy Brock, "Nakedness and Clothing in Early Encounters between Aboriginal People of Central Australia, Missionaries and Anthropologists," *Journal of Colonialism and Colonial History* 8, 1 (Spring 2007), https://doi.org/10.1353/cch.2007.0015; Philippa Levine, "States of Undress: Nakedness and the Colonial Imagination," *Victorian Studies* 50, 2 (Winter 2008): 189–219; and Philippa Levine, "Naked Truths: Bodies, Knowledge, and the Erotics of Colonial Power," *Journal of British Studies* 52, 1 (January 2013): 5–25.

48 Undated and unaddressed letter fragment, Tommy Norbury to parent(s), typescript page beginning "ill & hope he pulling round," BCA, MS-0877, Norbury family, box 1, file 1.

49 Billy and Tommy Norbury to mother, Tobacco Plains, 16 August 1888, BCA, MS-0877, Norbury family, box 1, file 3. For other notable examples of personal encounters refracted through colonial tropes, see Tommy Norbury to mother, Tobacco Plains, 6 December 1887, BCA, MS-0877, Norbury family, box 1, file 2; and Tommy Norbury to mother, Fort Steele, 16 June 1892, BCA, MS-0877, Norbury family, box 1, file 7.

50 Tommy Norbury to sister Nell, Tobacco Plains, 6 January 1888, BCA, MS-0877, Norbury family, box 1, file 3.

51 My thinking on "colonial toolkits" comes from the 2014 conference "Hard and Soft Power: Questions of Race, Intimacy and Violence in the Comparative Colonial Toolkit," organized by Emily Manktelow at the University of Kent.

52 Personal letters were not the only medium used for such inquiries. See also Elizabeth Jane Errington, "'Information Wanted': Women Emigrants in a Transatlantic World," in *Canada and the British World: Culture, Migration, and Identity*, ed. Phillip Buckner and R. Douglas Francis (Vancouver: UBC Press, 2006), 10–28.

53 Tommy Norbury to father, Fish Lakes, 23 February 1895, BCA, MS-0877, Norbury family, box 1, file 10.

54 Tommy Norbury to brother Coni, Tobacco Plains, 10 February 1888, BCA, MS-0877, Norbury family, box 1, file 3.

55 Ibid.

56 Tommy Norbury to parent(s), first page with addressee and date missing, page begins "2 from you," likely spring 1888, BCA, MS-0877, Norbury family, box 1, file 3.

57 Undated and unaddressed letter fragment, Tommy Norbury to parent(s), page beginning "ill & hope he pulling round," BCA, MS-0877, Norbury family, box 1, file 1.

58 Tommy Norbury to father, Fort Steele, 4 July 1890, BCA, MS-0877, Norbury family, box 1, file 5.

59 Tommy Norbury to brother Coni, Tobacco Plains, 10 February 1888, BCA, MS-0877, Norbury family, box 1, file 3.

60 Quoted in Tommy Norbury to parent(s), first page with addressee and date missing, page begins "2 from you," likely spring 1888, BCA, MS-0877, Norbury family, box 1, file 3.

61 Tommy Norbury to father, Fort Steele, 1 May 1891, BCA, MS-0877, Norbury family, box 1, file 6.

62 Tommy Norbury to brother Coni, Tobacco Plains, 10 February 1888, BCA, MS-0877, Norbury family, box 1, file 3.

63 Tommy Norbury to father, Fort Steele, 1 May 1891, BCA, MS-0877, Norbury family, box 1, file 6.

64 Tommy Norbury to sister Betty, Cranbrook, 30 October 1887, BCA, MS-0877, Norbury family, box 1, file 2. Emphasis in original.

65 Tommy Norbury to father, Tobacco Plains, 13 November 1887, BCA, MS-0877, Norbury family, box 1, file 2.

66 I am grateful for Adele Perry's insight on this point.

67 Tommy Norbury to mother, Fort Steele, 10 October 1890, BCA, MS-0877, Norbury family, box 1, file 5.

68 Tommy Norbury to father, Fort Steele, 1 November 1890, BCA, MS-0877, Norbury family, box 1, file 5.

69 Tommy Norbury to mother, Fort Steele, 17 January 1891, BCA, MS-0877, Norbury family, box 1, file 6.

70 Tommy Norbury to brother Coni, Tobacco Plains, 10 February 1888, BCA, MS-0877, Norbury family, box 1, file 3.

71 Tommy Norbury to father, Fort Steele, 1 May 1891, BCA, MS-0877, Norbury family, box 1, file 6.

72 Tommy Norbury to mother, Fort Steele, 10 February 1892, BCA, MS-0877, Norbury family, box 1, file 7.

73 Tommy Norbury to mother, Fish Lakes, 21 February 1896, BCA, MS-0877, Norbury family, box 1, file 11; and Tommy Norbury to father, Fish Lakes, 7 February 1898, BCA, MS-0877, Norbury family, box 1, file 13.

74 David A. Gerber, "Epistolary Masquerades: Acts of Deceiving and Withholding in Immigrant Letters," in *Letters across Borders: The Epistolary Practices of International Migrants,* ed. Bruce S. Elliott, David A. Gerber, and Suzanne M. Sinke (Basingstoke, UK: Palgrave Macmillan, 2006), 148–50.

75 Tommy Norbury to Augusta Grasett, The Norrest, 23 June 1916, LAC, MG29 C22, Michael Phillipps.

76 C.M. Edwards to Tommy Norbury, Baynes Lake, 19 July 1916, LAC, MG29 C22, Michael Phillipps. Michael Phillipps and Rowena David Phillipps (d. 1935) were buried in the Roosville Cemetery. See death registration, Rowen [sic] Phillipps, 25 May 1935, BCA, 1935-09-510730; Michael Phillipps, Roosville Cemetery, Find a Grave Memorial 131682825, https://www.findagrave.com/memorial/131682825; and Rowena Phillipps, Roosville Cemetery, Find a Grave Memorial 131684727, https://www.findagrave.com/memorial/131684727. I am grateful that Patricia A. Goulden photographed and documented the graves on the Find a Grave database.

77 C.M. Edwards to Tommy Norbury, Baynes Lake, 19 July 1916, LAC, MG29 C22, Michael Phillipps.

78 White, *Speaking with Vampires,* 77.

Conclusion

1 The following family history has been compiled from Henry Hunter Murdoch, "My History," and David Carruthers Murdoch, recollections, both in the author's private collection.

2 Henry Hunter Murdoch, "My History," 8–9, author's private collection.

3 See E.M. Collingham, *Imperial Bodies: The Physical Experience of the Raj, c. 1800–1947* (Cambridge: Polity, 2001); Elizabeth Buettner, *Empire Families: Britons and Late Imperial India* (Oxford: Oxford University Press, 2004); and Margot Finn, "Anglo-Indian Lives in the Later Eighteenth and Early Nineteenth Century," *Journal for Eighteenth-Century Studies* 33, 1 (March 2010): 49–65.

4 See Buettner, *Empire Families,* ch. 5.

5 See Jason Patrick Bennett, "Apple of the Empire: Landscape and Imperial Identity in Turn-of-the-Century British Columbia," *Journal of the Canadian Historical Association* 9, 1 (1998): 63–92; and Jean Barman, "Unpacking English Gentlemen Emigrants' Cultural Baggage: Apple Orchards and Private Schools in British Columbia's Okanagan Valley," *British Journal of Canadian Studies* 16, 1 (2003): 137–49. On settler colonial retirements from India, see Buettner, *Empire Families,* ch. 5; and J.F. Bosher, *Vancouver Island in the Empire* (Tamarac, FL: Llumina, 2012).

6 David Carruthers Murdoch, recollections, 4, author's private collection; and W.R. Carruthers, "Edward Maurice Carruthers, J.P.," *Thirty-Second Report of the Okanagan Historical Society* (1968): 63–66.

7 David Carruthers Murdoch, recollections, 19, author's private collection.

8 Ibid., 14.

9 See David Lambert and Alan Lester, eds., *Colonial Lives across the British Empire: Imperial Careering in the Long Nineteenth Century* (Cambridge: Cambridge University Press, 2006).

10 Mary A. Procida, *Married to the Empire: Gender, Politics and Imperialism in India, 1883–1947* (Manchester: Manchester University Press, 2002), 5.

11 While our subjects and their past and present vulnerabilities differ significantly, my reflections here owe much to Jane Nicholas, "A Debt to the Dead? Ethics, Photography, History, and the Study of Freakery," *Histoire Sociale/Social History* 47, 93 (May 2014): 139–55.

12 This is a nineteenth-century phrase explored further in Marilyn Lake and Henry Reynolds, *Drawing the Global Colour Line: White Men's Countries and the International Challenge of Racial Equality* (Cambridge: Cambridge University Press, 2008). See also Adam McKeown, *Chinese Migrant Networks and Cultural Change: Peru, Chicago, and Hawaii 1900–1936* (Chicago: University of Chicago Press, 2001); Erika Lee, "Orientalisms in the Americas: A Hemispheric Approach to Asian American History," *Journal of Asian American Studies* 8, 3 (2005): 235–56; Henry Yu, "Refracting Pacific Canada: Seeing Our Uncommon Past," *BC Studies* 156/157 (2007): 5–10; Andrea Geiger, *Subverting Exclusion: Transpacific Encounters with Race, Caste, and Borders, 1885–1928* (New Haven, CT: Yale University Press, 2011); Kornel Chang, *Pacific Connections: The Making of the US-Canadian Borderlands* (Berkeley: University of California Press, 2012); and David C. Atkinson, *The Burden of White Supremacy: Containing Asian Migration in the British Empire and the United States* (Chapel Hill: University of North Carolina Press, 2016).

13 See Emma Battell Lowman and Adam J. Barker, *Settler: Identity and Colonialism in 21st Century Canada* (Halifax: Fernwood, 2015).

14 Here, I again play with the idea of being "at home with the empire," explored in Catherine Hall and Sonya O. Rose, eds., *At Home with the Empire: Metropolitan Culture and the Imperial World* (Cambridge: Cambridge University Press, 2006).

Bibliography

Legal cases

Brighouse v. Morton, [1929] SCR 512, 1929 CanLII 27 (SCC), http://canlii.ca/t/21v1h.

Morton v. Brighouse, [1927] SCR 118, 1927 CanLII 37 (SCC), http://canlii.ca/t/21v65.

Morton v. Brighouse and Moxon, Court of Appeal, in E.C. Senkler, *The British Columbia Reports, Being Reports of Cases Determined in the Court of Appeal, Supreme and County Courts and in Admiralty, with a Table of the Cases Argued, a Table of the Cases Cited, and a Digest of the Principal Matters Reported under the Authority of the Law Society of British Columbia,* vol. 36 (Victoria: Colonist Printing and Publishing, 1926), 231–37.

Databases and online archives

British Colonist. Digitized at http://britishcolonist.ca/.

Canadian Great War Project, Canadian Expeditionary Force soldier database, compiled from Library and Archives Canada, RG 150, http://canadiangreatwarproject.com/.

Columbia Basin Institute of Regional History database, https://www.basininstitute.org/home/index.html.

Find a Grave database, https://www.findagrave.com.

FreeBMD database, Civil Registration Index for England and Wales, https://www.freebmd.org.uk.

Hudson's Bay Company Archives. Employee Biographical Sheet, Michael Phillipps, https://www.gov.mb.ca/chc/archives/hbca/biographical/p/phillips_michael.pdf.

Legacies of British Slave-Ownership database, University College London, https://www.ucl.ac.uk/lbs/.

Memory BC database, catalogues for British Columbia archives, https://www.memorybc.ca/.

National Archives database, catalogues for United Kingdom archives, http://discovery.nationalarchives.gov.uk/.

Archival Sources

British Columbia Archives (BCA)

GR-3097, Crown Land Grants

MS-0055, Crease family

MS-0060, Mary Susanna Moody

MS-0061, Birch family

MS-0142, John Christie

MS-0369, Alexander David Pringle

MS-0441, Alben Hawkins

MS-0505, Helmcken family
MS-0877, Norbury family
MS-1077, Newcombe family
MS-1101, Mary Susanna (Hawks) Moody
MS-1151, Nation family
MS-1236, Lomas family
MS-1463, Alexander Harris
MS-1963, Jane Fawcett
MS-2044, Deaville family
MS-2047, Thomas Porter
MS-2073, Samuel O. Beeman
MS-2112, John Evans
MS-2166, Jessie Chambers
MS-2167, T. Roger C. Hays Hicks
MS-2436, Victor Robinson
MS-2443, Frederick Dally
MS-2797, John Brough
MS-2819, Cornelius Bryant
MS-2879, Crease family
MS-2894, O'Reilly family
MS-2897, Trutch family
PR-1509, Papley family
PR-1540, Annie Deans
PR-1616, Felicite Caroline (Bayley) Wolfenden
PR-1617, H. Leonard Witherby

British Columbia Archives, vital events registrations (BCA)
1877-09-001296, marriage, William George Pinder and Annie Marie Heurielle Devereux
1879-09-092583, marriage, Felicite Caroline Bayley and Richard Wolfenden
1895-09-009846, death, Julia Trutch
1916-09-184035, death, Michael Phillipps
1935-09-510730, death, Rowena Phillipps

British Library, India Office Private Papers (BL)
Eur MSS Photo Eur 60, Franklin Richardson Kendall
Mss Eur C176, Henry and Annette Akroyd Beveridge
Mss Eur D830, Major-Gen. Sir William George Lawrence Beynon
Mss Eur F528, Mary Caroline (Pollie) Holloway Keen

City of Vancouver Archives (CVA)
AM-23, Goepel family
AM-24, Cornelius Bryant
AM-54-S11-3, Major Matthews
AM-111, Sam Brighouse
AM-114, McCleery family
AM-245, Quine family
AM-860, Morton family
AM-875, Edward Lloyd

City of Victoria Archives (CVIC)
PR-24, John Barnsley
PR-35, Rattenbury family
PR-76, Cridge family
PR-118, Charles Hayward

Fort Steele Heritage Town Archives (FSHTA)
MS-3, Michael Phillipps

Library and Archives Canada (LAC)
MG29 C22, Michael Phillipps
MG30 C165, vol. 1, Wilfred Bastyan Rowell
RG 10, Indian Affairs
RG 31, Census of Canada, 1891

National Archives, United Kingdom (NAUK)
RG9, Census Returns of England and Wales, 1861 (digitized by Ancestry, https://www.ancestry.co.uk)
RG12, Census Returns of England and Wales, 1891 (digitized by Ancestry, https://www.ancestry.co.uk)
CO305, Colonial Office: Vancouver Island Original Correspondence (digitized by Colonial Despatches of Vancouver Island and British Columbia 1846–1871 digital archive, University of Victoria, https://bcgenesis.uvic.ca/)
CO60, Colonial Office: British Columbia Original Correspondence (digitized by Colonial Despatches of Vancouver Island and British Columbia 1846–1871 digital archive, University of Victoria, https://bcgenesis.uvic.ca/)

New Westminster Archives (NWA)
144, Discrete item collection
IH1993.40, Official Administrator (New Westminster, BC)
IH2007.151F.2 (1/2), Peebles family

Private collection, author
David Carruthers Murdoch, recollections
Henry Hunter Murdoch, "My History"

University of British Columbia Rare Books and Special Collections (UBCSC)
RBSC-ARC-1322, Langley family
RBSC-ARC-1561, Trutch family
RBSC-ARC-1702, Royal Fisk

Books and Articles

Aids to Epistolary Correspondence, or, Familiar Directions for Writing Letters on Various Subjects: Also Rules of Punctuation. Quebec: C. Darveau, 1887.

Akrigg, G.P.V. and Helen Akrigg. *British Columbia Place Names.* 3rd ed. Vancouver: UBC Press, 1997.

Amyot, Chantal, Bianca Gendreau, and John Willis. *Special Delivery: Canada's Postal Heritage.* Hull, QC: Canadian Museum of Civilization, 2000.

Amyot, Chantal, and John Willis. *Country Post: Rural Postal Service in Canada, 1880–1945.* Gatineau, QC: Canadian Museum of Civilization, 2003. https://doi.org/10.2307/j.ctv16pj9.

Anderson, Clare. *Subaltern Lives: Biographies of Colonialism in the Indian Ocean World, 1790–1920.* Cambridge: Cambridge University Press, 2012. https://doi.org/10.1017/CBO9781139057554.

Anderson, Kim. *Recognition of Being: Reconstructing Native Womanhood.* 2nd ed. Toronto: Women's Press, 2016.

Anderson, Michael. "The Social Implications of Demographic Change." In *The Cambridge Social History of Britain,* vol. 2, *People and Their Environment,* edited by F.M.L. Thompson, 1–70. Cambridge: Cambridge University Press, 1990.

Arnold, David. "Deathscapes: India in an Age of Romanticism and Empire, 1800–1856." *Nineteenth-Century Contexts* 26, 4 (2004): 339–53. https://doi.org/10.1080/0890549051233 1329349.

Atkinson, David C. *The Burden of White Supremacy: Containing Asian Migration in the British Empire and the United States.* Chapel Hill: University of North Carolina Press, 2016.

Auerbach, Jeffrey. "Imperial Boredom." *Common Knowledge* 11, 2 (Spring 2005): 283–305. https://doi.org/10.1215/0961754X-11-2-283.

Babe, Robert E. *Telecommunications in Canada: Technology, Industry, and Government.* Toronto: University of Toronto Press, 1990. https://doi.org/10.3138/9781442680425.

Ballantyne, Tony. *Orientalism and Race: Aryanism in the British Empire.* Basingstoke, UK: Palgrave Macmillan, 2002. https://doi.org/10.1057/9780230508071.

–. "Strategic Intimacies: Knowledge and Colonization in Southern New Zealand." *Journal of New Zealand Studies* 14 (2013): 4–18.

–. *Webs of Empire: Locating New Zealand's Colonial Past.* Wellington: Bridget Williams, 2012.

Ballantyne, Tony, and Antoinette Burton, eds. *Moving Subjects: Gender, Mobility, and Intimacy in an Age of Global Empire.* Urbana: University of Illinois Press, 2009.

Banivanua Mar, Tracey, and Penelope Edmonds, eds. *Making Settler Colonial Space: Perspectives on Race, Place and Identity.* Basingstoke, UK: Palgrave Macmillan, 2010.

Bannet, Eve Tavor. *Empire of Letters: Letter Manuals and Transatlantic Correspondence, 1688–1820.* Cambridge: Cambridge University Press, 2005.

Baptist, Karen Wilson. "Diaspora: Death without a Landscape." *Mortality* 15, 4 (2010): 294–307. https://doi.org/10.1080/13576275.2010.513162.

Barclay, Krista. "From Rupert's Land to Canada West: Hudson's Bay Company Families and Representations of Indigeneity in Small-Town Ontario, 1840–1980." *Journal of the Canadian Historical Association* 26, 1 (2015): 67–97. https://doi.org/10.7202/1037198ar.

Barman, Jean. "Beyond Chinatown: Chinese Men and Indigenous Women in Early British Columbia." *BC Studies* 177 (2013): 39–64.

–. "Ethnicity in the Pursuit of Status: British Middle and Upper-Class Emigration to British Columbia in the Late Nineteenth and Early Twentieth Centuries." *Canadian Ethnic Studies* 18, 1 (1986): 32–51.

–. *French Canadians, Furs, and Indigenous Women in the Making of the Pacific Northwest.* Vancouver: UBC Press, 2014.

–. *Sojourning Sisters: The Lives and Letters of Jessie and Annie McQueen.* Toronto: University of Toronto Press, 2003.

–. "Sophie Morigeau: Free Trader, Free Woman." In *Recollecting: Lives of Aboriginal Women of the Canadian Northwest and Borderlands,* edited by Sarah Carter and Patricia McCormack, 175–95. Edmonton: Athabasca University Press, 2011.

–. "Taming Aboriginal Sexuality: Gender, Power, and Race in British Columbia, 1850–1900." *BC Studies* 115/116 (Autumn/Winter 1997/98): 237–66.

–. "Unpacking English Gentlemen Emigrants' Cultural Baggage: Apple Orchards and Private Schools in British Columbia's Okanagan Valley." *British Journal of Canadian Studies* 16, 1 (2003): 137–49.

–. *West beyond the West: A History of British Columbia.* 3rd ed. Toronto: University of Toronto Press, 2007.

Barman, Jean, and Bruce McIntyre Watson. *Leaving Paradise: Indigenous Hawaiians in the Pacific Northwest, 1787–1898.* Honolulu: University of Hawai'i Press, 2006.

Bartrip, Peter. "Food for the Body and Food for the Mind: The Regulation of Freshwater Fisheries in the 1870s." *Victorian Studies* 28, 2 (1985): 285–304.

Battell Lowman, Emma, and Adam J. Barker. *Settler: Identity and Colonialism in 21st Century Canada.* Halifax: Fernwood, 2015.

Beattie, James. *Empire and Environmental Anxiety: Health, Science, Art and Conservation in South Asia and Australasia, 1800–1920.* Basingstoke, UK: Palgrave Macmillan, 2011. https://doi.org/10.1057/9780230309067.

Beattie, Judith Hudson, and Helen M. Buss, eds. *Undelivered Letters to Hudson's Bay Company Men on the Northwest Coast of America, 1830–57.* Vancouver: UBC Press, 2003.

Bedikian, Sonia A. "The Death of Mourning: From Victorian Crepe to the Little Black Dress." *Omega: Journal of Death and Dying* 57, 1 (2008): 35–52. https://doi.org/10.2190/OM.57.1.c.

Belasco, Warren. *Food: The Key Concepts.* Oxford: Berg, 2008. https://doi.org/10.5040/9781350042148.

Belich, James. *Replenishing the Earth: The Settler Revolution and the Rise of the Anglo-World, 1783–1939.* Oxford: Oxford University Press, 2009. https://doi.org/10.1093/acprof:oso/9780199297276.001.0001.

Belshaw, John Douglas. *Becoming British Columbia: A Population History.* Vancouver: UBC Press, 2009.

Bennett, Jason Patrick. "Apple of the Empire: Landscape and Imperial Identity in Turn-of-the-Century British Columbia." *Journal of the Canadian Historical Association* 9, 1 (1998): 63–92. https://doi.org/10.7202/030492ar.

Bickers, Robert, ed. *Settlers and Expatriates: Britons Over the Seas.* Oxford: Oxford University Press, 2010. https://doi.org/10.1093/acprof:oso/9780199297672.001.0001.

Bickham, Troy. "Eating the Empire: Intersections of Food, Cookery and Imperialism in Eighteenth-Century Britain." *Past and Present* 198, 1 (2008): 71–109. https://doi.org/10.1093/pastj/gtm054.

Boddice, Rob. "Manliness and the 'Morality of Field Sports': E.A. Freeman and Anthony Trollope, 1869–71." *Historian* 70, 1 (2008): 1–29. https://doi.org/10.1111/j.1540-6563.2008.00201.x.

Bosher, J.F. *Vancouver Island in the Empire.* Tamarac, FL: Llumina, 2012.

Boucher, Ellen. *Empire's Children: Child Emigration, Welfare, and the Decline of the British World, 1869–1967.* Cambridge: Cambridge University Press, 2014. https://doi.org/10.1017/CBO9781139649582.

Boyce, Robert W.D. "Imperial Dreams and National Realities: Britain, Canada and the Struggle for a Pacific Telegraph Cable, 1879–1902." *English Historical Review* 115, 460 (February 2000): 39–70. https://doi.org/10.1093/enghis/115.460.39.

Bracken, Christopher. *The Potlatch Papers: A Colonial Case History.* Chicago: University of Chicago Press, 1997.

Bradbury, Bettina. *Wife to Widow: Lives, Laws, and Politics in Nineteenth-Century Montreal.* Vancouver: UBC Press, 2011.

Brant, Clare. *Eighteenth-Century Letters and British Culture.* Basingstoke, UK: Palgrave Macmillan, 2006. https://doi.org/10.1007/978-1-349-74050-5.

Bridge, Kathryn. *Henry & Self: The Private Life of Sarah Crease 1826–1922.* Victoria: Sono Nis, 1996.

Bridge, Kathryn Anne. "Being Young in the Country: Settler Children and Childhood in British Columbia and Alberta, 1860–1925." PhD dissertation, University of Victoria, 2012.

Briggs, Asa. *Victorian Things.* Chicago: University of Chicago Press, 1989.

Britten, Liam. "UVic to Rename Trutch Building Because of Colonial Politician's Racist Legacy." CBC News, 6 June 2017. http://www.cbc.ca/news/canada/british-columbia/uvic-trutch-joseph-1.4147789.

Brock, Peggy. "Nakedness and Clothing in Early Encounters between Aboriginal People of Central Australia, Missionaries and Anthropologists." *Journal of Colonialism and Colonial History* 8, 1 (Spring 2007). https://doi.org/10.1353/cch.2007.0015.

Broomfield, Andrea. *Food and Cooking in Victorian England: A History.* London: Praeger, 2007.

Broughton, Trev Lynn. "The *Bengal Obituary*: Reading and Writing Calcutta Graves in the Mid Nineteenth Century." *Journal of Victorian Culture* 15, 1 (April 2010): 39–59. https://doi.org/10.1080/13555501003607677.

Broughton, Trev Lynn, and Helen Rogers, eds. *Gender and Fatherhood in the Nineteenth Century.* Basingstoke, UK: Palgrave Macmillan, 2007. https://doi.org/10.1007/978-0-230-20785-1.

Brown, Jennifer S.H. *Strangers in Blood: Fur Trade Company Families in Indian Country.* Vancouver: UBC Press, 1980.

Browne, Christopher. *Getting the Message: The Story of the British Post Office.* Stroud, UK: A. Sutton, 1993.

Brownlie, Robin Jarvis. "Intimate Surveillance: Indian Affairs, Colonization, and the Regulation of Aboriginal Women's Sexuality." In *Contact Zones: Aboriginal and Settler Women in Canada's Colonial Past,* edited by Katie Pickles and Myra Rutherdale, 160–78. Vancouver: UBC Press, 2005.

Buettner, Elizabeth. "Cemeteries, Public Memory and Raj Nostalgia in Postcolonial Britain and India." *History and Memory* 18, 1 (Spring/Summer 2006): 5–42. https://doi.org/10.2979/his.2006.18.1.5.

–. *Empire Families: Britons and Late Imperial India.* Oxford: Oxford University Press, 2004.

Burbank, Jane, and Frederick Cooper. *Empires in World History: Power and the Politics of Difference.* Princeton, NJ: Princeton University Press, 2010.

Burnett, John. *Destiny Obscure: Autobiographies of Childhood, Education and Family from the 1820s to the 1920s.* First published 1982; republished Abingdon, UK: Routledge, 2013.

–. *Plenty and Want: A Social History of Food in England from 1815 to the Present Day.* London: Thomas Nelson, 1966.

Burton, Antoinette, ed. *Archive Stories: Facts, Fictions, and the Writing of History*. Durham, NC: Duke University Press, 2005.

–. *Dwelling in the Archive: Women Writing House, Home, and History in Late Colonial India.* Oxford: Oxford University Press, 2003. https://doi.org/10.1093/acprof:oso/9780195144253.001.0001.

–. *Empire in Question: Reading, Writing, and Teaching British Imperialism.* Durham, NC: Duke University Press, 2011.

Canada, Department of Indian Affairs. *Annual Reports,* 1884, 1887, 1888, and 1890. Digitized by Library and Archives Canada, http://www.bac-lac.gc.ca/eng/discover/aboriginal-heritage/first-nations/indian-affairs-annual-reports/Pages/introduction.aspx.

Canada, Postmaster General. *Canada Official Postal Guide: Comprising the Chief Regulations of the Post Office, Rates of Postage and Other Information, Together with an Alphabetical List of Post Offices in Canada.* Ottawa: Maclean, Roger, 1887.

–. *Canada Official Postal Guide: Comprising the Chief Regulations of the Post Office, Rates of Postage and Other Information, Together with an Alphabetical List of Post Offices in Canada.* Ottawa: Government Printing Bureau, 1914.

Canada, Royal Commission on Indian Affairs for the Province of British Columbia. *Agency Testimonies.* Digitized by the Union of British Columbia Indian Chiefs, http://gsdl.ubcic.bc.ca.

Carruthers, W.R. "Edward Maurice Carruthers, J.P." *Thirty-Second Report of the Okanagan Historical Society* (1968): 63–68.

Carter, Sarah. *The Importance of Being Monogamous: Marriage and Nation Building in Western Canada to 1915.* Edmonton: University of Alberta Press and Athabasca University Press, 2008.

Cavanagh, Edward. *Settler Colonialism and Land Rights in South Africa: Possession and Dispossession on the Orange River.* Basingstoke, UK: Palgrave Macmillan, 2013. https://doi.org/10.1057/9781137305770.

Cavanagh, Edward, and Lorenzo Veracini, eds. *The Routledge Handbook on the History of Settler Colonialism.* New York: Routledge, 2017.

Chang, Kornel. *Pacific Connections: The Making of the US-Canadian Borderlands.* Berkeley: University of California Press, 2012.

Chesterfield's Art of Letter-Writing Simplified: Being a Guide to Friendly, Affectionate, Polite and Business Correspondence. London, ON: W. Bryce, 1886.

Chilton, Lisa. *Agents of Empire: British Female Migration to Canada and Australia, 1860–1930.* Toronto: University of Toronto Press, 2007.

–. "Canada and the British Empire: A Review Essay." *Canadian Historical Review* 89, 1 (March 2008): 89–95. https://doi.org/10.3138/chr.89.1.89.

–. "Travelling Colonist: British Emigration and the Construction of Anglo-Canadian Privilege." In *Empire, Identity and Migration in the British World,* edited by Andrew S. Thompson and Kent Fedorowich, 169–91. Manchester: Manchester University Press, 2013.

Chung, Tzu-I. "Kwong Lee & Company and Early Trans-Pacific Trade: From Canton, Hong Kong, to Victoria and Barkerville." *BC Studies* 185 (2015): 137–60.

Clarkson, Chris. *Domestic Reforms: Political Visions and Family Regulation in British Columbia, 1862–1940.* Vancouver: UBC Press, 2007.

Cleall, Esmé. *Missionary Discourses of Difference: Negotiating Otherness in the British Empire, 1840–1900.* Basingstoke, UK: Palgrave Macmillan, 2012.

Cleall, Esmé, Laura Ishiguro, and Emily J. Manktelow. "Imperial Relations: Histories of Family in the British Empire." *Journal of Colonialism and Colonial History* 14, 1 (Spring 2013). https://doi.org/10.1353/cch.2013.0006.

Codell, Julie F., ed. *Imperial Co-Histories: National Identities and the British and Colonial Press*. Madison, NJ: Fairleigh Dickinson University Press, 2003.

Cohen, Deborah. *Family Secrets: Living with Shame from the Victorians to the Present Day*. London: Viking, 2013.

Colley, Linda. "Britishness and Otherness: An Argument." *Journal of British Studies* 31, 4 (October 1992): 309–29. https://doi.org/10.1086/386013.

Collingham, E.M. *Imperial Bodies: The Physical Experience of the Raj, c. 1800–1947*. Cambridge: Polity, 2001.

Colquhoun, Kate. *Taste: The Story of Britain through Its Cooking*. London: Bloomsbury, 2007.

Comacchio, Cynthia R. *The Infinite Bonds of Family: Domesticity in Canada, 1850–1940*. Toronto: University of Toronto Press, 1999.

Combs, Mary Beth. "'Concealing Him from Creditors': How Couples Contributed to the Passage of the 1870 Married Women's Property Act." In *Married Women and the Law: Coverture in England and the Common Law World*, edited by Tim Stretton and Krista J. Kesselring, 217–39. Montreal and Kingston: McGill-Queen's University Press, 2013.

–. "*Cui Bono?* The 1870 British Married Women's Property Act, Bargaining Power, and the Distribution of Resources within Marriage." *Feminist Economics* 12, 1–2 (2006): 51–83.

–. "'A Measure of Legal Independence': The 1870 Married Women's Property Act and the Portfolio Allocations of British Wives." *Journal of Economic History* 65, 4 (December 2005): 1028–57. https://doi.org/10.1017/S0022050705000392.

Compton, Wade, ed. *Bluesprint: Black British Columbian Literature and Orature*. Vancouver: Arsenal Pulp Press, 2001.

Conway, Alan. "Welsh Gold-Miners in British Columbia during the 1860s." *British Columbia Historical Quarterly* 21 (1958): 51–74.

–. *The Welsh in America: Letters from the Immigrants*. Cardiff: University of Wales Press, 1961.

Coombes, Annie, ed. *Rethinking Settler Colonialism: History and Memory in Australia, Canada, Aotearoa New Zealand and South Africa*. Manchester: Manchester University Press, 2006.

Cozzi, Annette. *The Discourses of Food in Nineteenth-Century British Fiction*. Basingstoke, UK: Palgrave Macmillan, 2010. https://doi.org/10.1057/9780230117525.

Curl, James Stevens. *The Victorian Celebration of Death*. Newton Abbot, UK: David and Charles, 1972.

Cvetkovich, Ann. *Depression: A Public Feeling*. Durham, NC: Duke University Press, 2012. https://doi.org/10.1215/9780822391852.

Darian-Smith, Kate, Patricia Grimshaw, and Stuart Macintyre, eds. *Britishness Abroad: Transnational Movements and Imperial Cultures*. Melbourne: Melbourne University Press, 2007.

Daschuk, James. *Clearing the Plains: Disease, Politics of Starvation, and the Loss of Aboriginal Life*. Regina: University of Regina Press, 2013.

Daunton, M.J. *Royal Mail: The Post Office since 1840*. London: Athlone, 1985.

Davidoff, Leonore. *The Best Circles: Society, Etiquette and the Season*. London: Croon Helm, 1973.

–. "'Close Marriage' in the Nineteenth and Twentieth Century Middle Strata." In *Kinship Matters,* edited by Fatemeh Ebtehaj, Bridget Lindley, and Martin Richards, 19–45. Cambridge: Hart, 2006.

–. "The Legacy of the Nineteenth-Century Bourgeois Family and the Wool Merchant's Son." *Transactions of the Royal Historical Society,* Sixth Series, 14 (2004): 25–46.

–. *Thicker Than Water: Siblings and Their Relations, 1780–1920.* Oxford: Oxford University Press, 2012.

–. *Worlds Between: Historical Perspectives on Gender and Class.* New York: Routledge, 1995.

Davidoff, Leonore, and Catherine Hall. *Family Fortunes: Men and Women of the English Middle Class 1780–1850.* Rev. ed. London: Routledge, 2002.

Davidoff, Leonore, Megan Doolittle, Janet Fink, and Katherine Holden. *The Family Story: Blood, Contract and Intimacy, 1830–1960.* London: Longman, 1999.

Daybell, James. *The Material Letter in Early Modern England: Manuscript Letters and the Culture and Practices of Letter-Writing, 1512–1635.* Basingstoke, UK: Palgrave Macmillan, 2012. https://doi.org/10.1057/9781137006066.

de Leeuw, Sarah. "'If Anything Is to Be Done with the Indian, We Must Catch Him Very Young': Colonial Constructions of Aboriginal Children and the Geographies of Indian Residential Schooling in British Columbia, Canada." *Children's Geographies* 7, 2 (2009): 123–40. https://doi.org/10.1080/14733280902798837.

Deaville, A. Stanley. "The Colonial Postal Systems of Vancouver Island and British Columbia, 1849–1871." *British Columbia Historical Association Annual Report and Proceedings* 3 (1925): 45–59.

Decker, William Merrill. *Epistolary Practices: Letter Writing in America before Telecommunications.* Chapel Hill: University of North Carolina Press, 1998.

Devereux, Cecily, and Kathleen Venema, eds. *Women Writing Home, 1700–1920: Female Correspondence across the British Empire.* Vol. 3, *Canada.* London: Pickering and Chatto, 2006.

Dickason, Olive Patricia, with David T. McNab. *Canada's First Nations: A History of Founding Peoples from Earliest Times.* 4th ed. Don Mills, ON: Oxford University Press, 2009.

Dierks, Konstantin. *In My Power: Letter Writing and Communications in Early America.* Philadelphia: University of Pennsylvania Press, 2009. https://doi.org/10.9783/9780812201758.

Dua, Enakshi. "Exclusion through Inclusion: Female Asian Migration in the Making of Canada as a White Settler Nation." *Gender, Place and Culture* 14, 4 (2007): 445–66. https://doi.org/10.1080/09663690701439751.

Dunae, Patrick A. *Gentlemen Emigrants: From the British Public Schools to the Canadian Frontier.* Vancouver: Douglas and McIntyre, 1981.

Earle, Rebecca. *The Body of the Conquistador: Food, Race and the Colonial Experience in Spanish America, 1492–1700.* Cambridge: Cambridge University Press, 2012. https://doi.org/10.1017/CBO9780511763359.

–, ed. *Epistolary Selves: Letters and Letter-Writers, 1600–1945.* Aldershot, UK: Ashgate, 1999.

Eaton, Arthur Wentworth Hamilton. *Good Form: Letter-Writing, Its Ethics and Etiquette, with Remarks on the Proper Use of Monograms, Crests and Seals.* New York: Frederick A. Stokes, 1894.

Edmonds, Penelope. "'I Followed England Round the World': The Rise of Trans-Imperial Anglo-Saxon Exceptionalism, and the Spatial Narratives of Nineteenth-Century British Settler Colonies of the Pacific Rim." In *Re-orienting Whiteness,* edited by Leigh Boucher, Jane Carey, and Katherine Ellinghaus, 99–115. New York: Palgrave Macmillan, 2009. https://doi.org/10.1057/9780230101289_8.

–. *Urbanizing Frontiers: Indigenous Peoples and Settlers in 19th-Century Pacific Rim Cities.* Vancouver: UBC Press, 2010.

Elkins, Caroline, and Susan Pederson, eds. *Settler Colonialism in the Twentieth Century: Projects, Practices, Legacies.* New York: Routledge, 2005.

Elliott, Bruce S., David A. Gerber, and Suzanne M. Sinke, eds. *Letters across Borders: The Epistolary Practices of International Migrants.* Basingstoke, UK: Palgrave Macmillan, 2006. https://doi.org/10.1057/9780230601079.

Elliott, Gordon R. "Henry P. Pellew Crease: Confederation or No Confederation." *BC Studies* 12 (Winter 1971–72): 63–74.

Epstein, James. *Scandal of Colonial Rule: Power and Subversion in the British Atlantic during the Age of Revolution.* Cambridge: Cambridge University Press, 2012. https://doi.org/10.1017/CBO9780511760204.

Erickson, Charlotte. *Invisible Immigrants: The Adaptation of English and Scottish Immigrants in Nineteenth-Century America.* Leicester: Leicester University Press, 1972.

–. *Leaving England: Essays on British Emigration in the Nineteenth Century.* Ithaca, NY: Cornell University Press, 1994.

Erickson, Lesley. *Westward Bound: Sex, Violence, the Law, and the Making of a Settler Society.* Vancouver: UBC Press, 2011.

Errington, Elizabeth Jane. *Emigrant Worlds and Transatlantic Communities: Migration to Upper Canada in the First Half of the Nineteenth Century.* Kingston and Montreal: McGill-Queen's University Press, 2007.

–. "'Information Wanted': Women Emigrants in a Transatlantic World." In *Canada and the British World: Culture, Migration, and Identity,* edited by Phillip Buckner and R. Douglas Francis, 10–28. Vancouver: UBC Press, 2006.

–. "Webs of Affection and Obligation: Glimpse into Families and Nineteenth Century Transatlantic Communities." *Journal of the Canadian Historical Association* 19, 1 (2008): 1–26. https://doi.org/10.7202/037424ar.

Eustace, Nicole, Eugenia Lean, Julie Livingston, et al. "AHR Conversation: The Historical Study of Emotions." *American Historical Review* 117, 5 (December 2012): 1487–1531. https://doi.org/10.1093/ahr/117.5.1487.

Eyford, Ryan C. *White Settler Reserve: New Iceland and the Colonization of the Canadian West.* Vancouver: UBC Press, 2016.

–. "'Close Together, though Miles and Miles Apart': Family, Distance, and Emotion in the Letters of the Taylor Sisters, 1881–1921." *Histoire Sociale* 47, 96 (2015): 67–86. https://doi.org/10.1353/his.2015.0012.

Fedorowich, Kent, and Andrew Thompson, eds. *Empire, Migration and Identity in the British World.* Manchester: Manchester University Press, 2013.

Finn, Margot. "Anglo-Indian Lives in the Later Eighteenth and Early Nineteenth Century." *Journal for Eighteenth-Century Studies* 33, 1 (March 2010): 49–65. https://doi.org/10.1111/j.1754-0208.2009.00210.x.

Finn, Margot C. "Colonial Gifts: Family Politics and the Exchange of Goods in British India, c. 1780–1820." *Modern Asian Studies* 40, 1 (February 2006): 203–31. https://doi.org/10.1017/S0026749X06001739.

–. "Family Formations: Anglo India and the Familial Proto-State." In *Structures and Transformations in Modern British History,* edited by David Feldman and Jon Lawrence, 100–17. Cambridge: Cambridge University Press, 2011.

Fischler, Claude. "Food, Self and Identity." *Social Science Information/Information Sur les Sciences Sociales* 27, 2 (June 1988): 275–92. https://doi.org/10.1177/053901888027002005.

Fitzpatrick, David. *Oceans of Consolation: Personal Accounts of Irish Migration to Australia.* Cork: Cork University Press, 1994.

Forbes, Bruce David. *Christmas: A Candid History.* Berkeley: University of California Press, 2007.

Ford, Lisa. *Settler Sovereignty: Jurisdiction and Indigenous People in America and Australia, 1788–1836.* Cambridge, MA: Harvard University Press, 2010.

Forest, Timothy S. "Highland Warriors or 'Scotch Coolies'? Hebridean Crofters in British Columbia, 1887–1893." *Pacific Northwest Quarterly* 102, 2 (2011): 79–90.

Francis, Daniel. *The Imaginary Indian: The Image of the Indian in Canadian Culture.* 2nd ed. Vancouver: Arsenal Pulp Press, 2011.

Freeman, Victoria. "Attitudes toward 'Miscegenation' in Canada, the United States, New Zealand, and Australia, 1860–1914." *Native Studies Review* 16, 1 (2005): 41–69.

Furniss, Elizabeth. *The Burden of History: Colonialism and the Frontier Myth in a Rural Canadian Community.* Vancouver: UBC Press, 1999.

Gage, John T. "Vestiges of Letter-Writing in Composition Textbooks, 1850–1914." In *Letter-Writing Manuals and Instruction from Antiquity to the Present: Historical and Bibliographic Studies,* edited by Carol Poster and Linda C. Mitchell, 200–29. Columbia: University of South Carolina Press, 2007.

Galois, Robert, and Cole Harris. "Recalibrating Society: The Population Geography of British Columbia in 1881." *Canadian Geographer* 38, 1 (March 1994): 37–53. https://doi.org/10.1111/j.1541-0064.1994.tb01516.x.

Geiger, Andrea. *Subverting Exclusion: Transpacific Encounters with Race, Caste, and Borders, 1885–1928.* New Haven, CT: Yale University Press, 2011.

Gerber, David A. *Authors of Their Lives: The Personal Correspondence of British Immigrants to North America in the Nineteenth Century.* New York: New York University Press, 2006.

–. "Epistolary Ethics: Personal Correspondence and the Culture of Emigration in the Nineteenth Century." *Journal of American Ethnic History* 19, 4 (Summer 2000): 3–23.

–. "Epistolary Masquerades: Acts of Deceiving and Withholding in Immigrant Letters." In *Letters across Borders: The Epistolary Practices of International Migrants,* edited by Bruce S. Elliott, David A. Gerber, and Suzanne M. Sinke, 141–57. Basingstoke, UK: Palgrave Macmillan, 2006.

Ghosh, Durba. *Sex and the Family in Colonial India: The Making of Empire.* Cambridge: Cambridge University Press, 2006. https://doi.org/10.1017/CBO9781139878418.

Gillis, John R. *A World of Their Own Making: Myth, Ritual, and the Quest for Family Values.* Cambridge, MA: Harvard University Press, 1997.

Golden, Catherine J. *Posting It: The Victorian Revolution in Letter Writing.* Gainesville: Unviersity Press of Florida, 2009. https://doi.org/10.5744/florida/9780813033792.001.0001.

Good, Cassandra A. *Founding Friendships: Friendships between Men and Women in the Early American Republic.* Oxford: Oxford University Press, 2015. https://doi.org/10.1093/acprof:oso/9780199376179.001.0001.

Goodstein, Elizabeth S. *Experience without Qualities: Boredom and Modernity.* Stanford, CA: Stanford University Press, 2005.

Goody, Jack. *Cooking, Cuisine and Class.* Cambridge: Cambridge University Press, 1982. https://doi.org/10.1017/CBO9780511607745.

Goose, Nigel, and Katrina Honeyman, eds. *Childhood and Child Labour in Industrial England: Diversity and Agency, 1750–1914.* London: Routledge, 2016.

Gordon, Eleanor, and Gwyneth Nair. *Public Lives: Women, Family and Society in Victorian Britain.* New Haven, CT: Yale University Press, 2003.

Gust, Onni. "The Perilous Territory of Not Belonging': Exile and Empire in Sir James Mackintosh's Letters from Bombay, c. 1804–1811." *History Workshop Journal,* 86, 1 (October 2018): 22–43. https://doi.org/10.1093/hwj/dby013.

–. "Remembering and Forgetting the Scottish Highlands: Sir James Mackintosh and the Forging of a British Imperial Identity." *Journal of British Studies* 52, 3 (July 2013): 615–37. https://doi.org/10.1017/jbr.2013.114.

Hall, Catherine. *Civilising Subjects: Metropole and Colony in the English Imagination 1830–1867.* Chicago: University of Chicago Press, 2002.

–. "Commentary." In *Haunted by Empire: Geographies of Intimacy in North American History,* edited by Ann Laura Stoler, 452–68. Durham, NC: Duke University Press, 2006. https://doi.org/10.1215/9780822387992-018.

–, ed. *Cultures of Empire, A Reader: Colonisers in Britain and the Empire in the Nineteenth and Twentieth Centuries.* Manchester: Manchester University Press, 2000.

–. *Macaulay and Son: Architects of Imperial Britain.* New Haven, CT: Yale University Press, 2012.

Hall, Catherine, and Sonya O. Rose, eds. *At Home with the Empire: Metropolitan Culture and the Imperial World.* Cambridge: Cambridge University Press, 2006. https://doi.org/10.1017/CBO9780511802263.

Hall, Catherine, Nicholas Draper, Keith McClelland, Katie Donington, and Rachel Lang. *Legacies of British Slave-ownership: Colonial Slavery and the Formation of Victorian Britain.* Cambridge: Cambridge University Press, 2014.

Hamilton, Carolyn, et al., eds. *Refiguring the Archive.* London: Kluwer, 2002. https://doi.org/10.1007/978-94-010-0570-8.

Hamilton, J.H. "The 'All-Red Route,' 1893–1953: A History of the Trans-Pacific Mail Service between British Columbia, Australia, and New Zealand." *British Columbia Historical Quarterly* 20 (1956): 1–126.

Harper, Marjory. *Adventurers and Exiles: The Great Scottish Exodus.* London: Profile, 2003.

Harper, Marjory, and Stephen Constantine. *Migration and Empire.* Oxford: Oxford University Press, 2010. https://doi.org/10.1093/acprof:oso/9780199250936.001.0001.

Harris, Cole. "How Did Colonialism Dispossess? Comments from an Edge of Empire." *Annals of the Association of American Geographers* 94, 1 (2004): 165–82. https://doi.org/10.1111/j.1467-8306.2004.09401009.x.

–. "Moving Amid Mountains, 1870–1930." *BC Studies* 58 (Summer 1983): 3–39.

–. "Towards a Geography of White Power in the Cordilleran Fur Trade." *Canadian Geographer* 39, 2 (June 1995): 131–40. https://doi.org/10.1111/j.1541-0064.1995.tb00408.x.

Harris, R. Cole. *Making Native Space: Colonialism, Resistance, and Reserves in British Columbia.* Vancouver: UBC Press, 2002.

–. *The Resettlement of British Columbia: Essays on Colonialism and Geographical Change.* Vancouver: UBC Press, 1997.

Harris, R. Cole, and Elizabeth Phillips, eds. *Letters from Windermere, 1912–1914*. Vancouver: UBC Press, 1984.

Harvey, Megan. "Story People: Stó:lō-State Relations and Indigenous Literacies in British Columbia, 1864–1874." *Journal of the Canadian Historical Association* 24, 1 (2013): 51–88. https://doi.org/10.7202/1024997ar.

Headrick, Daniel R. *The Tools of Empire: Technology and European Imperialism in the Nineteenth Century*. New York: Oxford University Press, 1981.

Heaton, J. Henniker. "A Penny Post for the Empire." *The Nineteenth Century: A Monthly Review* 27, 160 (June 1890): 906–20.

Hendrickson, James E., ed. *Journals of the Colonial Legislatures of the Colonies of Vancouver Island and British Columbia, 1851–1871*. vols. I–V. Victoria: Provincial Archives of British Columbia, 1980.

Henkin, David M. *The Postal Age: The Emergence of Modern Communications in Nineteenth-Century America*. Chicago: University of Chicago Press, 2007.

Herbert, Christopher. *War of No Pity: The Indian Mutiny and Victorian Trauma*. Princeton, NJ: Princeton University Press, 2008.

Hogg, Robert. *Men and Manliness on the Frontier: Queensland and British Columbia in the Mid-Nineteenth Century*. Basingstoke, UK: Palgrave Macmillan, 2012. https://doi.org/10.1057/9781137284259.

How to Write: A Pocket Manual of Composition and Letter Writing. London: William Horsell, 1857.

Howe, Stephen, ed. *The New Imperial Histories Reader*. London: Routledge, 2009.

Howland, Douglas. "An Alternative Mode of International Order: The International Administrative Union in the Nineteenth Century." *Review of International Studies* 41, 1 (January 2015): 161–83. https://doi.org/10.1017/S0260210514000114.

Hudgins, Nicole. "A Historical Approach to Family Photography: Class and Individuality in Manchester and Lille, 1850–1914." *Journal of Social History* 43, 3 (Spring 2010): 559–86. https://doi.org/10.1353/jsh.0.0298.

Huggins, Mike. "Sport and the British Upper Classes c. 1500–2000: A Historiographic Overview." *Sport in History* 28, 3 (2008): 364–88. https://doi.org/10.1080/17460260802315470.

Hyde, Anne F. *Empires, Nations, and Families: A History of the North American West, 1800–1860*. Lincoln: University of Nebraska Press, 2011.

Iacovetta, Franca, Valerie J. Korinek, and Marlene Epp, eds. *Edible Histories Cultural Politics: Towards a Canadian Food History*. Toronto: University of Toronto Press, 2012.

Igler, David. *The Great Ocean: Pacific Worlds from Captain Cook to the Gold Rush*. Oxford: Oxford University Press, 2013.

Ikebuchi, Shelly. *From Slave Girls to Salvation: Gender, Race, and Victoria's Chinese Rescue Home, 1886–1923*. Vancouver: UBC Press, 2015.

Ipsen, Pernille. *Daughters of the Trade: Atlantic Slavers and Interracial Marriage on the Gold Coast*. Philadelphia: University of Pennsylvania Press, 2015. https://doi.org/10.9783/9780812291971.

Ireland, Willard E., ed. "Gold-Rush Days in Victoria, 1858–1859." *British Columbia Historical Quarterly* 12, 3 (July 1948): 231–46.

Ishiguro, Laura. "'Growing Up and Grown Up ... in Our Future City': Discourses of Childhood and Settler Futurity in Colonial British Columbia." *BC Studies* 190 (Summer 2016): 15–37.

–. "How I Wish I Might Be Near: Distance and the Epistolary Family in Late Nineteenth-Century Condolence Letters." In *Within and Without the Nation: Canadian History as Transnational History*, edited by Adele Perry, Karen Dubinsky, and Henry Yu, 212–27. Toronto: University of Toronto Press, 2015.

–. "Relative Distances: Family and Empire between Britain, British Columbia and India, 1858–1901." PhD dissertation, University College London, 2011.

Jackson, Will. "Not Seeking Certain Proof: Interracial Sex and Archival Haze in High-Imperial Natal." In *Subverting Empire: Deviance and Disorder in the British Colonial World*, edited by Will Jackson and Emily J. Manktelow, 185–204. Basingstoke, UK: Palgrave Macmillan, 2015. https://doi.org/10.1057/9781137465870_10.

Jalland, Pat. "Bereavement in the English Family 1850–1980: Exploring Change over Time." *Family Science* 4, 1 (2013): 4–11. https://doi.org/10.1080/19424620.2013.819224.

–. *Death in the Victorian Family*. Oxford: Oxford University Press, 1996.

–. "Victorian Death and Its Decline: 1850–1918." In *Death in England: An Illustrated History*, edited by Peter C. Jupp and Clare Gittings, 230–55. Manchester: Manchester University Press, 1999.

John, Richard R. *Spreading the News: The American Postal System from Franklin to Morse*. Cambridge, MA: Harvard University Press, 1998.

Johnson, Olga Weydemeyer, ed. *The Story of the Tobacco Plains Country: The Autobiography of a Community*. Rexford, MT: Pioneers of the Tobacco Plains Country, 1950.

Johnston, Anna. *Missionary Writing and Empire, 1800–1860*. Cambridge: Cambridge University Press, 2003. https://doi.org/10.1017/CBO9780511550324.

Jones, Bill. "Writing Back: Welsh Emigrants and Their Correspondence in the Nineteenth Century." *North American Journal of Welsh Studies* 5, 1 (Winter 2005): 23–46.

Jones, William D. "'Going into Print': Published Immigrant Letters, Webs of Personal Relations, and the Emergence of the Welsh Public Sphere." In *Letters across Borders: The Epistolary Practices of International Migrants*, edited by Bruce S. Elliott, David A. Gerber, and Suzanne M. Sinke, 175–99. Basingstoke, UK: Palgrave Macmillan, 2006. https://doi.org/10.1057/9780230601079_10.

Jorgenson, Mica. "'Into That Country to Work': Aboriginal Economic Activities during Barkerville's Gold Rush." *BC Studies* 185 (2015): 109–36.

Joyce, Patrick. *The State of Freedom: A Social History of the British State Since 1800*. Cambridge: Cambridge University Press, 2013. https://doi.org/10.1017/CBO9780511843914.

Keating, Andrew Prescott. "The Empire of the Dead: British Burial Abroad and the Formation of National Identity." PhD dissertation, University of California, Berkeley, 2011.

Kershen, Anne J., ed. *Food in the Migrant Experience*. Aldershot, UK: Ashgate, 2002.

Kilian, Crawford. *Go Do Some Great Thing: The Black Pioneers of British Columbia*. Vancouver: Douglas and McIntyre, 1978.

Knowles, Valerie. *Strangers at Our Gates: Canadian Immigration and Immigration Policy, 1540–2007*. Rev. ed. Toronto: Dundurn, 2007.

Lai, David Chuenyan. "From Downtown Slums to Suburban Malls: Chinese Migration and Settlement in Canada." In *The Chinese Diaspora: Space, Place, Mobility, and Identity*, edited by Laurence J.C. Ma and Carolyn Cartier, 311–36. Lanham, MD: Rowman and Littlefield, 2003.

Laidlaw, Zoë. *Colonial Connections 1815–45: Patronage, the Information Revolution and Colonial Government.* Manchester: Manchester University Press, 2005.

Lake, Marilyn, and Henry Reynolds. *Drawing the Global Colour Line: White Men's Countries and the International Challenge of Racial Equality.* Cambridge: Cambridge University Press, 2008. https://doi.org/10.1017/CBO9780511805363.

Lamb, W. Kaye. "Letters to Martha." *British Columbia Historical Quarterly* 1 (January 1937): 33–44.

Lambert, David, and Alan Lester, eds. *Colonial Lives across the British Empire: Imperial Careering in the Long Nineteenth Century.* Cambridge: Cambridge University Press, 2006.

LaRocque, Emma. *When the Other Is Me: Native Resistance Discourse, 1850–1990.* Winnipeg: University of Manitoba Press, 2010.

Lee, Erika. "Orientalisms in the Americas: A Hemispheric Approach to Asian American History." *Journal of Asian American Studies* 8, 3 (2005): 235–56. https://doi.org/10.1353/jaas.2005.0051.

Leong-Salobir, Cecilia. *Food Culture in Colonial Asia: A Taste of Empire.* New York: Routledge, 2011.

Lester, Alan. *Imperial Networks: Creating Identities in Nineteenth-Century South Africa and Britain.* London: Routledge, 2001.

Levine, Philippa. "Naked Truths: Bodies, Knowledge, and the Erotics of Colonial Power." *Journal of British Studies* 52, 1 (January 2013): 5–25. https://doi.org/10.1017/jbr.2012.6.

–. "Sexuality, Gender, and Empire." In *Gender and Empire,* edited by Philippa Levine, 134–55. Oxford: Oxford University Press, 2004.

–. "States of Undress: Nakedness and the Colonial Imagination." *Victorian Studies* 50, 2 (Winter 2008): 189–219. https://doi.org/10.2979/VIC.2008.50.2.189.

Lindgren-Gibson, Alexandra. "'I Wish I Could See You as Often as I Could See Your Letter': Imperial Anxieties and Working Class Family Life in the Raj." *Journal of Colonialism and Colonial History* 17, 3 (Winter 2016). https://doi.org/10.1353/cch.2016.0039.

Little, J.I. "West Coast Picturesque: Class, Gender, and Race in a British Colonial Landscape, 1858–71." *Journal of Canadian Studies/Revue d'Etudes Canadiennes* 41, 2 (Spring 2007): 5–41. https://doi.org/10.3138/jcs.41.2.5.

Loo, Tina. *States of Nature: Conserving Canada's Wildlife in the Twentieth Century.* Vancouver: UBC Press, 2006.

Lutz, Deborah. "The Dead Still among Us: Victorian Secular Relics, Hair Jewelry, and Death Culture." *Victorian Literature and Culture* 39, 1 (March 2011): 127–42. https://doi.org/10.1017/S1060150310000306.

Lutz, John Sutton. *Makúk: A New History of Aboriginal-White Relations.* Vancouver: UBC Press, 2008.

Lyall, Francis. *International Communications: The International Telecommunication Union and the Universal Postal Union.* Farnham, UK: Ashgate, 2011.

Macdonald, Charlotte. "Intimacy of the Envelope: Fiction, Commerce, and Empire in the Correspondence of Friends Mary Taylor and Charlotte Brontë, c. 1845–55." In *Moving Subjects: Gender, Mobility, and Intimacy in an Age of Global Empire,* edited by Tony Ballantyne and Antoinette Burton, 89–109. Urbana: University of Illinois Press, 2009.

Macdonald, Charlotte J., ed. *Women Writing Home, 1700–1920: Female Correspondence across the British Empire.* Vol. 5, *New Zealand.* London: Pickering and Chatto, 2006.

Mackie, Richard. "The Colonization of Vancouver Island, 1849–1858." *BC Studies* 96 (Winter 1992/93): 3–40.

Mackie, Richard Somerset. *Wilderness Profound: Victorian Life on the Gulf of Georgia.* Victoria: Sono Nis, 1995.

Magee, Gary B., and Andrew S. Thompson. *Empire and Globalisation: Networks of People, Goods and Capital in the British World, c. 1850–1914.* Cambridge: Cambridge University Press, 2010. https://doi.org/10.1017/CBO9780511805868.

Mahoney, Deirdre M. "'More Than an Accomplishment': Advice on Letter-Writing for Nineteenth-Century American Women." *Huntington Library Quarterly* 66, 3/4 (2003): 411–23.

Manktelow, Emily J. *Missionary Families: Race, Gender and Generation on the Spiritual Frontier.* Manchester: Manchester University Press, 2013.

Marcus, Sharon. *Between Women: Friendship, Desire, and Marriage in Victorian England.* Princeton, NJ: Princeton University Press, 2007. https://doi.org/10.1515/9781400830855.

Marks, Lynne. *Infidels and the Damn Churches: Irreligion and Religion in Settler British Columbia.* Vancouver: UBC Press, 2017.

Mars, Valerie. "Parsimony amid Plenty: Views from Victorian Didactic Works on Food for Nursery Children." In *Food, Culture and History,* vol. 1, edited by Gerald Mars and Valerie Mars, 152–62. London: London Food Seminar, 1993.

Matsuda, Matt K. *Pacific Worlds: A History of Seas, Peoples, and Cultures.* Cambridge: Cambridge University Press, 2012. https://doi.org/10.1017/CBO9781139034319.

Matthews, Major James Skitt. *Early Vancouver.* Vols. 1–7. First published 1932–56. Vancouver: City of Vancouver, 2011. City of Vancouver Archives, http://former.vancouver.ca/ctyclerk/archives/digitized/EarlyVan/.

Mawani, Renisa. *Colonial Proximities: Crossracial Encounters and Juridical Truths in British Columbia, 1871–1921.* Vancouver: UBC Press, 2009.

McCabe, Jane. *Race, Tea and Colonial Resettlement: Imperial Families, Interrupted.* London: Bloomsbury, 2017.

McCarthy, Angela, ed. *A Global Clan: Scottish Migrant Networks and Identities since the Eighteenth Century.* London: Tauris, 2006.

McDonald, Robert A.J. *Making Vancouver: Class, Status, and Social Boundaries, 1863–1913.* Vancouver: UBC Press, 1996.

McIntosh, Alex. "The Family Meal and Its Significance in Global Times." In *Food in Global History,* edited by Raymond Grew, 217–39. Oxford: Westview, 1999.

McKenzie, Kirsten. *Scandal in the Colonies: Sydney and Cape Town, 1820–1850.* Melbourne: Melbourne University Press, 2004.

McKeown, Adam. *Chinese Migrant Networks and Cultural Change: Peru, Chicago, and Hawaii 1900–1936.* Chicago: University of Chicago Press, 2001.

McLeod, Anne Burnaby, and Pixie McGeachie, eds. *Land of Promise: Robert Burnaby's Letters from Colonial British Columbia 1858–1863.* Burnaby: City of Burnaby, 2002.

Mennell, Stephen. *All Manners of Food: Eating and Taste in England and France from the Middle Ages to the Present.* Oxford: Basil Blackwell, 1985.

Menzies, Charles R., and Caroline F. Butler. "Working in the Woods: Tsimshian Resource Workers and the Forest Industry of British Columbia." *American Indian Quarterly* 25, 3 (2001): 409–30. https://doi.org/10.1353/aiq.2001.0051.

Miller, Naomi. "Michael Phillipps: Prominent Kootenay Citizen." In *The Forgotten Side of the Border: British Columbia's Elk Valley and Crowsnest Pass,* edited by Wayne Norton and Naomi Miller, 29–39. Kamloops: Plateau, 1998.

Millions, Erin. "'By Education and Conduct': Educating Trans-Imperial Indigenous Fur-Trade Children in the Hudson's Bay Company Territories and the British Empire, 1820s to 1870s." PhD dissertation, University of Manitoba, 2017.

Mintz, Sidney W. *Sweetness and Power: The Place of Sugar in Modern History.* New York: Viking, 1985.

Morgan, Cecilia. *Building Better Britains? Settler Societies in the British World, 1783–1920.* Toronto: University of Toronto Press, 2016.

–. "Creating Interracial Intimacies: British North America, Canada, and the Transatlantic World, 1830–1914." *Journal of the Canadian Historical Association* 19, 2 (2008): 76–105. https://doi.org/10.7202/037749ar.

Morgensen, Scott Lauria. *Spaces between Us: Queer Settler Colonialism and Indigenous Decolonization.* Minneapolis: University of Minnesota Press, 2011. https://doi.org/10.5749/minnesota/9780816656325.001.0001.

Morley, John. *Death, Heaven and the Victorians.* Pittsburgh: University of Pittsburgh Press, 1971.

Morris, Robert. *Men, Women and Property in England, 1780–1870: A Social and Economic History of Family Strategies amongst the Leeds Middle Class.* Cambridge: Cambridge University Press, 2005. https://doi.org/10.1017/CBO9780511495953.

Mosby, Ian. "Administering Colonial Science: Nutrition Research and Human Biomedical Experimentation in Aboriginal Communities and Residential Schools, 1942–1952." *Histoire Sociale/Social History* 46, 91 (May 2013): 145–72.

Mouat, Jeremy. *Roaring Days: Rossland's Mines and the History of Mining in British Columbia.* Vancouver: UBC Press, 1995.

–. "Situating Vancouver Island in the British World, 1846–49." *BC Studies* 145 (Spring 2005): 5–30.

Murdoch, Lydia. "'Supressed Grief': Mourning the Death of British Children and the Memory of the 1857 Indian Rebellion." *Journal of British Studies* 51, 2 (April 2012): 364–92. https://doi.org/10.1086/664195.

Neary, Kevin. "Newcombe, Charles Frederic." *Dictionary of Canadian Biography Online.* Vol. 15. University of Toronto and Université Laval, 2000. http://www.biographi.ca/en/bio.php?id_nbr=8309.

Nelson, Claudia. *Family Ties in Victorian England.* Westport, CT: Praeger, 2007.

Nelson, Jay. "'A Strange Revolution in the Manners of the Country': Aboriginal-Settler Intermarriage in Nineteenth-Century British Columbia." In *Regulating Lives: Historical Essays on the State, Society, the Individual, and the Law,* edited by John McLaren, Robert Menzies, and Dorothy E. Chunn, 23–62. Vancouver: UBC Press, 2002.

Neylan, Susan. "Colonialism and Resettling British Columbia: Canadian Aboriginal Historiography, 1992–2012." *History Compass* 11, 10 (2013): 833–44. https://doi.org/10.1111/hic3.12084.

–. "Unsettling British Columbia: Canadian Aboriginal Historiography, 1992–2012." *History Compass* 11, 10 (2013): 845–58. https://doi.org/10.1111/hic3.12085.

Nicholas, Jane. "A Debt to the Dead? Ethics, Photography, History, and the Study of Freakery." *Histoire Sociale/Social History* 47, 93 (May 2014): 139–55.

Norman, Alison. "'Fit for the Table of the Most Fastidious Epicure': Culinary Colonialism in the Upper Canadian Contact Zone." In *Edible Histories Cultural Politics: Towards a Canadian Food History,* edited by Franca Iacovetta, Valerie J. Korinek, and Marlene Epp, 31–51. Toronto: University of Toronto Press, 2012.

O'Connor, Kaori. "The King's Christmas Pudding: Globalization, Recipes, and the Commodities of Empire." *Journal of Global History* 4, 1 (2009): 127–55. https://doi.org/10.1017/S1740022809002988.

O'Reilly, Susan McLeod. *On Track: The Railway Mail Service in Canada.* Hull, QC: Canadian Museum of Civilization, 1992.

Ogborn, Miles. *Indian Ink: Script and Print in the Making of the English East India Company.* Chicago: University of Chicago Press, 2007. https://doi.org/10.7208/chicago/9780226620428.001.0001.

Ormsby, Margaret A. "Moody, Richard Clement." *Dictionary of Canadian Biography Online.* Vol. 11. University of Toronto and Université Laval, 2000. http://www.biographi.ca/en/bio.php?id_nbr=5715.

Osborne, Harvey, and Michael Winstanley. "Rural and Urban Poaching in Victorian England." *Rural History* 17, 2 (2006): 187–212. https://doi.org/10.1017/S0956793306001877.

Parnaby, Andy. "'The Best Men That Ever Worked the Lumber': Aboriginal Longshoremen on Burrard Inlet, BC, 1863–1939." *Canadian Historical Review* 87, 1 (2006): 53–78.

Parr, Joy. *Labouring Children: British Immigrant Apprentices to Canada, 1869–1924.* Toronto: University of Toronto Press, 1980. https://doi.org/10.2307/j.cttlwlvn3g.

Pearsall, Sarah M.S. *Atlantic Families: Lives and Letters in the Later Eighteenth Century.* Oxford: Oxford University Press, 2008. https://doi.org/10.1093/acprof:oso/9780199532995.001.0001.

Peckham, Robert, ed. *Empires of Panic: Epidemics and Colonial Anxieties.* Hong Kong: Hong Kong University Press, 2015. https://doi.org/10.5790/hongkong/9789888208449.001.0001.

Perry, Adele. "The Autocracy of Love and the Legitimacy of Empire: Intimacy, Power and Scandal in Nineteenth-Century Metlakahtlah." *Gender and History* 16, 2 (August 2004): 261–88. https://doi.org/10.1111/j.0953-5233.2004.00341.x.

–. "Canada and the Empires of the Past." *History Compass* 1, 1 (2003): 1–4. https://doi.org/10.1111/1478-0542.008.

–. *Colonial Relations: The Douglas-Connolly Family and the Nineteenth-Century Imperial World.* Cambridge: Cambridge University Press, 2015.

–. "From 'the Hot-Bed of Vice' to the 'Good and Well-Ordered Christian Home': First Nations Housing and Reform in Nineteenth-Century British Columbia." *Ethnohistory* 50, 4 (2003): 587–610. https://doi.org/10.1215/00141801-50-4-587.

–. "Hardy Backwoodsmen, Wholesome Women, and Steady Families: Immigration and the Construction of a White Society in Colonial British Columbia, 1849–1871." *Histoire Sociale* 33, 66 (November 2000): 343–60.

–. *On the Edge of Empire: Gender, Race, and the Making of British Columbia, 1849–1871.* Toronto: University of Toronto Press, 2001.

–. "The State of Empire: Reproducing Colonialism in British Columbia, 1849–1871." *Journal of Colonialism and Colonial History* 2, 2 (Fall 2001). https://doi.org/10.1353/cch.2001.0028.

Perry, C.R. *The Victorian Post Office: The Growth of a Bureaucracy.* London: Royal Historical Society, 1992.

Phegley, Jennifer. *Courtship and Marriage in Victorian England.* Santa Barbara, CA: Praeger, 2012.

Phillips, Richard. "Settler Colonialism and the Nuclear Family." *Canadian Geographer* 53, 2 (Summer 2009): 239–53. https://doi.org/10.1111/j.1541-0064.2009.00256.x.

Pike, Robert M. "National Interest and Imperial Yearnings: Empire Communications and Canada's Role in Establishing the Imperial Penny Post." *Journal of Imperial and Commonwealth History* 26, 1 (1998): 22–48. https://doi.org/10.1080/03086539808583014.

Pleck, Elizabeth Hafkin. *Celebrating the Family: Ethnicity, Consumer Culture, and Family Rituals.* Cambridge, MA: Harvard University Press, 2000.

Plotz, John. *Portable Property: Victorian Culture on the Move.* Princeton, NJ: Princeton University Press, 2008. https://doi.org/10.1515/9781400828937.

Porter, Mrs. Adrian [Rose]. *The Life and Letters of Sir John Henniker Heaton.* London: John Lane, 1916. https://doi.org/10.5479/sil.282443.39088008213639.

Porter, Bernard. *The Absent-Minded Imperialists: What the British Really Thought about Empire.* Oxford: Oxford University Press, 2004.

Potter, Simon J. *News and the British World: The Emergence of an Imperial Press System, 1876–1922.* Oxford: Oxford University Press, 2003. https://doi.org/10.1093/acprof:oso/9780199265121.001.0001.

Pratt, Mary Louise. *Imperial Eyes: Travel Writing and Transculturation.* London: Routledge, 1992. https://doi.org/10.4324/9780203163672.

Pritchard, Allan, ed. *Vancouver Island Letters of Edmund Hope Verney, 1862–65.* Vancouver: UBC Press, 1996.

Procida, Mary A. *Married to the Empire: Gender, Politics and Imperialism in India, 1883–1947.* Manchester: Manchester University Press, 2002.

Racette, Sherry Farrell. "Nimble Fingers and Strong Backs: First Nations and Métis Women in Fur Trade and Rural Economies." In *Indigenous Women and Work: From Labor to Activism,* edited by Carol Williams, 148–62. Champaign: University of Illinois Press, 2012.

Raibmon, Paige. *Authentic Indians: Episodes of Encounter from the Late-Nineteenth-Century Northwest Coast.* Durham, NC: Duke University Press, 2005.

–. "Living on Display: Colonial Visions of Aboriginal Domestic Spaces." *BC Studies* 140 (2003): 69–89.

–. "The Practice of Everyday Colonialism: Indigenous Women at Work in the Hop Fields and Tourist Industry of Puget Sound." *Labor* 3, 3 (Fall 2006): 23–56. https://doi.org/10.1215/15476715-2006-004.

Rappaport, Erika. "'The Bombay Debt': Letter Writing, Domestic Economies and Family Conflict in Colonial India." *Gender and History* 16, 2 (August 2004): 233–60. https://doi.org/10.1111/j.0953-5233.2004.00340.x.

Ray, Carina E. *Crossing the Color Line: Race, Sex, and the Contested Politics of Colonialism in Ghana.* Athens: Ohio University Press, 2015.

Reid, Robie L. "Captain Evans of Cariboo." *British Columbia Historical Quarterly* 2, 4 (1938): 233–46.

Richards, Christopher. "Richards of Wexford and Other Families," Rootsweb, http://homepages.rootsweb.ancestry.com/~cmricha/fam5391.html.

Richardson, Ruth. *Death, Dissection and the Destitute.* 2nd ed. London: Phoenix, 2001.

Rifkin, Mark. *Settler Common Sense: Queerness and Everyday Colonialism in the American Renaissance.* Minneapolis: University of Minnesota Press, 2014. https://doi.org/10.5749/minnesota/9780816690572.001.0001.

Robertson, Leslie A. *Imagining Difference: Legend, Curse, and Spectacle in a Canadian Mining Town.* Vancouver: UBC Press, 2005.

Robertson, Leslie A., with the Kwagu'l Gixsam Clan. *Standing Up with Ga'axsta'las: Jane Constance Cook and the Politics of Memory, Church, and Custom.* Vancouver: UBC Press, 2012.

Robertson, Megan. "Epistolary Memory: First World War Letters to British Columbia." *BC Studies* 182 (Summer 2014): 125–51.

Robinson, Howard. *Britain's Post Office: A History of Development from the Beginnings to the Present Day.* London: Oxford University Press, 1953.

–. *Carrying British Mails Overseas.* London: G. Allen and Unwin, 1964.

Rothschild, Emma. *The Inner Life of Empires: An Eighteenth-Century History.* Princeton, NJ: Princeton University Press, 2011. https://doi.org/10.1515/9781400838165.

Roy, Susan, and Ruth Taylor. "'We Were Real Skookum Women': The shíshálh Economy and the Logging Industry on the Pacific Northwest Coast." In *Indigenous Women and Work: From Labor to Activism,* edited by Carol Williams, 104–19. Urbana: University of Illinois Press, 2012.

Sabatos, Terri Renee. "Images of Death and Domesticity in Victorian Britain." PhD dissertation, Indiana University, 2001.

Sanders, Valerie. *The Brother-Sister Culture in Nineteenth-Century Literature: From Austen to Woolf.* Basingstoke, UK: Palgrave Macmillan, 2002. https://doi.org/10.1057/9780230513211.

Sandwell, R.W. *Contesting Rural Space: Land Policy and Practices of Resettlement on Saltspring Island, 1859–1891.* Montreal and Kingston: McGill-Queen's University Press, 2005.

Schor, Esther. *Bearing the Dead: The British Culture of Mourning from the Enlightenment to Victoria.* Princeton, NJ: Princeton University Press, 1994. https://doi.org/10.1515/9781400821488.

Schuurman, Nadine. "Contesting Patriarchies: Nlha7pamux and Stl'atl'imx Women and Colonialism in Nineteenth-Century British Columbia." *Gender, Place and Culture* 5, 2 (1998): 141–58. https://doi.org/10.1080/09663699825250.

Scott, Elizabeth A. "'The Ill-Name of the Old Country': London's Assisted Emigrants, British Unemployment Policy, and Canadian Immigration Restriction, 1905–1910." *Journal of the Canadian Historical Association* 26, 1 (2015): 99–130. https://doi.org/10.7202/1037231ar.

Shah, Nayan. *Stranger Intimacy: Contesting Race, Sexuality and the Law in the North American West.* Berkeley: University of California Press, 2011.

Sleigh, Daphne. *The Man Who Saved Vancouver: Major James Skitt Matthews.* Surrey: Heritage House, 2008.

Smith, Dorothy Blakey, ed. "Harry Guillod's Journal of a Trip to Cariboo, 1862." *British Columbia Historical Quarterly* 19, 3–4 (1955): 187–232.

Smith, Woodruff D. "Complications of the Commonplace: Tea, Sugar, and Imperialism." *Journal of Interdisciplinary History* 23, 2 (1992): 259–78. https://doi.org/10.2307/205276.

Snell, K.D.M. "Gravestones, Belonging and Local Attachment in England 1700–2000." *Past and Present* 179, 1 (May 2003): 97–134. https://doi.org/10.1093/past/179.1.97.

Spacks, Patricia Meyer. *Boredom: The Literary History of a State of Mind.* Chicago: University of Chicago Press, 1995.

Stanley, Liz. "The Epistolarium: On Theorizing Letters and Correspondences." *Auto/Biography* 12, 3 (2004): 201–35. https://doi.org/10.1191/0967550704ab014oa.

Stanley, Timothy J. "'Chinamen, Wherever We Go': Chinese Nationalism and Guangdong Merchants in British Columbia, 1871–1911." *Canadian Historical Review* 77, 4 (1996): 475–503. https://doi.org/10.3138/CHR-077-04-01.

Steel, Frances M. "Via New Zealand around the World: The Union Steam Ship Company and the Trans-Pacific Mail Lines, 1880s–1910s." In *Coast to Coast: Case Histories of Modern Pacific Crossings,* ed. Prue Ahrens and Chris Dixon, 59–75. Newcastle upon Tyne: Cambridge Scholars, 2010.

Steinbach, Susie L. *Understanding the Victorians: Politics, Culture and Society in Nineteenth-Century Britain.* 2nd ed. New York: Routledge, 2016.

"Sticker Campaign Targets 'Racist' B.C. Lieutenant-Governor." CBC News, 14 August 2012. http://www.cbc.ca/news/canada/british-columbia/sticker-campaign-targets-racist-b-c-lieutenant-governor-1.1205660.

Stoler, Ann Laura. *Along the Archival Grain: Epistemic Anxieties and Colonial Common Sense.* Princeton, NJ: Princeton University Press, 2009.

–. *Carnal Knowledge and Imperial Power: Race and the Intimate in Colonial Rule.* Berkeley: University of California Press, 2002.

–. "Tense and Tender Ties: The Politics of Comparison in North American History and (Post) Colonial Studies." *Journal of American History* 88, 3 (December 2001): 829–65. https://doi.org/10.2307/2700385.

Stoler, Ann Laura, and Frederick Cooper. "Between Metropole and Colony: Rethinking a Research Agenda." In *Tensions of Empire: Colonial Cultures in a Bourgeois World,* edited by Frederick Cooper and Ann Laura Stoler, 1–56. Berkeley: University of California Press, 1997. https://doi.org/10.1525/california/9780520205406.003.0001.

Storey, Kenton. *Settler Anxiety at the Outposts of Empire: Colonial Relations, Humanitarian Discourses, and the Imperial Press.* Vancouver: UBC Press, 2016.

Strange, Julie-Marie. *Death, Grief and Poverty, 1870–1914.* Cambridge: Cambridge University Press, 2005. https://doi.org/10.1017/CBO9780511496080.

–. *Fatherhood and the British Working Class, 1865–1914.* Cambridge: Cambridge University Press, 2015.

Szreter, Simon. *Fertility, Class and Gender in Britain 1860–1940.* Cambridge: Cambridge University Press, 1993.

Tarlow, Sarah. "Landscapes of Memory: The Nineteenth-Century Garden Cemetery." *European Journal of Archaeology* 3, 2 (2000): 217–39. https://doi.org/10.1179/eja.2000.3.2.217.

Teneese, Margaret. "Michael Phillipps' Original Records Donated to the Ktunaxa Nation Council Archives." *NationTalk,* 25 November 2015. http://nationtalk.ca/story/michael-phillipps-original-records-donated-to-the-ktunaxa-nation-council-archives.

Thrush, Coll. "Vancouver the Cannibal: Cuisine, Encounter, and the Dilemma of Difference on the Northwest Coast, 1774–1808." *Ethnohistory* 58, 1 (2011): 1–35. https://doi.org/10.1215/00141801-2010-062.

Tosh, John. *A Man's Place: Masculinity and the Middle-Class Home in Victorian England.* New Haven, CT: Yale University Press, 2007.

–. *Manliness and Masculinities in Nineteenth-Century Britain: Essays on Gender, Family and Empire.* Harlow, UK: Pearson Longman, 2005.

Trimble, Sabina. "Storying *Swí:lhcha:* Place Making and Power at a Stó:lō Landmark." *BC Studies* 190 (2016): 39–66.

Trouillot, Michel-Rolph. *Silencing the Past: Power and the Production of History*. Boston: Beacon, 1995.

Van Kirk, Sylvia. "From 'Marrying-In' to 'Marrying-Out': Changing Patterns of Aboriginal/Non-Aboriginal Marriage in Colonial Canada." *Frontiers: A Journal of Women Studies* 23, 3 (2002): 1–11. https://doi.org/10.1353/fro.2003.0010.

–. *Many Tender Ties: Women in Fur-Trade Society in Western Canada, 1670–1870.* Winnipeg: Watson and Dwyer, 1980.

–. "Tracing the Fortunes of Five Founding Families of Victoria." *BC Studies* 115/116 (Winter 1997/98): 149–80.

Veracini, Lorenzo. *Settler Colonialism: A Theoretical Overview.* Basingstoke, UK: Palgrave Macmillan, 2010. https://doi.org/10.1057/9780230299191.

Vibert, Elizabeth. "The Contours of Everyday Life: Food and Identity in the Plateau Fur Trade." In *Gathering Places: Aboriginal and Fur Trade Histories,* edited by Carolyn Podruchny and Laura Peers, 119–48. Vancouver: UBC Press, 2010.

–. "Real Men Hunt Buffalo: Masculinity, Race and Class in British Fur Traders' Narratives." *Gender and History* 8, 1 (1996): 4–21. https://doi.org/10.1111/j.1468-0424.1996.tb00221.x.

–. *Traders' Tales: Narratives of Cultural Encounters in the Columbia Plateau, 1807–1846.* Norman: University of Oklahoma Press, 1997.

Vincent, David. *Literacy and Popular Culture: England 1750–1914.* Cambridge: Cambridge University Press, 1993.

Vizenor, Gerald, ed. *Survivance: Narratives of Native Presence.* Lincoln: University of Nebraska Press, 2008.

Vogt, David, and David Alexander Gamble. "'You Don't Suppose the Dominion Government Wants to Cheat the Indians?': The Grand Trunk Pacific Railway and the Fort George Reserve, 1908–12." *BC Studies* 166 (2010): 55–72.

Wagner, Kim. "'Treading Upon Fires': The 'Mutiny'-Motif and Colonial Anxieties in British India." *Past and Present* 218, 1 (2013): 159–97. https://doi.org/10.1093/pastj/gts026.

Walvin, James. *Fruits of Empire: Exotic Produce and British Taste, 1660–1800.* Basingstoke, UK: Macmillan, 1997. https://doi.org/10.1007/978-1-349-25451-4.

Wanhalla, Angela. "The 'Bickerings' of the 'Mangungu Brethren': Talk, Tales and Rumour in Early New Zealand." *Journal of New Zealand Studies* 12 (2011): 13–28.

–. *Matters of the Heart: A History of Interracial Marriage in New Zealand.* Auckland: Auckland University Press, 2013.

–. "Rethinking 'Squaw Men' and 'Pakeha-Maori': Legislating White Masculinity in New Zealand and Canada, 1840–1900." In *Re-Orienting Whiteness,* edited by Leigh Boucher, Jane Carey, and Katherine Ellinghaus, 219–34. New York: Palgrave Macmillan, 2009.

–. "Women 'Living Across the Line': Intermarriage on the Canadian Prairies and in Southern New Zealand, 1870–1900." *Ethnohistory* 55, 1 (Winter 2008): 29–49. https://doi.org/10.1215/00141801-2007-045.

Wheeler, Michael. *Heaven, Hell, and the Victorians.* Cambridge: Cambridge University Press, 1994.

White, Luise. *Speaking with Vampires: Rumor and History in Colonial Africa.* Berkeley: University of California Press, 2000.

Whyman, Susan. *The Pen and the People: English Letter Writers, 1660–1800.* Oxford: Oxford University Press, 2010.

Wilkinson, Myler, and Duff Sutherland. "'From Our Side We Will be Good Neighbour[s] to Them': Doukhobor-Sinixt Relations at the Confluence of the Kootenay and Columbia Rivers in the Early Twentieth Century." *BC Studies* 174 (Summer 2012): 33–59.

Wilson, Deborah. "Change Urged to Victoria Street Named for 'Racist' Figure." CBC News, 16 January 2018. http://www.cbc.ca/news/canada/british-columbia/trutch-bc-street-name-change-racism-indigenous-1.4489550.

Wilson, Kathleen, ed. *A New Imperial History: Culture, Identity and Modernity in Britain and the Empire, 1660–1840.* Cambridge: Cambridge University Press, 2004.

Wolfe, Patrick. "Settler Colonialism and the Elimination of the Native." *Journal of Genocide Research* 8, 4 (December 2006): 387–409. https://doi.org/10.1080/14623520601056240.

–. *Settler Colonialism and the Transformation of Anthropology: The Politics and Poetics of an Ethnographic Event.* London: Cassell, 1999.

Yu, Henry. "Refracting Pacific Canada: Seeing Our Uncommon Past." *BC Studies* 156/157 (2007): 5–10.

Zastoupil, Lynn. "Intimacy and Colonial Knowledge." *Journal of Colonialism and Colonial History* 3, 2 (Fall 2002). https://doi.org/10.1353/cch.2002.0053.

Zlotnick, Susan. "Domesticating Imperialism: Curry and Cookbooks in Victorian England." *Frontiers: A Journal of Women Studies* 16, 2/3 (1996): 51–68. https://doi.org/10.2307/3346803.

Index

Note: "(i)" after a page number indicates an illustration or map. "Norbury" in subentries refers to Frederick Paget (Tommy) Norbury; "Phillipps," refers to Michael Phillipps.